THE EIGHTH NIGHT
OF CREATION

THE
EIGHTH NIGHT
OF CREATION

Life on the Edge of Human History

Jerome Deshusses

TRANSLATED BY

A. D. MARTIN SPERRY

THE DIAL PRESS

PUBLISHED BY
THE DIAL PRESS
1 DAG HAMMARSKJOLD PLAZA
NEW YORK, NEW YORK 10017

This work was first published in French as *Délivrez Prométhée*
by Flammarion in France. © Flammarion, 1978.

Translation copyright © 1982 by Deneau & Greenberg Publishers Ltd.

Design by Ann Gold

LIBRARY OF CONGRESS CATALOGING IN PUBLICATION DATA
Deshusses, Jerome.
The eighth night of creation.
Translation of: Délivrez Prométhée.
1. Civilization, Modern—1950–. 2. Human ecology.
3. Twentieth century—Forecasts. 4. Man—Influence on nature. I. Title.
CB428.D4613   909.82   81–12570
ISBN 0–385–27206–5   AACR2

The research necessary for the completion of this book was made possible by the assistance of the Pro Helvetia Foundation, to whom the author's thanks are due.

Contents

THE EIGHTH NIGHT
OF CREATION

INCIPIT AQUARIUS
(Introduction)

I

The heroes and gods have not yet been born. Sprung from a desire or a fear—and thus from a future yet to come—the myth precedes History as much as it proceeds from it; one of its first names, legenda, means that which will be read. In the same way that roots account for a flower less than they are implied by it, that the end of a sentence alone justifies its beginning, and that every arrival is simultaneously the motive for the departure and the motive force for the voyage, so the meaning of a symbol is more to come in the future than here with us in the present, less rich at its birth than in its decline, and never more clearly determined than at the moment when everything is terminated. Two unknowns echo each other, two images answer each other from one end to the other of this night in time that interrupts the day before yesterday and recommences the day after tomorrow. That which appeared formerly is reflection, not glimmerings of light. Eros, Orpheus, and Daedalus are calls, not memories. If the immemorial acts on human beings as a guarantee, it is because it alone resembles that of which it speaks to them and because to see into the infinite future is inconceivable in respect of anything that has not first receded into the infinite past.

The sources lie upstream. They have already touched us, but we have not yet reached them. The false doctrine that History preaches is so full of approximation that History increasingly resembles the truth it wished to know. The lyric prophet and the epic poet, one turned towards the future and the other towards the past, face each other like the East and the West that respectively give birth to

1

them; however, it is from the same sun that the first draws its canticles and the second his cantilenas. As the future of the dawn is the past of the twilight, so prophecies are myths disguised, and myths disguised eschatologies. Day and night, good and evil, high and low: nothing exists except by virtue of its opposite—that is to say, its reflection. We only see one term of each couple because these are whole concepts, because we are partakers thereof, and because a partaker implies a part taken.

Incipit Aquarius. The age of the Water Bearer is dawning. This Latin chapter title, heraldic and solemn after the manner of votive steles and milliary columns, indicates what has come down to us today from the Babylonian grimoires as modern prognostication and from popular rumor as cliché. Only the earliest days of Christianity offer a comparable image. The Fish, the sign of the Christ and His followers, suddenly came into vogue in a time so disorganized that the masses were unable to exorcise what lay in store for them except by returning to the most ancient and the least rational of expectations. Yet even the fall of the world proved to be nothing but a threat worn threadbare by generations of alarmists, and the most confused of analogies became merely disconcerting when there was no longer any need to sound the alarm. The dawn of the third millennium henceforth evokes for everyone what the dawning of the first must have been like. It is merely a matter of magnifying the smoke of the barbarians into sulphurous vapors, the listlessness of the patricians into depressive neuroses, the orgies of the circus into televised sports, and the disintegration of the Roman Empire into the collapse of the human race.

This time it is Life itself that risks everything. It does so in order to have everything. Father of utopias and patron of floods, offering the stars with one hand and spreading disaster with the other, closely connected with Prometheus whose victory he invokes at last, at once the Second Coming and the Last Judgement, the Water Bearer begins by destroying, for it is thus that a world is created. The Universe itself is an explosion.

II

Etymologically, a catastrophe is something that turns or returns against me. Every obstacle is thus catastrophic in nature, though not necessarily in extent. Now, a living or mechanical system cannot enrich itself unless it obtains information, and it cannot obtain information except by a retroaction—an action that retreats from an obstacle.

The distinction between nature and artifice is itself artificial. Not only is it impossible to find an objective criterion for distinguishing them; above all, we ourselves are Nature incarnate, and our action— whatever its mechanism—is simply the latest of the methods that the Universe chooses to ascend more rapidly towards its prime cause and ultimate objective, self-awareness. Prime cause and ultimate objective are but one, as I hope to show adequately in the most speculative sections of this book. Certainly, this concept of Alpha and Omega is embedded deep in our common parlance; all we need is for an objective to become an ideal, and we call it a cause.

Cybernetics sprang from the established, evidential fact that an amoeba, a green alga, and a computer function according to the same rules. Machina ex deo. The bat that emits ultrasonic waves and picks them up in altered form, the pseudopod that takes its shape from the impacts it experiences, the cellular protoplasm (such as human skin) that serves as a protective membrane when it dies—all these are examples of immediate retroactions. Ultimately, however, what is a reflection, an action, or a considered thought if not—as the words imply—a reflection, action, or thought that we both originate and receive, enriching ourselves with what obstructs us? Everything discloses itself by its close or determines itself by its term; all awareness is awareness of limits; that which applies to nothing is nothing. Intelligence has never appeared anywhere without being provoked by and then dismissing an obstacle. Catastrophes or nothingness. Information is always retroactive, retroaction is always a short circuit, a short circuit is always a breakdown.

If the idea of a cyclical world gratifies mediocrity, it is because the circle is a flat figure whose exact middle is a center and whose total enclosure is a perfection. Everything recovers there: the present is superimposed on the past, and the lessons of History are reduced to recipes. All we lack is one dimension—but that is a serious lack, the only one that counts. The third dimension turns this circle into a spiral. History continues to revolve but grows larger as it does so; it overlaps itself, rising upwards the while; it lives—and thus it respires.

Its journey appears as a perpetual obstacle, since only a difference in inclination distinguishes a rising slope from a vertical wall. Moreover, its very path is a series of obstacles overcome—and in the world of the irreversible, that which once overcomes rises forever. Looking at things on the Universe's scale, we can see how closely its progress resembles the ascent of a ladder. The first cells combined only in the face of a material and logical obstacle: the growth of their surfaces implied a similar increase in their volume, and the latter forced them to choose between extension by symbiosis and extinction by isolation. The young Earth knew dragonflies with a meter-long wingspread; a change in the atmosphere eliminated them. Each glaciation erected an unscalable wall in front of giant species; thus died the dinosaurs and the mammoths. The present biological balance is created by innumerable forces, each of which, in the absence of the others, would become a scourge. Every previous catastrophe has merely enriched the vital current of reflexes and then of reflection, so that from each eclipse Life has surged back more vital than before. Thus Chance, the absolute enemy of Awareness, has ultimately worked only on behalf of the latter, which itself has worked only through the former.

Our existence has no price; neither has truth. One serves as payment for the other, and the whole of Human History, the figurehead of Natural History, tells us only that. By this means and this means alone we have learned that Nature has its laws. What we have not yet deduced is that it must have a justice of its own. We still believe that it opposes us, whereas in reality it poses, composes, and supposes us all at the same time. We take it for our field of action, whereas it is our action itself; for a fixed point, whereas it is movement; for an enigma, whereas it is a sphinx. It is Nature that chooses the questions, we who miss the point as we reply. All this would be nothing but a game if "question" did not signify, when necessary, "torture."

All human jurisdictions at least recognize forgetfulness as cancellation of a debt and pardon as prolongation of credit. Nature, however, does not pardon, does not forget anything, does not return blow for blow. It may withstand a thousand blows and then suddenly render not an eye for an eye but an apocalypse for a mere flick of the finger. All the damned of the Earth end up ready to negotiate, but the damned Earth remains deaf, dumb, blind, un-wavering. Vanished species never return, errant plutonium counts its radioactive future in millennia, a lake used as a sewer will over-whelm twenty generations with the miasmas of our generation. We are perforce interdependent in space; we are also so in time, and by a force yet more binding. The accumulation of horror is merely a bill to which each subterfuge, each delay, each technological pseudo-palliative simply adds a zero. The hundreds of yesterday are already the thousands of today; we shall manage to invent no new evasions before everything collapses under the millions of tomorrow.

III

However terrifying they may be, overkill armaments, the demo-graphic cyclone, and pollution are merely images. It is, of course, necessary to list them in this book, if only in summarized form. It is not the first time they have been tallied, but any plan to counter these calamities obliges the writer to repeat what they themselves reiterate so constantly. But it is even more necessary to say what they represent: a still-bestial Humanity whose ideas, standards, and laws are all lies.

Thus, the reader will find, side by side in this work, first the inventory of our world's material disasters and then the inventory of their causes. The latter includes most current institutions, knowl-edge, and beliefs, not in a discussion of their deployment, but in the articulation of their principles, which, considered as prejudices, are nonetheless ideas and are thereby dependent on a philosophy. Let no one accuse me, therefore, of claiming to know everything or of oversimplifying. In the first place, a knowledge of the law of gravity makes it unnecessary to examine each of the countless possible falls to which this law applies. Second, one single objection, clear and simple, can be enough to shatter a whole system (this was the insult that Galileo's inclined planes paid Aristotle's Physics). Argumenta-tion of the false is always more complex than its refutation; evidence slashes the ramifications of an error to ribbons. The very idea of truth would be illusory without the complementary idea that truth has a single aspect, whereas there are an infinity of ways in which two and two do not make four.

To believe that it is impossible today to think of the world as a whole is to believe that a general concept is the result of particular concepts—which is absurd. To imagine that modern scholarship is too heterogeneous to allow any synthesis whatever is to imagine that concepts such as time, causation, chance, or determinism vary from one scientific discipline to another. Ultimately omniscience is what is imposed upon us by the world, which we consequently think of as a whole with the help of clichés: the collective unconscious, the curvature of space-time, the class struggle, scientific sociology, abstract art, the formation of concepts. We must choose one of two attitudes: accepting these ideas just as they are or stripping them bare. In exactly the same way, we must choose between only two philosophies: common sense, which is totally false, and critical sense, which is a little closer to the truth.

However, "divide and rule" is the motto of the prevailing disorder, so the great ruse of departmentalized ideologies lies in what they describe as their general views of the world. In actual fact, they have made generalizations about the world without having seen it, while dismissing in advance any criticism that is not specialized. Thus, our culture is made up of systems that exclude or are unaware of each other. Each manages to perform the same miracle: to contain the whole truth, of which each of them forms in fact but a part. Consequently, philosophy is led into decay—and no one can understand why it is dead.

The antiphilosophies of today so ignore actual manifestations of reality that visitors to Earth after a cataclysm would have no idea of what ecological disaster had occurred if the only information available were the writings of our so-called philosophers. Yet Voltaire could find subjects in the Lisbon earthquake or the murder of the Calas. And as for the questions of traditional metaphysics, they have been left to Science; we shall see later how Science has handled them. Totally occupied in the frenetic exegesis of ancient works, refusing to produce anything that is not second-class literature, the antiphilosophers feel they would soil their hands were they to grasp the world. Details, especially statistics, fill them with utter horror. On the other hand, there are authors whose works abound in statistics and other details, but they have a horror of philosophy and even of thought, so reading books on ecology is an aesthetic and logical torture. They simply fatten a report written for no one.

This would matter less were the same gap not found between literature and the sciences. The algebraic sign is an intimidation, the biological reference a lack of taste, cybernetics an avowal of technocracy. The literati consider simple facts gathered by scientific observation not worthy of a thought and so seek to get rid of them by ignoring them, in order the more nobly to carry out the totally inconsistent plan of soaring into space.

In this work, I have tried to make do with a bare but sufficient minimum of complexity. I have not tried to make up for the bareness by expounding a philosophy, even a first philosophy, for a first philosophy begins by seeing what it deals with and by laying hands on it. This book does not display rubrics; it embodies them. I could not avoid, especially in regard to Science, making the text somewhat heavy reading here and there, owing to the number and diversity of the principles involved. It would have been totally useless to undertake any one demystification without completing them all, for the lie has only one objective—self-interest—while every truth has only one function—sharing.

Before long the only choice left to History will be that between the horror of its own racket and the path of confession—in other words, between two humiliations, one of which would at least bring salvation. In this respect we live in a shameful but providential age. Since the Human's beginnings, the Ideal has no more power than Power has ideals. That which called to us in vain from the highest level of the Spirit we now find waiting, peremptory, murderous, and definitive, at the lowest level of Matter. Humanity, in a word, is trapped on all sides simultaneously. It is the enormous living spiral that continues to move upwards. Because we resist this spiral, we see it coming at us in the opposite way: namely as the turn of a screw.

GEHENNA

I

When the Christ of the Gospels spoke of Hell or the Last Judgement, one of the words he used was *gehenna*. Usage and erosion of the language have made this word a general term for torment, but it originally had an exact meaning: the municipal wastes of Jerusalem. Think of a garbage dump filling a whole valley, infested with rats, contaminated with mosquitoes, breeding perpetual epidemics among the hovels that surrounded it, stinking of decayed food, excrement, and tar. It was often set on fire, and then it was asphyxiating, making the whole city reek when the winds blew, leaving pestilence behind when they died down. It was damnation itself. The "fires of Gehenna" did not purify; they contaminated.

For the Jerusalem of Christ's day this constant threat of death was the reverse of a way of life, just as a reflection in a mirror is the reverse of a face. Trade was already a balance of terror, the markets swarmed with middlemen, and the exchanges were centers of extortion. Fresh water was never so dear as when it was in short supply, slaves were never so cheap as immediately after a battle, supply and demand conspired together like a pair of thieves, and the public weal was in the hands of bureaucrats whose administration had swindling as its objective and notoriety as its ideal. The principles of modern political economy were already in full gear. So anyone who could glimpse, from afar or from on high, the mountain of refuse on one side and the ancient city on the other had only to dream of justice to hope that the latter would one day turn into the former.

8

The image contained too much horror to retain its content while nascent Christianity shed its own. The invisible hell, like the hereafter that comes after my death and the flood after my life, can always wait. Garbage will not wait: it activates itself, it works itself up, it ferments, it attacks. Not having been the concern of anyone in particular, it becomes the product and problem of all of us. It blends particular vices into a single general scourge that crushes quibbling under catastrophe, creates fusion through panic, strikes the blind as they grope, and uses the death it carries to awaken the dead who are ourselves. Thus Gehenna epitomizes everything: segregation and profit, lies and theft, unawareness and negligence. It leads from "every man for himself" to "headlong flight." It shows where hell is to be found—which is where we are now. It prospers from our doubts about it, waxes fat on our subterfuges, grows stronger from our silences, changes evasions into obstacles, and increases through being minimized, until the day when everyone struggles hopelessly in its clutches for want of ever having known how to fight it or been willing to do so.

The modern Gehenna is disordered without a doubt. Pollution, overkill armaments, and blind growth are disorder itself. The sinister panorama of the following pages is no longer up-to-date even as I sketch it for you, since it surpasses itself with every day that passes. Neither is it news, since it uses known, quasi-official data. In bygone days one could only imagine the hell to which wrongdoing would lead one in the end. Today one comes face to face with hell straightway. We are being driven down into the depths of Gehenna, the meeting place of all the evil deeds that have brought us here.

II

Plants and marine plankton produce all the Earth's oxygen. Today they are able to produce less and less of it, though our consumption grows greater and greater. Each year concrete covers an area of grassland the size of Holland. California's new roads and freeways reduce its arable land by the equivalent of a sidewalk one kilometer long for each new resident. The Sahara advances more than 40 kilometers annually; other deserts throughout the world are generally growing at the same rate. Each year in the United States alone, the pulp and paper industry destroys enough forest to cover Jamaica —and paper is not the only industry that eats up trees. Ocean plankton, which produces nearly four fifths of the globe's oxygen, is disappearing even faster than forests and grasslands.

Our technology and science do not know how to manufacture oxygen, even in small quantities, without expending more of it than they make. Even if we were to master photosynthesis, the usefulness of an artificial process would be doubtful, given the enormous quantities of oxygen that the world needs. Thus we remain completely dependent on plants and plankton. Whoever destroys a plant-bearing surface injures Humanity, no matter what property rights he or she is exercising. The whole problem of pollution lies in the struggle between ecology and the economy.

The source of oxygen is diminishing through abuse of consumption, while consumption is increasing through ignorance of the source. An automobile consumes as much of the life-supporting element as thirty humans; our planet gets one million new cars each month—and six million extra inhabitants. All imaginable forms of combustion—fires, bombs, industrial processes—increase constantly in number and intensity, burning up quantities of oxygen that are literally incalculable. A jet plane uses 35 tons of oxygen in crossing the Atlantic; more than three thousand of these huge planes fly regularly all over the world. Less than half the oxygen consumed in the United States and Europe is replaced, and the situation is almost as bad in the U.S.S.R. Oxygen is free, but crops earn profits and are not going to grow any less profitable.

Human activity has already destroyed more than two billion hectares—one quarter of all the arable land on this planet, and today our parasitism is more widespread than ever before. It has also become noxious. We do not only take oxygen from the air; we also return it in the form of poisons.

Thus, Nature ceases to be useful only to become toxic. This phenomenon first became evident in the fate of the freshwater lakes. Lake Erie was once crystal clear and drinkable; it has suddenly become a sewer. It is not even like the Dead Sea, which is at least aseptic. A swim in Lake Erie now could be fatal. When fresh water "changes sides," it does so completely: as soon as it stops being wholesome, it becomes viral. Similarly, seawater cannot break down

even a fifth of the pollutants it receives today, and additional pollution is the price of whatever breaking down it does accomplish.
Water's efforts at self-rehabilitation use up a tremendous amount
of oxygen (a liter of crude oil absorbs as much of it as 400,000 liters
of unpolluted sea water). Once its oxygen supply is depleted,
anaerobic bacteria gain the upper hand, and the death struggle
begins. The resurrection of a single lake would take five or six centuries, even if it were theoretically and practically possible.

As for the atmosphere and the stratosphere, nobody knows what
kinds or quantities of gaseous emissions they can tolerate without an
upset in the climatic balance. Just 5 percent more oxygen in the air
would turn each fire into a catastrophe, if not each flame into a
conflagration. But 1 percent less oxygen? No one knows. The climatic balance depends on an infinitely tenuous balance of factors,
which are subject to chain reactions. Their intricacies are such that
even if we were to enter a glacial or diluvial era, Science would be
unable to decide whether to blame pollution or cosmic chance, for it
knows as little of the latter as it does of the former. It is logical to
assume, however, that if the Earth's environment is attacked by
enough gases akin to those of volcanic action, it will support
only simple, primitive life forms, those that originated in periods
when oxygen was scarce and volcanic craters abounded. An arthro-
pod is generally better equipped to deal with pollution than a
vertebrate.

Only the most obvious catastrophes or retroactions give birth to
an understanding that can laboriously and gradually raise itself to
the level of Nature, which already has that understanding. Take
the case of the massive drainage program in Ceylon in the 1950s. It
was "successful," and the malaria-carrying mosquito died out—and
so did the other insects. For want of insects, the geckos perished; for
want of geckos, the cats moved away; for want of cats, rats swarmed
everywhere, dying only from hunger and overcrowding. Consequently, plague-carrying fleas, which were parasites of the rats,
started jumping onto humans, who resorted to rat poison—so the
plague made even better progress. The authorities hastily parachuted in thousands of cats, who finally restored the balance. It was
the same story in China, where the whole rural population chased
away sparrows, making considerable use of rattles and scarecrows.

Thus "protected," the crops were destroyed the following year by hundreds of kinds of now equally protected parasites.

Similar retroactions have occurred all over the world. The U.S.S.R. hastily irrigated 12 million hectares; over 3 million of them were drenched in saltwater, which scorched the crops that were supposedly being nurtured. The Aswan Dam let water evaporate too quickly from its lake, so it developed a crack in a place which had been considered impregnable. Moreover, it held back nutritive sediments from the Nile, making it impossible for fish to survive there and hence for fishermen to earn their livings. It also changed many kilometers of river into marshland, suffocated the Mediterranean, recreated a desert on the seashore, and enouraged the breeding of the worms that inflict the riparian population with bilharziasis. As for the electric power the dam produced, Egypt had so little need of it that in the end all the country could use it for was to stop the river, which has kept Egypt alive for so long, from killing it in a quarter of a century.

In northwest China the destruction of huge forests freed the Yellow River of its natural obstacles. It soon ate away thousands of tons of rich earth and turned them into mud, thus transforming the river banks into slag heaps and killing off a fertile plain equal in area to Cambodia. Any flooding is now a cataclysm.

Deforestation in France means that in some years the Seine washes up to 40 hectares of arable land under the bridges of Paris every day for months on end. For the same reason, the Arno is no longer a threat to Florence alone, but to all Italy; one third of Italy's land surface is liable to flooding—and by poisoned waters.

On the seashores bathing beaches, jetties, and marinas produce the same effects. Slag heaps bury reeds, sea wrack, and rushes, drive away waterfowl, and cover the mud which had fed worms and shrimp, which in turn had fed flounder and salmon. The water renews itself less effectively than before, and is polluted more quickly. The tides diminish in their range and hence in their mixing effect, which normally fills the backwaters and brings silt to the sea bottom. Coastlines are deteriorating in thousands of places all over the world. For example, at Anaheim Bay in California, changes in the tidal action are resulting in an annual loss of 20 kilometers' depth of coast. This 30 million cubic meters of sand is the equivalent of a good-sized desert. (Desert, it is true, is the thing we lack the least.)

The retroactions I have just cited are among the most simple that are occurring on our planet. There are many others that are infinitely more complex. They are also slower and more serious, which is logical since they are circuitous, and a detour is not the shortest road from one point to another.

These changes have already brought us to a level at which Science is almost inarticulate. Even if it were not almost totally devoted to serving industry and management, it could do nothing against the industrialists and governments who, imitating those under their jurisdiction, pollute as much as they can. The minute someone speaks to them of pollution, they think only of thinking no more about it. Even when scientists pretend to prefer the truth that threatens their jobs to the lies that provide them with employment, they find no difficulty in giving their employers the benefit of the doubt, for they have literally enough and to spare of doubt—and as much profit to make. If their overworked abilities were not as self-seeking as they are fictitious, they could always find in our cowardice justification for their own. Before Nature we are illiterates, but the best way of destroying a library is still not knowing how to read.

III

Since the beginnings of written History, at least 120 species of mammals and 150 species of birds have disappeared under the pressure of humanity, which, though restrained for millennia, has doubled during the last fifty years and will quadruple during the next twenty, while our pickaxes become bulldozers and our appetites bulimias.

A major oil spill now occurs ten or fifteen times a year and is always a calamity, and countless leakages from oil tankers, which happen all the time, have the same effect. The life expectancy of a fish in Tokyo Harbor is no more than four hours. One drenching with detergent is enough to kill off albatrosses en masse. A few doses of radioactivity disorientate turtles permanently. The smell of oil upsets advanced species of fish, and in the oceanic environment this smell is ubiquitous. The oil itself kills marine fauna indiscriminately. What is the purpose of the puffin, the guillemot, the petrel, the albatross, and the turtle? What delicate balances do these links in the vast chain of life guarantee? We do not know. Nor do we know how cockchafers manage to fly in defiance of the known laws of aerodynamics. That is why Germany asked Switzerland to let her have a dozen of them in 1975. Fifteen years earlier, Germans had been destroying them by tens of millions.

Today, 280 species of mammals, 250 species of birds, and 20,000 plant species are in their death throes. This is double the number of species human beings exterminated in six millennia. When will this doubling become quadrupling? Once again, we do not know. Two thirds of the birds of Hawaii are extinct—and Hawaii is no exception. The black emu of Kangaroo Island is gone. The tall ungulate *dubale* that lived in southern Algeria is no more. The Galápagos tortoises are dying out. The monk vulture and the eagle can no longer be found on the steppes. The Swedish pygarg, which used to live off the sea, has succumbed to the mercury in it. The American beaver, the chinchilla, the sable, the marten, the antelope, the rhinoceros, the elephant, the bison, the camel of Turkestan, the ibex of the Alps, the bear of Europe, the lynx, the cachalot, the rorqual, the salmon, and even some of the most familiar kinds of bird—all these are nearly extinct. Yet even though the whole fabric of Nature is already ripped at this level without a soul in the world knowing how far the rent will run, we regard the destruction as a mere aesthetic scandal—one that has no real significance at all, since moral ugliness does not usually retreat before ugliness plain and simple.

Each year 22 million fur-bearing animals are massacred. When newborn seal pups are clubbed to death, the mother can always escape—by diving into sheets of fuel oil, from which she emerges with a black-lined gullet. Two million sparrows are killed on the coasts of Aquitaine every year; the hunts are illegal, but the Nimrod who leaps out of his car armed like an infantryman is also a voter, sometimes even a president. More than two million turtledoves, swallows, and swifts that have escaped DDT are shot down each May in France. France has a Ministry of the Environment, but she also has two million hunters and issues thirty thousand hunting permits a year.

Mercury alone is enough to make all the fish in the sea toxic—

after it has decimated them. One out of every four tuna is judged too contaminated for sale in the United States. The swordfish is completely forbidden, the cod will be before long—and we are only just beginning. A fish caught in Sweden may contain a hundred times the "permissible" dose (permissible by commercial complacency, of course), and twice the fatal dose. Yet Swedish standards would shut down nearly all Danish fisheries. Science shows a curious change of opinion when it crosses frontiers (rather like the effect of the Pyrenees on Pascal).

At the end of its career, a species dies out because of a mere nothing. It was a mere nothing that caused the dodo to vanish, that rendered the passenger pigeon extinct, that made the great penguin, the quagga, and the aurochs disappear into the garbage can of History (which puts one less and less in mind of a history and more and more of a garbage can). In one year a lighthouse keeper's cat, in Cook Strait, got the better of an entire species of seminocturnal sparrows, birds that had been living there for thousands of centuries.

Human beings, animals, and plants alike now face dire threats from both air and water. The two dangers are inseparable: one cannot change the oceans into sewage dumps without transforming the atmosphere into a gas chamber. Foul water does, of course, catch the imagination more readily than vitiated air because it strikes down organisms more quickly. The prospect of drought or the reality of infection, it matters little: we confront them both.

Water covers nearly three quarters of the globe, but only 3 percent of it is fresh water, and most of this 3 percent is ice. Water that is really potable, even after purification treatment, does not represent a hundredth part of the remainder, and it is under simultaneous attack from industry and pollution—with the former wasting resources, the latter poisoning sources. It takes 1,000 liters of water to make one kilo of milk, 900 liters to process 5 kilos of oil, 200 liters for one kilo of paper, 100 liters for one kilo of sugar, 20,000 liters for a single gram of fissionable material. A steam-generating plant swallows up 20 million liters a day. A paper mill fouls as much water in one day as does the entire population of France. Making one ton of steel requires 250 cubic meters of pure water. Abattoirs use 500 liters per animal; they take their water in fresh and discharge it contaminated. The butter, milk, sugar, and cheese industries also discharge water full of germs and viruses that represents one fifth of all river pollution. Who decides to exchange fresh water for sugar refined for nothing, for wrapping paper made for nobody? Precisely: nothing and nobody—the two pillars of the great human family.

With water as with other things, purification is a myth. A treatment plant can cleanse the effluent from a single factory or even a group of buildings, but when the liquid volume is as large as that of a river, treatment is no longer possible. Even in the production of potable water, no one has managed to stop pesticides, the most aggressive pollutants, from passing from the lakes to the underground water tables and thence to the human body. The same is true of radioactive isotopes and most viruses and germs, as we shall see.

Chicago, which has the most modern treatment plants in the world, discharges as much polluted water into the Des Plaines River as a city of a million inhabitants which carries out no treatment *at all*. The waste water of New York contains, *after* treatment, ten times more bacteria than it did twenty years ago. (The multiple would be forty rather than ten if much of the bacteria-ridden effluent were not discharged into the open sea.) The Atlantic is four million times more polluted at Le Havre than at Tréport, despite large treatment plants in the Seine-Normandy basin.

Deposits of hydrocarbons (crude oil and its derivatives) form a film on the surface of the water; the result is a lack of oxygen, which prevents it from purifying itself. And even if all the necessary oxygen were available, this natural self-purification would be impossible in many places. Nuclear power stations and many industrial complexes warm the water in their vicinity so it absorbs still less oxygen. Consequently, organic matter decomposes poorly or not at all, the flora change, the fish die, and sewage does the rest. This lack of decomposition is particularly serious in the U.S.A., where three quarters of the potable water comes from surface waters, and almost equally so in Germany, where the surface waters receive 50,000 tons of hydrocarbons a year. Rains no longer renew water; they are nearly always polluting, and sometimes seriously so. While potable (that is, "purified") water in all industrial countries often contains hormones from birth control pills (I hardly need say that these hormones retain their effectiveness), New York's running water contains radioactive substances.

Most of Europe is a little better off, for many areas depend on underground water tables and one out of three of them is still unharmed (or at least potable without purification). But water tables, the last repositories of pure natural water, are unfortunately sensitive. They can be contaminated by pestilential waters fermenting tens of kilometers away. And because they are fed mainly by woodlands, they die as a result of deforestation. Moreover, some areas do not wait for these indirect forms of corruption to affect their water supply; they pour their sewage into tables that until now have been protected by the soil's filtering action. That filtering is not infinite in its capacity. Neither is it infallible: gasoline, for example, penetrates the earth six times as quickly as water, goes down as deep as 40 meters, and spreads easily over an area 10 kilometers across. Since we know that Germany alone cuts down 50,000 hectares of forest each year (each hectare can feed a well) and that deterioration is progressing even more quickly in America, how can we be surprised that universal rationing of fresh water is already in sight?

Nearly 80 percent of the water used in the world is dirtied, colored, heated, and infected before it is discharged without having undergone any treatment whatsoever. It goes into the sea, like everything else, but much of it gets there via the rivers, which are being killed right under our eyes. (In contrast, the death throes of the oceans are hardly visible.) More than fifty kinds of fish have disappeared from the Seine. The Moselle, the Allier, the Orne, the Marne, the Rhone are polluted and are polluting themselves with ever increasing speed. The waters of the Lys, the Deûle, the Alzette in Luxembourg, and the Donietz in the U.S.S.R. cannot be used for irrigation or even as coarse wash water in metallurgical works. It is impossible to water one's garden with water from the Sorgue, which springs from the Fountain of Vaucluse—which according to legend was rejuvenating. The Maine was all but poisoned from one end to the other by a single bottle of blood which contained viral hepatitis serum. The total of toxic matter dumped into the freshwater resources of France alone would fill ten thousand trains of 600 tons each. All the tributaries of the Po are on their way to putrefaction. Around Ferrara, a district full of sugar mills, there is no longer a single stream which is not more or less a germ-ridden canal, with water that resembles the flow in a trunk sewer. The Escaut, the Meuse, the Sambre are near biological death. The rivers which flow into the Adriatic near Ravenna and Ancona are almost as toxic as Lake Erie. The Bidassoa spews 15 tons of organic and industrial waste into the sea every day.

At the very spot where a Hyères treatment plant discharged its *treated* effluent, five kilometers of beach had to be closed in 1972. Often the insignificant efficiency of a so-called treatment plant is reduced to nothing, as was notoriously the case at Vitrolles, and as is secretly the case elsewhere. It is simply impossible for planners to foresee the nature of pollutants. Industry invents new ones every day.

Now the "need" for pure water (quotation marks here because we are dealing mostly with the needs of industry) in France, for example, has risen in fifteen years from 18 to 30 billion cubic meters; one can list hundreds of germs transmitted by insects which reproduce only in polluted water; cholera, dysentery, and typhoid germs permeate this water with or without insects. Yet a city such as Paris does not treat one third of its waste water, and the purified water it uses is never pure. Half of that city's potable water comes from rivers into which flow twenty-eight communal sewers and the waste water from some sixty factories. Other European capitals are hardly any better provided for, and some are worse off. Nevertheless, the consumption of water is increasing in almost geometric progression (and an American "needs" twice as much as a Frenchman). In brief, demand is increasing while supply decreases. Nature has no sense of business, and vice versa. . . .

A strain of poliomyelitis found recently in the water supply of a large French city was sufficient to prepare a vaccine. Tap water all over the world may yield lead, selenium, cadmium, and even benzopyrene, which rains carry to surface waters. Arsenic sometimes comes out of the taps in Latin America. Fluoride, which is put into drinking water to reduce dental caries, does not stop tooth decay, but it does become toxic if the planned strength is exceeded only slightly. Lead pipes are responsible for colitis, insomnia, and cancer. Reservoirs contain unbelievable quantities of metals; associated with them are asphalt and tar, which are carcinogens. To complete the list of the more commonplace substances contained in purified, piped drinking water, we must add pesticides and various isotopes such as strontium 90.

Every day the Potomac receives a million cubic meters of wastes that it would be unable to break down even if it were a living river. The area around St. Louis no longer uses the waters of the Mississippi for agricultural purposes. The Cuyahoga is viscous. The list of facts and figures could go on forever. It seems sufficient to note that Canadian and American authorities describe their coastal watercourses with a single laconic but clear phrase: 60 percent pollution. In the U.S.S.R., 300,000 kilometers of rivers (nearly eight times the circumference of the world) are unusable or noisome. In France putrefaction extends over 2,000 kilometers of waterways at low water, and over 500 all the time. Similar foulness is found everywhere in Europe.

Pesticides and other contaminants are a constant, ubiquitous threat to water reserves. One quarter of the 100,000 tons of the powdered copper sulphate that French vineyards use annually ends up in watercourses and water tables. Recently, residual liquor from a distillery in France percolated through a chalky substratum to contaminate wells a dozen kilometers away. European brewers use water tables for waste disposal so freely that they treat them with antibiotics lest they become exhausted too rapidly. In the state of New York, 230,000 liters of highly radioactive liquid wastes leaked from so-called secure reservoirs a few years ago and now have centuries in which to contaminate many water tables for all eternity. Any drilling for oil can spell doom for underground water dozens of kilometers away.

All the great lakes of Europe, America, and the U.S.S.R. are approaching an irreversible state of pollution. They receive contaminants from the water tables and rivers as well as plenty of their own—phosphates, nitrates, heat, and all the rest. Lake Michigan could be fatal to swimmers. Decaying Lake Superior releases into Lake Huron the filth it no longer needs to ensure its own death. The Tergensee in Germany, the Schliersee in Austria, Lake Balaton in Hungary, Lake Zurich in Switzerland—all these and hundreds more are dead or dying. In the U.S.S.R., Lake Baikal is slowly becoming cloudy, while huge rivers, such as the Kama, the Volga, the North

Dvina, the Donietz, and the Neva on the outskirts of Leningrad, and all the watercourses near the towns of Omsk, Novosibirsk, and Kermerovo, are moving towards the fetid and soon-to-be familiar sluggishness of the waters of Europe and America.

The Rhine, with at least four countries contributing pollution, is well on its way to death, bringing poisons with it as it goes. As early as 1970, it carried 85,000 kilos of mercury and a million kilos of arsenic. It receives 20,000 kilos of potash a day from the mines of Alsace and a ton of various insecticides per month from German, French, and Dutch factories, not to mention the contributions of the Swiss chemical industry. An estimated 60 percent of Germany's domestic waste water, saturated with varied, highly toxic pollutants, passes into her rivers without treatment of any kind. By the time the waters of the Rhine reach Holland, they contain so much chloride that they can no longer be used to desalinate the polders. (For their drinking water, the Dutch must use underground water tables—while there are still some left.) The river finally flows into the North Sea charged with 60 million tons of waste *a day*.

A *temporary* cleanup of the Rhine basin would cost 900 million French francs. Reclamation of France's watercourses—which would be virtually impossible because of the volume of toxic mud alone (where could one put it?)—would cost four times the total budget of its Ministry of the Environment for the next twenty years. Faced with expenses of this magnitude, governments merely argue among themselves on the rare occasions they do not preserve a stony silence. The united Europe of nations is making no headway, but the united Europe of the viruses has already arrived.

Furthermore, the financial agencies that administer waterways manage to make every intervention a catastrophe. They fell trees, build embankments, bulldoze banks to straighten them—and each action adds its bit to industrial and urban wastes. Many also have unforeseen results. The U.S.S.R. took 28 billion cubic meters of water from the basin of the Caspian Sea to meet the demands of irrigation and industries. The consequent silting up of ports, lowering of the water level, and increased salinity forced the so-called competent authorities to repeat the operation—this time on the rivers of the north at double the volume. One step forwards, two steps back—that could well be the motto of the whole world.

IV

The United States creates nearly four billion tons of waste each year; disposing of it costs as much as all its hospitals and schools together (Europe, Japan, and the U.S.S.R. are not far off the same figures). The Hudson alone discharges 2.28 million cubic meters of toxic waste into the Atlantic. The wastes carried into San Francisco Bay daily include a ton of chrome, copper, and other metals, as well as 60 tons of oil. Various watercourses enrich the seas annually with some 3 million tons of lead, 2 million tons of manganese, and 7 million tons of phosphorus.

In the average modern city 300,000 automobiles burn 3,000 tons of oil every year, forming a harmful viscous slime; most of it reaches the sea, either directly or through sewers. Day in and day out a million inhabitants produce 2,000 cubic meters of filth that cannot be treated and, therefore, gets down to the sea.

Each month, thousands of tons of detergent reach all the oceans in the world. They deprive the water of its oxygen and consequently of its power to clean itself. Thin layers of detergent float as far out as the open ocean; they immediately kill a third of the fish in the area, down to a depth of three meters, where most marine fauna live. Biodegradable detergents destroy bacteria which are thenceforth unable to break down anything else; so laundry products sold with "antipollution" labels are, in fact, even more polluting than the other kind.

Benzopyrene, which cars give off to the atmosphere in enormous quantities, ends up in estuaries, where it is concentrated by shellfish. Painting two square centimeters of skin with a weak (1 percent) solution of benzopyrene once a day almost invariably produces cancer within a month.

There is much worse to come. One milligram of DDT in a cubic meter of seawater reduces the oxygen-producing ability of its plankton by one quarter. As we have seen, three quarters of the Earth's oxygen comes from plankton—which for all intents and purposes no longer exists in the Mediterranean, in the North Sea, or at many points in the oceans. The marine environment today contains nearly 300,000 tons of DDT, enough to cut off the production of oxygen in a hundred thousand million cubic meters of water forever. It is impossible to stop the migration of pesticides, which travel on the winds and in the rains. The most complex treatment plants can do nothing against DDT, which from now on will be present in our underground water tables, in our foods almost without exception (whether they be "natural" or not), in the soil, in the air, in the snows of Alaska, and in the fat of the penguins in the Antarctic. But we shall come back to pesticides later. . . .

Hydrocarbons are hostile to all marine life because they overwhelm and then destroy the bacteria that should break them down. Every day 300 tons of hydrocarbons are discharged off the coasts of France alone; worldwide, the estimated figure reaches 90,000 tons. Nearly one tenth of the globe's petroleum production ends up in the oceans. "Marine graveyard" is becoming a pleonasm. Seabirds are being decimated; in Europe, oil (by no means their only enemy) kills more than a million of them every year.

Benzopyrene (once again!), fixed by algae and diatoms, concentrates all along the alimentary chain, poisoning the fish that eat the algae and the people who eat the fish. Oil tankers have a habit of cleaning out their bunkers in midocean. (The fine they risk by doing so represents only a tenth of the savings they gain. The penalty is less than 20,000 francs in France, a mere 100 rubles in the U.S.S.R.) The bunkers of hundreds of tankers sunk during the Second World War are slowly disintegrating; to the 5 to 10 million tons that escape from them must be added leaks from the new undersea oil wells, which have already destroyed oyster beds and shrimp banks along the shores of California, Texas, and Louisiana. In the Bay of Mexico alone, 8,000 drilling rigs are at work. Now, an average 8,000 drillings will cause at least 23 catastrophic accidents and about 100 less serious accidents; the United States has recorded sixteen real horrors since these rigs were built. And they keep being built in ever-increasing numbers.

Similarly, one can reckon, on average, on one collision per tanker of at least 30,000 tons; there are 12,000 oil tankers continually ploughing the world's oceans. A single accident at Ensenada seriously affected 150 marine species and wiped out 7 of them completely. Yet as long as oil tankers exist, there is no way to eliminate these accidents, even in theory; statistics—the law of large numbers

—ordains them. The march to death thus becomes a race, just as the race for profit becomes a death. And although the inevitable oil spills alone are certain to dump more than a million tons in the ocean each year, any other method of transporting petroleum would be worse.

No international law could do much, even if it were meticulously respected. Furthermore, no such law is likely to replace commercial cowardice. The latter is now at its peak. For example, at the time of the catastrophic stranding of the *Torrey Canyon* (March 18, 1967), while towns on either side of the Channel were being mobilized to fight the oil spill, two tankers were caught taking advantage of the oil slick by adding the sludge from their bunkers to it in the dead of night. The same thing happened in March 1978, when the Breton coast was hit by the most widespread spill ever recorded, five times as big as that caused by the *Torrey Canyon*.

It would be wrong, however, to think that only oil tankers are involved in polluting the oceans. *All* ships repay the ocean for carrying them by discharging mineral oils and fuel oil (the latter contains nickel, which makes it more corrosive than crude oil). Warships, cargo boats, and passenger steamers pump water into their tanks, as ballast in exchange for their fuel, whose by-products their engines spew liberally into the air—which means, after a short delay, into the sea. Before refilling the tanks, all one need do is pump out the dirty water.

The degassing of oil tankers in port is a myth. A plant specially built for this purpose, such as the one at Le Havre, handles about twenty-five tankers a year out of a possible 1,500. The ships would lose three days being cleaned. Since they are always in a hurry— more often than not their crews get a bonus for a fast passage— owners and sailors prefer to dump 1 percent of the cargoes into the sea while under way. Jets of hot water under pressure scour the sides of the bunkers, forcing a thick blackish layer (a ton of concentrated toxic material) onto the surface of the water. It immediately makes fishing impossible, but local fishermen are compensated. For them, fish merely represent money, and money can always come to an understanding with money.

Another source of petroleum pollution is underwater drilling. In 1980 more than a quarter of the world's total oil production will come from undersea "fields." One single blowout from such a rig produced a devastating oil slick along 45 kilometers of the California coast in 1969. The wells were sealed off, but the pressure threatened to make them blow, and they had to be opened up again immediately.

At Kirkuk, in 1972, an undersea well released 12,500 tons of oil per day. In the North Sea, in 1977, the drilling rig *Bravo* did not achieve this daily rate but kept it up longer. In fact, the danger to the oceans from underwater wells is even greater than that from oil tankers. The point is academic, however, since both of them are going to go on multiplying, whatever we do.

Industry is also currently prospecting undersea for coal, natural gas, copper, sodium, and calcium; such mines pose the same dangers of escaped material and poisonous side effects. There are already about sixty marine coalfields in the United States, and probably as many in the Soviet Union. Their effluents contain acid reducing agents that accelerate the massacre in the seas; reducing agents can be resisted only by species that require little oxygen—in other words, primitive species, which multiply quickly when the death of their competitors leaves them room to do so (much like the human race). Any escaped mineral matter forms an alluvial cone that quickly eliminates all life to a depth of hundreds of meters. Calcium sulphate, which industry spews forth in great abundance, produces a hypersaline environment closely akin to the Dead Sea—a somewhat premonitory analogy. The red sludges of boric and phosphoric acids do the same, but they do it much better.

If the list of oceanic contaminants seems interminable, the reason is that, in the final analysis, *all* terrestrial pollution ends up concentrated in the oceans: oil derivatives carried by surface drainage water; wastes from refineries; the outpourings of burst oil pipes, overfills at service stations, groundings, sinkings; myriad industrial wastes; sewage in a million different forms; runoffs and accidental spills of herbicides and pesticides. (Pesticides are so lethal to the marine environment that a single spill of the same volume as the average oil spill would probably get the better of the whole Atlantic. Yet in Vietnam the Americans used some 71,000 tons of toxic agents more powerful than any pesticides imaginable and actually delivered them by plane.) And then there is rain, just as filthy as the miasma-ridden atmosphere from which it comes; each year it pours 90 million tons of poison into the seas.

Thus, in marine environments today there is nothing, or almost nothing, that can be saved, to a depth of more than a hundred meters. As I write, a ship has just been sunk off Otranto carrying the threat of immediate death to the Mediterranean (which, without this, would have had about twenty years of life left to it). The ship contains 250 tons of tetraethyllead, an antiknock agent for automobiles and a deadly poison. After the sea eats away just one more millimeter of metal, everything will escape. In the last resort salvage would cost about as much as one day's maintenance of the German army. Yet this price may be considered too high, just for saving a sea that is already half-dead.

Many forms of pollution are responsible for the dizzying imbalances among living things in the oceans. Approximately two tons of lead and hundreds of kilos of mercury, selenium, cadmium, copper, tin, and arsenic fall into the sea every hour in the form of microscopic dust; it asphyxiates algae and plankton, upsetting the natural equilibrium. In Holland the Rhine already carries some 200,000 germs per cubic centimeter; the situation in the seas can only be worse. On the other hand the 100,000 tons of phosphorus and the 500,000 tons of nitrogen that the U.S.A. alone discharges annually into the Atlantic make algae in other places thrive all too well; this is the well-known phenomenon of eutrophication, which, like all cases of particular wealth amid general poverty, usually spells misery in the long run. Incredible quantities of viruses and bacteria are retained by shellfish or released directly into the water. At Arcachon, in 1972, there were nearly 10,000 streptococci per liter; at Le Moulleau in the same year, 20,000 coli bacilli. Rome's waste water is discharged into the Tiber, the mouth of which is a tourist beach: in the summer, 10 cases of viral hepatitis, 2 of typhus, and 25 of enteritis occur every day. Off Beirut, Trieste, Messina, Naples, and Tel Aviv the water is 100 percent polluted, though it is crystal-clear. Tourists prefer to close their eyes to the fact that sulphuric acid is equally clear. Most pollution, in fact, is transparent. The exceptions include a few unfortunate kinds of slag and minerals such as copper, which concentrates in oysters and turns them green—at least making them easy to recognize.

All the lamellibranchs filter an enormous volume of water and thus become foci of infection, causing hundreds of epidemics every year; one, which started in Naples in 1973, turned out to be cholera. Through the medium of shellfish, salmonellosis has increased the number of its victims tenfold in twenty years, and its incidence is growing apace.

On the other hand organic wastes kill crustacea, by blocking their branchiae. The Crown of Thorns starfish can devour twice its surface area of coral in a single night; since the death by pollution of its natural predators, this formerly nocturnal creature has been working during the day as well. Coral reefs used to form the richest of all marine environments, sheltering hundreds of kinds of fish; now they are at the point of death. Near the island of Guam, only one tenth of these dwelling places remain on a coastline 60 kilometers long; a third of the famous Great Barrier Reef, a former zoological marvel, has already disappeared.

We cannot leave the subject of marine destruction without mentioning nuclear pollution, a problem which will be examined in more detail later on. Atomic fallout crosses all boundaries, and the duration and the variety of its effects frustrate all attempts to keep track of it. By 1970 atomic tests in the atmosphere had already ravaged the oceans as if a nuclear reactor had been functioning there for ten years without any shielding. The number of factories discharging radioactive wastes into estuaries and watercourses is constantly (and obviously) on the increase. The phosphorus 32 that *normally* used to escape from the U.S.A.'s Hanford power station was concentrated 2,000 times by plankton, 50,000 times by full-grown ducks, 150,000 times by fish, and 1,500,000 times in the yolks of ducks' eggs.

Radioactive wastes are stored at the bottom of the sea, encased in ridiculous containers. By 1965, 100,000 tons were there, ten times more than in 1960. These dumpings, which involve ten industrial countries, are "supervised" by an international commission whose powers are about on a par with a stamp club's. The British power station at Sellafield has secretly released frightening quantities of nuclear wastes into the Irish Sea. The U.S.S.R. accuses the U.S.A. of authorizing wastes five times more radioactive than her own. China is not even present as an observer. But there is nothing to observe: a rat race is a rat race.

The height of absurdity is that every sea in the world now harbors thousands of kilos of resins, which lie there crumbling away after having been used to "purify" radioactive wastes. Sardines and mackerel are very fond of these resins. Suppose that the world's volume of fish were 50 million tons and only one fish per million has happened to absorb a few grams of this kind of substance; then 500,000 people would each eat 100 grams of radioactive fish—which can be enough to cause cancer.

Another danger is nuclear-powered vessels. As early as 1970 there were 300 of them sailing the seas, dumping wastes from their reactors along their way. The number of these vessels increases every year—and consequently the amount of waste and the risk of an accident.

When the *U.S.S. Thresher* and the *U.S.S. Scorpion* sank in 1963 and 1968 respectively, all their nuclear fuel went down with them. The public knew about these incidents because it was impossible to hide the truth from them. But on the subject of general marine radioactivity, as on the subject of accidents which can be concealed, no government has ever said anything to the people—who do not wish to know anything anyway. The fact of the matter is that the rulers themselves do not know much more about these subjects than the man on the street.

In fact, nobody knows where or how to dispose of nuclear wastes safely. In 1972 it was discovered (once again, by accident) that out of 1,800 concrete containers the Saclay station used to enclose its wastes on land, 500 had been cracked, damaged by frost, or eroded by rainwater. Now marine corrosion, as one can imagine, is infinitely stronger than atmospheric attacks. And radioactive liquids boil furiously and give off heat that eats away at their containers. The slightest leak kills off the surrounding flora and fauna and poses unbelievable problems of cooling and settling; any irradiated fish that are still alive can carry their radioactive loads hundreds of kilometers away.

All this doomsday material, thousands of tons of it, is accumulating at the bottom of the sea, along with the innumerable deposits of poisons that are already there. For example, 7,000 tons of arsenic, three times enough to wipe out the human race, was dumped into the Baltic forty years ago; 400,000 tons of yperite, a hundred times enough to do the same job, was engulfed in the Atlantic in 1970, and so on. As early as 1960 two members of the Parisian Academy of Sciences stated that algae, plankton, and oceanic bacteria were carrying a "fantastic" load of radioactivity. Sure enough, the news was greeted as a fantasy. Yet some of the marine bacteria used as agricultural fertilizer concentrate cobalt 60; they are as radioactive in our food as they were in the sea.

The general poisoning is complicated by out-and-out plundering of marine life. Nearly all fisheries have become exterminating operations. They use sophisticated military equipment to track down the last fish that can be called edible. But this greed does not stop catches from diminishing constantly. The blue whale, the cachalot, the rorqual, and many other species are dying out. The volume of the Brazilian crayfish catch has not increased since 1950. The tonnage of sole taken in France has dropped by almost a quarter over the last five years. In Sweden one is more and more frequently advised not to eat the fish. A fifth of the American crop of mollusks and crustaceans is already condemned. In 1977 Iran announced that its production of caviar had decreased by half as the result of oil pollution. The reserves of pearl oysters in French Oceania are almost exhausted. A carnivorous fish consumes, through its prey, the equivalent of 200 kilos of plankton per day—double poisoning. The spectre of viral hepatitis threatens all shellfish. Certain oysters multiply the concentration of DDT in their environment by 100,000.

In general, over the last twenty-five years, the globe's marine life has lost at least one quarter of its resources; in the Mediterranean, the loss is at least half. In the seas as elsewhere the downward movement is accelerating. Some experts see the oceans as humanity's sole hope for nutritional survival. They must think, then, that the race's future lies behind it—and perhaps they are not mistaken.

V

The atmosphere is a volatile sea that can clean itself only by fouling the other sea beneath it. The marine rubbish dump thus depends very largely on the atmospheric gas chamber.

As the whole world knows (or at least suspects), the iron and steel industry alone emits an enormous quantity of gases. The worst among them are often the least easily detected, such as carbon monoxide, which is odorless and colorless. Steel manufacture, in addition to wasting fresh water, also produces penetrating reddish-brown fumes that include sulphur dioxide, which attacks birds and people alike, sulphur (which is also produced by the Lacq process of "clean" gas extraction), and many other elements that react with ultraviolet rays in the stratosphere to generate a whole chemistry of unexpected, harmful substances.

Domestic heating exudes heavy hydrocarbons and tiny particles of tarry slag that slowly destroy trees and grass. In fact, nearly half the pollution that ravages our bronchial tubes is caused by the cut-rate precautions we take against the cold. When the catastrophe-ridden cities finally turn to solar energy for help, the sun may no longer be visible to give it.

The automobile is another offender. During the last fifteen years the number of automobiles in the world has more than doubled: from 136 million in 1966 to at least 300 million in 1980. As we have seen, one automobile "breathes" as much as thirty humans; city air owes half its toxicity to motor vehicles, the waters of the sea one fifth of theirs. And the latter figure does not take account of pollution resulting from the transport of oil, lead, asbestos, and so on, activities that exist only because of the existence of the internal combustion engine.

An automobile in operation spews out an interminable list of poisons—and the quantities, even for a single vehicle, are enormous. Among its hypertoxic products is asbestos. This mineral is so dangerous that people almost everywhere have thought of banning its use even in modern construction and industrial processing. But they have *thought* about a ban—and too late, at that. Automobiles grind asbestos to powder in their brakes and clutch plates. Once it gets into human respiratory passages, it is *never* resorbed. Among the many illnesses that can be attributed to it, cancer takes pride of place.

The very wear of tires is also harmful. Each year it produces at least a half-million tons of carbon black—a carcinogen, though one less virulent than benzopyrene and methylcholantrene, which are among the most virulent cancer agents known, and which, thanks to the winds, can now be found on the ice packs of the South Pole. All by themselves, automobiles are saturating Earth's atmosphere with lead; thanks to them, the amount of this poisonous metal in Green-land today is five hundred times greater than that of 1910. They also give off huge quantities of carbon monoxide; an 11 HP motor emits more than 1,500 liters of it per hour. Air that is 4 percent carbon monoxide can kill a medium-size bird; a concentration of scarcely more than 2 percent doubles the rate of breathing in human beings. Nitric oxide, which the automobile emits in enormous quantities, has similar effects and also leads to lung cancer and the slow deteriora-tion of the nervous system. All these airborne poisons are, of course, bombarded by ultraviolet rays in the stratosphere, producing new pollutants that Science finds even more disquieting than the old ones—which is saying a good deal. Their harmfulness is only re-vealed by large numbers of victims and immediate affliction. Sud-den, widespread damage taught us, for example, that peracetyl nitrate, a product of automobile exhaust gases after treatment in the stratosphere, is deadly dangerous to all forms of plant life; it is also, of course, highly carcinogenic.

The automobile thus ranks with nuclear energy as one of the worst factors in the general poisoning of the world. "Antipollution" exhaust devices, which industry promised in 1972 for 1975, were still not in existence in 1977. They will never exist, for all combustion spells pollution. A French campaign against automobile pollution proudly claimed partial success in 1977. "Partial" is about as much as one can say since the "part" turned out to be almost exactly 1 per-cent.

Today there is no city that the automobile has not turned into a vast parking lot, no avenue that is not a rectilinear traffic artery bordered by concrete sidewalks and strips of sickly, dying, dusty, greyish grass. It will soon be impossible for people to talk to each other in the street except by walkie-talkie, impossible to breathe except high up in the mountains (where the air is only a little less toxic than elsewhere, and cars will soon be as numerous as tourists, anyway), impossible to cross a lane without thinking of the danger of being run down and killed, impossible to regard other human beings as other than so many pilots nattering away behind their windshields, so many Sunday mechanics mucking about underneath the artificial armor of their coachwork.

At the wheel of a car people are threatened physically, morally, and financially. Anything that brushes against them frightens them, anything that touches them harms them; they have the soul of a mollusk in the shell of a crustacean. The shinier and more cumbersome their car, the louder the purr of its motor, the more impressed they are. They are either a peacock in the poultry yard or a sparrow among the peacocks. Cooperation, courage, brotherhood—these are unthinkable concepts in the world of the automobile. A few years ago, a man lying wounded on a road in France was finished off by being hit by about fifty cars in succession. Every day a driver who has just killed someone makes a fast getaway. Aggressiveness is obligatory; it is veiled and low profile but always ready. Several times a year a bump between two cars ends up in murder by a bullet or a knife. Crowds, backfires, asphyxia, traffic jams—all recreate in their image the humanity that fashioned them in its own. The Ego is inflated in proportion to the size of the metal box it drives; each make of car signifies a particular social status. The Other is a challenge, a danger, an opportunity for victory—an enemy. Two cars stopped at a red light are two racers at the starting line: being passed is an insult that calls for redress; being first off the mark is a ceremonial triumph.

Hands gripping the steering wheel, eyes glued to the speedometer as the radio blares, the driver can no longer use speech. The semantics of the automobile is skimpier than the language of prepaleolithic society. Of its dozen or so elementary signals, some nine of them are nothing but surrogate blows that signify intimidation, anger, and fright (for example, the index finger circling at the temple as the driver passes another car with a blast of the horn or a flash of the headlights). There is only one—a sort of Boy Scout salute—that more or less expresses thanks.

Medically speaking, a driver has no single organ operating in its natural state. At a hundred kilometers per hour, tension becomes almost tetanic. The adrenaline content of the blood rises, the digestive system ceases to function, the coronary arteries constrict (this is the prelude to a heart attack). The nervous system goes on a state of alert, and awareness is fully mobilized, for the rules of the asphalt chessboard are grim. Each error must be paid for; the lightest penalty means one's purse, the heaviest one's life.

Space is eaten up, counted carefully, weighed in the scales: so many liters per hundred kilometers. Timetables grip the traveller like the jaws of a vise; the automobile made them possible, now they make the automobile indispensable. Time is measured in cans of oil, slopes in degrees of inclination from the horizontal, hairpin curves in the number of gear shifts—and everything is measured in money. A highway has plenty of reading material: lies on the billboards, figures denoting kilometers, police orders, military instructions. One is held to ransom all the way from the toll bridge to the service station, and what with motorized *brigades* and police *patrols* and electronic *controls*, one might as well be in a barracks. "Caution," "dangerous curve," "squeeze right," "no passing," "no standing," "stop," "60 maximum," "go," "pull over," "yield," "switch off headlights," "do not blow horn." On top of all these injunctions come the threats of calamities ahead: "avalanche," "slippery road," "school crossing," "falling rocks," "factory exit," "concealed side road," "fog," "major accident 1 kilometer ahead" (and one can see those sinister red lights blinking). It is impossible for the drivers to avoid catastrophe if they miss their exit so they must watch for the signs: only one kilometer to go, slow down, only 500 meters, shift down, take care, right turn signal on, sharp bend, scissors motion with the feet, grip the steering wheel tight. What remains of awareness must be directed towards the machinery: they must know where the distributor is, be prepared to get their hands covered with grease changing a spark plug, be able to use a jack and wrench to change a tire, to clean a windshield that is sticky with the entrails of mosquitoes and moths. An eight-hour trip leaves them with shaky legs. Their expression is set, they are drooping with fatigue, their nostrils have gone dry in the tepid, polluted air, which is often laden with stifling smells of plastic, benzine, and burnt rubber. The intersections are maddening, the curves irritating, the trees along the roads pillories. The countryside doesn't matter—they can't see it, anyway. Grey as tombs and smooth as billiard tables, the freeways asphyxiate meadows, woods, even villages. Each section of the road means the death of a thousand trees. The French Autoroute A–86, in the Yvelines, cost four hundred hectares of forest.

Each lineup of cars, each traffic jam spells irritation, anger, impotent powerless rage. The horn blasts seem to multiply all by themselves; the driver's lungs fill with benzopyrene from the car ahead, which is going flat out but still seems impatient. In New York and

Los Angeles during the evening rush hour, signs light up instruct-
ing drivers to switch off their engines: the air is becoming dangerous. Yet nothing discourages the craze for the automobile. Many
attempts have been made in the United States to penalize the lone
drivers; it costs them more to cross the Golden Gate Bridge, but
they remain alone. The authorities in Osaka have considered making
gas masks obligatory, but people would go on driving even if they
had to wear scuba gear.

Residential suburbs and vacation homes depend on the automobile, which has become a necessity. Our lives are organized by and
for the monster. We pay for parking lots, for thousands of kilometers of concrete roads, for whole hospitals, and even for the progressive disfigurement of our cities by the foaming tide of this gaily
colored scrap iron. If all the public squares in Paris were excavated
two to five storeys deep, they would provide parking for fewer cars
than the city's annual increase in them. A six-lane freeway has about
the same price tag as an electric train but carries thirty times fewer
people. A section of throughway costs as much as a thousand residential units or a 520-bed hospital. Transporting a thousand tons
(from Paris to Marseilles, for example) requires a fifty-car freight
train operated by two people or some sixty trucks with 100 to 120
drivers working shifts. The latter method risks an accident on each
of some 4,000 bends along the way, poisons Nature as well as Humans, and costs considerably more; in consequence, it is the one that
gets chosen all over the world.

Not only does the automobile degrade everything and everybody,
not only is it dirty, not only does it stink; it is also ugly in all its
styles. A car's "beauty" is reckoned by its price, its speed, and its
comfort—in other words (in order) by cash, competition, and flash.
As with "beautiful" refrigerators and "beautiful" washing machines,
bad taste and charlatanry combine to give the machine exactly what
the customer expects to find in it. They recall the excessive elegance
of bygone days in an attempt to compensate for the gas gauges and
all the bric-a-brac of extraterrestrial pseudotechnology. Thus, the
assembly lines drip paint, solder, and chrome, turning out hundreds
of thousands of mauve cabriolets, cabbage-green coupés, and violet
sedans. But the ideal hidden beneath this disguise is always the
rocket, the shell, the tank.

Modern warfare is also the only equivalent for the scenes of horror that the automobile accident has made familiar. Pools of blood, bodies cut to shreds by broken glass and seared by burning gasoline, death rattles drowned by ambulance sirens: fatal accidents occur at the worldwide rate of ten per minute. But the dead, the wounded, the permanently crippled will avail nothing—for nothing will be of any avail. The automobile means autonomy, and the time it gains for us is priceless. The money that it has swallowed since it first saw the light of day would by now have been enough to give us a near-perfect network of subways and trains linking all the important places of the world. The air would be pure, the boulevards would look like those of Monet and the quays like those of Corot. The automobile turns all these scenes into a single identical picture. The picture represents us, but we are losing our identity.

I shall be accused of exaggerating the evils of the automobile and taking too little account of other forms of pollution. But they are not *other*; they are the same. Whatever the car owners know about emissions of their vehicle, they will not give it up, not today, not tomorrow, not ever, because they need it and because they are *theirs*. Neither is there a nuclear power station, a pesticide factory, nor an oil tanker in the world that the owners do not need and that is not *theirs*.

VI

This is the reason that 300,000 tons of sulphur dioxide fall on Paris every year, along with 100,000 cubic meters of sulphuric acid and 13,500 tons of greasy dusts with bases of arsenic, chlorine, mercury, selenium, and so on. Half this sulphur dioxide comes from a supposedly nonpolluting form of energy; an electric power station near Saint-Ouen gives off nearly 9,000 tons of it per month. As early as 1966, 200,000 tons of lead were getting into the atmosphere in the U.S.A. and thence into the oceans. The tonnage of dusts given off annually by major cities is staggering: in 1973, London averaged 276 tons per square kilometer, Osaka 390. (Osaka's dusts would fill 140 garbage trucks every day.) While the polluters compete against each other, the pollutants combine. The result is other pollutants that are more concentrated and usually have cumulative effects. The human body does not eliminate them completely, and there are some, such as asbestos, that it does not eliminate at all. Thus, the toxic doses add up. During a few months of walking along traffic-ridden streets, a pedestrian completely absorbs (and only partly eliminates) the equivalent of one bottle of sulphuric acid, one briquette of anthracite, one flask of arsenic, and 300 grams of verdigris—not to mention radioactive isotopes and various elements whose harmfulness is still not well known.

There are more and more of the latter. One is beryllium. This light metal has killed hundreds of workers who handled it—and their so-called protective clothing has contaminated thousands more. (Asbestos does the same things though more slowly.) But manufacturing secrets make a complete study of beryllium's effects impossible. Only profit can stop progress, and one does not stop profit. In 1973 the Dutch authorities intercepted trucks with 78 tons of beryllium packed haphazardly under their gas tanks in rusty, cracked drums. A few days later it was all put into new drums and shipped to Anvers. The destination of the consignment was kept secret; the truck drivers attacked indiscreet TV cameramen from a German station.

Aerosol sprays have been in general use for fifteen years. The alarm has now been sounded. They emit a gas called Freon that attacks the respiratory passages; worse, it is eating away the layer of ozone without which the sun's ultraviolet rays would destroy all life on Earth. Since there is no question of banning these highly profitable devices, which already exist in millions of millions, commercial science calms the public by telling it that lightning in the upper atmosphere continually recreates ozone. Will Freon spur it on to recreating even more?

Fluorine, one of the by-products of manufacturing aluminum, is toxic (and naturally, carcinogenic) in very small doses. It kills conifers or renders them sterile. One single aluminum works can cost 700 hectares of forest, but paying damages is cheaper than neutralizing fluorides.

Ultraviolet rays oxidate the escaped gases, which then bring on hemorrhages and pulmonary edemas. Spending three hours in a city with heavy traffic raises the carbon content of human blood by a third (it is this high carbon content that encourages hemorrhages and edemas). Respiratory diseases, excluding tuberculosis, are responsible for one third of the lost working hours throughout the world. In the United States the number of deaths attributable to bronchitis and emphysema doubles every five years. In France bronchopulmonary attacks wreak more havoc than heart attacks, although the latter are constantly increasing. More and more, plants are developing strange malformations. The leaves become cankered under a layer of sticky lacquer and then drop off.

Around 1870 Parisians could expect twenty-three days of poor visibility per year. By 1914 this figure had almost doubled, and in 1958 it was 125. Today Paris is capped year round by a gaseous dome 2 kilometers high and 40 across.

We can forecast climatic changes on a global scale (though not their exact nature). The ozone layer is sensitive not only to the Freon in aerosols, but also to nitrogen oxide; the big supersonic jets emit one ton of it during each hour of flight. With so many planes in the air, the total volume of cirrus clouds has increased by 6 percent in the last ten years, and the cloud layer over the North Atlantic is now 10 percent heavier than normal.

Houses, walls, monuments—all are growing darker in color. Three statues over the royal portal of Chartres Cathedral have had to be replaced by copies, and it will not be long before the others need replacing too. A urinelike yellow is the clearest color a cathedral can retain, even if it is properly maintained. An Egyptian obelisk exposed to the air in New York has deteriorated more during the last eighty years than it had during the previous three thousand. The Acropolis in Athens has crumbled so that it threatens to collapse completely; there are plans to give it a plastic coating. Every Parisian pays 30 francs a year towards the resurfacing of the city's façades; worldwide, the chemical damage suffered by roofs alone costs 15 million francs annually. Florence is turning brown; Michelangelo's marbles are crumbling. Statues everywhere are turning black, a sort of caries is gnawing away even at granite, a blackish froth issues from the mouths of stone Christs, a brown edging transforms Madonnas into gargoyles and Apollos into street cleaners, while bas-reliefs resemble impressions, and Gothic frontispieces seem to date from the Carboniferous age. In just one quarter of Venice during 1967 alone, 250 paintings, frescoes, and statues deteriorated from contact with the air; 6 percent of the city's sculptures fall into dust each year. Old masters, however, are of little account since today's artists have learned to adapt and are not afraid to expose their spray-paint compositions and straw sculptures to the open air.

When a country the size of France receives an annual fall of 2 million tons of sulphur dioxide, 5 million tons of carbon monoxide, 1 million tons of nitrogen oxide, and another million of various other chemical dusts, can one be surprised to learn that there are 500,000 bacteria in a cubic meter of air in Montsouris Park, whereas the same volume of air contained only 75 in 1900? Along the major boulevards, the usual count is now a million bacteria per cubic meter; in public squares it fluctuates between 6 and 8 million. These bacteria date from the first flood of minerals, and they thrive wherever lead, nitrogen, or cadmium creates a void.

Another aspect of Gehenna is noise. The principal component of noise pollution is obviously the sounds made by automobiles. They lower intellectual efficiency by one fifth; in some offices the number of typing errors triples when the windows are opened. The consequences of noise are psychological and so incalculable, but they are identifiable, since they are identical from one human being to another. Noise upsets cardiac rhythm, brings on progressive deafness (which itself encourages a heightening of noise), makes conversation impossible while reducing the language to a series of onomatopoeic syllables, distracts attention, produces dizziness, disturbs or prevents sleep, and causes depression and hostility. It even makes fetal hearts beat faster, because of nervousness, *before* the mothers are affected by it. Irreversible organic problems set in when the noise level is above 80 decibels. In Paris's Place de l'Opéra, the din now reaches 90 to 100 decibels around 6 P.M. At Orly, a school off the end of a runway receives a wave of 54 to 114 decibels every five minutes. While a suave voice is asking businessmen to fasten their seat belts, the teacher down below has to shout to make herself heard by the children, who are on their way to becoming schizophrenics (later on, psychoanalysis will explain their mental disorders by Oedipal fables). People who live under the most frequented air traffic lanes go deaf. The population of New York's Long Island perceive a range of frequencies that is four times narrower than that perceived by the inhabitants of the Sudan. The effect of supersonic booms on animal species can be measured by what they produce on breeding farms: convulsions, spastic deaths, sterility, accelerated aging, and so on. Windows, roofs, furniture, chinaware—everything breaks, cracks, comes apart. The monuments that airplane noise has affected or destroyed in France are counted in hundreds. But the profits of the airlines are counted in millions.

Finally, garbage. In both Europe and North America, the weight per town is doubling every five years. (Industry is very generous; it provides two thirds of the amount.) The daily trash of Paris would form a pyramid a hundred meters high with the Place de la Concorde as its base. There is no need to describe the disorder all this rubbish produces. Nine tenths of Germany's solid wastes are disposed of quietly in some fifty thousand public dumps; for the most part they are situated well out in the countryside. In America six million cars per year are piled up near landfills and on waste ground. Only partially treated, since money is involved, this refuse attracts rats (there was nearly a panic in Texarkana, Texas, when they recently increased thirtyfold) and serves as a culture medium for microbe strains and a dwelling place for billions of disease-carrying insects.

Incineration of all these pollutants has only one inconvenient thing about it: it is itself a source of pollution. The thousands of kilograms of poisonous mercury incinerated each year (in junked batteries, thermometers, electrical parts, and so on) evaporate almost completely—and fall gently back to earth. The incineration of refuse inevitably releases both sulphur dioxide and nitrogen peroxide and can thus contribute up to one quarter of a city's total pollution.

Certain materials, such as plastics, do not decay when buried and are toxic when burnt. For example, polyvinyl chloride, the substance used for phonograph records among other things, gives off hydrochloric acid. Glass and aluminum call for special treatments, which are costly—and incomplete anyway. Industrial packaging has doubled in weight over the last ten years and will quadruple in five years' time.

Any new material poses new disposal problems. Of every *thirty* products that world commerce launches, it has only *one* of them analyzed, and this analysis is never concerned with recycling the product in the form of garbage. Such are the laws of profit. This is why only harmful substances seem able to proliferate at the same rate as the merely superfluous.

VII

World production of pesticides has quintupled during the last fifty years and will double its present level over the next fifteen. Meanwhile, these poisons will continue to demonstrate their astonishing durability and pervasiveness. Arsenic used fifteen years ago to treat a tobacco plantation filtered into the soil and can still be found in cigarette smoke. Pesticides of all sorts find their way into the underground water tables and onto the ice packs; the Antarctic holds thousands of tons of them.

Soluble in fats but not in water, DDT concentrates in mammals in the suprarenal glands, the thyroid, the liver, and the mesentery. A diet of DDT at 1 ppm (1 part per million or 1 milligram per kilo) can produce loadings of 100 ppm in these organs. Nothing escapes it—neither embryos nor mother's milk. A small dose can simultaneously attack the liver and inhibit an enzyme essential to the functioning of the heart. A recent investigation of workers in a plant manufacturing DDT and other pesticides established that one out of three was "on the threshold of mental abnormality." In the U.S.A. pesticides are directly responsible for the deaths of 1,000 people a year, and they poison more than 100,000 others. Henceforth, we will be able to deduce a person's nationality from the DDT content of the tissues. For all of us, not even excepting the Inuit, this content is so high that our bodies are inedible under international butchers' standards. A breast-fed baby takes in an almost fatal dose of DDT, arsenic derivatives, mercury salts, heptachlor, and so on (logically, therefore, breast-feeding should be increasingly discouraged).

Pesticides attack us in three ways: through our vegetables, which contain them; through the animals we eat, which concentrate them; through the air we breathe, which distributes them. Eggs are contaminated by the grass hens peck at and by the grain they eat; fish by algae and plankton, which in turn have been contaminated by winds and rain. The animals that give us our meat take in pesticides not only with their fodder but also by breathing the air as we do, by drinking the water as we do. Each time an animal devours another animal's flesh, the predator's body further concentrates the pesticides already concentrated in its victim's body, and so on in succession, *da capo senza fine.*

We are not far from the point of no return. The poisons that are replacing DDT are more destructive without being any less penetrating. They get into fruit and vegetables, and no amount of washing can get them out. PCBs are five times as toxic as DDT. Lindane kills bees at a distance and attacks the hearts of roots and tubers, such as radishes and potatoes. Its presence in the muscular tissues of the French has just been confirmed. Chlordane is even more harmful; it penetrates the skin just on handling. Dieldrin, forty times more violent still, directly destroys the nervous systems of insects— and of humans. Aldrin settles in the liver and the kidneys; only infinitesimal quantities are involved but just a few traces are sufficient to sterilize a man or a woman, and a female dog can barely tolerate 2 or 3 ppm in her body (her pups die the first time she feeds them). Endrin has already poisoned a large number of wells in the United States and left underground water tables beyond recovery. Malathion, regarded as inoffensive when it was put on the market, becomes more destructive than DDT if it combines with certain products containing phosphorus; now wheat is often treated with pesticides containing phosphorus, yet malathion, like lindane, is still supposed to be a wheat *preservative.*

Parathion is so lethal that 5 milligrams in a liter of air kills rats in a few minutes. A chemist volunteered to ingest an infinitesimal dose of it while holding a syringe of the antidote in his hand; he died as though struck by lightning before he could inoculate himself. A splash of parathion in the eye can be instantly fatal. Potatoes pulled from soil treated four months earlier with parathion still contain the chemical; so does olive oil.

Lindane is in the air Londoners breathe. Just sitting in a field that has been recently sprayed with this pesticide can be deadly. Carrots disinfested with lindane contain up to 6 milligrams per kilo of this poison; 10 percent of them become sterile, and their carotene content falls. Herbivorous animals get unbelievable concentrations in their tissues.

Milk, butter, eggs, animal fats—all these may contain up to forty times the so-called permissible dose of any pesticide, especially of DDT. When several hectares of Canadian forest were recently sprayed with DDT, about a million salmon died in a nearby river; nobody knows why. Another example: a French firm dumped its lindane wastes into a gravel pit; within a few months, 70 tons of potatoes, thousands of liters of milk, and an underground water table were contaminated. In 1964 near Paris twenty thousand colonies of bees died after a compound containing phosphorus was used on a field in the area; no more than a few thousand nectar gatherers could have foraged in this field, but bees constantly touch each other's antennae and breasts. This is why pesticides are found in honey. But, of course, they are found everywhere.

By 1968 American production of DDT had reached 63,000 tons. Half of the vast hoard of poison was intended for export even though the whole world knew by then that this pesticide is no better than a plague. The production of DDT finally ceased in 1978, but its results are still with us around the world. Cahow petrels, which live on a desert isle in the Bermudas, have enough DDT in their bodies to ensure that their fertility's dropping 3 percent a year; extinction is inevitable. Concentrations of the deadly chemical have caused the eggshells of one quarter of the recorded species of birds to become increasingly thin and fragile. The sparrow hawk, the golden eagle, the peregrine falcon—already rare species—have lost 60 percent of their numbers through the action of organo-chlorates. The wild duck, the robin, and the osprey are becoming sterile in the same way. Out of 1,200 pelican chicks in Anacapa in 1969, only 5 survived. Millions of birds are slaughtered each year—not by sterility but by direct poisoning. They are doing only one thing wrong: they cannot distinguish DDT-laden insects from the others—if there are any others.

The point of no return approaches everywhere. The pesticide that penetrates the soil is absorbed by bacteria and by the flesh of mushrooms; these feed animals that in turn feed other animals. At each stage the concentration increases. Eight years after an area is treated with DDT, half of it remains in the ground, and part of this has sunk down deep. (For benzene hexachloride, the figure is eleven years.) And 1 gram of DDT buried in the ground is as virulent as 40 grams in the open air.

Thus, even though no more DDT is being produced, the quantity of this pesticide in the soil will increase worldwide until 1986. Only then will it drop off slowly. Fish will have to struggle against it increasingly until 1989 and will not regain their 1978 level of concentration until 2003. DDT concentrations in all animals, including the Human, will rise for an even longer period. As the curve ascends, how many species will fall by the wayside and perish? As usual, we do not know.

What we do know is disquieting: the only animals totally immune to pesticides are insects. Henceforth, flies, cochineals, and fleas will be able to resist enormous doses, since they have had hundreds of generations in which to adapt through Darwinian selection. Even now at least 200 species of pests are no longer really harmed by the worst of poisons. Now, out of a million different species of insects, only some 3,000 are considered harmful to crops. Perhaps 500,000 others are rather more useful to agriculture than not; they may die indiscriminately. The resistant species are not only continuing their ravages but also transmitting pesticides like an infectious strain. Furthermore, the meal they offer their predators, who are interested only in whether their prey is alive, is a poisoned one. Should these predators happen to be chickens, for example, the last guests at that particular table will be ourselves.

Ironically, although pesticides act rather indiscriminately, allowing mites and caterpillars to multiply because of the destruction of carpocapsas and sparrows respectively, the pest-fighting techniques of Nature are both successful and selective, even though they are still not fully understood. Wasps combat the San José louse better than pesticides, mites are infallible against the woodworm, a single ant's nest in a dying forest can cure it in one season. But treatment with wasps costs ten times as much as treatment with DDT. The rules of the commercial game of grab, rigid between individuals, harsh between companies, implacable between nations, do not allow any such entomological fantasy at any level. The economic reality is that Pakistan cannot choose to breed hymenoptera as long as Canada uses lindane. In any case, thanks to the winds, lindane in either of these countries would end up killing the wasps in the other— while, of course, sparing the fleas.

VIII

Whatever a poison makes profitable, someone is going to market. Thus, additives prolong the life of pesticides. One additive in four is carcinogenic, and laboratory tests show that nearly all of them attack the liver, heart, spleen, or kidneys, invariably resulting in stunted growth, anemia, myocarditis, liver changes, and arrested testicular development. Each year, we eat nearly *two kilos* of additives.

One brand of rice currently on the market contains nitric acid, sodium glutamate, monoglycerides, propylene glycol, and antioxidants. What is sold as orange juice sometimes has 20 percent orange juice, sometimes none at all (dozens of additives make up the rest). Besides, half the time orange juice is made by pressing the citrus fruit with its skin still on and still coated with diphenyl—for nothing must be allowed to go to waste. Insoluble in water, diphenyl is soluble in alcohols; orange liqueurs contain it. Even weak doses interfere with the functioning of the kidneys. Carrots are most frequently preserved by irradiation with cobalt 60, which destroys their vitamin E, some of their vitamin C, and their carotene. In Europe an apple or a pear undergoes an average of twelve to fifteen treatments.

The meat we eat is almost as toxic as our own flesh. Antibiotics used to treat animals are still found in their meat six weeks later, along with the usual pesticide derivatives of arsenic, mercury, organo-chlorate, and so on. Also present are estrogens, enzymes, and even tranquillizers (sedating pigs makes butchering them easier). The chloramphenicol used to blanch meat can be directly lethal—it splits bone marrow—it can also immunize intestinal flora against antibiotics so they are no longer effective in combatting serious illnesses, such as typhoid. France has banned the use of antibiotics for foodstuffs; 168 tons of them were used on livestock in 1967 alone. The animals were reported suddenly sick, and, of course, they had to be cared for. . . .

In Europe eight out of ten calves are treated with estrogens because this hormone makes female calves grow fat (just as overly strong birth control pills make women grow fat). Estrogen stays in the meat after it is butchered. In laboratory tests male organisms subjected to estrogen acquire feminine characteristics. It is pure chance, of course, that the number of hormone imbalance cases in France increased 150-fold in the decade 1963–1973. Pollution is becoming a habit with us.

Were it not fortified with vitamins, today's milk would be no more than whitish water, distinguishable from mineral water only because of its paucity of minerals and its richness in pesticides. Some 500,000 bacteria can often be found in one cubic centimeter of commercial pasteurized milk, in which only the natural vitamin P remains intact (doubtless because it is the only one that serves no useful purpose).

Onions are bombarded with cobalt, ham with gamma rays, flour with X rays. Wheat, grapes, tomatoes, cucumber seeds, chickens, and steaks are all irradiated. Standard procedure, but a procedure that is uncontrolled and almost uncontrollable. Instant soups are treated with antioxidants. The potatoes we buy in plastic bags go through baths of bisulphite of soda and carbon dioxide. Colza, soya, and linseed oils are pressed without a binding agent and thus almost completely deprived of their nutritional value; they are also deodorized with sulphuric acid. Most table oils are extracted with aviation fuel. An Italian process allows the manufacture of olive oil that is 3 percent olives; the rest of it is mainly bone fat and slaughterhouse wastes, treated with Vaseline, oil, and carbon. The fraud is almost undetectable, and the fines, however heavy, never outweigh the profits.

Most makers of foie gras cram their geese with a mash that contains arsenic derivatives and antimony; it fattens up the birds' livers and produces functional changes in human livers. French cheeses often contain nisin and pimaricin, which are banned in nearly every other country—French science cannot understand why.

The methyl-4-imidazole found in caramels sends mice into convulsions. The powder dusted on candies brings on cancers and pneumoconioses in laboratory animals. The Dulcin in chocolates produces cancer in rats and makes the females abort. The liquid paraffin used to polish coffee grains and the smoke used to darken them are both carcinogenic. So is the benzoic acid through which purees, fruit juices, preserves, berries, salmon caviar, and sprats are passed and the sulphuric acid used in the treatment of ciders, wines, fresh, dried, and candied fruit.

The sooty deposits on smoked foods are responsible for gastrointestinal cancers, as are the emulsifiers contained in three out of four brands of margarine. Certain additives encourage the body's absorption of others. Sodium nitrate and ascorbic acid are sometimes found together, making it possible for a child to absorb four times the so-called permissible daily dose of sodium nitrate, a source of arterial hypertension. Selenium compounds, which are often responsible for serious genetic damage, are found in the majority of edible plants. There is no flour made that has not had hydrogen, benzol, peroxide, chlorine dioxide, and oxides of nitrogen added to it. Sliced bread may contain ninety-six different additives.

Then there are the involuntary additives. Strictly speaking, these include all the pollution to which the animal and vegetable worlds are subjected, and which these worlds pass on to us to swallow. We know that crustaceans, mollusks, and fish contain mercury, but this hypertoxic metal also invades cereals through the action of the wind. Traces of cadmium can also be detected in rice, wheat, and millet, not to mention certain seafoods that are as rich in poisons as all the seas and all other foods. Cadmium is used in the plating of food cans, and it gets into the contents, as tin does into canned soft drinks. Just a few millionths of a gram are enough. . . . Cobalt, which brings on heart attacks, is still used to settle the froth on beer. In Quebec in 1965 such a beer sent forty-eight people to hospital in one evening; twenty of them died.

These examples are a short excerpt from an inexhaustible catalogue. No food exists today without additives, and additives have made possible the appearance of more than 10,000 new food products. This commercial chemistry is literally uncontrollable. Suppose the number of food additives in the world were one thousand (in fact, it is four or five times that number); assuming only three additives per commodity, testing each would be a scientific effort beyond the powers of the human race. In addition, it would be useless. No country can control all its producers, nor can the producing countries achieve control among themselves. Chemistry in the service of profit will follow its employers' wishes: each year we shall eat a little less real food and a little more sham. When the wealth of nations is ending in the ruination of the world and private profit in public deficit, it is only to be expected that one additive should be regarded as counterbalancing several subtractions.

As is also to be expected, there is also a constant increase in the number of recorded food-poisonings, both mass and individual. The latter only come to light by chance (which means only in exceptional cases). Such phenomena must be both large scale and rapid—such as the catastrophes at Minamata or Seveso—if they are to be noted and diagnosed correctly. Otherwise Science, which cannot bring itself to trust anything but statistics in this area, can no longer find the real cause of a specific incident; the possibilities are in the millions when Humanity is collectively and simultaneously being poisoned on all fronts.

Yet even if diagnosis were possible, the remedies would not be effective. The World Health Organization has published blacklists banning certain chemicals for use in all food products; nevertheless, many of these substances, such as boron and salicylic acid, are still ubiquitous. Germany, England, and the U.S.S.R. have passed outline laws concerning the pollution of foodstuffs, but it is on the increase, as those responsible admit. Although the United States' Food and Drug Administration (FDA) is considered the most powerful control organization in the world, it has been bought off on many occasions, most notably by twenty-one large milk distributors in 1968. It has also shown many times that policing the American fishing industries is a bad joke, that supervision of fish canneries is a mediocre do-it-yourself performance, that one out of five chickens sold as ready for eating is not fit for consumption, that those responsible for various cases of food poisoning will not allow their premises to be inspected. All in vain. . . .

We find the same state of affairs in the sphere of pharmaceuticals—and for the same reason: this sphere is private property. Out of a hundred drugs, scarcely four are studied in depth in the United States (once again, this information comes from the FDA). We can imagine what things must be like in Europe or the U.S.S.R.

Now, during the twenty-five years or so it takes, on average, to reject and ban a harmful drug, tens of thousands of others come onto the market. And knowing that pharmaceutical products are even less controlled than foodstuffs (still according to the FDA), we may conclude that new poisons are allowed to circulate almost freely. Any guarantees as to their harmlessness are almost worthless, as are the incredible statements about tolerated dosages (which almost always vary from one country to another, depending, of course, on how much each country is raking in from a particular item). What sort of alimentary control is it that permits DDT in bread, mercury wastes in flour, lindane in milk, and orange juice that contains no oranges?

In this sort of world the struggle against addictive drugs, even heroin, is a disaster, full of lies which it tries to pass off as motives. It is difficult to understand why societies that are destroying the Earth are so anxious to prevent us from dying. Few of the so-called hard drugs are actually lethal, but even if they claimed a hundred times more victims each year than they do, the total would not be half the number of fatalities caused by drunks, not to mention those caused by alcoholism itself. Alcoholics account for a third of the expenditures of all the clinics in France. They are responsible for at least three out of every ten fatal accidents. Every ten minutes, another Frenchman dies of alcoholism or its effects: delirium tremens, premature aging, cirrhosis of the liver, and so on. In every industrial country at least one in every twenty-five persons is an alcoholic. If heroin caused even 0.1 percent of the deaths caused by alcohol, the press and public opinion would cry out against such a scourge.

Moreover, no drug, not even any of the opiates, can produce effects that compare with those of overindulgence in alcohol. The worst narcotics merely induce stupor; alcohol releases everything, including violence. Opium and heroin sometimes induce sleep but leave the intelligence untouched; alcohol also induces sleep, but after having made a drinker lose reason and good sense, after having changed the person into a drooling, infantile, repetitive, forgetful wretch. Cocaine exalts, but alcohol causes delirium. Tranquillizers tranquillize, alcohol reduces a man to flabby fatuity, gives rise to uncalled-for fraternization, motiveless joy, and shoddy sociability, generates the forgetting of miseries, then the forgetting of that forgetting. Baby, *bibere*, imbibe, bottle. The experience of a drink that fills one to saturation and then induces sleep is reserved for only two kinds of people: newborn babes and drunkards. The tosspots no longer have what the babies do not yet possess. They are without honour, without conscience, without identity, without wits. They are like village idiots: happy when they make people laugh, pleased when people listen to them, frenzied when people speak to them.

When the police go into an alley to arrest a young man for possession of three grams of hashish—three grams of a completely harmless medicinal plant (Washington grew it all his life, and our grandmothers used to ask their doctors for it as a remedy for headaches)—they are quite likely to step over half a dozen drunkards covered in vomit. You see, the young man was seeking a psychic effect, whereas all that is wrong with the drunks is that they were *thirsty*.

Therein lies the whole difference. No drug in small doses—not even a cigarette lightly treated with heroin—has a greater effect than a single glass of alcohol. But when people are ashamed of what they are looking for, they must pretend to be looking for something else. Only alcohol, which masquerades as a food, lends itself to this hypocrisy. A whole mythology helps. That which parodies burning is classed as fire: since love is a flame, spices and alcohol, which are inflammatory, must be aphrodisiacs. (Similarly, since adolescent acne involves little organic volcanoes swelling up and spewing forth matter, it must be symbolic of sex.) Alcohol must help digestive fermentation since it is itself fermented, and it must help digestion, which is a slow combustion, since it is combustible itself. The words *stewed*, the familiar story of the drunkard whose breath catches fire, the flaming punch bowl—all these are irresistible, as analogies usually are. A cellar in which bottles are fermenting has something intestinal about it. Wine has a sanguineous connotation which is also found at the heart of the Christian liturgy; the West could think of no better way of extolling its favourite drug than by making the blood of its god into an alcoholic drink. In the same way, one must drink red wine with red meat and white with white-fleshed fish. As for the fetish of dusty old bottles covered in cobwebs, it is a reminder of an authorization—the authorization that the drunkenness of the past gives to the drunkenness of the present.

Everything here is false, of course; digestives hinder digestion, aperitifs do not whet the appetite, and no organ of the body greets any liqueur or wine as anything but an enemy. We eat by salivation; we digest by anesthesia. What makes us eat, what relaxes us (and thereby sometimes facilitates digestion) is happy drunkenness. The real indigestion is put off until the morrow, with its sticky mouth, its heartburn, its coated tongue, and its dully aching head.

"So long as one gets drunk" is the only truth of alcohol. Only drunkenness allows one to eat sumptuous meals while harbouring cirrhosis of the liver; only drunkenness stimulates sexual desire while excusing it, like everything else, from coming to a successful conclusion; only drunkenness accounts for the wealth of hypocrisy poured out over millennia about the hundreds of tastes, thousands of bouquets, and myriads of fragrances in wine.

If we insist on classing alcohol as a food, the fact is that we are dealing with one of the most polluted foods available. This is true even leaving aside hard liquor and aperitifs, which are the products of real industrial chemistry. The wine currently offered under medieval-looking labels is thickened with ferrocyanide and treated with tannin, albumen, gelatine, alginates, calcium phytate, sodium monosulphite, oxygen, sulphur dioxide, citric acid, sorbic acid, and potassium sulphate. It is also pasteurized, pseudoaged, cut with water, and embellished with essential oils, glucose, colouring matter, and synthetic aromatics. A bottle of French wine may contain as much sulphur as a whole box of matches.

The ceremonies with which wine glorifies itself are merely a practical joke on the theme of intoxication, worthy of gastronomy in this age of aniline-dyed meat and pesticide-laden vegetables. Distinguishing one wine from another is no more difficult than distinguishing between two colouring matters—unless they turn out to be the same thing. For someone who is neither a drinker nor a smoker, there are no more good wines than there are good cigarettes. Children and animals know this; they like alcohol only for its effects. There has never been a drinking song that really mentions the taste of the wine. There are no eating songs. Rabelais' *Divine Bottle* is not divine by virtue of its gustatory properties. Neither Brueghel nor Jordaens extolls the delights of the palate. Verlaine and Horace do not commend wine tasting, but wine cooking. The sly Bacchus who clutters up our culture takes his daily nips with an air of loosening up his muscles, quenching his thirst, and stimulating his digestion, but if he lies in so doing, it is because he is ashamed of the very nature of his drug. All the metaphors for drunkenness suggest a fall into a bottomless pit: to be dead drunk, to be sloshed, to be tight, to be smashed, to be bombed, to be pickled, to roll under the table. Hangovers and lapses of memory bring on remorse: what did I

say, how did I behave? By the time drunkenness subsides into headache, the guilty conscience calls for punishment; Noah, drunk, threw
off his clothes—one indecency expressing another. Regression, decompression, and depression combine. Alcohol, the drug of guilt,
makes penitence desirable.

Thus, the most degrading drunkenness serves the most degraded
of societies, in which the cults of work as a punishment and leisure
as a drunken orgy explain each other. If alcohol and the automobile,
the pillars of our civilization, are as adequate to summarize it as
they are to support it, it is because they symbolize it, one through
the other, like two emblems. Incoherent, drooling, aggressive, and
myth-loving, launched lightless and at ever-higher speeds into an
ever-darker night, the whole world is guilty of drunken driving.

IX

After the merely frightening comes the terrifying. Under Gehenna
sits the fire which will set it alight. To contract lung cancer, it is
enough to breathe in 13 millionths of a gram of plutonium. This
danger would remain theoretical if industry never pulverized, diluted, or distributed plutonium, and if its containers were perfectly
leakproof—but this is exactly where the theory breaks down; the
idea of a perfectly leakproof container is ridiculous. The water passing through a reactor is *inevitably* charged with radioactive particles, and an infallible purifying process can *never* exist, just as a
machine can never achieve 100 percent, efficiency. In 1971 the
Commission des Communautés Européennes, proponents of nuclear
energy who are scarcely considered prone to exaggerating, predicted
that before the end of the century European power stations with
purification systems that do not yet exist will allow 20 to 100 kilos of
plutonium *per year* to escape in gaseous emissions to the atmosphere, in dilution in water, and in particles of dust into the soil.

This means that today 2 to 10 kilos of plutonium are escaping
annually in Europe alone—and those figures do not take into account accidents which have been kept a (literally) deadly secret.
Pluto is the god of the damned. To avoid any quibbling, let us
reduce every single minimum. Let us suppose that it takes not 13 but
20 millionths of a gram of plutonium to bring on a cancer; that,

contrary to the evidence, Europe now loses no nuclear material through accidents; that present-day purification processes are already as perfect as is envisaged for the year 2000; that the commission I mentioned before is composed of fanatical alarmists, and that the quantity of plutonium dispersed is not 2 to 10 kilos per year, but only one quarter of the lower of those two figures—only 500 grams. Now, we do the calculation and arrive at 25 million lung cancers per year. Of course, these are only nascent cancers, so they will not all show up immediately or even all at the same future time. But plutonium has time to wait: its radioactivity lasts 25,000 years. The quantity that will go through the world's reactors during the next twenty years will require 480,000 years before it is no longer equal to killing the entire human race, just once. Our planning is long-term. . . .

That we are not already dying off in larger numbers can be explained by a simple principle from the theory of probabilities. If one hundred black balls and ten thousand white balls are mixed together in an urn, no single draw is likely to pull all the black balls at once. But a limited number of drawings will pull them all out separately. Thus, although it is almost impossible for 25 million cancers to appear simultaneously, their progressive appearance is inevitable. No matter how immense the atmosphere, how infinitesimal the radioactive isotopes, the inevitability is there. Plutonium oxide is a molecule, and *with each breath* we take in molecules which have passed through the lungs of Julius Caesar, Shakespeare, or Napoleon. How can we expect the ones which have gone through a reactor to make a detour?

This absolute inevitability of nuclear pollution should be enough to make it the worst nightmare human action has ever produced. There are also accidents. In themselves, they are much less serious, but they are what make us recoil because they are what are visible. In 1957 the Brookhaven Report assumed a breakdown in which half the radioactive products escaped from a 150 MG power station. It estimated 3,400 dead, 43,000 cancer casualties, 500,000 evacuated from a 500 square kilometer area. Present-day power stations are at least seven times more powerful, and the danger zone around them is 400,000 square kilometers. Worse, if *one hundredth* of the material in the reprocessing station at Cherbourg were to escape when the wind was blowing in the direction of Paris, eight million Parisians and the whole of the population between Paris and Cherbourg would be forced to evacuate immediately. Still worse, a major accident in a single station of the same kind in the north of Germany could kill thirty million Germans, some ten million French, and the whole population of Switzerland at one fell swoop.

These nightmare scenarios could be ignored if nuclear accidents were just a legend, as the silence of the press and governments would lead one to think. But accidents, in power stations as in the whole atomic industry, are legion; they are increasing in number and in seriousness with increases in the number and power of nuclear reactors. Between 1945 and 1963 there were more than a thousand such accidents—and the figure omits "minor" accidents, which have only one inconvenient aspect: their effects are cumulative. In France alone, more than six of them occur every year. (We have somehow to manage to count them ourselves, for Pluto is not very talkative. . . .)

At Windscale, England, the discharge of a small amount of radioactive iodine put a stop to grazing on 500 square kilometers of nearby land. At Humboldt Bay, California, emissions of the same sort of iodine were 11 percent over the so-called tolerable amount in 1967; after considerable repair work, they were still more than 8 percent too high the following year. In Nevada a run-of-the-mill accident condemned 65,000 hectares of land for centuries, if not for millennia. In Lucens, Switzerland, in 1969, the reactor had to be hastily walled up forever, after thirteen hours of continuous operation. The average life of a power station is astonishingly short, taking into account inordinately long breakdowns. During 1973 it was announced in the U.S.A. that seven important reactors had had to be shut down, as well as seventy-seven experimental reactors—not to mention that a nuclear cargo boat was out of action and four submarines were possibly lost. In 1968 the Belgian power station at Chooz announced that an accident had been "minor" (as always!) but that repair work would take more than two years; in the same year the power station at Monts d'Arrée, France envisaged three years for its repairs. In 1969 a power station in Bavaria closed down for good after only three years of moderate activity. An accident at Oak Ridge in 1958 claimed a dozen victims immediately; there were also indirect and unchecked casualties. An explosion at Idaho Falls,

Idaho, in 1961 killed three and caused hundreds of other casualties, also indirect. In 1964 it was the same story at Wood River, another American power station: one dead and many contamination cases. At Windscale in 1973 forty people were contaminated despite their protective clothing. At Surry, in the U.S.A., the bursting of an ordinary valve killed two workers and caused a panic alert in 1972. The shutting down of several Japanese power stations in sequence in 1975 almost gave rise to a similar alert.

The whole subject of nuclear power seems to belong to the world of the thriller and the spy story; we almost never get to know anything about the accidents which lead to shutdowns. There was no announced reason for the accident that irradiated a physicist at Mol, Belgium, in 1966. When Van Waas, another physicist, revealed in 1971 that numerous leakages had occurred in the power station at Dodewaard, Holland, he was instantly dismissed. Only the evidence of seismographs or satellites reveals accidents in the U.S.S.R. and in China; those that are so recorded must be veritable catastrophes, such as the 1976 explosion of bombs carried on Soviet submarines. In 1978 the CIA did reveal that two nuclear catastrophes have, in fact, occurred in the U.S.S.R.: the first, in 1958, at Khystym in the Urals, claimed thousands of victims and contaminated more than 15,000 hectares; the second, in 1961, was even "more terrifying." The CIA explicitly stated that there are fourteen documents of the same nature, but it refuses to release them for "reasons of security." Such discretion is all the more reassuring in that a few days later a Russian satellite loaded with 50 kilos of uranium 235 set off the atomic alarm throughout the whole of the West. The satellite disintegrated over Canada, giving off radioactivity which the Canadian government asserted to be "very dangerous." On the very same day it inadvertently came to light that thirty people had been hospitalized in the vicinity of the Belgian power station at Tihange. There are some ten thousand satellite objects circling the earth; more than half of them are military, and nearly half of them are radioactive. Thus the conquest of our space seems to be beginning with the end of our species. . . .

France refuses to allow inspection of her stocks of uranium and plutonium. In 1974 a storm cast up some "highly toxic" drums on two French beaches; the authorities refused to reveal their contents.

In 1967 five commandos armed with submachine guns stood guard over a truck that had been in a road accident; it may have been carrying atomic bombs, although the authorities said the load was in no way nuclear. In 1966, at Palomares, Spain, the Americans accidentally dropped four H-bombs, two into the sea and the others onto land. The work of recovery lasted eighty days, plutonium was spread over 226 hectares, and the whole of the press told a pack of lies about the matter before lapsing into silence. The power station at Rocky Flats, Colorado, caught fire and spewed out plutonium; citizens' committees proved that the radioactivity released was a *thousand* times higher than what the owner (Dow Chemical) and the government admitted.

After a hushed-up alert at Visé, Belgium, in 1973, the drinking water of the region was 23,000 times more radioactive than water is elsewhere for a period of six months. The count has also been very high at Lake Elliott, Canada, on account of uranium wastes *habitually* disposed of in the lakes; in the state of New York, 230,000 liters of radioactive liquids have permanently ruined soil and underground water tables.

Authorities admitted a loss of "several kilos" of plutonium from the Sefor reactor in Arkansas in 1969, and a reprocessing plant in Apollo, Pennsylvania, discovered that 6 percent of its radioactive material had not been registered for six years. Two hundred tons of uranium disappeared between Anvers and Gênes in 1968; 100 kilos of plutonium went missing in England in 1970. The year before, the power station in Saint-Laurent-des-Eaux, France, revealed the loss of several kilos of enriched uranium—which is no small matter. In 1977 Washington admitted having "mislaid" 3,822 kilos of plutonium since 1945. Where are these hundreds of billions of lung cancers today?

In 1971 two employees at an English power station threw twenty nuclear fuel rods over the fence. In the U.S.A. in 1972 three air pirates threatened to blow up the Oak Ridge power station. In 1973 terrorists seized the power station at Atucha, Argentina, and threw bombs, which luckily did not hit the nuclear equipment. It was amateurish work: a big power station properly sabotaged would release 192,000 times more radioactivity than the bomb dropped on Hiroshima. In 1974 one individual contaminated the Vienna-Rome express with iodine 131 and indium 113; three days later a similar attack on the Vienna-Linz line affected twelve people.

In 1973 there were leaks of radioactive liquids in the United States at Idaho Falls, Idaho, Hanford, California, and Savannah River, Georgia. One year later the Savannah River reactor, now more closely supervised, released an enormous cloud of tritium which drifted slowly to a height of 70 meters. In Europe such incidents are two for a penny: for example, at The Hague, which received more than one hundred times the so-called permissible dose of iodine 131 in 1968; at Lingen, Austria, where the Ems became radioactive in 1969; at Grenoble, where the Siloé reactor released iodine and caesium in 1967. Working at one sixth of its capacity, the Humboldt Bay reactor in the U.S.A. developed twice the "normal" radioactivity in 1965. In 1973 the American Academy of Sciences revealed that in the vicinity of power stations radioactivity was gaining ground everywhere—in the water, in the air, and in the soil—and that it was at least five times more dangerous than had ever been admitted. But who ever admits anything?

In 1972 two trains loaded with enriched uranium were derailed—one in the United States, the other in Germany. Their tanks held out, but one ton of the material in them would have been enough to contaminate a town the size of Cologne. But imagine a multiple traffic accident, such as the one at Breda in 1972, which literally flattened whole lines of trucks and cars. What would then happen to a drum—even an armoured drum—containing 25 kilos of plutonium? It was in exactly this way that 19 tons of powdered uranium were spread over a road in Springfield, in the U.S.A., in 1977.

Twelve million tons of radioactive sand have been dumped into the Colorado River without any precautions. In the U.S.A. alone, 30 million tons of wastes have been dumped into abandoned mines. In Europe wastes are often buried in salt mines. Now salt is an excellent conductor of heat and also is ultracorrosive; neither ceramics nor steel containers can offer more than feeble resistance to the triple attack from the active energy enclosed within them, the heat surrounding them, and the heated salt eating them away. Authorities in Kansas had to improvise surface stockpiling in 1971 in order to prevent a salt mine filled with wastes from setting off a catastrophe.

The life of radioactivity is measured in millennia, while the best of containers are barely capable of lasting a half century. We have already mentioned the accidental discovery of 500 fractured containers at Saclay. A similar incident occurred in 1972 at Grenoble: 450 drums, cracked everywhere, were lined up in the open air a few meters from a freeway.

In 1972 a delivery truck containing radioactive elements was stolen in Marseilles, while in Perpignan children played with boxes containing strontium 90, which they had found on some waste ground. A box of iridium fell off a truck in Montreal in 1973. An Argentine workman picked up a shiny bolt in 1968; it was caesium 137, and he died after ten months of dreadful agony. Radioactive products were found in 1970 on a side road in France. A leakage of molybdenum 99 was not discovered in an airplane until after it had made nine flights in 1971; the contamination had come from a package being carried for the post. Similar radioactive packages were recently discovered at Aubervilliers; likewise, some were found, again by chance, in the cloakroom at Orly in 1972. A whole Mexican family died from some tiny pellets of cobalt 60 that a child had found while playing. Where did all this material come from? And how were such losses possible amid the ominous precautions with which the nuclear industry surrounds itself?

In 1973 a drum filled with cobalt 60 (capable of killing everything that approached closer than one meter) fell off a drilling rig in the North Sea and was swept away towards England. In 1974 Radio-Boulogne-Maritime warned all seamen to look out for a missing box that contained highly radioactive material. In June 1972 some Dutch fishermen netted a drum marked "Highly Radioactive." The Council of Europe was told in 1970 that observations had revealed "protective" casings half-open or even split apart at the bottom of the sea. France has sunk thousands of tons of radioactive wastes in the Gulf of Gascony, which happens to lie in a moderately active seismic zone. If air, which is not corrosive and exerts negligible pressure, causes or allows cracks to form in thousands of castings, how many of them do the depths of the sea produce? And what is happening to the wastes that are allowed to escape? Dumping wastes in a seismic zone is all the more serious in that nuclear wastes have a tendency to provoke earthquakes. The imagination boggles at what would happen if a volcanic eruption were to touch off the whole of this submerged, radioactive powder magazine. Yet such eruptions are commonplace under the seas. Furthermore, we must bear in mind that present-day tanks must be refrigerated if the energy fermenting inside them is not to leak out within a few hours; since the object is to avoid pollution of the water, their cooling systems are linked to devices that assure the venting of their radioactive gases to the atmosphere—for where else could they go? This system, of course, disperses them (but not before we have had time to breathe them), then redistributes them to the oceans in the form of rain.

Apart from accidents, the routines peculiar to power stations also have some dangerous secondary effects. At the power station at The Hague the cases of internal contamination increase each year; there were 206 of them in 1976. In 1971, the working periods there were three minutes long. At the end of 1973 it was announced that 3,700 workers employed in U.S. power stations had been discharged for alcoholism, use of drugs, and mental illness. For employees, the endless precautions, the omnipresent if invisible radioactive enemy, and the feeling that they are selling health and life are not conducive to good morale. According to the very moderate International Commission of Jurists, in Geneva in 1977, listening posts, spies, infiltrators, secret monitoring squads, tampering with private correspondence, hunting down extremist groups, blackmail, corruption, and occasionally torture are inherent in the nuclear society. Democracies are thus slowly turning into police states—a somewhat pleonastic phrase. Thus the lie reveals itself by its own logic. Pluto wants crime—and thus, truth. A death's head no longer needs a mask.

The secondary effects of the atom industry can be far removed. For example, the Welsh had to abandon their traditional algae-based preserves because they discovered the algae had become radioactive. Over the whole of England, the carbon 14 content in oats increased seventy times between 1955 and 1962, because of nuclear power stations. In the U.S.A. in 1970 the Dresden reactor was accused—with statistics supporting the claim—of having caused the death of 2,500 babies. Similarly, it was shown that Aliquippa, Pennsylvania, once sixty-fourth in the state for infant mortality, had risen to first place after the installation of a reactor whose effluents were contaminating the town's drinking water.

A bomb buried in Nevada in 1970 let a tiny part of its radioactivity leak out; three hundred people ended up in hospital, and a dangerous cloud hovered over twelve American states, although the experts had considered this particular accident impossible. When the Americans first scheduled nuclear explosions in the open air, the experts announced the fallout would be limited to the unpopulated part of Nevada where they were set off, and the test would be "without danger." We know today that such tests are unthinkable. Less than fifteen days after the explosion cows' milk in Salt Lake City was found to contain iodine 131, and two months later it was noted in children's thyroids. Although the radioactivity was not supposed to cross the Atlantic, it reached Europe. Every time an obvious nuclear peril appears, experts come forward and deny that it exists. This is what they did when the fractured containers were discovered at Saclay; as though to prove their claim, these wastes were immediately transferred to The Hague. At the beginning of the nuclear age, every government, supported by hordes of experts, announced that the immersion of radioactive wastes presented no risk; by 1972 all nations were banning disposal by immersion. It is still practiced here and there, but in those cases it is naturally quite harmless. . . . Much the same thing happened in a different sphere: in 1972 the American government dumped 2,500 nerve gas rockets into the Atlantic (a milligram of this stuff is enough to kill a person). Citizens organized committees and protested. Experts "proved" that even if the containers came open, seawater would gradually destroy the gas. The next day the government announced that never again would anything so dangerous be dumped in an ocean deep. And the *following* day, on government instructions, 5,000 tons of explosives went to the bottom of the sea, right next to the 2,500 rockets.

In 1956 the American government declared that "in the opinion of the most eminent scientists alive" nuclear test explosions were not a threat to Humanity. Eight years later, after the signing of a treaty banning these tests, the same eminent scientists were now of the opinion that such explosions would endanger the health "of the entire human race," even if they added no more than 5 tons of plutonium to the stratosphere. But since France still needed open-air tests at that time, thousands of French experts declared them to be harmless. In 1960 experts asserted that only atomic bomb tests gave

rise to radioactive iodine; two years later it was discovered in livestock in ten American states, and it was coming from power stations.
In 1953 the experts assured the U.S.A. that fallout could never cause
hereditary mutations; by 1957 they forecast as many as thirteen thousand such mutations per year—and they were still wrong, for more
than thirteen thousand are being recorded. In 1957 it was "evident"
that military tests would not produce radioactivity higher than 7
microcuries per square mile; in fact, they produced seven times that
figure. The same experts had announced that strontium 90 would be
dangerous only in the bone splinters of animal carcases—that is, in
butcher shops—but the highest concentrations were found in
dairies, with cows' milk far exceeding all the "expected" figures for
contamination. The Atomic Energy Commission experts also stated
definitely that strontium 90 would remain within the confines of the
U.S.A.; its highest concentrations were recorded in Italy. As for
caesium 137, they said, it would not spread beyond the immediate
vicinity of the explosions; the highest concentrations were discovered
among the Inuit (who eat reindeer, which eat lichen, which concentrates caesium).

If explosions in the open air, which threatened nobody, were
banned because suddenly they were threatening the whole of the
world, then underground explosions, which are authorized, must
surely be quite safe. Doubtless this is why the Soviet Union (which
no longer needs them) is beginning to mount a discreet campaign
for their suppression. *Independent* experts analyzed 171 underground tests, just one of which alone had produced more than ten
thousand earth tremors over a distance of 13 kilometers in 1968.
They discovered that 32 hours after any explosion of this nature,
tremors increased by an average of 62 percent, both in number and
in intensity. Twenty-four years after the construction of the Hanford
nuclear plant, it was learned that its 140 buried tanks, despite artificial cooling, had changed the hitherto neutral region into a zone of
moderate seismic activity. The subsoil is cracked more or less everywhere, and each crack contains radioactive wastes. And since the
tanks were built in accordance with the instructions of numerous
experts, they are *not* equipped to withstand seismic shocks—though
this would be more or less impossible, in any case.

If the story of nuclear energy is an endless series of faults and failures, of soothing speeches followed by deathly silences, of each statement's giving the lie to the preceding one and each denial's preceding another lie, the reason is that in this area the very word "expert" is a lie. The public continues to believe the physicists, whatever the danger, and they continue to play their little game with a dishonesty which is all the greater in that their competence in the matter is, to put it bluntly, nil. All that physics can know concerns the quantities of radioactivity being disseminated into the environment—and it knows even that imperfectly. What the environment (beginning with the human organism) does with radioactivity should be the province of biologists. But biology, which is not an exact science, can know little about an enemy hitherto unknown to Life itself because this enemy makes use of the whole labyrinth of vital cycles that belong to ecology—which is not a science at all. Therefore, there can be no such thing as experts in these matters even if, by a miraculous exception, the expertise is neither governmental nor industrial. The whole subject of pollution leads to no other conclusion.

This is why the growing concentration of radioactivity along the organic chains is among the phenomena which were not foreseen. In the Columbia River, which receives the waste waters from the Hanford reactor in the U.S.A., the algae are 90,000 times richer in strontium 90 than the water, the caesium content of the fish is 2,500 times higher than that of their surroundings, and the ducks are 1,000 times more contaminated with caesium 137 than the fish. (If two people ate one of the ducks, it could be a fatal meal for both.) In a Canadian lake the bones of perches and muskrats contain 3,000 times more strontium 90 than the water, which itself contains infinitely more than was anticipated. In the Clinch, into which the Oak Ridge power station pours its officially "inoffensive" waters, the plankton raises the multiplication factor to 10,000—a record beaten by the Columbia's caddis flies, which have concentrations on the order of 350,000 times. Swallows can be 75,000 times more radioactive than their environment.

Radioactivity is not the only problem around power stations; there is also heat. Every reactor must be cooled with some 200 to 300 cubic meters of water per second—almost the total flow of the Seine. Water temperatures can rise as high as 46°C in the neighbourhood of power stations and 35°C eight kilometers downstream. Now, even at 35°C, nearly all animal species disappear. Plankton is no longer found in the Connecticut River, which receives 1,800,000 liters of water per minute at only 22°C. All the water flowing into one river basin in the United States happens to pass through power station heat exchangers. Six reactors already release their waste waters into the Rhine. Radioactivity and its accompanying heat thus constitute the final solution to the problem of watercourses. . . .

When necessary, the experts contradict each other according to their nationality. United States experts have condemned the breeder reactor as being too dangerous. A breeder produces more plutonium than it consumes and can make 100,000 kilos of it per year. A bomb requires ten kilos of plutonium, so, in theory, a breeder means 10,000 bombs for sale in one year. (An American student proved in 1976 that small-scale production is possible; his bomb was one third as powerful as the one dropped on Hiroshima, and he had designed it himself.) France, which says it will never sell plutonium or bombs because it finds the arms trade repugnant, has built a breeder reactor which will never explode, as American experts fear, because that would be repugnant to French experts. . . .

For some time it was believed that with radioactivity, as with pesticides, it would be possible to reach agreement on "norms of tolerance," as these indices of complicity were called. But the evidence was too overwhelming: apart from iodine 131, which has a short half-life (eight days), radioactive elements accumulate for millennium after millennium. In the case of iodine 129 the half-life is more than 18 *million* years. Organisms mistake strontium 90 for calcium and carbon 14 for normal carbon; they concentrate radioactivity and retain almost all of it. In the environment in general no radioactive molecule will ever cease to be radioactive before its appointed time has elapsed (and we have seen how long that can be). The dosage of 0.17 rads, universally accepted as "normal" or "permissible" because something had to be accepted, can cause 32,000 secondary cancers each year, as well as 16,000 cases of leukemia and countless miscarriages and congenital deformities. The French nuclear tests up to 1962 alone irradiated humanity's ovaries and testicles with 0.08 rads and its bone marrow with 0.15. With that dosage alone we are already near the "norm"—and the 32,000 cancers that are attributed to it. But how can one guess the origin of a cancer when one has no idea what a cancer consists of and when millions of possible carcinogenic substances exist?

However, the incidence of cancer around power stations is quite striking. At Petroleum, Montana, leukemia occurs fifteen times more often than in the rest of America. At Garfield, miscarriages are two and a half times more frequent than elsewhere. Boise, Idaho, has four times more deformed, deaf, blind, and dumb babies than other locations, including big cities. At Caroll, Massac, and Shermann, congenital deformities are more than three times more numerous than the national average. According to Linus Pauling and others, the nuclear explosions to date (without counting power stations or wastes) will afflict 16 million children with mental illness, premature deaths, cancer, and so on. The first generation alone will see 160,000 children affected, and the harm will continue for millennia. These results would be inevitable, they say, even if every form of atomic energy were to disappear from the face of the globe today. When independent experts put forward figures like these, one imagines, at best, that they might be hypotheses. But when experts paid by industry or the government paint the nuclear future as an idyll, one accepts their arguments as being, at worst, entirely probable—and, hence, almost a certainty. Ecology is propaganda, but business tells the truth. That is why, a few years from now, Earth will be covered with power stations.

Given the nuclear device that broke up at Palomares in 1966; given the satellite that disintegrated over Africa in 1969, pulverizing a kilo of plutonium whose existence was not announced for three years; given the two nuclear submarines that have sunk with all their reserves of plutonium; given all the indications that nine out of ten nuclear accidents have remained completely unknown—then nuclear contamination cannot be evaluated. Addition is useless because the total would be incomplete. The incidence of cancer is useless because carcinomas do not announce their source. The measurement of radioactivity is useless because such measurement is very rare. Moreover, the figures would never be given out if they were catastrophic, for a radioactive catastrophe is, by definition, invisible, impalpable, and little short of undetectable—at least as long as the irradiation is fairly slow.

Since the wastes that have been buried or sunk are—of course—absolutely safe, it is rather surprising to learn that the American government recently considered sending all its radioactive wastes to the sun via a series of rockets. Only panic could explain such a crazy scheme. On average, one rocket-firing out of thirty is a failure, so such a means of disposal would be playing Russian roulette. Given the vast quantity of waste, so many rockets would be involved that the game would soon be over.

Then again, Russian roulette is unnecessary. The more industry looks to the atom for resources, the more the probability of catastrophes approaches certainty. Meanwhile we all plunge together into uncertainty even without the effects of power stations or explosions. Workers in Canada's radium and uranium ore refineries receive seven times the so-called permissible dose. If refineries elsewhere in the world had better methods of protection, Canada would have them too. These methods do not exist—but business is in a hurry. Painting watch dials with luminous paint can bring death to the workers involved. Just as the dangers from X rays are being discovered (after they have been employed without restraint for half a century), the use of the X ray diffractometer is spreading throughout industry—with little heed for the ravages it causes. In any case, risk bonuses are becoming more and more commonplace. To die sooner in order to live better is no more illogical than to lose one third of your life in order to pay for the other two thirds, or vice versa.

X

One suspects that the description of the world of pollution could go on forever—while remaining quite useless. Everything that strikes home is unsettling, but what is unsettling is not necessarily convincing. So I might as well cut this catalogue short here and now. Only Nature carries on with it tirelessly, and for a long time now Nature has been doing it as a countdown. . . .

We live by representations and not by ideas: anything not accompanied or at least emphasized by images cannot have any real effect on us. If the description of pollution in the earlier sections of this chapter corresponded with what we could actually *see*, it would

be a superfluous commentary; since it does not correspond, it risks
being dubbed a fairy tale. To begin with, one has the impression
that if all these horrors were true, the Earth would already be dead.
But the Earth is immense, so it is a long time a-dying. And its death,
which began long ago, is not only slow but invisible.

This last point cannot be overstressed: in pollution, what can be
directly observed is generally of no importance. Pesticides are invisible, food additives are invisible, radioactivity is invisible, industry's
worst gaseous emissions are invisible. Even the most harmful automobile exhausts, such as carbon monoxide, are invisible and inodor-
ous, while lead, benzopyrene, and methylcholanthrene can be
detected only with difficulty. By the time everyone can see that the
waters of a lake or an ocean are polluted, it is already too late. The
oil spills we read about are only an infinitesimal part of ocean pollution. Accidents in nuclear power stations can affect public opinion—
or rather public imagination—but their emissions are nothing in
comparison with the kilos of plutonium that power stations release
imperceptibly despite any possible system of purification. Nonsmok-
ers have no way of knowing whether the air they breathe will have
the same effect on them as smoking two packs of cigarettes a day. It
is the same with the disappearance of species: people campaign for
the protection of baby seals, whose deaths are spectacular, but not
for the protection of dolphins, which are being quietly killed off by
the tuna industry at the rate of 300,000 per year. Who has seen
forests disappearing? Who has seen marine plankton vanishing?
Who has seen the millions of tons of DDT gathered in the oceans?

Seeing nothing, we could compensate for this blackness by clear
thinking, but the rare ideas we do have are both nebulous and false.
The popular belief is that we could reduce overall pollution of the
environment to a certain level at which, in some way or other, it
would be absorbed and reabsorbed. In fact, most of the elements
that we are foisting onto Nature subdivide or combine there with
elements that are even more harmful or simply accumulate without
breaking down at all. Furthermore, the word "environment" is a
snare since it makes us think only of what is around us, just as the
word "Nature" makes us think of the animal and vegetable world. In
fact, neither "the environment" nor "Nature" is exclusive of Humanity. We are composed of cells, like any other part of the living
world, and we are animals—more sensitive and less protected than

the others by virtue of our complexity. Steel balls cause less damage
to a machine tool than to a computer. . . . The environment and
Nature are primarily ourselves: we are the center of the former, and
we represent a point in the latter.

Moreover, as the reader has no doubt noted, the most common
outcome of all forms of pollution is cancer. The more possible causes
there are for cancer, the less able one is to attribute it to one cause
rather than to another. Even if the guilty plutonium were to remain
fixed in the bodies in which it had caused cancer, medicine would
still be incapable of detecting it; there is too much cancer, not
enough plutonium, and no real method of detection. Anyway, detection is of no interest when it is a question of curing a cancer (an
ambition which is entirely utopian).

The problem of pinpointing causes is even worse when it comes to
the terrestrial climate. If that fluctuates, it will be, as I have already
noted, completely impossible to hold pollution responsible for it, still
less any particular form of pollution. The climate has suffered numerous upsets, often of unheard-of brutality, for which the causes
are unknown precisely because there are hundreds of possible ones
(galactic, solar, planetary), all equally plausible. This is not to say
that the first global effects of pollution will not be climatic. In fact,
they are likely under way already, but Science can tell us nothing
about them.

In any event, one should not now turn towards Science, whose
confusion will be examined later. When ecology threatens us with
an unprecedented *moral* revolution, we are driven to invoking imaginary *technical* reforms. "They'll think of something" means "someone else will pull something out of the hat." But when it comes to
pollution, especially at its most serious, technical palliatives are inconceivable—not in the way that a voyage to the Moon was inconceivable in 1900, but in the way that the equation $2 + 2 = 5$ will still
be inconceivable in a hundred millennia. It is impossible to purify
the seas completely, to reestablish a shattered climatic balance, to
build nuclear power stations that do not develop any leaks at all, to
bring a lake back to life in less than four centuries, to recreate
humus in less than the same period, to invent a nonpolluting form of
combustion (and hence, clean factory chimneys or car exhaust
systems).

To these theoretical impossibilities we must add more practical ones: producing increased quantities of paper without disturbing the forests, replacing paper with plastic without replacing wood with oil, building up substitute compounds by photosynthesis, burning or burying refuse without pollution, avoiding even localized dryness or cold, inventing pesticides whose harmlessness can be guaranteed in advance or additives that will surely be noncarcinogenic. We have seen that the French campaign of 1977 against automobile pollution ended up, at best, reducing it by 1 percent, a percentage far below that of the annual increase in the number of cars on the road. Does anyone really believe that more costly techniques would have enabled them to do very much better? The first effect of a massive recourse to solar energy, if such a thing were technically possible, would be to provide industries with the means to function better, and thus to pollute more. It would scarcely decrease the production of oil (the base for ever more numerous synthetic products), and it would not threaten the growing use of plutonium in weapons. The electric car would call for quantities of energy which we do not have; it would not prevent automotive pollution from asbestos, carbon black, and chrome, and it would likely make mercury a major pollutant at one fell swoop. Moreover, it would not make cars any less ugly, any less cumbersome, or any less noisy. Generally speaking, all the technical remedies that one can advocate are partial and hence nothing but disastrous lies. Yet until the final stampede, governments, industries, and the public will have no recourse other than these lies. They may be punctuated by a few facile, face-saving gestures—London's air freed of smog (though more polluted than before), the Thames partially rescued from becoming a sewer, the little French Lake Annecy spared in time—but overall pollution increases year after year, wherever one goes, whatever one does.

The fact that ought to be saved is that of health. A hundred years ago life expectancy was on the increase, thanks to vaccination and the discoveries of Pasteur; a little later, Fleming's work with antibiotics raised it further. True, individuals were not living very much longer, but our numbers were increasing through our not dying off too young. Now, life expectancy is the result of an "averaging" calculation. If one or two individuals can be expected to die at seventy and the other at only a few weeks of age, their joint life

expectancy is thirty-five years. If nine individuals will die at seventy
and only one at a few weeks, the life expectancy of all ten is sixty-
three years. In the second case the death of a single baby subtracted
seven years from the average life span of nine adults (and a hundred years ago the infant mortality rate was doubtless more than
one in ten). From the beginning of this century until 1950 life
expectancy increased four years every decade; it still went up one or
two years between 1950 and 1960; then it stayed stable until around
1970. At the present time, however, it is going down.

Never before has medicine had available so much equipment, so
many computers, so many pharmaceuticals, so many laboratories, or
so much available staff. Never before have tranquillizers been more
effective, antibiotics more efficient, the pharmacopoeia more inven-
tive. Never before has so much help been sought from homeopathy,
acupuncture, Zen, healers' herbs, and even the grimoires of the al-
chemists. We are rid of diphtheria, plague, malaria, leprosy, scurvy,
and a thousand other bugbears; we can transplant hearts, kidneys,
and livers; we are each of us credited with ten or twenty extra years
of life by dint of keeping alive newborn babes who in the old
days would not have lived two hours. Yet here we are on a descending slope which implies acceleration into a fall, and on which the
wounds we had healed are reopening and becoming infected with
the scourges we have created. The maladies that are on the increase
—cancer, infarction, mania, and all the rest—are new, complex, and
rapid, and it is not yet really possible to name their causes.

In every industrial country, for more than ten years, the death
rate has been rising at an ever increasing speed for men between
thirty-five and sixty—but not for women. Why? The question does
not even make sense: a phenomenon which may have ten thousand
reasons has no real reason. That medicine should capitulate before
the rising tide of allergies is only to be expected: it is not known
what an allergy really consists of. Neither is it known what skin
diseases are, though they too, including acne and psoriasis, are on
the increase. The same is true of colds and flu. But what is nothing
short of scandalous is that salmonellosis has increased its victims
tenfold in less than twenty years, that syphilis is making a silent
comeback in the company of typhus. These are diseases whose
agents we know, illnesses which we could, in theory, prevent. Only

no medicine exists which is capable of guaranteeing our survival in the middle of a septic tank.

It would be quicker to list the illnesses which are not on the increase than to name all those which are. These latter include diabetes mellitus, behaviour problems, cerebral vascular lesions, arteriosclerosis, heart disease, hypertension, cirrhosis of the liver, and *especially* congenital deformities. Maladies of the respiratory system no longer present a case of simple progression; they have become an explosion, as has the worst of modern scourges, the one that even obituary notices describe only in paraphrases: cancer.

Lung cancer was practically unknown in 1885. In 1952 this particular form of cancer killed six times more men in the United States than it had eighteen years before. During the same year it killed forty-four times more people in Switzerland than it had in 1900, and in England, thirty times as many. Other industrialized countries experienced increases of the same order. Since 1960, however, the proportion of lung cancers in the same countries has increased *10 to 15 times*. All forms of cancer, without any exception, are increasing. And if medical academies describe these tidal waves of cancer as "startling," what can be said about the number of mental illnesses, which has quadrupled in the last twenty years? What can be said about alcoholism, whose ravages grow more tragic every year? Of overuse of prescription drugs, which has become a world menace, especially among women? Of the craze for heroin and other hard drugs, which has blown up into a veritable cyclone? Of cases of food poisoning, which are multiplying more rapidly than the foods themselves? Of the crime wave, which is spreading with dizzying speed? Of suicide (in Switzerland today, as many people do away with themselves as are killed in road accidents)?

All these facts and figures would be useless if they did not force us to do some decoding. The vision of the world defaced would be completely in vain if it did not show us a face impossible for us not to recognize. It is in this mirror, and here alone, that there appears the collective reflection from which will spring the new Humanity— or from which will die the whole of existing Humanity—which at the moment is making this planet even more repulsive morally than physically. Striped with freeways like suppurating welts, pitted with quarries and mines, saturated with poisons, split by strangling na-

tional boundaries, abused by ignoble interests, treated like a slot
machine filled with counterfeit coins, asphyxiated, moribund, here
as ugly as sin, there completely filthy, the Earth is covered with
people. Is it really surprising that the face of the Earth is in Humankind's own image?

XI

As we have seen, it is impossible in nearly all cases to repair the
damage caused by past or present pollution. On the other hand, in
theory one can nearly always reduce or stop the most serious pollutant activities. Any chance for doing so, however, lies in the future, which—even more than the oceans—serves us as a universal
garbage dump.

Stopping any major form of pollution now is impossible because
each instance would mean a revolution, for which the initiative
would have to come from one of four nebulous entities: industry,
government, the people, or Science. Let us see why it will take
incredible cataclysms to make any of them able or willing to act,
catastrophes whose origins are clear and whose ravages are still
reparable.

First, let us note that certain forms of pollution cannot be suppressed today because they keep part of Humanity alive. For example, the World Health Organization (WHO) lists the perils of
DDT but still recommends it because it is the *cheapest* and most
certain pesticide and without it many diseases would again become
endemic, bringing hundreds of thousands of deaths in their wake.
For WHO, as for most people, these realities are more important
than the fact that 10 percent of the world's DDT ends up in the
oceans, where it puts a permanent end to the renewal of terrestrial
oxygen. The garbage dump future is also part of human concern.
But the ethics we display only deal with appearances: although we
are vaguely responsible in space, we are not so in time. The death of
future generations troubles our conscience less than the death of a
continent because we are not the *visible* cause. The suppression of
pesticides would mean not only epidemics but more famine than
ever before. Humanity lives above its means in order to survive at a
lower level than its ends. It is impossible to make it lower its stan-

dards—and who cares about the means? Our grandchildren will find better ones; just as they will retrieve plutonium out of thin air and bring the Atlantic back to life.

The situation is just about the same with regards to additives; they are almost indispensable for feeding the present world. All current sources of energy, even nuclear power, are nearly as necessary. If WHO haggles over the price of DDT, it is because it would not even dream of disturbing the world's economic equilibrium. What ecology calls for is exactly what no one in the world—not even the ecologists—is willing to grant it.

Certainly industry lacks goodwill. It is not only that companies do nothing; in fact, they do *everything* in order to do nothing. They always begin by denying everything they are accused of: they never give way except to court orders, and then only after having tried every method of intimidation—including, on occasion, murder. When their share of guilt is established, they put forward the cost of their antipollution measures (which are only moderately cleansing at best). They raise the spectre of unemployment (which is, it must be added, a genuine threat). If competitors are of a different nationality, negotiations become so bitter that they can no longer be carried out between governments. A typical example of industrial reaction to accusations of polluting is the story of the Montedison Company, which was dumping its "red sludge" off Corsica. Getting any reaction out of the company took a quasi-revolution, complete with threats of attacks and armed expeditions. Then the company announced that installing purification devices (barely effective ones at that) would increase its capital expenditure by 150 percent. The French government's hands were tied because it was dumping the same toxic sludges in the Pas de Calais and the estuary of the Seine. But everyone was satisfied by the final solution: dumping wastes farther out to sea and at a greater depth. Several faces were more or less saved, with absolutely no attempt to fight general pollution. Notice that the actors in this sorry farce represented every quarter from which something might conceivably have been expected: an industry, a government, citizens, and scientific researchers.

Since the whole of world pollution is industrial, it should not be surprising that it is also governmental. After all, there are only two alternatives: either a country is collectivist and its industries are run by the same people that run the states, or it is not and the people that run the state are themselves under the thumb of big business. The imperatives of profit, production, sales, and standard of living are stricter for a country than for a company—the latter is not threatened with a revolution if it goes bankrupt, or even with bankruptcy in the event of a revolution. A nation is nothing but a huge commercial enterprise poisoned by patriotism. A hundred conglomerates could be formed in the time it takes two countries to form a sketchy federation, and all the corporations in the world could conclude complicated negotiations among themselves in less time than it takes United Nations members to communicate with each other (unless, of course, the latter are insulting each other or saying nothing at great length). The ideal of the "balance of trade" is perforce the same for all: each country must export more than it imports, and the prosperity of one half of the world depends directly on the deficit of the other half, although no capitalist theory, however savage, would prescribe that.

Whether an enterprise is communist or not is obviously of no importance. The way in which a national organization is run does not make nonpolluting processes any less costly—or any more necessary. China is polluted. The rivers and lakes of the U.S.S.R. are as filthy as those of Europe. Hungary has a National Bureau for Nature, but Lake Balaton is on its last legs, and Budapest is one of the most unhealthy cities in the world. In Czechoslovakia industrial complexes have already razed 100,000 hectares of forest and made half the watercourses stink. Furthermore, a communist country is so communal that public opinion there is muzzled—and what can the people say about a matter of which they know nothing? Pollution goes on all the more efficiently as a result. . . .

Pollution also benefits from the existence of international boundaries. Take the ubiquitous discrepancies between "standards" of purity, alimentary and others. Such differences would be inconceivable for companies within a single nation because they would condemn (and hence restrain) each other in the most unrestrained way possible. But the United States will not condemn France, for the amount of mercury it is willing to tolerate in fruits, although (and sometimes because) this makes these fruits unacceptable for marketing in the U.S.A. The same is true of the Swedish attitude towards Danish fish. An industry can only voice internal, fairly moderate censure, but a government—especially a communist government—has complete freedom. It has to sell its polluted beaches and its polluting power stations. There is no authority above it, few critics below. If Germany or France wish to arm Pakistan, they can do so. There is no lack of tricks, no lack of indulgence—and industrial espionage still has a great deal to learn from international espionage.

Let us imagine a world conference urgently convened to prevent or palliate an ecological catastrophe. How big would such a disaster have to be? The death of Lake Erie does not stop Norwegians from sleeping. If the Mediterranean became a septic tank, the Chinese would not be worried. The Arabs would not consider it their business if the South Pacific were at its last gasp. Let us imagine, then, that there was an immediate threat to the whole of the Earth's atmosphere and that by some miracle, all the nations of the Earth considered themselves equally responsible for the situation.

If the solution to the crisis lay in reorienting the automobile industry, would Algeria pay Germany's costs? If the sale of arms were prohibited,.would Nigeria recompense France? Would the strongest countries relinquish their supremacy under coercion by the weakest? Would Hungary prevent the U.S.S.R. from stealing its uranium? Would Chile force the U.S.A. to recompense her for the damage that American destroyers inflict on her coastal fauna? Would even the members of the Common Market agree? It is justified by the identical financial and geographical interests of its partners, but they can vacillate over setting a standard process for manufacturing chocolate. What would things be like in an assembly where some members still hated each other, where the Pakistanis would be at loggerheads with the Germans and the Russians with the Chinese? Remember that the objective would be the precise opposite of forwarding *any* particular interest and that each of the biggest powers —who would alone be able to get anything done—would be facing the possibility of losing at least half its national income. Moreover, some processes, such as the production of "clean" electricity, are possible only under geographical conditions that exist in some countries but not in others, so a global solution would require the first group being willing to sacrifice themselves for the second. As one can see, the only successful conclusion to our imaginary conference would be to abolish frontiers and profits—a utopia which we would consider only slightly preferable to death. And that is why death alone will be able to impose it in the long run.

Meanwhile, consider the conclusions of the United Nations Conference on the Environment, held in Stockholm in 1972. There the states gathered, proposing to protect Nature—rather like hunters getting together to preserve wildlife. Matters were aptly summed up in Paragraph 21 of the final resolution: "The States have the sovereign right to exploit their own resources, and the duty to ensure that their actions cause no damage in other States." To put it another way, a paper mill can pollute *its* river to death provided that it does not harm the nearby cement factory, which is putrefying *its* lake. But in the long run this parcelling out of the polluted Earth is hypothetical, for there is no form of pollution which is not international. When a government puts huge smokestacks on smelters and factories to prevent gases from falling back to earth *directly* next to them, it is the whole Earth's atmosphere that is being used as a garbage can. The slightest blow struck anywhere at the sea is a likely blow against the world climate. The fish of Norway are dying from the fumes of the Ruhr, which are making acid rain fall on Sweden. After an atomic test in China, the whole of Humanity gets a dose of proletarian strontium 90 in its bones. When Germany sells cars to Brazil, it is the skies of Brazil and then of the world that turn grey. If Brazil wishes to cut down half of Amazonia (which means one out of every eight trees on earth), she merely has to ask any protesters to reforest their own countries—which, for regions like the Sahel, would obviously pose no real problem. . . . Thus, governments and industries work hand in glove.

Of course, chiefs of state and industrialists have always had the reputation of being Machiavellian. The people, however, are generally credited with goodness and innocence. Since well before Rousseau—indeed, from the times of the Greek idylls—it has been maintained that those who do nothing can do no wrong. *"Vox populi, vox dei."* Unfortunately, the voice of the people that is the voice of God no longer even lets us think that God is dumb; in recent times it has elected most ruling politicians when it has not been extolling, by turns, family, country, work, treachery, war, and genocide. The minorities who consider themselves the elites may well be detestable, but the veiled envy and anonymous resentment that are responsible for their being detested are even worse than they are. "The People" may or may not be a myth, but once they have become the power in the land, they demand and receive exactly the same boot-licking as any other dictators. In order not to appear to be putting oneself above the masses, one has to defend them: they have done nothing, said nothing, wished for nothing, and are nothing but the victims of what happens to them. They are humble, infinitely humble, in everything, and all they need do in order to be good is to have nothing: such is the underlying motive— one might call it the humble ideology—at the heart of any party, revolutionary or reformist, whose object is mobilizing a population.

Of course, it is obvious that pollution, like everything else, is merely the filth of the rich fashioned from the blood of the poor for the martyrdom of the humble. It is the powerful—people who were not given power by others—carrying the world off in their claws. It is Hitler alone mesmerizing the German people who were powerless in his hands; it is Stalin alone enslaving the people of Russia against their will. A myth means a lie, and a collective lie can only be explained by its ability to organize the whole world. "The captive audience" is created by public opinion polls, by the opinions of the majority of the lowly. "Forced consumption" depends on a demand that is meekly anonymous and generalized; the police have never compelled anybody to go into a department store (though one sometimes sees them erecting barricades against the crowds at sale times). "Pressure to buy" does not make us buy electric toothbrushes, any more than "hard sell" makes us change our brand of cigarettes. The "silent majority" loves silence and has nothing to say. "Status" is the obsession of the masses. Of course, the ideology of the meek is at the heart of the most radical political movements, which "manipulate" the masses by a variety of permanent, hypercomplex conspiracies, always invisible and undetectable, controlled by the powers-that-be. Hence, the calculation of a "tolerance of repression" in advanced societies. Hence, the "enslavement" of women, whereby they allegedly count for nothing (although since time immemorial they have been charged with the education of the human race). Hence, the postulate of psychoanalysis (the one that makes it successful): the good qualities which humble persons ascribe to themselves come from within, while the failings they recognize in themselves stem from their education and environment.

Meanwhile, the French people are proud of their atomic strength. The Swiss vote down a bill aimed at banning the export of arms. In the same country it has taken almost a century to get civil rights for women because the government cannot impose them, as elsewhere, but must receive the assent of the *people*. If the people of the United States had their way, they would bring back the death penalty. The German people voted in favour of their nuclear power stations. After two years of horrifying TV news films, the majority of Americans still supported the war in Vietnam. In the same way the American workers regularly support the most reactionary candidates for the presidency. In the U.S.S.R., ordinary people revile and denounce the intellectuals who dare to jeopardize the orderly progress of the regime: are not intellectuals, by definition, the elite? In China one word of command is enough to set a billion computers applauding. *"They"* have deceived all these people, who are victims of geography, of the economy, of a set of traditions. The people themselves have never done anything, since the meek cannot do anything; thus, they have nothing to give but their total submission in return for the total remission they are offered. Such is the double benefit we humble ones obtain from our anonymous society.

The automobile, which sends tons of toxic concentrates down to the decaying kingdom of the dolphins and the noctilucae, which turns the atmosphere corrosive and surrounds every single person with dozens of cubic meters of ugliness, din, and mortal danger— the automobile is the ideal of the meek. Communist parties make their governments promise that the people will never be short of gasoline when they go on vacation. Sport—symbol of the economic game of grab—electrifies the meek. When hundreds of hectares of forest have to be changed into sparse scrub to let three million imbeciles know that a prizefighter and a millionairess are leading a cat and dog life together, who is forcing the meek to read this gutter press? When the meek revel in obscene spectacles on TV, such as *Twenty-Four Hours at Le Mans*, but complain to high heaven over the obscenity of a naked body, who then is manipulating them? If they cannot see the oceans dying through a haze of gasoline, are we to force them to exchange their best sellers for ecological primers? They know that car exhausts are harmful—everyone knows that you can commit suicide in a garage—but the atmosphere is a *big* garage, and my car is not the only one there.

The truth is that the meek adore everything that makes up the horror of the world pollution: rivalries, authorities, kudos for the winners, evasions, noise, a devil-may-care attitude, brute force. Others know better than they do, so technicians will surely invent antipollution systems, what the experts say is true, statesmen have secret and complicated reasons for their actions. Bread and circuses for the meek, and let other people worry about everything else: responsibility, loneliness, powerlessness, and despair. Someone else has perverted their culture, someone else has lied to them, someone else has manipulated them, someone else has taught them all wrong. The invisible elite forces the meek to choose rock music instead of Beethoven; belonging to the working class gives one a taste for boxing matches; work hinders thought, rather than thought making work possible; an hour's concentration on a book is out, but eight hours' concentration on a freeway is a Sunday pastime. The people hate the mention of pollution *and* demand that it be done away with *and* insist on the very things that create it: white veal, fruits more sweet than natural, aerosols, supersonic planes, plastic everything, paper in ever growing quantities. Several years ago Ford perfected a vehicle in which it was almost impossible to kill oneself; the car looked like a cross between a soft-boiled egg and some sort of Moon machine—and the public spurned it from the word *go*. But it is only industry that is guilty. The people are merely bullied, and when they buy what industry produces and thus induce industry to produce more and more for them to buy, they are acting like sleepwalkers.

That the ex-damned of the Earth are cowards, that the masses are even flabbier than the parasites they vote into office, that the insulted dream only of becoming insulters, that the humiliated adore and justify humiliation—that is what exasperates their advocates to the point of bringing them face to face with the perpetual contradiction: how can one not see that everything that threatens Earth with an ignominious death is both summarized and rooted in the ignominy of so many victims who would like nothing better than to become victimizers. How can one not see that nothing can be expected from four billion men each of whom expects everything from all the others? How can one use all one's eloquence to decry mass leisure activities, mass consumption, mass media, and massive inertia, when the only recourse imaginable against these scourges is a mass revolution? How can one believe in the cause of people who regard whole populations as their enemies?

If the production of automotive engines falls off, the trade unions start complaining. If a factory that produces artillery shells discharges a thousand employees, they will threaten riots unless their workshops are reopened. The workers are not interested in knowing what use will be made of the shells or the engines. Try replacing road transport with rail transport, and you will have truckers barricading all your roads. The worldwide interests of small business are not what interests small business people. "Our 12 percent raise," say the labourers, "our profit margin," the bosses reply—and they negotiate at 10 percent increase and a slightly reduced profit margin. Every man for himself, and sulphur dioxide for all.

The industrialists have no wish to interrupt the fabrication and sale of the lie; their clientele have no wish to be stopped from consuming it, from working to produce it, and from using their earnings from this work to consume even more of it. The bosses are not willing to yield anything, the workers are not willing to lose anything. The people are not responsible—nor are their industries or their governments, since each of these categories simultaneously represents the other two. The wheel turns, the whole world is innocent, and all that is left for us to do is to die. But at least some crafty legends will die at the same time we do.

We shall have seen the enemy and know that "he is us." We shall know that all the oppressed of the world were losers in the same race; that we allowed a small number of vampires to suck vast hordes of victims; that the powerful elites manipulating the powerless majorities were, from start to finish, alibis for our assents and our silences. We shall know that Stalin was Russia personified from the twenties to the fifties, Hitler a representation of Germany during the thirties, the "ecological" war in Vietnam a portrait of the America of the sixties—and that pollution is the image of Humanity throughout time, reflecting the whole social scale, from top to bottom.

Faced with a Europe in ruins in 1918, Kaiser Wilhelm II stammered, "I didn't want this." Nationalist writers had not wanted it either, nor had the millions of the meek who had left with flowers in their rifle barrels, bawling patriotic songs. Nobody had wanted anything—and yet it had happened. As always, the means got the better of the end. None of our descendants will know what our objectives were—and it will be better so—but pollution, which is our means, will still remain their lot. The whole story of Life leads to no other conclusion: only the means count, and the end cannot but resemble them. The huge dinosaurs certainly had every intention of surviving, the unicellulars showed the same intention of becoming organisms as inexpensively as possible. But an intention that fails is a wrong intention—in the human sphere, we call it hypocritical. Christianity in power is merely Power; revolution through violence ends up as violence; the dictatorship of the proletariat is still dictatorship; liberty organized by the Mafia ends up in the Mafia; nuclear tests—capitalist and socialist alike—end up in radioactivity. And nothing is more admirable than this constant defeat of human bad faith in the face of the serene honesty of the Universe. *Vox Naturae, vox dei.*

So of our four protagonists, the only one left is that scattered elite known globally as Science, which we regard, in desperation, as standing guard over the human race. The truth is that the race has come to regard itself as some stately ship, whereas likening it to a life raft would actually be too flattering. Science perforce resembles it. The scientific researcher is the perfect hireling. Even the money attached to a Nobel prize is not enough to finance a laboratory, and even the largest personal fortune in the world is insufficient to buy a proton synchrotron. No scientist can earn a living from research work alone, and the idea of a completely independent scientific researcher is almost as absurd as that of a traffic cop working at his own expense. In other professions, moral scruples can make one refuse the best offer; after all, two firms will probably not offer a chartered accountant very different work. But the firm that promises the highest salaries to researchers is nearly always the one that gives them the best possibility of continuing their own particular work. This is the explanation for the "brain drain" to the U.S.A.

This is also why, throughout the world, one scientist in five works directly for the military, while the other four are employed by industry, which is indirectly supported by the military. The proportion is the same for engineers and technicians. Research is directed, laboratories are opened conditionally, patents are buried in file drawers or launched onto the commercial circuit. To put it another way, if Science is to concern itself with the environment, it will do so only because its patrons wish it to. That, one suspects, is almost never the case, certainly as soon as the estimates for a job exceed what a firm—even a generous firm—is prepared to pay.

So the struggle against what is killing us depends on the infinitesimal proportion of researchers who are independent, which means those at universities. And not only does this tiny corner of Science have to exist on the crumbs of others; it is also subject to crumbling itself. Specialized books and journals are its only outlet. Science has never managed to unify itself, although what it has to face is always united. Knowledge in itself has never made any one incorruptible, and scientific knowledge, by its very nature, tends towards separation, for to analyze is to divide. The result is a division of work which is not better compensated for by a single objective. Naturalists occupy themselves with marine flora and fauna, chemists with seawater, physicists with tides and currents, engineers with hydromechanics. Hygiene depends on the public health services, which depend on their governments, and the *management* of the oceans depends on the economists, who depend on their governments or on industry. Secrets, professional or not, and jealousies, personal or not, reign over everything. Only pollution is interdisciplinary.

So scientists are in the habit of confining themselves to a prudence which in turn confines itself more or less to cowardice. So even the most distinguished among them—like Heisenberg or Teller—have worked on the worst horrors without questioning the ends to which they would be put, preferring to cultivate for their own benefit the metaphysics of the bazaar and the humanism of elderly spinsters. So Science today has sold out lock, stock, and barrel to business and the arms industry. And even if it had not done all this, even if, having grasped that action is essential, it had the power to act, it would still have to make a groping assessment of its most urgent objectives. And it could not achieve, even if it recognized them, because of the lack of time, staff, and money. Take only the problems of the seacoasts. We do not know much about turbulent dispersion nor about advection by currents; we have scarcely an inkling about sedimenta-tion, flocculation, the innumerable exchanges between plants and animals, bacteria and diatoms, bacteria and viruses. If all this knowledge could be acquired in a flash and if the poisoning pro-cesses were not outstripping analysis of their consequences, then perhaps one could foresee some of the ultimate effects of pollution—foresee, but not prevent. Even though we can fix with some exacti-tude the arrival of a cyclone, identify the portents of an earthquake, and anticipate a melting of the polar icecaps, it still remains impos-sible to prevent them.

Up till now, Science has quite simply *never* foreseen a single one of the phenomena we lump together under the name of pollution. It is, as Oppenheimer said, "the sum of the errors that will not be repeated." But pollution is also the sum of the errors we have not yet made and those it is in our interest to make again.

XII

"Pollution is the price of progress"; "pollution is the inevitable appendix of the universe of technology"; "pollution is Nemesis to man, the sacrilegious Faust"; "pollution is the other side of the capi-talist coin"—all lies. "Return to Nature," "Science, the sorcerer's apprentice," "Science, runaway technology"—also lies.

One can understand why we try ceaselessly to ward off the evil with the same swindles that have brought it on. The name of Faust honours a world of profiteers. The word "progress" is too good for the game of economic grab, whose advances have sprung up like roses emerging from a compost heap. The word *technology* fits in very conveniently between human inertia and what it produces by an interposed technique. Capitalism, whether liberal and private or repressive and state-run, continually exchanges the substance for the shadow. Enslaved and consenting Science raises no complaint when its myopic, grocery clerk's dreams are disguised as the cosmic visions of the sorcerer's apprentice, just as the schedules, the profits, the crowds, the asphyxia, and the hubbub which make Humanity both prosperous and ill are called "civilization" by those who know no better. In fact, "return to Nature" is as meaningless as "squaring the circle." Nature exists only because it is the exact *opposite* of a return.

Three billion years of incredible, ever-more-rapid struggle—it is that sum total of accumulated risks which is proposed as our refuge. The journey ahead of us would have to be made with our engines in reverse.

Practical examples of this attitude are already among us. It is no longer possible to feed the Humanity of today with the techniques of only ten years ago, so small groups are reverting to feeding themselves away from pesticides; they remain quite separate while preaching generosity. Since all pollution stems from individualism and the spirit of sectarianism, it is as individuals or sects that we must escape it: *I* shall survive the Flood. Similarly, since Nature is merely a vast, confusing technology that has never stopped widening and changing, we must counter it with human techniques, which are intrinsically perverse. Returning to the sources would enable Humans to survive by turning them into animals—as though the mammals had outlived the dinosaurs by reverting to the invertebrates. We would be pretending to say, "Leave it to Nature," while thinking, in common with all religions, "Leave it to Chance," even though we know (for it is impossible *not* to know) that Chance and Nature work through each other only when they work against one another.

Thus the anti-God of religion is called Chance, and Providence becomes the reverse of foresight, in the same way that matter and the human mind are the reverse of divinity. Reproduce by chance, make a fortune by chance, trust in chance—what do these lies matter if they allow the cult of Death to exorcise sex? It is by sex that Life defends itself, so one must consign the one to asceticism when one wishes to doom the other to failure. This obsession would be negligible if it were merely religious, but we do not need Jehovah to preserve the family, the couple, or especially property. The jealous God can, without inconvenience, delegate his powers to Jealousy itself, in exactly the same way that the idolatry of Chance, barely forsaken by faltering theologies, has no better method of prolonging itself than by faith in free competition. Nothing resembles baccarat as much as speculation, nothing parallels roulette more than dabbling on the stock exchange. And nothing is more apt than an accident of birth and fortune to make one believe that freedom is power of any kind, while making one forget one of Life's lessons: that power of any kind means not being anyone at all, that an amoeba is less free than a human because liberty, in the strictest biological sense, is a question of organization in the strictest organic sense.

For the same reasons we can do without the Devil. *Diabolos* means "the separator." No one could possibly be more separated than we are, or more humble. And humility has been the desire of all the so-called moralities and religions of a commercial humanity that, seeing everything in reverse, consigned everything to Hell after depicting God as a limitation, the Human Being as a slave, knowledge as pride, mediocrity as reality, real life as after-death, and Paradise as an affair of the deceased. At that rate we shall soon have paradise on earth, and "Thy Kingdom come" will have been fulfilled. Humble morality, which advises its devotees to seek death, could not ask for more.

We also find this humble morality in the idea that pollution is the price of progress. It is not we who are guilty but our instruments. The Nazi camps were not the price of Nazism but of Zyklon-B gas. The rush to install nuclear power stations everywhere stems not from the profit motive but from progress. Pesticides are aimed not at crop yields but at agricultural progress. An oil tanker dumps its fuel oil into the sea as a result of progress and not the attraction of profit. Antibiotics enrich the meat and not the butcher. And so on, ad infinitum.

If we are at a loss, in thought as well as in action, in the face of what is happening to us, it is because the phenomenon seems new. In fact, its principles date from the beginnings of the world of humans, perhaps even the world of animals. Every zoological group proliferates and consumes as much as it can, but only human power is undefined, and from that fact comes our gesture of malediction. The child who bumps into a chair hits and abuses it.

The gap we have created forbids our turning back. Meanwhile the human race has now reached such a great size relative to the globe that it is tantamount to a planetary organism in terms of harmful effects. That is the point at which we must begin—and what we have begun of necessity, we have no option but to complete of our own free will. We are without guarantees, but Life—or call it Evolution—cannot equip itself in advance with the means of confronting something it does not yet know of. Neither does it have any certainty of success.

I said at the beginning of this book that there is no conceivable reflection save through or over an obstacle, and that a refracted ray implies a refractory material. Even if nine tenths of the human race must die and I and my readers are not among the survivors, pollution would still be a benefit to humanity, a saving strangulation, a last resort accorded Conscience to help it scale the walls of its final prison. The individual Ego is not the last word of Life, whose ambitions have no reason to stop before the infinity from which they come. Whether we find these ambitions terrifying or exalting, we know that this is the way the life force has always worked. Each stopping point is a question of "double or quits," and each time quitting becomes a more serious matter and doubling, more crazy. Vertigo increases at each turn of the spiral, but nothing produces more vertigo than love and beauty; the awakening of the Universe is the divine work, which is the Universe itself. Day will come, or Night will swallow everything. This phrase may sound like a threat, but a threat is nothing but the reverse of a hope.

On the one hand, pollution has always existed; the Romans decimated the fauna of the Maghreb, the Greeks turned their well-wooded country into a desert, medieval people's use of the rivers brought pestilence to the towns. On the other hand, until now Humanity has lived in ignominy. Every economic exchange has been the balance of two thefts; there has always been privation in the adjective "private." Customs offices have always been ransom offices, states have always been born from pillage, fortunes and miseries have always stemmed from chance. There has been no social order that has not been a masquerade, no authority that has not been usurped, no morality that has not been hypocritical, no military or political triumph that has not been vulgarity enthroned. We have never stopped selling Nature. We have never stopped lying through our work, with its apparent objective always a pretext, and its ending unique, monotonous, piercing like the monosyllable "I" repeated indefinitely.

This lugubrious parade, which all the oppressed of History accepted as their fate, *had* to have an end. Earth, sacked for the profit of Profit, had to close itself over the El Dorado it had pretended to open up. The continual misuse of the world was marked down by its turning aside of progress, so progress had to expose us to an enemy that has no national boundaries in order to force us to abolish our own. With the rise of Science, matter half-opened its gates, as though to give a glimpse of infinity, and human rapacity rushed forward into the breach. It was a *trap*—the most intelligent, the most unforeseeable, and the most unavoidable that we have ever encountered. What we had taken for inertia is ensnaring us in a labyrinth. Matter, which our bookkeeping has never taken into account, which we have taken for something passive and infinitely malleable, is proving harder and more rigid than all the now inoperative moral laws; it is also identical with them. "That which is above is like unto that which is below," said Hermes Trismegistus, and all the philosophers who followed him had a presentiment, from the depths of their ghetto, that the spiritual and the material worlds are identical. They thought they could stifle the voice of the one, but they discovered the silent coldness of the other: and the voice and the silence said the same thing. God seemed to have stopped joking, and this barely forgotten philosophy turned into dictatorship. Such is the admirable convergence that delineates pollution, once and for all.

In a universe of rockets, it is impossible to survive with an anti-morality that is barely authorized by the speed of the horse and the galley. In the world of strontium 90 and parathion, it is impossible to operate business combines that can just about cope with pepper and cinnamon. In our dreams we wanted chemistry, and here it is—it turns those dreams into nightmares. We wanted Nature, and here it is—it is worse than egalitarian, it is organic.

Let us imagine an electric motor that has to attain its maximum power while functioning as follows. Right at the main switch, a small amount of current is diverted to produce multicoloured sparks; wherever two wires cross, a device produces musical notes without which there will be a short circuit; the insulators threaten to become conductive unless they are each given the chance to produce a spark; a transformer diverts half the energy it receives to surrounding itself with its own private electromagnetic fields; each gear protects its own teeth by driving the next wheel only if it can divert the heat it produces to its own benefit; a thousand useless relays pretend to be indispensable. That is how human communities work. We have not even attained the efficiency of machines, which themselves are not a quarter as effective as organisms. Moreover, thanks to nationalism, each of the unbalanced, dirty motors in our allegory sets itself against all the others, drawing off from them as much current as it can and then wasting it. And so—to switch metaphors for a moment—the terrestrial metropolis remains a hodgepodge of shantytowns.

If we change our allegory to organic images, the description of our own level would not even be that of a cancerous body, in which each cell (each human) imparts (sells) false information to the others. Rather, it must be a portrait of decay progressing until everything is topsy-turvy. Blood plasma collaborates in the cicatrization of a wound only in exchange for extra glucose, which it consumes on the spot or sets aside. Antibodies go on strike the minute a virus invades. The heart demands guarantee bonuses before it pumps blood into the arteries. The suprarenal glands create a scarcity of adrenaline so as to send the price up as need increases. The hypothalamus slows down its warnings so as not to disturb the muscles. The thyroid produces too much thyroxin and dumps the balance near the brain. The kidneys purify only 30 percent of the urine. The intestine voids its filth through the intestinal walls so as to maintain its competition with the liver, which gets rid of its bile in the same way. And so on and so on. That is the state of health of our social *body*. How could one expect this shadow of a corpse to have the smallest spark of soul?

When the body is going to pieces, the soul tends towards suicide. That is the last nail I have to drive home to create anything other than a prettied-up model of Gehenna.

XIII

Pollution is a combination of anarchy and rigidity with two poles: absolute disorder and systematic absurdity, or—to put it another way—overpopulation and armies.

During the next half-hour, the world will have seven thousand more babies and three thousand fewer people. Of its four thousand extra passengers, one third will not have enough to eat, half will never know how to read, one tenth—at the very least—will die because of war. Within a year the additions to the human race will form a population more numerous than those of Sweden, Switzerland, and France together—but a population in rags. Eight out of ten inhabitants of our planet are undernourished, while the other two eat twice as much as they should and must often use pharmaceuticals to help them slim down. An American dog gets more protein to eat than a Pakistani peasant.

We should plant more crops, but each year the amount of arable land is less. Moreover, erosion threatens more than half the world's irrigated soil; some of it is losing its layer of humus at the rate of 5 centimeters every six years, and it takes four to ten *centuries* to create 3 centimeters of humus. We should increase irrigation, but its average cost is $1,150 per hectare, a sum out of reach for the very countries that need it the most. We should feed these starving countries from the rich nations' surpluses, but the amounts needed are almost beyond comprehension. The U.N.'s Food and Agriculture Organization (FAO) launches appeals several times each year; a recent one for just six West African countries asked for 320,000 tons of cereals—an amount equal to 33 percent of the world's food reserves. In the event of a climatic accident, no country will have any cereals to give away: the whole world will be short of them. We should teach the vast masses of hungry people, so they can become autonomous and learn to feed themselves, but the ability to read does not perforce change aridity into fertility. Even though all governments have programs for eliminating illiteracy, the worldwide total of analphabetics has grown by 100 million in a decade and a half and is increasing each year. We should reduce the inequalities between the rich and the poor, but they are getting worse. Just try the operation within a *rich* country to get a faint idea of what it would entail in the others. The ditch that separates the "have" nations from the "have-nots" should be filled in, but it is growing wider and deeper—and changing into a septic tank, a potter's field. A baby in the West eats twenty-five times as much as one in the Third World (who is lucky to be eating at all). Death from famine becomes more frequent every day. When a population grows by 10 percent, its harmful effects grow by 40 percent. And human masses tend to concentrate in cities as their woes increase. As early as 1930 schizophrenia was seven times more frequent at the center of a metropolis such as Chicago than at its outskirts; alcoholic psychosis was six times more common, as were murders, armed assaults, and suicides. Every laboratory test repeats the results we can observe on a global scale: overcrowding both lowers the level of intelligence and breaks down the rules of ethics that are never broken by an animal species in the natural state. But what does it matter? In the natural state the human species already breaks every single one of them.

The blast of the demographic explosion stirs up universal pollution just as a strong wind aggravates a forest fire. And pollution and overpopulation have the same origins. Because it also pollutes, America is in no position to demand that Brazil reduce its population, and because it is overpopulated, Brazil is in an even worse position to demand that America stop polluting. So there will be no choice between famine and war: we shall have to undergo them both. The forecast is that 500 million children, ages one to fifteen, will die from one or the other during the next twenty-five years. Yet all the international conferences held to stem the tide of humanity decry the equivalence of large numbers and force. Misery seeks company in compensation. Every state regards its labour as capital ("cattle" might be an equally valid word) and is no more disposed to letting others become interested in this capital than to granting them control, even remote control, over its "exploitable resources"— in other words, over pollution. China insistently says that there is "no limit to the mastery [sic] of Man over his environment," while the Holy See keeps parroting its eternal phrase about "respect for life"— thanks to which fetuses can achieve the dignity of skeletons.

Who would ask their country to allow itself to be overwhelmed by others? Although the most paternalistic of industries can no longer count on the support of the workers whom they are exploiting, the least homogeneous of nations can still command the backing of the hundreds of thousands of ragamuffins whom it mobilizes. Now, overpopulation is patriotism itself (the word "matriotism" would be more appropriate here!); it also expresses human narcissism at its most basic. Although our species is the only part of Nature whose continuity we can guarantee without the least effort, it is precisely by that least effort that it swarms as it does. The renewable, which lives increasingly badly, takes precedence over the irreplaceable, which is dying out everywhere, while the do-gooders are still shouting that famine is preferable to pollution. Fortunately, we do not have to make a choice. What states are unwilling to do together for the purpose of curbing their industrial and agricultural surpluses, they are even more reluctant to do individually for the purpose of limiting their superfluous labour power. It matters little since nothing can be done individually, and since it is on separation, not agreement, that we have based the whole of our life and even, as we shall see, preparations for our death.

Almost all the large species that have disappeared from the Earth died from an overabundance of armour plating, an excess of armament, and a plethora of defensive equipment. The mammals that survived them were fragile but wiry, small but speedy. They illustrated the first law of the decalogue of evolution: all security imprisons, only risk sets free, liberty and consciousness are the two faces of a single form, neither of which can be reached without passing by the other. Thus, shells, protective but constricting, turned into internal skeletons, dangerous but liberating, and instinct, infallible but limited, gave way to consciousness, adventurous but adaptable.

Megaceros, a member of the deer family that was nearly three meters long, had to replace meter-and-a-half antlers every year; it died out in a period of scarcity because the regrowth of its antlers consumed all its calories. Brontosaurus was invincible to enemies of every kind save those the guardian spirit of its race had not foreseen: the rains and the frost. At the very moment when its energy was beginning to flag, this living fortress needed whole thickets to meet its colossal energy requirements, but it could no longer find anything but lichens. Survival in such circumstances is a lot to ask of a creature that weighs one hundred tons. We find ourselves in the same situation, except that the danger comes from ourselves. Armed to the teeth and more disposed to surrender our teeth than our arms, we are being attacked from the rear while the adversary in front of us immobilizes us as he forces us to mobilize.

The world's annual military expenditures, including the industrial, scientific, and technical efforts they give rise to, amount to at least *eight times* the total annual expenditure of the United States. Eight bountiful Americas! But the real America deprives the planet of this dream, only to organize a nightmare—imitated, of course, and often surpassed by China, Europe, and the U.S.S.R. Today the United

States and the U.S.S.R. alone possess enough weapons to kill every inhabitant of the globe 32,000 times over—an overkill capacity of 31,999 times four billion purely ornamental murders. In the event of war all people who are now at the point of death for want of a handful of rice would have the right to 25 tons of TNT each: enough to blow up a town of fifty thousand inhabitants or to feed a family in India for half a century. Since 1950 the world's population has increased by a factor of not quite 1.5, but the production of arms has at least tripled since that year. Now, in 1950 the Cold War was already said to be pushing overkill armament to the point of madness, and since then we have been enjoying a period of détente.

One tenth of the world's expenditures on armaments would cover the food and energy requirements of its forty poorest countries, but these countries have military budgets that add up to more than that tenth part. In fact, the Third World's arsenal costs five times more today than it did twenty-five years ago. In one way nothing could be more logical. Vietnam had to fight for thirty years in order to survive. One single day of the American bombing of North Vietnam cost more money than it would have taken to put that country's economy back on its feet. Meanwhile the United States, while helping the Third World with the same money it had extorted from it, wounded the entire planet by the chemical destruction of forests equal in area to half of Switzerland, by the poisoning of streams, by the elimination of fauna (elephants cannot live in jungles defoliated by dioxin), and by the collective torture of a people with napalm and antipersonnel bombs. But all that the First and Second World lost through this debauchery was their dignity—in other words, nothing. In all other respects they came out winners, since they sold enough arms to the poor countries to pay *twice over* for their international "aid."

As each country works continuously at perfecting new arms that call for ten to fifteen years of research, each can foresee dangers that do not yet exist; so can the enemy. Thus, this very foresight becomes a danger that calls for a reply, and so on ad infinitum. At this rate the military budgets of the year 2000 will reach today's gross world product. All this effort will not be wasted, however, for the number of victims of war is increasing rapidly with the number of localized wars. During the next fifteen years at least 100 million people will die as a result of war. Up to 1850, one man in a thousand died in this way; between 1850 and 1900, four men; between 1900 and 1950, twenty-one; between 1950 and 1975, about a hundred.

The average annual cost per soldier is eighty times greater than the average annual cost of education per child. This is only fair, since education is just a show, whereas the army is a professional opportunity: the military-industrial complex supports one American in five and directly employs one out of ten. During peacetime the army itself keeps nearly four million men permanently mobilized by letting them sit vegetating in 9,300 bases spread over the globe. The situation is naturally worse in the U.S.S.R. and China. It is impossible to distinguish industry from the army or the army from the schools in countries that draw no more distinction between a citizen and a soldier than between a police officer and a literary critic.

When it is possible to die 32,000 times over, the terminology of the politico-military lexicon can only be fictive. The way we are getting used to it is slowly sending us out of our minds (which would have the advantage of making war superfluous). We see "Communist tanks" in Asia and "Protestant bombs" in Ireland, we "clean" border strips with napalm, we bomb "demilitarized" zones, we flatten "refugee" camps, we cross "pacified" perimeters in force, we militarize "civilian" society to defend "civilization." Consequently, why should there not be a "Security" Council of the "United" Nations? Why should military competition not be called "peaceful" coexistence? Why should countries whose meat ration is decreasing not be in process of "development"? Why should the imbalance of the world caused by its anguish not be a "balance of terror"? And why should the name *disarmament* conferences not be given to meetings whose only objective (never attained) is freezing military expenditures at their current level—in other words, maintaining the status quo of the monstrous? In this connection here is a complete list of all these conferences' results so far: (1) the demilitarization and denuclearization of the Antarctic, which had never been militarized; (2) a ban on atmospheric nuclear tests, which France and China refused to interrupt and India began much later on; (3) an agreement on the nonproliferation of nuclear weapons, which then proliferated at an increased rate; (4) a ban on placing nuclear charges in space, which (alas!) is unenforceable, since in principle everything—even Moscow and Washington—is located in space; (5) a ban on military use of the ocean deeps, which are already covered in wastes (no doubt civilian) and which a nuclear submarine (no doubt tourist) can visit with impunity for months on end.

Either the states must disarm sequentially, which is impossible, or they must disarm simultaneously, which has been practically rejected. If leaders who have reached the stage of intimate confidences cannot manage to build a commercial Europe, how could China and the U.S.S.R., who hate each other, dismantle their political boundaries? Who would make good industry's deficit? If today's two great powers miraculously managed to agree on holding their armaments to present levels, why should China, India, Brazil, and all the rest follow their lead before they have war machines of equal power or a little greater (one can discuss things in more brotherly fashion from a position of strength)? Can one imagine the U.S.A. and the U.S.S.R. suddenly dividing into five parts what they have spent years sharing out so painfully between the pair of them? One-upmanship has no end.

This is why the military budget of the U.S.A. is at least 32 percent of its national budget, France's 18 percent, England's 21 percent, Germany's 22 percent, and that of all other countries together, from China and the U.S.S.R. to the Arab nations and those of the Third World, is estimated at about 40 percent. In other words, while Society shilly-shallies and Nature jeopardizes, one third of all Humanity's power serves at best to serve nothing and at worst to resolve our problems by war—just like dousing a fire with a flood.

But Science, smitten with an ideal, does not fritter away the immense fortune with which we other idealists keep endowing it. There is no point in detailing the world's macabre heavy artillery of phosphorus shells, rockets, bombs, and tanks teleguided by laser beams. This visible apocalypse is not worth the other, and secret arms are kept secret for good reasons. If the troops charged with their use realized what they are being made to do, their morale would be sapped. The gas used in Vietnam, one of the most innocuous, acts as follows: the nose runs, the chest feels constricted, sight is affected before being lost completely, salivating and sweating climax in vomiting; then urination and defecation can no longer be controlled, cramps and contractions seize the region of the heart, agonizing headaches make the victim cry out in pain, violent convulsions threaten to break bones. In the final stages coma sets in, breathing is cut off, and the victim dies.

The same results can be obtained from a milligram of Sarin gas, a Nazi invention, with which American and Russian arsenals are stocked to overflowing. Two hundred fifty tons of this gas would kill all the inhabitants of Paris, whether they were in enclosed premises or not. Arsine and Zyklon-B, which were used in Hitler's extermination camps, have been abandoned as ineffective. The defoliants used in Vietnam are a mere bagatelle compared to dimethylarsenic acid, one drop of which will annihilate a centuries-old oak.

Nobody knows how to save the ozone layer that protects the whole of terrestrial life against the sun's ultraviolet rays, but military science knows how to destroy it above a given territory. The region so affected becomes immediately and permanently like the surface of the moon—a true demilitarized zone. Nobody knows how to stop insanity from increasing its ravages fourfold every twenty years, but among the hundreds of secret chemical weapons there is not one that does not produce dementia. In a filmed experiment, an American battalion was given an LSD 25 substitute. The men went to pieces in less than an hour; they were seized with spasms of laughter, threw their arms down, shouted, wept, groaned, fainted from terror, and climbed trees. One kilo of LSD would be sufficient to plunge the population of London into this disarray, and the U.S.S.R. possesses substances that are much more powerful. The formulae of BZ and VX are available to all the Soviet, American, and European general staffs; they could set off epidemics whose victims would mostly end up dead or permanently demented. Pregnant women who had not absorbed enough to send them mad would give birth to monsters.

In 1957 a Russian colonel somewhat rashly announced that traditional weapons, the atom bomb, and chemical warfare all together would not equal the ravages of a biological war. That was all the U.S.A. needed to raise its funding for "military biology" from $35 to $150 million over seven years. In 1977 it was announced that the American army had made 250 open-air tests of bacteriological materiel on United States territory during the past twenty years. They were so successful that "inert" (i.e., inoffensive) bacteria had killed several people.

Today viruses and bacteria are regarded as operational weapons. Yellow fever, encephalitis, smallpox, and the most aggressive varieties of dengue, influenza, and typhus are available to the military. So are typhoid, undulant fever, cholera, and the plague in its most terrifying forms. A single charge of botulism toxin in a town's water supply would obviate the need for any other kind of attack; death would be general within a few hours. The merest smidgen of the R. Rickettsia Burneti can communicate "Q" fever, an extremely rapid and debilitating illness. Bubonic plague bacteria, in concentrations stronger than are found in the natural state, can destroy a country in two days, even a country as large as the U.S.S.R. Three grams of chicken embryo tissue impregnated with R. Burneti and other bacteria could start an epidemic that would kill off Humanity in three or four days—and there would be virtually no hope of checking it. An immunized saboteur would have no trouble spreading anthrax, which is 80 percent fatal if it is countered in the first few hours after the spores have been spread and 100 percent if it is not; its incubation period is only twenty-four hours.

The Pentagon announced in 1977 that it was studying "terrifying" arms (were the others benign?) that would swing the so-called balance of power in its favour; it was talking about laser beam weapons placed in orbit around the earth. The U.S.S.R. replied that it would do better and more quickly. It does, in fact, have at its disposal a "decompression bomb" that absorbs all the oxygen in the atmosphere within a radius of 500 meters; cannons, such as the GAU–8–a, that fire 4,000 uranium shells per minute; and a proton gun that has finally realized the dream of the "death ray" and destroys every target at ranges that have not been defined. Henceforth the neutron bomb becomes superfluous even though it can destroy all traces of life in concrete bunkers with ten meters' thickness of earth on top of them. Now they are talking about plans for computer-driven, crewless tanks filled with nuclear charges and protected by armour two meters thick. Official reports also envisage "bombs with retractile feet" that would clear ditches ten meters wide and move their atomic arsenals forward without the aid of human pilots—and thus without any hesitation.

We now know how to throw Nature off balance, to turn the climate upside down in a few hours, to cause earthquakes of hitherto unimaginable violence. The United States has not signed any agreement against the use of biological weapons, and the U.S.S.R. has reserved the right to use them against anyone else who uses them. Other countries have banned their manufacture, but not research work on them. Unfortunately, the only way of defending oneself against these weapons, like so many others, is to use them first, and the only suitable way of studying them is to manufacture them—and thus to have them. Nonproliferation of arms of any sort or description is a joke as vulgar as the "struggle against pollution," "protection of the environment," and "maintaining the quality of life."

It only remains for us to contemplate atomic weapons, armaments in their most spectacular guise, least secret, most costly, and before long the most common guise.

To crystallize our ideas, let us take the case of a European nation, say France. Who is going to attack France with traditional weapons? No country in possession of nuclear weapons. An outbreak of war between two nuclear countries would be a matter of minutes, at the most. Computers have already set the levels of alert, and the opening shots for a given level have been programmed even more inexorably. This forethought is logical since American military experts go so far as to forecast that a few seconds' lead will give "the advantage [sic] of half the enemy's territory destroyed." And they were talking about the territory of the U.S.S.R., the largest country in the world. So who then would attack France, who has the Bomb, unless they had it themselves? What kamikaze nation would do a thing like that? India, South Africa, Brazil, and others are too far away, so all we have left are the adjacent European countries. Now, hypothesize a traditional, nonatomic war in which Germany attacks France, Italy invades the Benelux countries, and—no more improbable—Switzerland strikes at Sweden. Since France and Germany today each have at least five times the firepower of the Wehrmacht in 1939, Europe would soon be covered with dozens of millions of corpses enveloped in an immense shroud of chemical dusts. All that would remain, after the rockets, the phosphorus shells, and the napalm, after the tank battles and the naval engagements, would be what remains of Carthage. And since Europe is already one of the high spots of world pollution, the Baltic, the Mediterranean, and the North Sea would become stinking swamps several years earlier than expected.

Of course, this hypothesis is utterly ridiculous, but can we suggest any others that are not in the same category? One additional example of futility should be enough. France's nuclear strike force, as General de Gaulle, its creator, recognized, is "a hundred times inferior" (a flattering estimate) to those of the two great powers. But, he added, "a wasp can terrify a bear"—and the French people swallowed that bear like a fly, only too happy to be worrying the U.S.S.R. and to forget that one wasp will not terrify a hundred swarms of hornets in the service of a bear bent on genocide. They were too delighted over the idea of dissuading an adversary with a force a thousand times smaller than theirs. It seemed a bargain without precedent in History, one that would be profitable even to a nation that had not, over the past half century, lost every battle in which its soldiers had been engaged.

There are, of course, two ways for a wasp to dissuade the enemy: mount a preventive strike or reply to the enemy's attack. In the first case Vladivostok disappears, but twenty minutes later France no longer exists. In the second France no longer exists, but twenty minutes later Vladivostok disappears.

The scenarios are the same whatever the countries: the U.S.S.R. and the U.S.A., the U.S.S.R. and China, China and the U.S.A., and so on. They all acquire and perfect atomic weapons to ensure that nuclear war never takes place. Therefore—the official reasoning goes —if there were suddenly no more atomic weapons, we would immediately be threatened with atomic war. But what matter? Distinctions between types of warfare have already become impossible. The neutron bomb, which attacks life but spares monuments, has entered the preserves of bacteriological weapons. Germany has recently perfected a nonnuclear device whose ravages equal those of the neutron bomb. There is no progress that does not imply some degree of convergency.

The theoretical war of our hypothesis may make us die laughing, but the real war will drive us to suicide. One single rocket with multiple warheads will be a thousand, ten thousand, twenty thousand times worse than Hiroshima and Nagasaki. The Earth will shudder and crack in a seismic dance such as History has never known. The whole sky will catch fire, blinding suns will shine everywhere simultaneously, the whole of Europe will be coloured in chalky white, pallid violet, fiery red. Fires will break out everywhere; forests will be an immense sheet of flame, factories will explode and give off every possible poison—sulphuric acid, nitrous oxide, phosphorus, titanium, beryllium, selenium, chlorine, and all the rest of Mendeleev's Table. Nuclear power stations will sow radioactivity like silent bombs, but there will be such a noise that no one will hear anything anymore anywhere because their eardrums will have burst. Similarly, 200 kilometers from the point of impact, eyes will melt from light a hundred times brighter than that of the noonday sun. The heat will spread in successive waves. If the bomb falls on Paris, the temperature will still be as hot as a volcano in eruption as far away as Dijon. Nothing will be able to withstand it: the groups of human beings huddled together in their so-called bomb shelters will be roasted as though in the heart of a furnace; the ground will quake and then turn to glass; trenches forty meters deep will open up in the middle of the streets; passersby will become screaming torches, gasping lumps of flesh, suppurating scabs. Walls, metallic debris, rain, water spurting from burst mains, gasoline from burning cars—everything will be radioactive. The survivors—one in ten—will run on shaky legs in all directions, unable to lean on anything without getting burnt, and doomed—again, one in ten—to die of fulminating leukemia in the hours that follow. Public squares will be one vast crowd that will prove fatal; there will be frantic confusion and panicked hallucination everywhere. Some people will be driven insane or lose their sense of orientation, the use of words, or memory; others will die of heart attacks on street corners, throw themselves out of windows (if there are any left) to escape cancer in the days to come (if there are any to come). The troops, struck dumb, paralyzed with terror, and looking like creatures from outer space in their protective equipment, will themselves be victims of dementia or wander aimlessly through the countryside. They will not be up to the task of defending their country—the supposed justification for the war—let alone their radioactive fields, their shattered homes, their cancer-stricken wives, their burnt children, or their monsters yet to be born. The occupying forces, of course, will be in no better shape. Eventually all the soldiers, no longer having a great deal to occupy or defend, will wage a guerrilla war on typhoid, plague, and madness and carry out raids for the conquest or reconquest of the Pompeii that was Europe, which will now consist of such archaeological sites as the shreds of freeways, the skeletons of cheap lodgings, and the remains of abbatoirs.

It is from the scientists that I have borrowed *every* single element of the above description, although they make it as eloquent as a pharmaceutical prospectus. When they wonder whether the remnants of the human race, scarcely more numerous than in the early days of the Roman Empire, would still be able to "climb back up the slope," what slope are they talking about? The whole Earth will be a vertical slide. Two thousand years ago, men and women lived on a verdant planet where the seas were rich, the forests vast, the animals numberless, the soil fertile, the springs crystal-clear, and all the resources intact. After a nuclear war, our bodies would retain their DDT and their mercury, our memories would preserve the images of an unspeakable horror, and our genes would have received enough radioactivity to ensure that our descendants, if any, would suffer from it for thousands of years. We would have nothing but irradiated oceans, probably empty, a soil a thousand times more poisoned than by all the pollution since pollution first started, toxic streams, some remnants of decrepit flora, a few insects, a few other arthropods, deserts overrun by foul miasmas, seasons without birds, our twisted and sick bodies, the idea of suicide rooted in our souls, and practically nothing from the past—no monuments or museums or libraries. And all of it in vain! For now people would not be able to close their eyes to the fact that the whole history of halberds, cannonballs, and royal dynasties led directly to the end of the world, just as the history of the merchants and provosts led straight to the poisoning of the world. He who wills the means wills the end.

The logic of Evolution consists of making the means more and more sinister until we understand how hideous the ends really are. We want our place in the sun—and we get "Everyone for himself" as our ideal. We want isolation—and we get solitude. We want solitary happiness—and we get the couple. We want the couple—

and we get the family. We want the family—and we get inequality. We want inequality—and we get competition. We want competition —and we get profit. We want profit—and we get pollution. We want closed communities—and we get countries. We want countries —and we get boundaries. We want boundaries—and we get armies. We want armies—and we get the nuclear arsenal. We want to loosen the screw as cheaply as possible—and it becomes even tighter. We want to see nothing any longer—and we understand nothing any longer. We lie to deceive ourselves—and the enormity of the lie deceives us. We close our eyes—and we are smitten with blindness.

Thus the silent seasons and the waves of suicides will come without the atomic bomb, as surely as anguish and cancer will extend their ravages. They will come for the same reasons that make the night around us grow ever darker, that make Gehenna glow red and settle itself, inexorably, on the millions of acts of cowardice, false pretenses, and imposture that called it into being yesterday, that maintain it today, and that will expand it tomorrow.

THE GAME OF GRAB

I

The equations could not be easier to grasp: more paper equals less
oxygen, more cars equal more carbon monoxide, more steel equals
less water. The race between Japan and the U.S.S.R. for cheap oil
equals the death of a whale every fourteen minutes, wealth for the
furriers equals the disappearance of leopards, tigers, and ocelots. All
gains are provisional, all losses definitive. Nature, on which our
survival depends, itself depends on us. It cannot survive except by
becoming our objective; that, of course, cannot be permitted by any
kind of commercial competition, whether between nations or groups
or individuals, because to work on behalf of Nature is to work
at a loss and because the objective of a business is necessarily a
pretext.

The extinction of the blue whale, the cockchafer, or any animal or
vegetable species, apart from its unforeseeable effects on the tissue
of Nature, means both the irremediable disappearance of a body of
aesthetics and the loss of irreplaceable techniques, of startling perfection. We do not know how cockchafers manage to fly in apparent
disregard of all known laws of aerodynamics or what system of
cybernetics they use to change course; neither do we know how blue
whales swim, breathe, or find their bearings. Few blue whales and
practically no cockchafers survive, butterflies are declining, and before long there will be no leopards, but women will be wearing
leopard-skin coats, and our axles will have been greased with whale
oil. Bach's musical scores were once used to wrap butcher's meat;

99

the story is repeating itself. It is the very foundation of our activity, which finds blindness advantageous since nothing can disappear unless it has been seen first.

Were our ecology and our economy not so completely opposed that the laws of one can be enunciated by reversing the laws of the other, we would have no need of cataclysms to identify (in both senses of the term) our interests and those of the Earth. They would always coincide. Even if the opposition could be reduced, we would not have to pretend either to know nothing about it or to understand it badly, even as we dream of extinguishing it by continued haggling, statistical prayers, and numerical incantations.

Supply and demand do nothing except perpetuate a dialogue of growing obscurity, which passes from unintelligible nonsense to complete uproar, to be overlaid in the end by the shouted protest that it has in fact said nothing. Unless one considers murder and war forms of human relationship, how can one not see that nothing in the sphere of social compacts could be more primitive, more false, or more opaque than the business contract, which, having achieved its purpose, has become so outdated that it now spends most of its time thwarting that purpose?

Profit, national boundaries, and wastefulness itself tighten the tissue of Society at a time when nothing more tangible could make men interdependent, when nothing more flexible could replace these threads, and when having a sense of the human species is as unthinkable as the scourges that will eventually arouse that sense. In the same way, when one talks of Nature in the global sense—the ensemble of the living world—one must not forget that this ensemble is merely a balance of brute forces. Although the organisms composing it possess a unity and integrity of cell and tissue greatly exceeding the social integrity of the human race, they behave, as individuals, even more blindly than we do. The history of the survival of the fittest, of competition, of the struggle for life is a *natural* history. Nature shows us an objective, not a method or even a starting point. It does not think of *itself* in its totality, except through us. Merciless battles have brought life to this point in History, but they will not carry it much further. The rough laws that sufficed for the conquest of the Earth are no longer valid now that the question is how keep the conquered Earth alive. Let us stop using the adjective "natural" as an excuse where we might reserve it to express an ideal. Jealousy is "natural," as is generosity; a drunken brawl is "natural," as are the works of Beethoven. It is still more natural to make a choice between the two. If Nature, after three billion years, had not channelled its millions of millions of choices into one single direction, it would not yet have reached the stage of the first Batrachia.

This is the way things are in all forms of commerce. Is not intrauterine growth natural? However, beyond nine months it would kill the embryo it has served to develop. Is not the flowering of appleblossom normal? Of course it is—but only if it ends in withering; perpetuation of the blossom would doom the fruit. It is true that Nature and History contain things that maintain continuity, but everywhere we see points of reflection at which former laws are reversed and suppressed. Action—reaction, expansion—contraction, diastole—systole, left—right; every step is limping, and each pace denies its predecessor. It was advantageous that insect behaviour should be engraved in a genetic code, but the opposite became essential with the appearance of the central nervous system. Man is born unequipped, malleable as virgin wax, and from our innate total ineptness comes our social dependence, the basis of our superiority to the rest of the animal world.

I have already noted that, whether we like it or not, Earth has become the equivalent of an organism for us. It has done so in negative fashion, in intaglio. The onus of finding the round—or, rather, of becoming it—falls entirely upon us. In the language of the scholastic philosophers, we have to cover an efficient cause by a final cause—to make an objective of a necessity. In Kant's day an organism was defined by the unity of its parts; now terrestrial unity rests only upon terrifying deficiencies, but it is precisely these deficiencies that will force it to extend and consolidate itself.

Again, it is not a question of making believe, in absurd fashion, that Nature *is* an organism. It is (which comes to the same thing) an equilibrium that we are compelled to preserve and to perfect. This equilibrium cannot then be other than an objective, and if the human race has only *one* objective, which alone justifies its unity, it is by definition organic. And it is to this objective that every possible kind of economic exchange and national partitioning is opposed.

In biology an exchange of false information is called cancer; in economics it is called publicity. Biological growth without an objective is known as a tumour; in economics it is called expansion. One says that a task is "interesting" when the objectives contained in it call for awareness; one calls a business "interesting" when it distracts awareness from the motives it conceals. Two groups of cells that do the same work are engaged in useless replication; two groups of people that do the same work and produce less than if they worked together are engaged in competition. When one part of an organism lacks a given substance, the whole body suffers from it; when one part of Humanity lacks an essential substance, everyone else profits from it. The cells keep the organism alive, and vice versa; we are killing the Earth, and vice versa. An organ takes only what is strictly necessary for its survival; whenever we can, we take even that which is necessary for the survival of others. When an organ needs help, help is given to it; the greater the need, the more generous the offer of help. When individuals or a community needs help, help is sold to them; the greater the need, the more unconscionable the price.

When water was plentiful, it was of no interest to financial circles; now that it begins to be in short supply, one can forecast its being quoted on the stock exchange. The U.S. government wants to set a minimum price on oil. Why? The reasoning is as follows: if the price of oil goes down, no one will be interested in looking for new sources of energy. In economics nothing can be of any interest by itself. The expression "to look at things from the viewpoint of economics" is meaningless, for things are what they are even when economics is not looking at them. If the age of pollution happens to be that of the decline of all the so-called commercial sciences, it is because pollution speaks the language of things, while business, despite the realism on which it prides itself, always perceives only one reality: its own.

The Solons of commerce have this as their axiom: to ask men to take the human race as their ideal (or to have any other sort of ideal) is asking too much of them. Society and the individual are opposed. People do not see that this antagonism is possible only in an advanced state of social organization. With infinite complacency, they profess to be saddened by the game of grab, in which they have had the misfortune to come out winners. "Men will always be like this" is a sigh—but a sigh of satisfaction.

A faint shadow of awareness makes quasi-perfect societies possible among many animals—bees, ants, termites, etc. For us, these societies are obsessions rather than models—as though our awareness, infinitely greater than the insects', were not already, by nature and by training, infinitely more collective. Since their first appearance, Humans have been more dependent on their group than any termite ever was on its termitary, and it is to this dependence that we owe our liberty—that is, our Egos. Similarly, the machine capable of the highest performance is the one most dependent on the perfection of its tuning: the almost monstrous prolongation of human childhood has no other *raison d'être*. We are language, education, tradition of all kinds, collective memory (and thus, History)—in short, we are culture. Apart from its philosophical meaning (which will be dealt with in another chapter), liberty means choice. But the number of choices possible, and hence the degree of liberty, can grow only as the degree of organization grows. It is for this reason alone that the history of the world goes from the simple to the complex. Life abandons instinct in favour of awareness—that is, restrictive infallibility in favour of limitless fallibility—only because it seeks its freedom.

There is less difference between a solitary ant and a social ant— since both of them are ants—than there is between a wolf child and an ordinary child—since the former has nothing of Humankind about it except its shape. Alienation, singularity, criticism, and even verbal rejection of social norms are possible in complex societies such as those in which we live, but unthinkable in a primitive ethnos. The liberty of the savage, a popular prejudice interpreted rather than introduced by Rousseau, Morelli, Lahontan, and a hundred others, is the reverse of reality, as is its corollary, the idea of "the return to Nature." What is frightening within the beehive is the eclipse of the individual hive dweller, to which we compare *ourselves*, instead of comparing *it* to the solitary bee. Were we to do the latter, we would discover that the hive dweller has more choice and therefore more freedom than the solitary. In every society Nature has produced (including human societies), the individual and the group have grown by means of one another. How could the discovery of our Ego make this process impossible for us, when it was from such a process that our Ego was born?

If the group and the individual were not mutually sustaining, the function of intelligence, contrary to the etymology of the word (Latin: *intelligere*—"to bring together within") would be to separate us. Of course, this is what we generally use it for. . . . We pretend not to see what sort of force could sweep along a total and collective Humanity or to what destination. But millions of millions of people all working for themselves—that seems *natural*. Now, if the beehive seems ridiculous to us, it is simply because we do not see its objective: the ensemble, which makes it an organism. What haunts us in the human termitary is the systematic knot of human vipers; and what attracts us to it is the very thing that makes us afraid of it: our unsurpassable ideal of individualism.

I must stress the absurdity of the idea that Humans should *dominate* Nature. We do not have to dominate what we are; indeed, we are required to yield to it if we are to lead its progress. Again, the phrase "domination of Nature" yields this equation: Nature = Chance. This is implied, for example, in the expression *natural catastrophe*, which expresses Nature's objective about as adequately as the expression *trade deficit* defines the objective of commerce. Avalanches, earthquakes, glaciations, floods are things that Nature is defined as being *against,* or that it allows to slip through by chance. In fact Nature itself dominates Chance. Therefore to "dominate" Nature, the very antithesis of Chance, would be to thwart its purpose, which, from the start, has been the diminishing of Chance by increasing awareness. If we miss our mark, the whole of Life will come to grief, but if we wish to hit the mark, the battle against Chance must start with ourselves. We think we are too civilized to go back to Nature when we are not even civilized enough to resemble her. Chance is not on Nature's side, but on ours. In the same way that no living organism has an efficiency as poor as our machines', no natural association—molecular, cellular, or social—has ever authorized, even within a limited sphere, the wastages, the approximation, or the failures that economics allows us on a global scale. There is no qualitative difference between Chance and wastage, Chance and currency fluctuations, Chance and duplication (or triplication) of effort. Our organization is merely a disorder in the midst of organism.

II

All progress in Nature magnifies both the good and the bad; we infinitely surpass animals in the worst *and* in the best, in our capacity for suffering *and* in our capacity for joy. History follows the same path: war *and* culture become more refined; commerce has civilized the world *and* now threatens it with death. But the threat was inherent from the start in the principle of commerce itself.

The commercial contract is the immediate successor to pure terror, but the remaining terror is scarcely less pure, since the contract is based entirely upon it. Ethnology will never prove the contrary: so-called primitive societies (in reality older than ours, but arrested) observe no customs that are not self-seeking, if sometimes only in a religious sense. Even the potlatch is merely a mutual blackmail. Business replaces the extortions that used to follow warfare; the reign of armed robbery gives way to that of robbery pure and simple in which arms serve as a guarantee rather than as an instrument. What is won by an act of violence is preserved by established violence. There can be no property without police, for the fundamental pugnacity of Paleolithic society merely awaits the opportunity to break out again. Hope has changed sides several times, but the struggle has never had a change of heart. When two equal violences cancel each other out, business and politics become—as Clausewitz never said—two ways of prolonging war by other means. We talk things over because there is no longer anything to be gained by a brawl, but as regards our objective, a brawl and a discussion are the same thing. Any exchange can be translated as follows: "I hold hostage what you need until you give me what I want."

Barter may seem pure in comparison with money transactions when one insists, as usual, on mistaking simplicity for technical sense and innocence for moral sense, but it is still conditioned deprivation, just as appropriation is violence, property is theft, and selling is blackmail. Negotiators can only become business people— that is, pass from looting to business, from outright war to ritual war—by granting the force of law (under pain of losing everything) to the rule of the strongest: yield the minimum of what one has in return for the maximum of what one wants, deprive one's opponent of as much as possible while enriching oneself as much as possible. The spirit of this law has not in any way been changed by ramifying each of its paragraphs to infinity. A subtraction multiplied by ten thousand remains a subtraction.

Merchants who do not raise their prices as demand increases violate the elementary rules of business, which are more relevant to the economics of barter than to the era of multinational corporations. The expression "black market" is a pleonasm, since every market is black as often as it can be, and none has ever been governed (or rather burlesqued) by regulations, except against merchants' objections. For example, when demand for housing is greater than supply, only rent controls protect tenants from having to pay their entire incomes for accommodations. In this area, barter has the same reasons for remaining relatively moral as an armless man has for keeping his hand clean.

In a barter situation, in commerce as in Nature, the middleman always oscillates between parasitism and pseudosymbiosis. As often as he can, he creates the very obstacles he later overcomes, and each of his demands is in reality an extortion. But there are limits to the wealth he can accumulate in the form of land, livestock, or equipment, even with equivalent increases in power. To go from 100 sheep to 600 means increasing the number of one's employees, but a herd of 600,000 becomes overwhelming even for a king. In an economy based solely on barter, loans and savings would be impossibly intricate, as would be the adjustment of prices. For twenty different commodities, it would be necessary to fix several hundred vague equivalences. Merchants would be obliged to be perpetually on the alert, to make incessant reevaluations and impossible accumulations (monetary reserves of eggs, pigs, agricultural equipment, etc.). In Marxian terms, the ideal currency would be an exchange value with absolutely no use value: not even metal, but paper, certificates, signatures. The Egypt of the Ramessides used the bull as the yardstick of value, the Mesopotamia of the second millennium B.C. ushered in the modern concept of money, and the eighteenth century finally saw universal acceptance of the letter of exchange, the discount, and the promissory note.

Thus, money came into being as a superior degree of abstraction, and it plays exactly the same role in the sphere of exchange as algebra plays in relation to numerical operations. Algebra's x can take the place of any number just as money can represent anything at all. The agreed value of x, like the value of a currency, immediately dictates all other values, although in itself it is nothing but a convention. Furthermore, algebra does more than universalize and generalize: it offers the beginning of an indefinite upwards surge generally and universally, while allowing the mathematician to get further and further away from numbers. In the same way, money allows business a boundless ascent, which implies a growing distance between seller and buyer, producer and product—from which comes, in the end, obligatory business lies and forced business pollution.

But since boundless ascent cannot come into being without growing distance, Evolution accepts them both. The essential thing for exchange is to keep on multiplying since the rise of Life, the rise of awareness, and ever more numerous interconnections are all one and the same. Life never has a choice between progress and the risks it entails. It can only grab hold of progress and then try to eliminate the risk, turning this elimination itself into a secondary progress. A step forward is always a fall arrested.

Thus money uplifts all the dubious techniques of exchange, while sweeping away all its limitations, rather in the way that the appearance of firearms uplifted the equivocations of war and did away with most of the traditional constraints of strategy. When war is treated thus by the methods it demands, it ends up in atomic bombs —and that is its only chance of being abolished. Commerce, treated in the same way by similar methods, leads to pollution, which will render it obsolete. The blind alley is the same. . . . Wars are intensified by the progress of Science, which is enhanced by the progress of wars. Scientific research had never been more active than it was during World War II. Business expands by the progress of technology, which is increased by the progress of business; the proliferation of patents has never been more rapid than it is today. Ultimately, Humanity is going to find itself in possession of a science and a technology, a system of war and a checkerboard of trade; under pain of death it will have to retain the first two and rid itself of the others. It will have to arrest the beginning of the final fall and turn it into the start of the final step.

III

Money is obviously nothing but a symbol. What grows worse in its name—and has been doing so since the earliest days of the civilized world—can only be blamed on the increasing complexity of this very world, of which it is merely an instrument. In the Middle Ages the slightest fraudulent practice in the area of foodstuffs laid one open to torture. A statute of 1574 governing the pastry cooks of Bruges forbade the use of saffron because this spice might make the purchaser think that the bakers had used eggs when they had not. Today it is impossible to find prepackaged sliced bread that contains fewer than ten additives—two of which are carcinogenic, while each of the other eight is more harmful than all the spices in the world put together. But the miller of 1574 was responsible for his flour and the baker for his bread, but today it is hard to know whether it is the bread, the flour, or the additives that one is grumbling at (one really needs a laboratory). Even if one *does* know, it is a difficult matter to reach the appropriate department of the company concerned—the switchboard refers you to a secretary, who informs you that the executive vice-president is in conference.

Under Louis XI, in 1481, sellers of rotten eggs were sentenced to the pillory, where they were pelted with their own wares. A seller of adulterated butter was exposed to a fire until butter placed on his head had melted, and a wine merchant who watered his wine was compelled to drink his own wares in public until he collapsed. In those days this type of exemplary punishment existed everywhere. Today our wines are chemical concentrates, our butter is even richer in food dyes than in DDT, and one egg yolk in three is artificial. But the more of a nobody you are, the more you are nobody; no one knows whom to punish today—manufacturers, bribed legislators, wholesalers, distributors, retailers, or even foreign industries.

In Geneva, four centuries ago, speculators whose profits exceeded 20 percent could be sentenced to have their hand cut off. In the same city today, the man whose business has a yield of 200 percent can reasonably aspire to a seat on the Great Council. Naturally, an endless labyrinth has taken the place of direct, verifiable profit. One sells a property to a corporation of which he or she is a director;

this company resells the same property to a development company of which the original seller is president; it finally disposes of the property to a public corporation for three times its original price. The tenants just have to work a little harder to pay their rent. If by some miracle they protest, the landlord can overwhelm them with a thousand watertight technical arguments.

In the thirteenth century interest-bearing loans were condemned by St. Thomas Aquinas, then forbidden by the Vatican on pain of excommunication. The papal anathema made fortunes for Jewish moneylenders, who had not expected it, just as Calvin's "Letter on Usury" later brought good luck to Protestant bankers, who had been waiting for it. St. Thomas is still the theological authority in Rome, but the Holy See, which is adamant, more adamant than he, on contraception and abortion, owns a lot of stock certificates. The biggest single transaction made on the New York Stock Exchange in 1975 was worth $16.8 million: it was carried out by the Vatican. When usury became a habit, the Church had to choose between the Stock Exchange and Life. Though its soul was torn in twain, it chose the Stock Exchange. The Angelic Doctor had been unrealistic. . . .

In 1382 Charles VI banned all industrial fumes and smoke from the vicinity of towns, and the edict was strictly enforced. Today, heads of state encourage industries that produce fumes a thousand times more toxic in quantities a thousand times larger. But in the fourteenth century, the ruling nobility had no sympathy with the merchant bourgeoisie (which had no merit, since it was based on slavery), while a political leader today can scarcely be other than an industrial executive.

In itself money merely permits the accumulation of profits (i.e., the amassing of extortion payments) and usury (i.e., the extortion process squared). To be worthy of the dictum that holds it to be odourless, money must become the leaven of a whole infrastructure that commerce develops. All the spider's web of industry had to be called into play to stop people from accusing themselves of infanticide when a profitable but defective talcum powder killed a dozen babies. A whole smokescreen had to be laid when a prominent defender of the Rights of Man banked a large sum of money with a financial institution that invested in a racist business in Johannesburg. The cover-up had to involve not only banks and stock exchanges but the world of technology as well—otherwise the whole thing would have been too transparent, for banks are merely cashier's desks and stock exchanges public meeting places. The Swiss know approximately what lies behind their banks' secrecy and numbered accounts, but they could not bear to know all the details. One may say that people are unclean but not that the inhabitants of the next village are people—especially not the mayor.

Yet all these veils and periphrases do not profit from having a bad conscience. From one end of the vocabulary to the other, commerce is treated with ignominy. "Profiteer" is an insult, *Mäkler* (German for "promoter") is another. A self-interested approach must pretend to be nothing of the sort. To talk about money is a kind of shamelessness. People do not allow themselves to be called a "usurer" these days. "Butcher's weight" is synonymous with shortchanging. Today's slang puts businessmen alongside the mackerel and the codfish (as the French contemptuously term their pimps and prostitutes); they are *sharks, barracudas, piranhas,* or *leeches.* Even children's banks are shaped like pigs. *Noble* and *disinterested* have almost the same meaning, while *interest* merely produces antiheroes: Harpagon, Shylock, Plautus's Carthaginians. A child who lacks for nothing is *spoilt.* To be *sated* is almost as serious as to be a *traitor.* One is *stiff* with cash or *loaded* with money, and caricaturists see wealth only in the form of plethora or indigestion—the boa constrictor taking its siesta. *Big* shareholders or *big* industrialists: it is always *big* and not *great.* The satisfaction of the *powerful* and the *parvenus* is never far from stupefaction, which is itself close to degradation. There is always something obscene about the Ego when it is swollen with the idea that *to be* means only *to have.*

But although I may know, and even try to picture in my mind, the fact that an earthquake in the Antipodes has killed twenty thousand people, I shall *never* be as sensitive to that tragedy as I am to a brawl beneath my window. Everybody knows this law, and it enables anyone to deal with all the world's immorality by conjuring away outward appearances. Thus, we do not see a bank loan as an extortion, even though we know it is one; neither do private property and inequality appear to be thefts, publicity an outright lie, nor pollution murder. Our morals are not well thought out; they are sensitive and therefore self-interested—that is to say, in the strict sense of the term, bestial. Even if our morals seem to be getting lower as a result of technical progress, the present state of things only reflects a previous state of mind. In this respect, our present state is like the transition from barter to money: the new technique did not itself create shady transactions; indeed, it was only the absence of an appropriate technique that had prevented their appearing earlier. One can refuse degradations one after the other, but increasingly competitive bids keep imposing new ones. It is the same mechanism that perpetuates inflation and thus makes it worse. Eventually habit sets in, getting the better of everything. Though no one now regrets the urban landscapes of the nineteenth century, because there is no one left who has seen them, we can be sure that our most hideous suburban buildings will soon fail to shock; those who were born in them will need something worse. Similarly, usage degrades commercial habits (*sit venia verbo*). Those who degrade themselves become wealthy, and their wealth dictates their law, just as those who raise their prices by swindling and their costs by fraud force everyone else to do the same. Furthermore, in order to compensate for the increasing ignominy of commerce, businesses must become veritable purification plants. The full extent of the evil disappears as myopia increases.

Machines directly applicable to industry, such as Kay's flying shuttle, Hargreaves's spinning jenny, or Crompton's mule, were acquired at the cost of a fortune, that is, at the cost of slavery—and they renewed both. The peasants who had never owned their own land, their own equipment, their own home, or even their own body, became the worker slaves (for whom Marx and Engels would play the part of the Gracchi); their only asset was their labour, and they could not survive unless they sold it. The shareholders succeeded the landlords, and the march towards anonymity continued: the landlords saw their serfs or at least knew they existed, but the shareholders exploited no one because they neither knew nor saw anything. Their money worked for them. They did not see it take the shape of a thirteen-year-old child vomiting his guts out as he lay dying at the mouth of a mine shaft. But this new form of servitude carried within it something that would alter the basis of enslavement. The workers toiled together, and so their solidarity grew. They were near the cities, so their misery became visible. They gradually acquired an expertise on which production would finally depend. So they became important.

Thanks to the introduction of techniques such as *puddling*, which accelerated the production of cast iron and steel, those who owned land and money could build a factory, equip it, exploit it, and end up owning more and better property than ever. Watt's steam engine gave impetus to metallurgy and the textile industry; the demand for weaving machines stimulated the demand for steel, which stimulated the mining of coal, which stimulated investments in all these sectors simultaneously—which accelerated the transformation of agricultural serf into industrial slave. But the economy of growth soon overwhelmed the economy of stagnation: goods began to circulate, and money contaminated the working class itself, just as it was emerging from its black misery without revolution. All was ready for an upwards surge of the third sector, whose members—administrators, supervisors, providers of services, retailers of rights, financial backers, and patent seekers—clustered in ever growing numbers around the old nucleus of usurers and pawnbrokers. The middlemen could henceforth dispense with their perilous careers as brigands; they no longer needed to hold wagon trains for ransom. Violence was useless—dissimulation had been discovered. Henceforth, anyone could shelter beneath the ever broadening fabric of industry and technique—the front and the back of one, indivisible piece of embroidery. The calculation of annuities passes common understanding, as does the fixing of prices or the steps by which the working capital for a megafarm is borrowed from one bank and passed through a trust company and a factory. Competences and compromises are sold at prices as uncontrollable as their controllers are incompetent and compromised.

That Marx could believe, right up to the end, in the pauperization of the proletariat is explained by the need he felt for a revolution that was mechanically inevitable, and by his ideas on the mechanisms of economics. The dynamics of capitalism, he thought, would concentrate wealth in hands that were less and less numerous and more and more powerful; thus the mass of dispossessed workers would grow until it became equivalent to the human race itself. On that basis alone, the workers would be able to seize power. And until the end of the nineteenth century, no one could foresee any other outcome.

Growth, however, encouraged businesses to reinvest their surpluses instead of accumulating them. Meanwhile it gradually became not only possible but necessary to continued growth to let employees share in the profits (fear of revolutions played no part in this strategy). Since what was gained from the viewpoint of reform was lost from the viewpoint of revolution, the ideology of the first trade unions was merely a lyrical reformism, in which only the lyre was revolutionary. How could it not be foreseen that a claim half satisfied could easily bring three quarters satisfaction to everybody? That the damned of the Earth would be tempted by Purgatory if Paradise was slow in coming? That social inequalities would no longer cry out for revolution once their lowest term rose above zero? That at a certain salary level nobody would fight for a higher salary at the risk of losing what they already have?

The workers have thus become watchdogs, less zealous in their support of capitalism than their petty bourgeois colleagues, but just as faithful. Their class consciousness is a myth. One of the most unfounded Marxist ideas is the one that expects the utter destitution of the humblest elements of the mass (the famous *Lumpenproletariat*) to make them allies of power. First, the only revolutions that have succeeded have been the work of the truly wretched. Second, if misery did ally itself to power, what would it stand to gain except accession to that state of poverty at which revolution is considered to become attractive? Finally, if the "proletariat in rags" can be bought, it is hard to see how any other proletariat could escape this rule. The best way to protect the industrial cake from the workers is to give them the crumbs. Marx's error lay in thinking that a process in which humans are implicated can have the attributes of a physical law. He also mistook timing. Because he regarded people as things, he was unable to foresee that, under the aegis of the most proletarian party in the world, revolutions would break out only where there were few proletarians—that is, where people were really dying of hunger.

Meanwhile, the industrial world, relieved of the Marxist spectre, commits the reverse of Marx's mistake: it regards things as people. Thus it paves the way for the real revolution. The more it ponders reforms, amendments, and moratoria, the more it lays itself open to catastrophes; one cannot negotiate with carbon monoxide, no half-measures will appease the chemistry of the oceans, and an organochlorinated molecule will never be tempted by a profit-sharing plan.

The principal actor is missing from the "Dialectic between Master and Slave" whose success astonished Hegel; it is the material world itself. By using technology to broaden the scope of robbery and then sharing the spoils, whole nations end up today on the side of the Masters, not only in relation to other nations (the Third World is the serf of the other two), but vis-à-vis the technological universe as a whole. It has been estimated that the average Westerners live today as though they had two or three hundred slaves each at their disposal. As Masters then, we can only be gratified by a world in which separation remains a rule, revolutions are watered down into trade union movements, utopias are weakened by demands for pay raises, injustice is toned down to ensure that it does not completely disappear, and accommodation with theft and lying has become the basis of a universal code of morals. It has taken us centuries of effort to get this far: at last we can sit back and catch our breath.

It is at this moment that the real ruin sets in. Our two hundred slaves flout us, here by heart attacks and cancer, there by depression and madness. And they revolt blindly, without law, without order, without motive, and without distinction. We were making a fortune from the sale of foodstuffs—and now we have become prisoners of the food chain. Our spirits tamely allow themselves to be downcast as the inert world kicks over the traces. Like the Demiurge of the gnostic legends, who sought to shape matter to his own purposes after refusing to serve his Creator, we believed ourselves to be at the end of our endeavour; but having gone so far, we are no longer able to stop, and we begin to hear, as from an abyss, contumacious matter murmur like an echo, "I will not serve." The more deeply commerce, competition, deceit, the bickering of nations and their technical pandemonium burrow into the heart of the universe, the more they will find what they were not intended to find, and the more terrible will the murmuring become.

So long as Humanity lives on the immediate surface of the world and makes do with biological products in restrained quantities, Nature recycles them. A bit further on, when it begins cashing in on the outer layer of atoms, say through mineral chemistry, Humankind leaves the labyrinth of Life, and the retroactions become sinister.

And when we get down to the kernel of the atom, to nuclear forces themselves, then Death looms up with all the paraphernalia of apocalypse, of damages that are invisible, unavoidable, irreparable, insidious to the point of deranging the understanding, and no longer to be measured save in millennia. Only a Humanity organized in superior fashion—an organic Humanity—can take this step. Once again, it is matter at its most primitive and hence apparently most neutral whose demands are most strict and inflexible. It is as though the moral law that can and must govern the future of the world were already inscribed at the furthest limit of its past: "I am the Alpha and the Omega." High and low, beginning and end, pure matter and pure spirit are but one. Our inclusion in this unique canvas is surely the only thing that robbery has not stolen from us.

IV

Taking human baseness as a postulate and believing oneself a realist; foretelling the past rather than taking a mortgage on the future; rebutting by platitudes; pondering the best method of getting some absurd machine to work and considering oneself a benefactor thereby; dressing up a set of race tout's morals with borrowings from Science and imagining oneself a scientist; piling misunderstandings on top of commonplaces and deeming oneself a philosopher—that, to all intents and purposes, describes the function of a political economist. Keynes, who seems to soar so high when he deals with everyday matters because he deals with them in detail, fails for the same reason to get off the ground when he tries to touch lightly on the universal. The muse of business disguised as a metaphysical pythoness, selling philosophy under the pretense of philosophizing about selling, is a caricature that justifies Nietzsche's horror of John Stuart Mill. To defend something that exists on the grounds that something else exists—the loftiest mind would make itself ridiculous pursuing such a task: witness Hegel's dismaying *Philosophy of the Right*. Marx went through economics not to demonstrate the excellence of revolution, but its necessity; it was a useless detour. When one asks *why* (and not how) one man becomes richer than another, when one asks why (rather than in what manner) the inhabitants of Earth fail to work with a single objective in view, all one can do is to wait for the answers. Once one has established that these answers are not and cannot be, in any possible philosophy, anything other than naïve or hypocritical nonsense, then one knows all one needs to know. Thus, the question "How can we obtain an earthly society that is also a society of equals?" is pointless; it is useless to wonder how to attain an objective that literally nobody wants. Yet this is the only "how" that economics cares to worry about when it becomes idealistic. We shall encounter the same pseudoproblem more than once later on.

Among the many myths that current economics endorses, though it has not created them, we find that of the complexity of the modern world. Technology *is* complex, but economics is merely complicated. This apparently Byzantine nuance is really of prime importance. Complexity produces structure; complication merely produces disorder. A multicellular organism is more complex than a paramecium because it is more structured, but a thousand paramecia are no more complex than one; a beehive is more complex than a solitary bee, but a swarm of flies is no more complex than a single fly—it is only more complicated. Flies merely form an indifferent, apparent whole; a beehive forms a whole within itself. It is complex (or—which comes to the same thing—structured) because it is *something other* and *more* than the sum of its parts. The structure is possible only because it is the objective and the criterion of the information its parts exchange.

Commerce spreads a growing volume of counterinformation—of lies—into the human environment. In this way it opposes the technology while also using it, thus satisfying the definition of a parasite. Its complication shelters behind a complexity whose progress it impedes. What makes economics exist is exactly what economics perpetuates: general confusion in the face of the generating organization. Technical or natural Humanity is a structure, but economic Humanity is a fluctuating juxtaposition of individuals, equal to each of its parts as regards principle but considerably inferior to their sum as regards action. It is the counterorganization par excellence for its elements would form a simple ensemble (and not a structure) if they were added together. In fact, their only aim is subtraction because they function only by their differences and every difference is the result of a subtraction. Until now, economics has stimulated social progress only in the way that inert matter stimulates Life: by serving it either as a refuge or as an obstacle. But Life has pushed the limits of the inert universe back as far as possible, while all social progress until now has merely broadened the extent of the economic universe.

A landowner sells a few hectares to a promoter, who resells them to a third party, who resells them to someone else, who resells them to an agent, who sends the necessary papers to the government, which returns them together with a building permit. All this requires the intervention of five or six lawyers. Then management commissions a contractor, who calls on fifty different firms for glazing, insulation, architecture, electricity, masonry, plasterboard, and so forth and so on. Finally, the whole lot is designated the "price of construction" in a purchase agreement. These activities constitute an example of what passes for complexity in the world of commerce. Fifty ransoms levied in passing by fifty kinds of interests, identical and divergent, have as their objective the support of fifty tradespeople, all of whom want their publicity, their offices, their profits—in short, their independence, which in the language of economics means their faculty of *separation*. The only interest that may be foreign to all of them is the house itself. Of course, technical progress justifies a growing specialization, and hence a growing separation. But this separation, instead of being compensated for by better coordination, is aggravated at every stage by a spirit of one-upmanship.

Speculation can easily represent 60 percent of the cost of a building; soundproofing would represent 3 percent, but no one does it. Soundproofing a building is complex, but anyone can walk on tiptoe. In the old days three or four trades were enough to build houses with thick walls, high ceilings, and big windows. Today, it takes about a hundred to crowd the maximum number of thin-walled apartments into the minimum of space: a mathematical problem that justifies resort to computers. When the technical possibilities are multiplied by two, the possibilities of profit are increased tenfold. Why do subsubcontractors keep multiplying? Ask an architect why government departments exist, question a government department as to the real usefulness of contractors, get a contractor to comment on the exact role of architects—the only possible conclusion is that the whole comedy is being played by understudies who are twenty times better paid than real actors; that these indispensable founts of knowledge serve no purpose save in their own eyes; that, from a strictly technical viewpoint, it *would* be possible for a group of workers and supervisors, controlled by a single computer, to build any type of house whatsoever. No wonder the shoddy concrete cages that cover the world with their majestic uniformity all resemble so many garages. Each of them is the work of an artist whom the imperious financiers forced, alas, to do only what the others were doing. An ever larger snarl of red tape supports the parasites; they also profit from legal protection (for example, the law forbids a contractor to pass himself off as an architect).

In former days, a peasant who bought a cart or agricultural implements could estimate their value himself. Today the purchasers of cars do not know the cost of steel, labour, advertising, machinery, or paint. Neither do they know the fluctuating rates of interest on the capital the manufacturer had to borrow to pay for all these items. All this is very obvious. But would it be desirable for a profit-oriented company not to profit from these thousand and one mysteries? Our only hope of seeing "fair" prices lies in the workings of competition. In the first place, however, competition does not question the innumerable parasite-ridden channels from which it draws its product. Second, it is compromised by contracts that are as complicated as they can possibly be made. Third, it resorts to retaliation, most of the time quite legal, against what it considers disloyalty. Fourth and most important, a company that wants to cut its domestic prices in half must more than double its production and export the surplus—a solution that fails to take into account the fact that, as soon as national commerce is at stake, customs barriers spring up (for the law always rushes to the rescue of the order that created it).

When I buy a medicine, I pay a ransom that brings the pharmaceutical industry profits of 400 percent or more. But what can I know about the rising costs of research, raw materials, and investment capital? I can assess the enormity of the theft only by counting up, in the laboratories, the managerial offices, and the advertising agency used by the firm—not omitting the residences of the corporation's directors—all the people whose incomes are fifty times greater than mine. From raw material to finished product, there is always room to make a thousand fortunes, for which I pay through never ending taxation. Wages are always low, but a public corporation is always rich. When a 3 percent increase in the cost of raw materials produces a final price ten times higher, who can fail to understand that at each step the increase has been increased? In fact, the original increase is exactly like the oil spills that tankers exploit as opportunities to clean out their bunkers. All this goes to show the natural "complexity" of economics. . . .

Nothing is more instructive than the attempts made by economists every three hundred years or so to determine the *true* value of merchandise and work: the Physiocrats on the production of profits; Ricardo on working time; Marx on the quality of work. We know today that these norms are fictitious, that if the value of a product or the value of work cannot be measured in terms of how sincerely Society believes that it needs that product or that work, then it cannot be measured at all. Now, Society needs pesticides, nuclear energy, and paper in increasing quantities. Economics cannot object to these needs, for in economics what Society desires is right. Furthermore, economics does not bother to find out, for example, whether electricity produced on a planetary scale in naturally favourable regions of the globe might not be twenty times less costly than it is at present: the existence of nations is not a matter for argument. Nor does it bother to determine how many of the hundred go-betweens who infest every process from oil exploration to plastics production are really necessary: no difference exists between something that has made itself indispensable and something that really is indispensable. Marx himself finally admitted that two different "quantities of work" should earn two different pay packets, which means that the motivation for work is gain and not the work itself or the services it performs. Thus, there is no real difference in spirit, in theory, or in point of departure between socialism and capitalism.

As for the needs of a society, how does one determine the relative necessity of an orchestra conductor, a diplomat, an athlete, a mathematician whose researches have not yet achieved success, and an engineer who specializes in flamethrowers? Four questions come to mind apropos Keynes's dictum that "the salary is equal to the value that would be lost if employment were reduced by one unit." Who determines the value of a machine gun factory or of armaments in general? For *whom* would this value be lost? How does one measure the loss incurred by reducing officeworkers from 500 to 499? And what occupations are we talking about? It is not possible to use Keynes's formula to determine appropriate incomes for support staff, much less for factory owners, directors, members of the liberal professions (whose studies must be paid for retroactively, which, incidentally, tells us something about the nobility of their objectives). What value would be lost and for whom if we did without ten managerial units, twenty lawyers' units—or all the units that make up a board of directors? But it is not the business of economists to organize production differently, to eliminate as many middlemen as possible, or to decide that a factory serves no useful purpose.

We could base our needs on Earth's resources and our ideas on Nature's objectives. We could develop a unified world technology, enriched by the millions of secrets that now fragment it, relieved of the thousands of commercial tasks that now confuse it, and spared the mobilization for war that now oppresses it. Such organization would acquire incredible power for it is Man who crushes Science and not the reverse. Human beings could work, at strictly equal salaries and without envy, towards the creation of a plain, simple production system in which machines would assume responsibility for mechanical work. (It has long been technically possible, for example, to run a spinning mill without personnel.) For the time being the most thankless tasks could be parcelled out like housekeeping chores. How many people, who today would not work in a mine for five times the going wage, would go down once a week if Society's objectives reflected their own?

Such a world would be the utopia to end all utopias, of course. But it is not impossible on technical grounds. The very people for whom this picture produces a certain skeptical amusement are quite serious—and for the same reasons—about the depollution of the seas, which is inconceivable. Instead of trying to find ways in which Humanity could reach this ultimate stage (and it really *must* reach it), they list reasons why Humanity never will reach it. What nobody dares reveal is that behind all the criticisms that paraphrase "How can you expect it?" lies the implication "How can you expect it, when I don't want it myself?" People's horror of the objective towards which the road may be leading can only be attributed to the obstacles that lie along it. How can we abolish inequalities, when there are such and such gigantic problems to be solved (the most serious of which is that there can be no question of abolishing inequalities)?

Realism—the active aiding and abetting of the real—thus takes men as they are, as it would not wish to see them cease to be. In consequence, talk of utopia rates smiles from the realists—as long as realism refrains from killing them off. Meanwhile they can acknowledge the reign of Chance. It is pure Chance whether one is born rich or poor, pure Chance whether one gets the right end of the offer or the wrong end of the bid, pure Chance whether one makes or loses a fortune trying to outguess the whim of the Dow Jones index, pure Chance whether prices rise or fall in accord with or contrary to the prognostications of the most desperately probabilist of planners, pure Chance if one's work is worth something, and pure Chance if its market value drops to zero. There is nothing but Chance. . . .

The world is thus a game of chance, and the Earth a casino. Each of us makes his or her play in fevered anguish, double or nothing. The whole of a country's industry can be staked on "pass," the whole of a people's savings on "red," hundreds of thousands of workers on "even"—is there not some risk in every venture? And the merchants, ever more and more peripatetic, whom we call businesspeople—do they not justify their power by the risks Chance makes *them* take?

Of course, no control over the players is possible. Governments are on the scene as croupiers, as flunkeys, or as participants. Financial groups are run from a post office box, from a yacht on the high seas, or from a fictitious desk drawer in an imaginary house in Liechtenstein. Company X, which is registered in Liberia, was run by an Indian from a bunker on the shores of Lake Lugano, then sold through Lebanese middlemen to some Swedish and Mexican investors, is perfectly capable of evading Liberian justice, which is tied to the purse strings of high finance in the United States. Similarly, the U.S. government, even if it wants to, cannot control a subsidiary of an American bank that is jointly owned by Japanese,

Swiss, or Norwegian banks. The First National City Bank, whose operations doubled in volume between 1969 and 1975, draws more than half its revenues from some 310 overseas branches in sixty-five countries. It maintains more than 22,000 employees abroad; their freedom is absolute, and the parent company can barely follow their transactions because they are carried out so quickly.

The casino is cleaned out by emirs, tarts, the staffs of multinational corporations, the gangster captains of industry, and the pimp chiefs of state. The U.S.S.R. dabbles in the game more or less discreetly, and China more or less secretly. Moscow buys a vast amount of Swiss francs and tiptoes silently away, Peking chooses the right time to sell a little gold. The exchange brokers gamble on currency prices and can break their own banks by gigantic raids. Nobody knows what anybody else is doing; the whole world has joined the frantic play. A multinational corporation can transfer $20 million from a New York trust company it owns to a bank in Rome that is completely at its service and that will lend the money to English or French companies, control of which thus passes to the multinational. It is estimated that over $400 billion is flooding the world monetary "system," completely out of reach of any authority whatsoever.

The fact is that the money powers will henceforth dominate almost all others. The 140 largest American-based multinationals have a total sales figure that is higher than any gross national product in the world, excluding those of the U.S.A. and the U.S.S.R. Mitsubishi sales are three times the gross national product of Switzerland. General Motors has more clout than South Africa. Ford is more powerful than Austria. Exxon outstrips Denmark. ITT surpasses Portugal plus Peru. . . . How could industrial intervention in politics not be the rule? During the oil blockade of 1973 Exxon gave Saudi Arabia secret information, thanks to which King Feisal stopped supplying the United States with gasoline. In 1973 ITT drove Chile into chaos to checkmate Allende's socialism. This was nothing new: United Fruit had promoted the overthrow of a leftist regime in Guatemala twenty years before. Dow Chemical encouraged the American government to continue the war in Vietnam—for which Dow, among others, was making napalm and defoliants.

Rigging the market by twisting and evading the law goes without saying. A multinational cannot survive without having hundreds, even thousands of lawyers at its service or without corrupting and intimidating governments. When England refused a 50 percent price increase demanded by Shell Chemicals, the firm only had to threaten to stop its sales. After all, nations are merely uninationals. Westinghouse and others are building nuclear power stations and want to sell them; therefore, reluctant chiefs of state find it difficult to remain in power, and the public finds itself inundated by benevolent experts proclaiming the innocuousness of atomic energy.

To free oneself from these pressures, one has only to give in to them. Germany sells power stations to Brazil, who uses them to obtain materials to make bombs. France similarly supplies Iran; Canada has supplied India. Meanwhile the whole world sells conventional arms, including the superfirms known as socialist countries. Thus the baccarat table produces an arsenal, increasingly nuclear, that the players can use should they feel they have been cheated. The rock at Monte Carlo offers only suicide to the victims of roulette; henceforth The Bomb will offer them suicidal revenge—the victims will merely be a little more numerous. Thus economic realism degenerates into madness. Utopia is a dream; reality is a nightmare.

But before madness comes panic, and before suicide depression; economic depression precedes social panic. Tomorrow, *anything* can happen: the only law of Chance is the unforeseeable, all the more uncertain because there are consciousnesses' reaction with each throw of the dice. It would be impossible to foresee what hundreds of millions of people will do even if one had all their consciousnesses at one's disposal simultaneously. Nobody reckoned on the larger results of the Yom Kippur War of 1973 or the war in Vietnam, which were psychological rather than financial. All that probabilist evaluation can forecast is that catastrophes of this nature may very well grow both more numerous and more intense. Panic among investors can stem from myths as well as from realities. On a single day's notice, industry can lack raw materials for the manufacture of arms simply because of the use of those arms in a producing country. Prices may shoot sky-high tomorrow on account of a diplomatic incident, an environmental alert, a surprise revolution, an unexpected war, an unanticipated coup d'état. Successful speculation against a country's currency may make it worthless; the savings of another country may shrink in consequence; the multinationals may move out suddenly. The planetary casino can offer no guarantees, since it is the very absence of guarantees that makes it live.

Since it is fear that keeps the game of grab going, it is only just that the entire world should live in fear. When the moment comes, we shall be as interdependent as people in a room ringed around with fire. Actually, we are in that situation already. Fear of unemployment, fear of inflation, fear of devaluation, fear of a recession, fear of a boom, fear of underconsumption, fear of overconsumption —we pick our way through spectres and phantoms, my wife and my children and myself first of all. At least our protracted economic death distracts us from the impending death of Nature, and therefore a single objective—saving our skins—remains to justify and comfort us through the long *fermata* of our waiting. From 1919 to 1922 the value of the German mark was divided by 500 million million. Germany had had bad luck at the tables. Hitler was about to offer the replacement chips, from which the whole world would benefit. . . .

V

There is no robbery without lying, and thus there is no commerce without advertising. This was unimportant when merchants were merely a social category and their means of lying, images of their means of stealing, were limited to a few pieces of verbal claptrap. It turned deadly when the whole of Society became merchants and got the run of the vast machinery of technology. Nowadays we breathe in deceit just as we breathe in benzopyrene—the material and the moral versions of a single affliction. An opaque veil is coming down over the world: what poisons our bodies intoxicates our consciousness, and we do not see it any more clearly in the one form than in the other. The ineradicable bad luck that infiltrates everywhere gives us the jaundiced looks and the twisted, fatalistic souls of persons who are mistrustful of everything or benumbed for life. Nobody is willing to be held responsible for the tiniest amount of poisoning, but everything is done to ensure that we know nothing about it.

The means of persuasion are there—all one need do is use them. Only a century ago nobody would have believed that sellers displaying their wares could say anything but inoffensive nonsense that was very easily checked. Today it is impossible to check what they say, and their nonsense has become a course in organic chemistry. One cannot resist arguments decked out with physicians' signatures and presented in four colours on glossy paper as easily as one could laugh off the explanations of a snake oil peddler. Since the massive arrival of Science in the empty halls of mass culture, advertising has managed to grow into a falsification industry as powerful as Science itself and almost as costly. Thousands of doubly parasitic firms are absolutely indispensable so that we may be deceived visually, hoaxed verbally, and duped textually. Advertising consumes the greater part of the paper produced each year throughout the world (remember that throwaway packaging, which is proliferating at a stupefying rate, has no purpose other than advertising). Huge forests are levelled every day so that thousands of billboards can tell commuters : "You asked for it—you got it—Toyota."

A toothpaste boasts that it is the only one in the world that contains iridium, but what is in this mystical substance? Another launches a fad for chlorophyll; what purpose can chlorophyll serve in a dentifrice? A soap announces proudly that it has been designed for sensitive skins (sensitive to what?) and contains hexachlorophene. It is hard enough to imagine a laboratory "designing" a soap; how is one to guess that hexachlorophene is a major pollutant. Suddenly enzymes are everywhere; the ones that make a fortune for a certain detergent are rightly advertised as "greedy"—they attack the laundry itself. Of course, enzymes owe their popularity as much to the novelty of their name as to the occult character of their power. When fruits saturated in lindane, phosphorus, and verdigris are called "biological," who asks what a nonbiological fruit might be? Who can pretend to know how detergents act on the laundry—or on seawater? Or what products contain what dyes? Or what a "preservative agent" is or how products that claim to be free of them can nevertheless contain gelling agents, emulsifiers, and antioxidants? What is the point of adding lecithin to chocolate? Who knows what radiation is, what effect antibiotics have on meat, and so on ad infinitum?

So we buy with our eyes closed, like sleepwalkers. The content of what we buy escapes us, its real price is unknown to us, and the explanations given on both these matters are designed to confuse us. Whichever way we turn—free market or state market—there is nothing but hawkers' stalls and sales patter. Advertising here, propaganda there: no way to escape it. If the producers of foodstuffs can corrupt the government agencies that are set up to control them, as happens constantly, how can one believe that these companies have no power over the media, which must serve their advertisers? It is really quite simple: whatever the subject, we must turn our backs on the truth the minute a commercial interest becomes involved. Of course, everything that touches on the essentials of our existence is precisely (and for that very reason) of commercial interest. We receive our money through our work and are sold by the purchasing power it gives us.

Not a moment of our lives fails to remind us that we live in the midst of a market. The comedy of advertising is horrible enough in itself—but all the more so for the contrast it creates between a merciless reality and an endless Camelot. The gas-laden freeways of 5 P.M. are filled with happily smiling posters. Interminable treatises from advertising flunkeys flood our mailboxes—which otherwise might be empty (except, of course, for the bills). Every year this rubbish alone costs every one of us two tall fir trees or their equivalent. Whether advertising agents are pushing a cake of soap or life insurance, they always adopt the same tone: they are thinking only of you, they have made the greatest possible sacrifices for you, they thank you in advance, work has been their whole life, they beg you to test the product, they promise to change your life, they do not have the thousand faults of their competitors, they operate almost at a loss, and so on. Ubiquitous on the television and radio, as intrusive as one of those tunes that keep on running through your head, advertising constantly repeats "new, new, new." Everything is new. Yet the visible protagonists of advertising, willing wimps who posture like clowns, capable of laughing, weeping, groaning, and jumping up and down on cue, do it all for motives that never change; Shakespeare's Timon of Athens encourages his fellow diners with the words, "Uncover, dogs, and lap!" Which they do. . . . Lines of ballerinas flutter about while a quartet chants frenziedly that a laundry product contains two bleaching agents; a cheese appears in the sky, provoking orgasmic moans; cars are posed alongside a periwinkle blue lake (which their effluents will turn grey) or decorate rustic idylls (which they will turn into highways and bypasses). Mom and Dad and the kid are happy as usual, thanks to a savings bank. The dull ceremony of the family meal becomes a stupefying little feast thanks to So and So's instant coffee. Electric carving knife X is happiness, mineral water Y is relaxation, cigarette Z is freedom. But what can *we* say? The ad people would never have thought up all this rubbish if they had not noticed that on the whole we are willing to agree that happiness *is* an electric carving knife, relaxation *is* a mineral water, and freedom *is* a cigarette. . . .

Like popular films and bestsellers, advertising is not ominous because it develops habits (although it devotes infinite care to cataloguing, exploiting, and following them). Its danger lies in reflecting them. It is merely a ritual language to which we have the key. It makes faces for money just as we work, overwork, hold our peace, flatter, dissimulate, beautify, and uglify for money. The projective lie, which consists of blaming things in order to exonerate human beings (an axiom, as we have seen, of the ideology of humility), makes it possible to believe that an advertisement designed for imbeciles produces imbecility. This lie works even better when the subject is fashion: no one has ever created fashion, everyone merely follows it—but following it is tantamount to creating it. When we know we are depressingly like everyone else, the easiest (and cheapest) way to differentiate ourselves is by our clothing, our cars, or our perfumes. Mediocrity is always on the lookout for a style and for a change. What would change, from one generation to the next, if outward appearances did not change? What would the press have to say to us, even (or especially) in the political sphere, if it allowed us to catch a glimpse of the sad reality beneath the worldwide camouflage of overall and ever increasing newness—the alternation between the giant dwarf and the dwarf giant? The Male, voluntarily imprisoned in the boredom of monogamy, wishes he had several different women; the next best thing is one woman dressed in several different fashions. Thus, each year millions of tons of synthetic fabrics just manage to meet the demand for autumn skirts, winter pullovers, spring handbags. Everywhere the same obsession: avoid change by making sham changes. Commerce is admirably placed to satisfy this obsession because it has a horror of real change and lives by the sale of shams.

Therefore radios and TV sets become outdated even before they are obsolete, just as cars become absurd even before they are worn out, in spite of industry's efforts to produce something already half-way to junk. The cars of three years ago looked like bathtubs, and the next year the makers turned to the flying saucer. The more Society becomes dully aware that it is marking time, the more fast, furious, artificial, and hysterical its changes of style become—and the more necessary. The wheels of industry must turn but without advancing, and industry must devour its millions of tons of mercury, wood, chrome, and steel in the service of the collective ideal that gets us all up bright and early in the morning: nothing.

VI

"One has to live." "Reality is not so simple." "Beware lest you lose the substance by grasping at the shadow." It is impossible to measure the complacency masked by these apothegms of resignation. Many people—those who live far better than they ought to be living, those whose existence is excessively more simple than not-so-simple reality, and those who conjure up shadows because they hold the substances—are extraordinarily modest before the complexity of reality—except, of course, when it is a question of selling it. Then the most complex chemical products suddenly become simple enough to launch onto the market without analysis.

In a society that was without profit and thus without national boundaries, a staggering number of professions would become unnecessary: money changers, bankers, tax inspectors, stock exchange clerks, insurance agents, promoters, moneylenders, lawyers, judges, customs employees, managers, dress designers, advertising people, prostitutes, estate managers, administrative consultants, wholesalers, retailers, arms manufacturers, and so on and so forth, not to mention the employees of one firm in three—and, of course, the vast, incoherent, and irremovable bureaucracy. Not only is the profit motive responsible for all the wastage and parasitism it can possibly arrange, not only does it pillage Nature a second time and maintain a whole string of professions in order to effect, by lies, the sale of what it has produced by robbery; it also devotes the careers of millions to its own safekeeping. To possess is not enough—something worth possessing must be possessed. A benefit is nothing if it is not protected, if it is not defended under and by the law, if it is not hedged around with quibbles, nourished by a thousand umbilical cords, sanitized by a thousand quarantine lines, sheltered behind twenty police cordons. Half an active society is thus employed maintaining social inequalities, and the world spends half its best efforts preserving what its own weakness has caused.

Property, which is power, constitutes the essential basis of every code of laws in the world. It is no use talking of class struggles: a class is merely a fortuitous collection of individuals who belong to it only by virtue of their selfish interests, and whose occasional solidarity has no basis other than those interests. The object of the game remains the Ego. In the aggregate, however, selfish interests create what are ludicrously known as "political opinions"; they create them in series, in a manner so stereotyped and so caricatural that each slablike segment of opinion provides the definition of a class. Every torture session in the world is ordered by interests at bay; every revolt, every repression stems from the same source; everything military or political results from self-protective interests; every philosophy carries their stamp; every religion acts as their mask—and in all this bloody and vulgar farce no one ever asks "why?" and no one dares to give the true answer: "for me."

The worst swindle is surely the one that consists of talking about communist countries in the same way that they talk about themselves: representing them as attempts, even if failed attempts, at egalitarianism. The fact must be insisted on: in the whole of History, the idea of absolute equality has only been put forward once—by Babeuf during the French Revolution (and he went to the guillotine). It never caught the attention of Marx, in whose view each man should be paid according to the amount of work he supplies. This criterion is derisory both in its form, because the amount of work supplied by an intellectual, an artist, a scientist, and so on, is indeterminable, and in its very basis, because it preserves the principle of working for money rather than for the work itself. This principle turns the whole of contemporary Society into a universal

Cold War, in which nothing is discussed because everything is disputed.

Never, simply never, has a community described as socialist or communist known the faintest shadow of real equality. The narrowest range of incomes recorded in History obtained until recently in China, where the highest salaries were four or perhaps five times greater than the lowest. In Russia today, the range is wider than in Sweden. The readers are invited to multiply their own income by four, and to ask themselves whether they consider those enjoying that enhanced figure their equal. No need to go as far as four times: two times is enough, or even one and a half. In fact, it is enough for one member of Society to have a better salary than another. Nor is income the only measure of inequality of employment; distinctions in power and prestige—even the post itself, if it is a sinecure—can all serve as counters in the game of grab. That communism and capitalism are alternatives is, therefore, perhaps the most astonishing lie that the intelligentsia of this century has been pleased to reconsider. Communist ideology and practice in all their various shades are fundamentally and strictly unequal—and it is impossible for them not to be so.

The fact is that any nation, however vast, that tries to introduce egalitarianism will find its position among nations to be rather like that of a person who insists upon playing checkers at a chess tournament. In the first place, no country can allow itself to go bankrupt. Moreover, it must arm itself to deter invasion, and this necessity alone presupposes the whole of modern technology and the industry that goes with it. A nation pursuing egalitarianism must reintroduce the imperative of yield and hence the various stimulations this imperative calls for. The more autarchical its way of life, the less it can count on assistance, and the more it needs an agriculture, a transport system, and plans that work. Every lack of material recompense is equivalent to an increase in police surveillance; mistrust, denunciation, prison, and concentration camps are all introduced at the same time. What a "free" economy loses in energy for maintaining its own incoherencies (i.e., profit), a state-run economy loses in repression, in controls, and in propaganda. Justly enough, this last usually fails to convince many people; it is better to work for oneself alone than for a patriotic Self, in whom the lower strata of such a society have every reason not to recognize themselves. Communist countries thus have good reason to suppress records of absenteeism, of sinecures established, of sabotage through negligence. Their technical slowness and inefficiency are equally logical. To get up early every morning, to pay more than an onerous tithe, and to serve more than a year of military service just to become entitled to censorship, secret police, televised boredom, and courses in Marxist-Leninism—that is enough to make one feel himself the victim of a historic injustice that cannot be put right easily.

No society can work at a loss, so the only situation in which the word "profitable" could lose its meaning would be that of a Society in which each man, whatever he did, received exactly the same pay. This would mean a society without nationalities, without armies, without competition, a society in which capabilities had replaced powers, in which organization had supplanted hierarchy. . . . No, it is impossible to picture it, because a really panoramic social criticism is a necessary preliminary, and because not a single facet of life then would resemble what it is today.

All this parenthesis with respect to communist countries was necessary to establish that all nations are presently involved in profit, self-interest, the reign of disorder, cheating, and chance. The primary and inevitable argument that holds up China and the U.S.S.R. as examples of what happens when profit and private interests are suppressed is completely void. Communism, as an ideal and as a reality, is discussed in greater detail later. In this chapter it is time to return to the general bickering, as a reality and as an ideal.

Under the aegis of profit and self-interest, Society is undergoing an increasingly severe partitioning. This process is characterized by massive duplications of effort and a corresponding fragmentation of energy—the components of a sham progress that precludes and reverses real progress. Each profession becomes a game preserve circumscribed by customs entitled patents, titles, qualifications, rights, licenses, and diplomas. Whatever I do, I must consider myself indispensable. All professional claims stem from this principle. The desiderata are work and salaries and nothing else. If the building industry has no more work, monuments end up being endangered. Apartment houses can go up and come down three times in twenty years. Small business wants to survive just as it is, and it matters little to it what it sells; the staff wish to remain staff, and they do not care why. Society must serve its constituent parts, even when it no longer needs to be constituted of them. Firefighters, police, and hospital staffs can strike. Like individuals, nations and businesses can only do what they must do. For the sake of the principle of competition, almost any sector of industry will stop another sector from making progress. Industrial espionage, which is suspected of costing industries as much as fiscal fraud costs governments (that is, more than the world spends on the "struggle" against pollution), has no other objective. A jealously guarded thousand secrets are worth more than the disappearance of the jealousy that guards them.

Similarly, many industries now have numerous specialists whose only task is to design machinery that breaks down more quickly than it should. A prewar car was much more solidly built than the cars of today; a more or less everlasting electric light bulb would present no insoluble technical problems. Generally speaking, everything mass-produced is designed to ensure mass production at as fast a pace as possible. Inventions pile up in filing cabinets because one must be made to pay off before another (and its successors) can be exploited—to the full limit of their profitability, which a product loses as soon as it requires too much attention on the assembly line. In this way profit and competition stimulate technology.

Industry could give us a single brand of transistor radio or refrigerator that incorporated all the good qualities technology can offer; rather, we have about a hundred, each with one good quality. The World Health Organization stated in 1975 that all but about 500 pharmaceutical products are useless or superfluous. Since every country in Europe has at least 100,000 different drugs at its disposal, each must have had 99,500 research efforts, 99,500 market studies, 99,500 publicity promotions, 99,500 printings of prospectuses, 99,500 packaging designs, 99,500 settings-up of production lines—*all for nothing*. A manufacturer of polyethylene tries to turn out ten thousand tons a year instead of one thousand. The intention is to reduce the unit cost and the manufacturer overlooks the fact that twenty other manufacturers throughout the world have the same idea. We get twenty factories that produce ten times more polyethylene than can be sold; therefore most of them must disappear. Two different TV colour processes compete with each other instead of combining;

the price of sets goes up and their technical quality goes down. Disagreement over the gauge of railroad tracks has cut Europe in two and severed the U.S.S.R. from the rest of the world. Raw materials, notably copper, are running out, but Chile produces copper and intends to enrich herself with it—it is not interested in others.

Even the multiplication of demands, a process that requires the active complicity of the public, approaches exhaustion. The day will dawn when there is nothing more to be said. . . . One Japanese firm produces typewriters that cannot be repaired; another has considered making cars that would only last a year. Pocket calculators proliferate, tape recorders pile up, discotheques get in each other's way. Western babies, surrounded by their hundred toys, protected by absorbent paper diapers and plastic pants, poison themselves (though apparently bursting with health) by eating commercial foods laced with glutamate and yawns in front of a TV showing educational games. Marvelling at technology is no longer fashionable. The field of potentially spectacular inventions has narrowed. The landing of the first human being on the Moon aroused only a feigned enthusiasm, and that was a decade ago. Industry mobilizes a good part of its resources in quest of a few feeble ideas, a few slight innovations upon which to pounce in lieu of a new continent to cover with cars, radios, and household electrical appliances. The depletion of Nature, even for the pot, is planned and thus profitable: in the U.S.S.R., a synthetic caviar appeared just in time to make up for the progressive disappearance of the sturgeon from the Caspian Sea; in the U.S.A., a cubical tomato is making up for the scarcity of other tomatoes because it is easier to package; and green tomatoes, which are more or less impervious to decay, are coloured red at the last moment. Growth and full employment, at all cost and in every way: Keynes's ideal is also the motto of cancer.

VII

Monday, Tuesday, Wednesday, Thursday, Friday, 9 A.M., noon, 1 P.M., 5 P.M. This endless cycle, which guarantees the sameness of our present and of our past, does at least guarantee something. No doubt it would have provoked the envy of the martyrs of the first textile mills, in the same way that a modern prison would make galley slaves jealous. In a few years' time, to be sure, we shall all be working less, but a false principle does not become correct because its consequences diminish any more than a judicial error is put right by a commutation of sentence. We are over the worst, it is true, but who feels particularly happy at escaping something that is no longer a threat? Furthermore, the evil seems less only because it is more widely shared. Working for wages, which in the beginning was the lot of only a few and was, in any case, regarded as superior to serfdom (without that being much of a consolation to anybody), has spread to the whole body of Society without gaining any direction in the process. To the contrary: work, although no longer an obvious calamity, still seems like a curse. We thought we were late for Paradise; now we are afraid that we are merely deferred from Hell.

It is no longer enough for us simply to sell our labour; we must now suspect that its sale is both temporary and in vain—that our work is passing slowly from the useless to the harmful. It is no longer enough for us to devote two thirds of our time to buying the right to kill the remaining one third (in the expectation that the latter will do the same for us); we are also obliged to watch the fearful results of this inescapable activity unfold under our eyes—on the TV, in the papers, in the countryside, in our very foods—like a statement of bankruptcy (which only a surplus of work allows us to escape). Workers in a company on the road to liquidation, we cling to the idea that we must not think of the final outcome of our work—and it is easy enough not to think of nothingness. Nature is dying, Society is collapsing. It is in order to escape this double spectacle that we pay our lives for the prolongation of our existence.

The individual who wishes to move forwards has one of two motives: pleasure or an ideal. Humanity, which should grow larger from our work, has no recourse to either. It is condemned to pick up our crumbs. It cannot move at all except by appealing to our interests—and our interests are not its own. Hence comes the most edifying of contrasts: we have never been so busy in business, so hard-working in work. The more excited the human race becomes, the more it grows agitated and overworks itself; the more it applies itself to the task that serves it as a pretext, the less it fulfills it. Our individual movements are rapid, precise, complex; our collective movement is Brownian.

New communication techniques do not make us more communicative, but they do speed up the billing and routing of merchandise, reminders, and orders; thus they accelerate the rates of work and production. So what? The acceleration of History does not necessarily stop it from becoming interminable. Napoleon's Europe came and went in a few years, while present-day Europe has been tottering along for nearly four decades. Vietnam fought longer against the West than two Western nations have fought against each other since the seventeenth century. No dictatorial regime in modern history has been more repressive, or proved more durable than those in power in the U.S.S.R. and China. Pushing a stick into an anthill makes the ants scurry to the rescue of their collective organism, but in the human anthill the stick is everywhere and the organism nowhere; one must scurry to one's own rescue.

Instead of rendering any service to the planet, this state of planetary alert only perfects its peril. Most of our feverish activity, simultaneously abetted and nullified by technology, is worse than useless. Modern drugs act with unprecedented efficacy and swiftness, but the aircraft that deliver arms fly faster than those of the Red Cross—even though the latter are flying only because of the former. Conferences on disarmament are of a geological slowness despite Telex and computers, thanks to which stock exchange transactions go through with lightning speed. Convoking vague assemblies to mull over an embryo of international justice or a sketchy outline of how to save the seas takes a year or two, but launching a new plastic toy or compressed-air corkscrew takes scarcely half an hour, and the whole world loses its breath trying to keep pace. The builders of the Future go off to the Antipodes in supersonic planes; they hold conferences by telephone with simultaneous translation and can read New York Stock Exchange quotations from luminous displays. But none of us would know what we were supposed to do if universal equality of salaries were suddenly decreed. All this hectic activity would collapse into inertia, and all we would have to show for it would be a few hospitals in working order. Such is the vast project in which we all collaborate, and such is the spirit of the work to which we are forced to sell our souls.

The word *travail* (which English took from the French word for work) comes from the Latin *tripalium*, which means "instrument of torture." One can be either a victim or a user of this machine: the worst thing of all is to be both. As old as the world or at least as old as the abolition of slavery, the myth of pleasant work is naturally coextensive with the obligation to work; one has to be a little fond of what it is impossible to abolish. In reality, people only like their work when they can consecrate themselves to it without hope of gain. Strictly speaking, only work in the Arts and Science meet this criterion. Useful handicrafts are the best of a poor lot; the decorative ones are only slightly better than boredom (the word "pastime" fits them nicely). Leisured, fortunate people have never pursued handicrafts seriously, and the most fanatical members of the guilds of yore would have abandoned their trades for an aristocratic name and the status and money that go with it. But artists and scientists, leisured or not, noble or not, would have remained what they were. Depending on how much of an artist the craftspeople of old were they may or may not have been able to swallow the pill of work with its coating of productivity. Today even this pretext is insufficient; in the absence of profit, the skilled craftsperson, the assembly-line worker, and the unskilled labourer lay down their tools together.

Thus, the only pleasant work is that which we never actually perform as workers, and which does not count socially as work. It is interesting simply because it is disinterested, because one likes it for the objectives one assigns to it or for the joy one gets out of it—in other words, for an ideal or for pleasure, which are usually combined. Therefore, to compare the handicrafts of yesterday with the compartmentalized work of today is absurd: first, because there has been no development of the former into the latter—for our workers are descended not from craftspeople but from serfs—and second, because pleasure in a craft is possible only when one does not make one's living from it. As work, crafts have always depended solely on commerce and have never resisted its progress; after all, it was craftspeople who built the first factories and got assembly lines under way.

Marx levelled two reproaches at the working world of his day (and of ours): "private ownership of the means of production" and "division of labour." Both perpetuate a naïve mythology. Owning a cement factory in common would not give workers a new sense of purpose, except in the sense that they would not look directly for profits instead of being satisfied with their salaries. For a time, self-management can change a factory's personnel into a troop of egalitarian *and* interested boy scouts, freed from paternal tutelage and submitted to that of competition, but it cannot change making guns into a work of peace. Even if workers owned all the means of production, neither profit nor growth, nor boredom nor pollution would cease to be the rule. As for the "division of labour" and the myth of "alienating work" (a pure pleonasm), the only bearing they have is on the *manner* in which we work, and that is of no importance. People claim our work today is alienation because it no longer permits us to sign the things we make, to "create" them instead of "producing" them, to follow their development from genesis to completion. A modern industrial process is split up into a thousand steps, none of which has any meaning in itself, they say, and so condemns us to a thousand identical and insignificant gestures, etc., etc., etc. But how much satisfaction could we expect to find in signing Russian nesting dolls, electric toothbrushes, irons, or cans of sardines? How much nobility would we gain by following these noble objects from their birth to their completion, as though we were their creators? Does the ineffable personality of a craftsperson who turns out a handsome vase crush the anonymous scientific team that draws up a program of ethological experiments?

The manner of work matters little. In most cases it is even to our advantage not to know too clearly what we are doing—and there is the true madness. An automatic rifle is an automatic rifle, whether it is signed or not, put together by an assembly line of workers or by a craft association. A plastics factory is a polluting, profitable, and generally useless business, whether it is run by big business executives or the workers themselves. The assembly-line workers who produce rifles, cursing their work while they do it, do at least save their souls, whereas the craftspeople who fuss over a handmade rifle and sing as they do so dishonour theirs. Turning things out for money is less ridiculous than turning them out for a false ideal: the "family factory" is a swindle much worse than the "sweatshop," and one must have a servile identity—or none at all—to identify with the accounts department of an instant coffee factory.

Work can have only one noble objective—its own abolition by cybernetics. And it must be for the ends at which nobody can ever smile: Humanity, Earth, Life. This is what Marx did not see: that the curse of work cannot be lifted by purely technical means, that the solution must be of a purely moral nature, that the problem is not one of manner but of fundamentals. A society in which everyone knew how to do everything and had to do everything (an old Marxist—and Maoist—dream) would be a machine running in neutral. No object can be an end in itself, and endless work is work without an object. If I can only work for the Individual, it might as well be for myself; as long as the most venturesome utopians can only imagine a social body whose sole objective is to make its members happy, then this social body, be it a phalanstery or the Abbey of Thélème, is nothing but a bottleneck. Rabelais' "Do as thou wilt" could well be inscribed on the façade of stock exchanges. Fourier's "happiness of men" might as well begin with mine. "Socialism" and "country" are merely echoes of egos, good only for justifying censures and planning wars. All these plurals can be reduced to collections of singulars, in which I am always the first person.

That most men "love" their work is to be expected. That retired sexagenarians frequently go into decline is also to be expected. From infancy to old age, we are taught that the leisured life is also an idle life, yet it is leisure that teaches us how to occupy our days. But we have not had the leisure in which to learn it. Interesting work is generally thought to be "varied" work: a little filing, a little typing, a little bookkeeping, a little letter writing, a few phone calls. Doing several things is worth more than doing only one—just as several zeros are worth more than a single zero. Eight hours a day of work, during which we at least meet other people, generally mean eight hours a day less of married life, which is solitude. These two ways of life are made for each other as by an equilibrium of terrors; the alternative need not arise—we already have alternation.

The requirements of production impose regular hours on us for meals, leisure time, sleep, and travel; their very regularity seems so essential that we hesitate to infringe them—indeed, our doctors go so far as to recommend them as biological rhythms. We wear our masks with pride, especially since they cover wounds. Most police, airline stewardesses, and bus drivers would feel dispossessed of themselves if their uniforms were taken away from them. We find it natural to comply with all the imposed disciplines, to which we are devotedly attached; to obey all the orders, which we respect; to support every hierarchy, which we love. Sometimes we are not pleased that So and So is our leader, but only because we would like to see someone else—or ourselves—in his place; we do not contest the institution of the place itself.

A business is a feudal organization that comprises vassals and suzerains indefinitely interlocked. Thus, we find it logical that standing and salary coincide, that earnings increase with the possession of power. We work obsequiously or silently for our class enemies because we dream of one day entering their circle and of making others suffer what we suffer now. While we wait, we can do mentally what employees of a Japanese company do in actuality: this firm gave its employees a cast of the boss's head that everyone can abuse from time to time, working off on somebody who is nobody the hatred that otherwise might have been vented on somebody who really is somebody. We pretend to feel deeply about our work, which is actually boring unless we happen to be doing something we would do even without being paid. We pretend to be urgently involved in things that we know have nothing to do with us. We treat our work as a means of self-preservation, though it is actually what keeps the world alive. We falsify things, we sabotage them quietly, we gut them of their substance—and when we are finished, commerce does the same thing by selling our work. Dressing Humanity, feeding it, supplying it with information or education: all pretexts. . . . Everything we see before us is nothing but a pretext, and not one of the objects that surround us has been its creator's true objective. We live in a world of sham.

A prison is not really confining when there is absolutely no hope of escaping from it. Thus, workers in past ages were simply dealing with Destiny. But our situation depends on a chronological chance —or mischance. The hazards of History are double the hazards of geography and triple those of society. What we do now, a machine will be able to do tomorrow—unless, of course, it can already do it today. I come cheaper than a robot. We are computer substitutes, deputy jackhammers, assistant telephone switchboards; the list of new professions grows longer every day. Without such proliferation, a machine could give the single correct answer to a question much too quickly to suit the demands of the modern workplace. Many specialized machine substitutes, however, can drag out the number of incorrect answers ad infinitum.

VIII

Another company is a *rival,* a product is *competitive,* prices are *unbeatable.* Rivalry, competition, and price wars cannot have become the basis of our economy without becoming the foundation of our moral code. The phrase *to strive together* can be used with two entirely different meanings: "People strive together towards the same objective" (the ideal meaning) or "People strive together among themselves" (the usual meaning). Even the formula "lend assistance" is rhetorical—we generally *sell* our assistance. The only assistance for which we do not insist on payment is the assistance we withhold so as to enjoy watching it being provided by others. We deserve some diversion in our arduous lives, one third of which we spend playing musical chairs, win or lose, heads or tails, double or quits, or tit for tat. Now, a diversion can be of two kinds: one makes you forget reality, the other glorifies reality in the form of a game. The first is dangerous. In the midst of a year of rhythms, cadences, norms, and schedules, spending one month away from one's usual surroundings can be tantamount to a shock, like a sudden silence interrupting a noise. On the other hand, rhythms, cadences, norms, and schedules offered as a world spectacle under the title of distractions—there you have the ideal entertainment.

From natural birth to national birth, our existence is a perpetual competition for major stakes, with the ground rules skewed by every possible kind of handicap. In addition, ritualistic images of the general game of grab accentuate it and provide competitions that serve us as relaxation, just as some loud noises serve as means of escaping the daily din and hubbub. These rites serve as comments on what they imitate by formulas such as: "Firm X allowed itself to be beaten at the post by Firm Y for the deal of the century"; "From now on there'll be no punches pulled between OPEC and the industrial nations"; "Will Europe ever overcome its handicap vis-à-vis the U.S.A.?"; "It's the final round between the two TV colour processes"; "Candidate A kicked off his election campaign." In the same way, economists are infatuated with "strategies for the Year 2000," "domination of the market," "price wars," and "the battle for raw materials."

Sport, from *dis-port* ("to carry elsewhere, to distract") used to mean *relaxation*. When, centuries later, the word returned to France from England via the snob vocabulary, it had all the competitive connotations that are all we recognize in it now. Only by convention do we still use the adjective *sporting* as a slightly military equivalent for *courteous, straightforward, polite*, or *playing fair*—without asking ourselves to what kind of real sport this epithet could possibly refer.

As we have seen, all our present defects sprouted—even flowered —in the past: primitive tribes chopped down trees and dirtied everything blindly, the termitary that was Sparta fulfilled the ideal of the fascist cantonment, genocidal war began with the Assyrians or in pre-Columbian America. Today's sport is no exception. It has two sources: one Greek, one Roman. The Olympic Games combined religious and civil goals, rubber-stamping prejudices and instituting the pretext of a sound mind in a sound body. The Roman games were more straightforward, with cruelty as their central attraction and madness as their *raison d'être*. Juvenal's *panem et circenses* was an Imperial adage: give the people bread and circuses, and let them mind their own business. The gladiators were charged with continually repeating the bloody pantomime that formed the glory of the Empire, and that would cause its decadence in due course. Up in the tiers of the amphitheatre, seated among the sellers of trash, the senators and courtesans, descendants of the Pax Romana, viewed the tarnished image of a success that stubbornly refused to become their own. Preplanned fights, mercenary deeds of valour, courage priced and totted up—none of these succeeded in deceiving; the inspiration was no longer there, and they had to call on wild beasts to conjure a sadistic reality unobtainable from military make-believe. It is a pleasant thing, wrote Lucretius, to watch a shipwreck, when you yourself are sitting on shore.

Bets could be placed on the *retiarius* (the "net man") or on the *secutor* (the "follower"), but money cannot replace fresh blood, and it was better to order these unwilling comedians to play their tragic roles in earnest, to have them actually put out their eyes in Sophocles' *Oedipus Rex* or refight the battle of Actium in the middle of a

Coliseum filled with water, with galleys going down in flames amid the groans of the dying.

Christianity put an end to the Olympiads and weakened the spectacle of the games by banning murder. All that is left of this tradition today is all-out wrestling, a buffoonery more vulgar than sinister, in which a flabby Angel of Death wears himself out as he brings down an Executioner of the Pyrenees of inexhaustible idiocy and mechanical malice. There also remains the bullfight; although it was celebrated for almost a century by a whole literature devoted to virility, alcohol, Spain, and fascism, it boils down to a grotesque exhibition by a butcher's boy in carnival costume. The more obvious the hideousness, the more honourable its name. Thus, boxing is called "the noble art" (art because it sells better than paintings, noble because it has post traumatic coma as its objective).

When one defends sports for their nobility, one invariably begins by detaching them from their competitive aspect. To whom does this distinction mean anything? The participants? For them, sports are distinguishable from competition only when they retire and practice gymnastics as a form of private relaxation. The fans? Then sports should interest them as a show: for example, the thirteen-second show of the 110-meter hurdles, the show of a fat, flabby giant busy lifting a wagonwheel, the show of a football scrimmage. In fact, the show *is* the competition. It is impossible to follow a boxing match without identifying with one of the boxers, or a football game without rooting for one of the teams. It is absurd to imagine an automobile race in which the drivers are anonymous, a hockey game between two teams whose nationality or hometown one does not know, or a match of any sort that will not be played to the end or whose result is known in advance. On the other hand, sports news reaches—and evidently gratifies—an immense public whom the show itself did not reach. Obviously, it is not aesthetics that fans appreciate in the high jump, the hammer throw, or an electronic scoreboard criss-crossed with names, nationalities, meters, and times.

If sports events were anything other than competitions, or even if fans did not participate vicariously in these competitions by taking sides, sports reporters would resemble literary critics or concert reviewers (though heaven knows what they would talk about). On the contrary, artistic criticism today is busily adopting a sports format; the reason such treatment has not yet discredited art by degrading artists is that art retains a certain amount of its content when even its acolytes have lost theirs. But what is the content of sport? What makes lifting a concrete flagstone, having big biceps or powerful calves, or high jumping 1.97 meters instead of 1.93 meters a basis for envy? If such performances are neither useful nor attractive, what are they then? Good for one's health? But athletes fall ill no less frequently than other people and live no longer. Necessary for our natural physical aptitudes? But adult animals, even in the wild, devote themselves to idleness as often as they can; they hardly ever make an unnecessary movement—and they are all the better for it. The people of past centuries, like the mountain, forest, and rustic tribes today, also never knew sport: walking, feasting, and sleeping were enough for them.

The people who put in forty hours in their office every week, plus ten hours of jogging, believe themselves to be in good health; they fall asleep from sheer physical fatigue instead of being kept awake by nervous insomnia. They think they are using physical tiredness to prevent nervous exhaustion, but what they are actually doing is combining two cults of effort for self-fulfillment, like abstinence and continence. Effort is good in itself, just as work, discipline, self-abasement, obedience, and militarism are good in themselves. The athletes achieve a "victory over themselves," say the alpinists—as though anybody who learns something does not achieve this victory. But playing the piano serves to make music, while climbing to the top of a mountain just to come down again serves no purpose. Furthermore, a "victory over oneself" should be a victory over the spirit of competition—of which sport, on the contrary, is the triumph. In the same fashion, skiers plead the beauty of the countryside, which is exactly what they are making hideous with their numbers—or they extoll the air they breathe, though they could breathe it still better without skiing. Do coaches give courses in aesthetics—or in ways to go fast, to come to a dead stop, to make sharp turns? To stay tense for hours on end in order to avoid getting one's face smashed up—that is relaxation. A slope one cannot see because one is going down it so quickly, a forest one speeds through like an automobile, a ski run that looks like a freeway—that is the beauty of the countryside.

Sports are said to be a safety valve and thereby a factor for peace.

Yet every play-off produces brawls; a match between two French towns ends up in murderous clashes; a friendly football game between two Latin American teams starts a ten-year war; a loss by the Brazilian national team sets off a rash of murders and suicides; and the public at a boxing match yells to the favourite: "Kill him!" The modern Olympic Games are fairs for national medals. A runner wins, and his country's newspapers announce: "*We* have a gold medal," though when a team withdraws for political reasons, commentators chant the traditional denunciation of confusing politics and sports. Do nationalism, competition, and the cult of military "values" in fact have something in common with politics?

Alexander the Great was once told about a sentry who could spear peas on needles from a distance of twenty paces; as a reward, the conqueror gave him a bushel of peas. The Soviet government gives its weight lifters not barbells but a fortune. It has seen clearly that an activity that can accomplish nothing, means nothing, and influences nothing offers the masses the best image of themselves, and that it would be dangerous to let a little daylight shine on this darkness. For owls, the dawn is a nightmare.

In fact, the owls have nothing to fear. Even though one out of two Westerners never opens a book, the daily press can no more survive without sports columns than it can without advertising. Sometimes it has to devote up to a third of its space to sports statistics—monotonous, sterile, ritual, narcissistic, lacking even the charm of a lie or the lively variety of the love affairs of pop stars and oil tycoons. The same orders, the same classifications, the same hierarchies that characterize every sector of our existence are offered here in all their nakedness, for themselves, to be fulfilled anew by fresh robot champions, each decked out with a little national flag, when another season comes round. If a dozen or so political officials really *are* the U.S.S.R., why should eleven football players not be Germany?

Thus, there is nothing surprising in the fact that an athlete's supreme joy consists in going up to a podium to the blaring of a military march, to receive medals and behold the raising of his or her national flag. Or in the fact that they play national anthems to honour people one would hope not to meet in a dark alley. The sporting fraternity is the fraternity of order: warm handshakes, backslapping, teamwork. Russians and Czechs congratulate each other after having come face to face in wholesome competition; it is not difficult to agree about nothing, but that is already something. . . . The more such confrontations multiply, the more the modes of confrontation must multiply as well. One day, perhaps, the Olympic Games will include sack races, bowling matches, and farting competitions.

On the other hand, it is also quite logical that sports should be the negation of everything that has the least touch of the tender, the feminine, the sensual, the delicate. The inept ideology of sports prefers not to know what fraternity would consist in if it stopped being represented by its caricature. Since sexual enjoyment is the exact opposite of effort and since sports are nothing without effort, the contradiction between sports and sex is the same as the contradiction between something and nothing.

Contradictions, however, do not stop us. From eroticism to music, there is nothing that we have not organized into a competition for the distribution of prizes. X is the biggest exporter of sugar; Y holds the record for steelmaking; one country heads the list for suicides; another has the largest GNP per capita. While music competitions grow more universal, they also grow more Olympic, and literary prizes will presently generate a marathon. Each year hundreds of good students come to try conclusions with Beethoven's sonatas or Chopin's preludes, picking up pass certificates, silver medals, or gold cups. Keyboards become running tracks for the fingers, and bows fly like rosin-coated javelins. The year's crop is gathered in by the record companies, which have their stables just as publishing houses have their "protégés": so many stars to be launched this season and replaced the next. . . . Female beauty is measured by the circumference of the bosom, the waist, or the calf, while the standards for intelligence are those of IQ tests: exercises in geometry and general puttering that rate chess players higher than composers because the creators of this rigmarole have no idea whether it is more intelligent to devote one's life to music or to the study of openings and gambits.

In brief, the system bespatters everybody. To single out a few: painters who call themselves anarchists receive state prizes; musicians who are considered revolutionary aim at promotions; writers who used to soar above the social free-for-all are happy to accept the Prix Goncourt, which is awarded by an association of feature writers. Records are ranked on the hit parade, books on bestseller lists. Read what is being read, do what is being done, make way for the top-ranking items. A head of state's political stock falls three points; one minister beats another by half a length. This, that, or the other nation grades its neighbours in this, that, or the other order of preference. Cities confront each other in televised sports events. And so on and so on and so on. How can one be surprised at the simultaneous rise of aggressiveness everywhere? Without aggressiveness, no competitions would be possible. Those who have sown the wind, says the Bible (which speaks from experience) shall reap the whirlwind.

The social scale, from top to bottom, is a greasy pole on which one slits one's throat in order to achieve one higher rank, one place up, one level of life forwards, and a few less kicks up the ass. Billions of threats echo one single cry—I, I, I—delivering the final word of the human adventure and threatening to become the word of its finale. We are sailing in search of terra firma on the raft of the *Medusa*. The lookouts are liars, the crew hate each other, the officers dream only of crossing swords with each other. We are without a compass, without a rudder, without a lighthouse or bell buoys, and yet we continue to believe in this cannibalistic skiff. Meanwhile night falls around us and the whirlwind draws nigh, the harvest of the wind we are still sowing.

THE BASIC CELL

I

Nothing is more repetitive than that which is permanent; that which is found everywhere always turns up everywhere. We have seen, apropos economics, that the parameters—profit, interest, competition, property—are constants and that the term "social structures" covers precisely those things that prevent human societies from being structures and make arbitrary juxtaposition triumph over organic wholes, organization over organism, complication over complexity.

Every structure exceeds the sum of its parts and constitutes their objectives. Yet Humanity and Nature are not our objectives but our pretexts, and the *raison d'être* for a billion people boils down to the *raison d'être* for each one of them separately. The gigantic struggle against Chance that is Life has always demanded unconditional cooperation, whether it be between cells or between social animals; the appearance of *reflected* awareness both increased and impeded this struggle. Since its creation, the mirror of awareness, which is fashioned above all out of language, has always reflected Human community while dividing Human Egos: speech has always served communication as well as lies; the first human was also the first recluse; Adam is also called Narcissus.

The word "natural" can be applied to what Nature is or to what Nature seeks to be; to put it another way, we may take Nature at its word or interpret its intentions. In the first usage, theft, jealousy, violence, and animality are natural; in the second, the only thing

147

natural is whatever opposes risks in every way possible. Humanity does homage to Death every time it honours Chance, no matter how much it calls it Nature. The fact is that Chance is a lottery, and this lottery has winners. Clearly self-interest—Egotism—is the equivalent of Chance and thus of death. Whatever is self-interested cannot act for logical reasons (a *me* does not follow reason), and anything that is without reason is Chance. Only the human mind, in the service of what should be serving it, can bring substance to this monstrous paradox: the organization of disorder. Our present problems of pollution, armaments, and demography illustrate and are provoked by economic, competitive, nationalistic conflict.

It remains to be seen what motivates this conflict. One Westerner out of ten is an alcoholic, or close to it. One Westerner out of three never opens a book. One human being out of three is illiterate. The tastes of nine out of ten are limited to television, sports, and the automobile. The majority of couples live in a state of permanent dissension and describe themselves as "deceived by marriage" (that is, by their own particular situation). Such are the educators of Humanity. Thanks to the sacred institution of the Family, young minds are in the charge of adult babies who fight over the result of a football game, drunkards who sow terror or depression all around them, automatons who are intimidated by reading a comic strip, greedy pigs who have never thought of anything but how much their spoils total, sectarians whose only dream is spreading the obscurity and suffocation they have turned into religion, neurotic couples disturbed by jealousy and rancour. Alas! This crowd boasts about their power over their children more frequently than the young souls they overload bewail the fact.

Thanks to the Family, one child is born in a mansion, has a hundred toys to play with, completes a higher education, becomes a manager, and so on and so forth, while another sees the light of day in a crowded two-room apartment, gets no proper education, and becomes an unskilled labourer. Thanks to the Family, a child is born to power or to be crushed by it. Thanks to the Family, Chance gives to a child a father who may be a bigot, a scientist, a mediocrity, a brute, or an intellectual, and a mother who may be a hen that soon turns into a hyena, a hysteric, a lymphatic case, an ignoramus, or a bluestocking. Thanks to the Family, Chance may allow death or choice to deprive a child of one or the other of these educators (although this loss may not actually constitute a deprivation). Chance may make this person an only child or surround him or her with a flock of brothers and sisters. Through Chance, a child may have the right to receive a religious education or to be inculcated in modern agnosticism, to play in the streets or to vacation abroad, to stay out all night or to meet a strict parental curfew, to speak three mother tongues or to know a vocabulary of five hundred words.

Society takes infinite precautions in matters of official education, demanding years of studies, diplomas, certificates of good moral character. But in matters of *real* education—fortune, name, social rank, mannerisms, habits, and all the rest of the things a child is steeped in and moulded by at the most malleable age—the actual educators may be vulgarity personified. They may spend their evenings fighting or their days hating each other. They may beat their children to the point of wounding or even killing them. Each year, two thousand American children die from parental abuse; the worldwide figure is five each hour. Such are the risks of Chance: these are the unlucky ones who draw a losing ticket in the Family lottery. Then there are the ones who do not die but suffer broken ribs, shattered livers, third-degree burns from hot irons, and so on. The official reports going into all these details are pointless; it is impossible to prevent what is impossible to foresee, and removing children from criminal parents would mean removing all children from all parents. So the victims perish. It does not matter that they would all still be alive and free from suffering if they were in the hands of professional educators. Neither does it matter that to blows, wounds, torture, and deaths, one must add sexual abuse, mutilations of all sorts, child prostitution, traumatizing scenes, violent exhibitionism, terrorist methods, intimidation, blackmail, and forced choices between two antagonistic parents. The Family must live on. It is Chance promoted as an institution that must be defended—like all our other institutions and because of all the others.

Thus, we not only approve of what we call "vital" competition; we even find it essential to tamper with the odds from the start, setting cripples against athletes, children born to poverty against those born to riches, the offspring of alcoholics, martyrs, and unwed mothers against the descendants of diplomats, princes, and industrial dynasties. We do not regard it as outrageous that the proverbial struggle for life, with its motto "May the best man win," is systematically rigged so that the best person does *not* in fact win, so that certain newborn babies already have a thousand careers closed to them, while others, not gifted in any special way, have the whole world at their feet. We see this situation as quite just, and we defend the Family for the only reason that keeps it going: like the automobile, like property, each of us has our own. In fact, the Family is anything but an institution; we inherited it from the animal world, so it never needed to be instituted. Its ties "transcend reason," as is said of the jealous passion called love, or of the pretended faith called religion —in short, of everything that is prosaically self-seeking. They are *mine*.

In the end, however, an enormous amount of obligation, duty, culpability, and thus shame enter into family feelings. No great gift of introspection is needed to realize this. Feeling obligated to love is an absolute contradiction, but it is what monogamy implies and the family imposes. We can at least choose our marriage partners, but not our parents, our sisters, our brothers. They break into our most private lives, exerting rights over us that we have not granted them. The dictum that a brother is "a friend given by Nature" overlooks the facts that a friend is not given but found, and that the majority of human beings refuse this gift. Considering the time that brothers and sisters must spend together, one can even marvel that they are in general so stubbornly opposed to friendship. Even when friendship does exist between siblings, family ties irk it rather than stimulate it; how can one be sure that something that should be the result of free choice is not actually the result of a debt? On the other hand, it is this debt itself that justifies the myth and the reality of brothers who are enemies. Eteocles and Polyneikes did not abuse each other solely because they were under an obligation to each other; their kinship increased the disparity of their natures in the same way that the force of repulsion between two electrical poles of the same sign increases as the distance between them grows less. Knowing each other too well, they could not forgive each other anything, and they shook the bond between them like a chain.

That we speak of a "debt of love" towards our parents or the state, that we talk of filial piety, that "Honour thy father and thy

mother" is a commandment—all these boil down to the same imperative. Familial love must be as blind as military obedience. It is
supposed to be an instinct that cannot be controlled, though it is
itself a control. It claims to be universal though it is partiality itself,
to be a form of justice though it is gross injustice, and to be a debt
though it is not owed. The ties of blood are binding to the extent
that nobility of blood is ennobling: both dictums exist by the decree
of God—that is, of the Ego sanctified. Mothers or fathers who admit
a preference for one or another of their children are allowing their
individual Egos to speak; when they do not admit any preference,
they are indicating that they prefer their children to all others for
the simple reason that they are *theirs*. That is the amplified, sanctified, institutional Ego—the Family—speaking. A united family resembles not a circle of friends but a clan, with all the complexity
and trouble that that word conceals. A circle of friends is not impenetrable; one can enter it freely, and one is chosen for it for
oneself. A clan, however, is closed by nature; one is a member of it
despite oneself, and one forms part of it for the clan. Egotism,
whether it be simple, familial, or national, always evokes the same
reactions; solidarity without reason leads to boundless mistrust, secret mutual aid leads to public suspicions. Reciprocally, isolating
leads to isolation, the Mafia leads to the ghetto.

Furthermore, note the curious fact that the most ardent defenders
of the Family with a capital *F* are, in reality considerate only of
their own families. They have no words harsh enough to describe
the majority of educational methods, couples, family surroundings—
in brief, the ensemble of families with a small *f* that is the real
Family with a capital *F*. Yet this is the cause they plead. The same
remark applies to the good souls who decry divorce without dreaming that the death of a parent is an equal deprivation for a child or
that deploring a phenomenon is not enough to make it disappear.
Let two parents separate, and a cry goes up that is a literary formula
half a century old: "Another Mozart is being slain." As though a
Mozart does not die every time he is born in a shantytown, or his
father is an alcoholic, or the walls of his room shake whenever planes
and heavy trucks go by. Yet Beethoven's father was under guardian-
ship, Hugo's parents were separated, the celebrated individuals who
have come from broken homes are numberless. But celebrated men

born to working-class families are extremely rare and were nonexistent until the end of the nineteenth century. Even if the presence of parents, whatever they may be like, or the nature of so-called methods of education had only a hundredth of the importance of social conditions. In the development of a human being, the only way of making divorce harmless would be to do away with marriage or at least the family.

Do away with the family? The inevitable question rears its head immediately; what would you replace it with? All anyone seems to know about outside the family circle are the infernal circles of orphanages, welfare agencies, and military service—institutions that coexist with family rights. The question shares in the hypocrisy of the one we already asked ourselves in relation to economics (here, it would be: how do we attain the objective of suppressing the family, given that we do not want to attain it?)

Moreover, our advice is not sought by Society, which, for a long time and despite itself, has been dooming the "institution of the family" to discredit and ruin. It is, in fact, paradoxical to think that we ought to preserve the role of something that is disappearing; a social form disappears when it no longer has any role to play. Today what is really worrying industrial countries, particularly those of Europe, is a problem that is not in the least idealistic. Rather, it involves a nationalistic or patriotic sphere: that of falling national populations.

A family of more than two children has become a luxury for simple reasons involving money and housing. A growing number of women are obliged to work outside the home—or at least prefer this role to that of being a housewife. Since a man is incapable of replacing a woman in this role, even if, by some miracle, he wants to, so the last foundations of family life are crumbling away. Already we have discarded the idea of old men as elders, and regard their experience as useless. They used to represent the collective memory of a family or village group; now they are pushed aside as drivellers because what they know is infinitely more vague than what is available in libraries, iconographies, and audiovisual media. (Besides, the only possible importance of the world of yesterday would be its allowing one to foresee the world of tomorrow through its similarity to the world of today.) Even during the last century, mandatory public education made inroads into the cultural (or anticultural) ascendancy of parents over their children. Today the omnipresent mass media, by spreading the same ideology, pointing the same morals, creating the same fashions everywhere, are gradually reducing the family to a simple transmission link in the immense chain of public life. However mediocre it may be, the TV screen has replaced traditional family conversation—and on the whole, has replaced it to good advantage.

Family and Society, who set each other up on the same pedestal, never stop setting traps for each other, one serving as a refuge from the other. The parents of students generally collaborate with their teachers as much as possible, but for all that, parents and teachers are antagonistic; in fact, they come near to being in opposition, a phenomenon that reveals itself, in acute form, in totalitarian societies. Communities do not want the increasing dissolution of the Family since they are all essentially based on matrimony and will do all they can to stay that way. Yet by their very nature, they will all do it in a disorganized fashion, and it is this very disorganization that is making an organized order (i.e., a social order) more and more necessary. Thus, as I have already pointed out, what leads to the "human collectivist ants' nest," which is really the opposite of a real ants' nest, is actually human individualism trapped by its own multiplication.

Familial-societal antagonism, however, has impassable limits. Taking complete charge of children from birth is something that no human community would dare to do (unless, as is quite likely to happen, the voluntary infecundity of a growing number of couples forces it to do so). All parents consider their children property par excellence. A child is primarily an object. Even if a child has not been conceived by way of a distraction, by a couple who were beginning to fall victims to boredom, he or she begins life by belonging to someone, in the strongest sense of the word. What a child discovers on making an entrance into the world is a couple; what he or she experiences before all other experiences is monogamy. "*My* child, *my* parents"—there are no pronouns more possessive than these. It is natural, from the start, to prefer one being to all others, and to be preferred by that being. Even education, which later will pretend to honour egocentricity, begins by inculcating in the child the duty to regard his or her parents as an expanded center of the world for the sole reason that the child is the real center of it and they are the child's immediate entourage.

Long before Freud we knew that a mother is never far from considering her child as one of her members and that this physical bond extends far beyond childhood, involving all kinds of trouble and irrationality. All literature testifies to this link, as does the observation of animals. The affectation that makes us admire the maternal instinct of animals, though with obvious mental reservations, pretends not to see that in humanizing the animal world we animalize the human world. "The first child prolongs the last doll," remarked Hugo. We come into the world as dolls; a woman who wants children does not want adults, but babies. The distinction would hardly be of importance if so many parents did not regret seeing their offspring pass from the status of toys to that of human beings.

The most decisive events of a human being's life take place inside this uncrackable social nucleus of early family life. For a long time now, statistics have highlighted family misfortunes; a worker's son or daughter has only a slim chance of going to university, the child of an alcoholic is also threatened with alcoholism, an uneducated couple pass on their lack of education to their children, children in all these circumstances at the very least suffer some form of handicap as adults. Notice that in all this, educational methods play practically no role. This is first and foremost because a human story is the story of the results of a choice, and although such choices are essentially free, what they can have an impact on is not. Moreover, these choices do not depend on what the parents do, but on what they are obliged to do. The same education can form two totally different characters, but social conditions and involuntary influences are far more restrictive. They make use of the prodigious powers of assimilation and mimicry, which the child has from earliest infancy. Even adolescents who reject all their parents' advice still retain their intonations, their accents, their gestures, their inevitable facial expressions. It is a being and not a manner of being that a child first notices. A hysterical mother and a calm mother may well use the same rules—strict or permissive—but the primary thing that they transmit is hysteria or calm. An uneducated father and a learned father may well use the same kindly manners, but they communicate lack of education or erudition much more positively than kindliness. It is known that a child's ability to learn languages decreases after the age of twelve, that age eight is, for all intents and purposes, too late to start training to be a musical virtuoso, and that, generally speaking, the younger the human being, the more likely he or she is to absorb, without resistance or criticism, anything that is fed. The child's parents are the sample of humanity put forward for this admiration; it is they whom the child learns, from his birth, to imitate as perfectly as he can. This mimicry goes as far as physical permeation, as is shown by the way most adopted children acquire an air of "being part of the family." Only general mediocrity, in the guise of individual excellence, considers itself worthy of being stamped into this soft wax.

The majority of couples who bring up children really have nothing to teach them. Hoping that the child will go further than themselves, they offer them the same starting conditions they had. Wishing to see them escape the education they themselves underwent, they never think that their own parents may have had the same wish and that what they imposed or did not impose might well have been worse. Moreover, education boils down to transmitting the fears and taboos that make the world what it is. As we shall see in a later chapter, the cult of psychoanalysis has merely aggravated its inept prejudices as it strengthens the ideology of the family with its emphasis on the importance of the Father and the need for the child to do the "Oedipus thing," its hypocritical identification of sexual liberty with nudity, its pseudonatural attitude that the sexual organ is "just an organ like the others" (which is exactly what it is not, as any child knows). And, of course, anything that parents say is nothing in comparison with the spectacle they offer. The fear of sex, the fear of "getting hooked," the fear of "bad company," the fear of coming home late, the fear of scholastic failure, the love of professional success, the cult of competition—all these are very easy to inculcate into a child's mind, which is already weighed down with the authority of school and of adults in general. The latter, simply by their behaviour, are educators at one step removed; what is the good of speaking out against military toys in a world in which their real-life models proliferate every month? What is the good of abolishing school report cards or grades (which, incidentally, does *not* abolish competition) when television is overrun with contests, sports competitions, comparisons of gross national products, and songs numbered on the "hit parade" according to their success?

Living with adults in a clumsy promiscuity that is without communication, whatever the parents may believe—*that* is what "the family circle" means to a child. It is a concept whose victim will be consenting more often than not and all the more victim thereby. The husband who becomes a father splits his realm in two unless the wife-mother forces him to abandon it. His work removes him even further from the center of the family, in which he thus becomes the drone. The couple have their habits and stresses, which make them utterly hasty in their shows of education; a few words of advice here, a few reprimands there, and then their adult life imposes its rhythm, its worries, and its prejudices. Two ways of life oppose each other here: children wear adults out with interminable questions, shouts, crazy laughter, endless recriminations, and transparent jokes; adults overwhelm children with their laboured despondency, preoccupation with business matters, the fall of the dollar, or the state of the stock exchange. They never have any idea how long an hour seems to a four-year-old or, on the other hand, how much pleasure a four-year-old can get from watching the same pussycat or the same cage at the zoo for hours on end. When parents try to enter the world of the child, they make it infantile by animalizing beyond all reason (those eternal stories about ducks and bears, which also appear on TV, of course), by using a fairy story or a fable to illustrate the prohibitions they intend to promulgate, or even by making the child an arbitrator (and a victim) of their inter-couple rivalry. How many women have brought up their children, in a more or less underhanded manner, to hate men? And how many men, when they have been able to do so, have done the same in reverse?

After childhood comes adolescence, and with it rivalry between father and son and between mother and daughter. The causes are shared equally (need I say?) between the rivals. Furthermore, they are quite clear; a father is his son's rival just as successive generations are rivals, and when he is jealous of his daughter's boyfriends, it is because he wishes to remain superior to them—because she is *his* daughter. Moreover, this jealousy may change, to his advantage, into a comradeship that can be pushed to exaggerated lengths. In the same way the mother sees her own youth blooming anew in her daughter, while she finds in her son the qualities lacking in her husband, and so on. Agreed, these are not hard-and-fast rules: but nobody can deny the widespread reality of the traditional image of the mother-in-law in conflict with her daughter-in-law or in collusion with her son-in-law, the somewhat more dramatic image of a man and a woman using a child as hostage, or the horrible image of a child beaten, tortured, and even assassinated by his parents. The last is so tragic that one would willingly relegate it to the realms of legend were it not for the statistics that force its acceptance as a reality. And thus the Family is completely unsupportable.

II

One could understand the defenders of the family if that were actually what they were trying to protect when they pretend to come to its defense. But such is not the case, not even in the courts. Even though the family may already be weakened and is regarded as slightly suspect here and there, the couple, which is what serves to support it, constitutes the ultimate ideal of humankind: No value is or ever has been more widespread or more powerful than the one called love, and no name has ever been or still is more radically usurped than that one.

Love passes for the highest of the *moral* sentiments, but if we hear a man telling another man he loves him, we at once wonder whether he is not a homo*sexual*. This attitude towards morals, which is also exemplified by the adjective "immoral" and the prejudices of censorship, is the basis for the most universal, the most venerated, and the most respectable of human sentiments. Minds and spirits are asexual but can become passionately fond of one another only when they are not of the same sex, and sex alone serves as the link between them. Love is a contagious enthusiasm, but just imagine Romeo's enthusiasm turning by contagion to Juliet *and* to another girl; Juliet's love changes quickly to hatred. King Mark wished most desperately for Isolde's happiness, but as soon as that happiness required Tristan, all he wanted was death all round. Take the most beautiful love poems that Humanity has produced, take all the apparently noble deeds that love has ever inspired, and remove sexual exclusivity from that love. Everything collapses, and *nothing* is left: the ecstasy was merely drunkenness, the gift merely a loan at exorbitant interest, the tenderness merely hypocrisy. I welcome one being to the exclusion of a thousand other beings; I offer her happiness while taking away her freedom, I appeal to her soul only in return for the monopoly of her body. The only impulse under which we may be capable of opening our arms is the one that most warmly invites us to clasp them tight. The hug is a double capture.

The old definition of the Family as the basic cell of Society applies even better to the couple, provided that here, as there, one uses the word "cell" not as a reference to biology but to prison. Nothing is more devoutly wished for, more carefully prepared, or better planned than the famous solicitude of the couple, for what is a couple except an isolation? It has everything: myself alone, nobody else, the dream of jealousy, and then—myself alone and nobody else, the nightmare of loneliness. Every family has a certain power of repulsion vis-à-vis other family clans, but the couple could not exist without this repulsive force, which defines its limit and thus its whole. Biological cells cooperate unconditionally when they are the base of something that transcends them, but nothing transcends unities such as the family and the couple unless it is the individual, a unity still further reduced. These unities are content to coexist under active surveillance—each man with his mate, each woman with hers, and let no one try to move.

A partner is first and foremost an appurtenance, and though the verb "appertain" has a whole flock of moral meanings, all of which are obviously specious here, its prime significance is physical; without that the others are worthless. When love ceases to be the equivalent of *droit du seigneur* pure and simple (somewhat more simple than pure), it is no longer the equivalent of anything but nothingness, and all the sublimity of the heart appears in its real shape, which is the shape of Envy with a capital *E*, as in Ego.

All this, of course, is "natural"—as in murder. But to liken jealousy to the territorial instinct of animals is to make at least three errors. First, we generally describe as instinct something that reason and human morals oppose, yet they are so devoted to jealousy that they have developed its animal beginnings into an ideology and a delirium. Next, the territory in this case is the Ego itself, so if one is to invoke an instinct, it must be the instinct of conservation. Finally, jealousy goes far beyond what really should be defended because it attacks without being attacked and because the due it claims is not far short of being the whole world. Envy, which improvises even more cryptic shapes upon the same foundation, springs up in every sphere, clad in every colour, without any necessary relationship to sex. Thus jealousy begins long before love and finishes long after it. Love is but a positive face of jealousy. Love is jealousy satisfied, but jealousy is considerably more than wounded love. And although the proverb says that love is blind, the fact is that jealousy, which serves as the basis of love, is extralucid or even visionary.

It is quite logical that possessiveness should be at its maximum when it is hard-pressed and when its objects are subjects (and thus liberties, and thus threats). But jealousy culminates like love and spontaneously acts like love in regard to sexual relations (and so one must term all relations, carnal or not, that carnal contact with third parties can call into question). These facts show that, despite all our talk, we consider ourselves more or less strictly as *bodies,* and that we are not able to believe in anything that is not physical. For us, "real" is almost the equivalent of "palpable" or "visible." Even our religions teach that the souls of the departed "leave the body," as though they were to be found *within* the organism; they pretend to pray for the spirits, but it is the corpses that they follow, bless, and inter, and tombstones read "Here lies X," rather than "here lies the ex-body of X." We believe that our thoughts are *inside* our heads, our Beyonds are always *places.* When individuals look at themselves in the mirror, they think, "That is *I* there"; when they walk, they say to themselves, "*I* am walking," and so on. Certainly, incarnation itself set this everlasting trap for us, and strictly speaking it is impossible to escape it. But material animality takes great pleasure in bestial materialism: knowing nothing closer than what is *physically* close to us; conceiving of no intimacy that is not sexual (although one says "intimate friends" as well as "intimate relations," it is understood that the second intimacy is both more real and more profound than the first); saying that a man "possesses a *woman*" when he enjoys her body or that a woman "gives *herself*" when she gives a man that enjoyment. Why do we dress our materialism up in all this angelic language and set it up as a supreme ideal? What is this pantomime aimed at? Having the angel mimicked by the beast; what already has wings may also have claws. Since it is incarnation that makes us all separate individuals, egotism and materialism go hand in hand, each with an interest in the other. And since the only relationships that we do not regard as academic are interested relationships, it is quite natural that the most interested should be the most strictly material. "Friendship" is the commonplace name of a very rare phenomenon, while "love" is the sublime appellation of an extremely general fact. What is the good of saying that the two words should be interchanged? Each is as tarnished as the other, and if tarnished words had to be made obsolete, we would no longer have a vocabulary.

"When one lacks one single being, the whole world seems empty of people": this is what I have found love does to me every single time that I have not been its object (and those times have been fairly numerous). All of us regard ourselves as being superior to everyone else (only the Ego is capable of this feat), and by a second miracle every human being who has chosen another in this fashion is convinced of the superiority of the chosen one. Thus, love is an example of obligatory bad faith. There is more than chance involved when a man or a woman has had ten or twenty amorous experiences in which there was no question of choice, since each experience was unique. But when "choice" is involved, by a third miracle it will never be called into question. I have known twenty partners and pseudochosen one of them; henceforth three billion other individuals can no longer interest me. Finally, there is a fourth miracle. In every other sphere but that of love, everyone agrees on the superiority of at least a few actions or ideas. But a human being tries in vain to be better than all others—because being so will not make him or her any more likely to be chosen by several, having already been chosen once by one single person. (This comparison is probably out of place, for aesthetic enjoyment asks only to be allowed to spread far and wide, while the other kind can only exist if it is *not* spread far and wide.)

Stendhal honours love's ability to erect idols with the word "crystallization." He does not add that a deliberate calculation is the basis of this phenomenon, which assumes the characteristics of an instinct par excellence. One is very chary of "crystallizing" on a crystal that belongs to someone else, just as one is chary of admiring scenery posted "Private Property," preferring to reserve one's resources of ecstasy for waste ground that is at least free.

My possessions remain dear to me, even when they fall to pieces, simply and only because they belong to *me*. I support many glories about which there is nothing special except that *I* support them. The mechanism of love functions in the same way. It is identification, doubled by a passionate *investment*, as the psychologists say (without realizing how right they are). Now, investments are not made without some hope of profit. That is the *gift* that is love, that is the objectivity of the choice that love makes, that is the inexplicable impulse for which any explanation would be fatal. To telescope two famous maxims, those are the reasons of the heart that Reason does not know, because the Ego is the strongest, and the reason of the strongest is always the best reason. The mysterious something that makes the loved one stand out from the others is simply being wanted, without mystery, as someone's private property. Give me today a number, an astrological sign, a colour, a cat, a car: by tomorrow these objects will have nothing in common with others like them because my *Ego* will have endowed them all with its own irreplaceable superiority. Such is crystallization, such is the purity of the crystal, such is love, and such, consequently, is the world. Since all the men in the world cannot spend their entire lives in bed with all the women, the compromise is monogamy. The Twoness of the couple is merely the refraction and the hypostasis of Oneness, of egotism. The first person singular takes over the first person plural: in simultaneous translation, *we two* means *I alone*. It would be all right if this arrangement could declare itself openly, but where then would it draw its enthusiasm from? If it could only dispense with lying—but then how could the lie dispense with itself?

Love's *Be with me* contains three dissimulations: *be* stands for *have sex*, *me* for *my body*, and *with me* for *not with another*. A reduction schema? Certainly—if by that one means that these essential conditions are not sufficient, and that possessiveness goes further, since a look, a thought, a past, even an object, if branded with the seal of a competitor, is enough to offend it. But if one means that a man and a woman can agree on other matters that are more noble, less egocentric, or more lasting, one must remember that sexual understanding is one of the most perfidious *mis*understandings possible. Then one must ask oneself: what are the more noble values that could outlast the ending of a couple's sexual relations or the end of their exclusiveness. How does it happen that a couple who agree on mutual possession always find ways to extend it over everything else, while the converse is so rare that one might as well disregard the fact the two are a couple? *With me* is less important here than *not with another,* without which crimes of jealousy would be inconceivable. The so-called territorial instinct takes offence at something that does not prejudice it in any way—for how does it hurt me if someone who loves me can *also* direct his love elsewhere? Why is it necessary that in love the friends of our friends should be our enemies? Thus love is the culmination of the most sinister of human laws: others must not have what we have, private property is only perfect when it is perfectly private.

Some readers may object that sexuality, at least in women, does not play as primordial a role as tenderness, the need for protection, or various moral qualities. But how then can one explain the fact that a woman no longer feels protected if her partner is also sleeping with another woman, that she then no longer believes in his tenderness or gives a damn for his moral qualities? How can one explain why, when it is a question of jealousy (and it is never a question of anything else), the cliché "that's all they ever think of" is as true for women as it is for men, even though men see the sexual act as an objective while women view it as a means? If a woman finds no pleasure in the act, she has an additional reason to make it the center of her jealousy. Another woman's having what she has is less devastating than his finding in it something she has not found.

Thus, love as an ideal is a mystification woven on the theme of egotistical, competitive, hate-filled, shameful drunkenness. Its thread underlies the story of Humanity. Who would want the participants in the great commercial and military free-for-all to have the ability to change themselves into idealistic dreamers because love has struck them? What is this thing that is supposed to transcend sexuality? Who knows a couple united by the meeting of their souls without the connivance of sex? The white wedding gown, the verb *to deceive*, the noun *fidelity*, the terms *modesty, customs, morals, intimacy, tenderness, charms, advantages, consummation of marriage, possession*, and a thousand others—do they allude to the world of sex or the world of the spirit? A passion that describes itself as a sickness, a stroke of lightning, a feverish attack, a devastating storm, madness, losing one's head, and so on can scarcely be more than an imperious, savage, and therefore unjust exaltation of the *material* Ego. Thus it would be strange if loving someone meant wishing that someone well enough to be willing to watch a third party ravish one's *property*. Love is said to be close to hate, and actually does turn to hate, as though reverting to its original form, as soon as the *object* of love realizes that his or her happiness lies in another sexual relationship. If love is noble (difficult, pure, generous), how can one explain the whole world's being capable of it? But when the whole world suggests that the sole objective of Life is choosing someone to take over as a personal possession, and being similarly chosen by that someone in return, one is left with practically no choice between this maneuver and solitude.

In fact, "choosing someone as a personal possession" does not tell the whole story. No collectors would dare treat the actual objects in their possession the way that jealousy-love can bring two human beings to treat each other. Unless they were crazy, any collectors would rather give up their masterpieces than see them destroyed. Love is more likely to choose the converse; in death, the former possession at least does not belong to anyone *else*. Thus, one can torture (morally or physically), spy on, imprison, and sometimes even kill because one *loves*. The courts make allowances for this type of crime. Murder motivated by jealousy—when the jealousy is "motivated"—is no longer exactly murder. Any jury is likely to make an extenuating circumstance out of a sentiment on which its members, like everyone else, have built their lives. People draw a distinction between a sordid crime and a crime of passion—as though it were not less sordid to kill human beings to take their money than in order to take their liberty. If murder is merely the instrument of theft, it causes horror, but when it is the objective itself, people find it more excusable.

Of course, love has inspired some great works of art. But bereavement, prison, and injustice have inspired just as many, as have the worst religious aberrations. None of these realities has any inspiration of themselves; it is the works that apparently spring from them that lend them the air of inspiration. Neither does an exaltation of the Ego by a Chopin or a Beethoven blossom out in beauty thanks to the Ego, but thanks to Chopin or Beethoven.

III

The fact that love is merely the lying ornamentation of jealousy, egotism, and sex would not matter if its expression in sex were not used as a basis for so many other lies and were not in itself a lie worse than all the rest put together.

Sexuality, especially male sexuality, has a long history of being compared to a hunger mixed with a fever, the whole being subject, like all fevers, to crisis, and like all hungers, to surfeit. Even today, sexual desire is called an "appetite." The language here is quite unequivocal, and in an essentially male society, it alludes to an obvious parallel.

Why does the comparison appear degrading? It is actually flattering because its other term is aesthetic in nature. Either the simple sex act is merely a comedy or it is infinitely closer to the pleasures of the palate than to artistic emotion, despite the emotion that can accompany it when it is more a sign than a simple act. There are three reasons for the separation of simple sex and aesthetic emotion. First, the sex act is essentially tactile and individual. Second, the sensations of which it is composed do not form a language but an objective (a note, an act, or a word is neither beautiful nor ugly in itself, but a taste, an odour, or a kiss is necessarily agreeable or disagreeable). Finally, it is self-serving and would die from the general distribution that enhances aesthetic enthusiasm. (All this is merely a glimpse of a subject that will be dealt with in a later chapter, the viewpoint that excludes gastronomy and eroticism from consideration as arts; for example, one of the conditions of pictorial nudity is that there must be no possibility of sexual excitation.)

Without wishing that sexual "appetite" cease to be an appetite or lose any of the characteristics of an instinct, one can wish that it corresponded with the use the couple wants to make of it, that it were renewable at pleasure, that it were as powerful in a year's time as it was yesterday, and, above all, that it were deaf to all other solicitation from the moment it finds its sole object. Starvation is the only reliable method of safeguarding an appetite in an atmosphere of monotony, and hypocrisy is the only way of disguising this sort of purposeful starvation. As long as he is not a particular woman's property, a man can desire all women or lust after several of them without inviting disaster, but let him make his choice, and the miracle must happen at once: he may no longer desire any other. Better still, his desire should continually increase for the thing he already possesses, and he should show no signs of tiring of a body he knows from head to foot. What would become of the couple—that agreement between two jealousies—if the man had to admit that temporary satisfaction had not changed his sexuality, that he continued to desire all desirable women, and that after a time (generally a very short time) he would prefer to sleep with hundreds of women other than his wife—were he not afraid that she would do the same, not out of desire, but out of revenge? If a hundredth part of friendship tempered the couple's love, if it rested on anything other than the sexual contract, this ominous mystification would not be indispensable. On the other hand, it is quite understandable that the woman has no trouble believing the man as to the reality of his desires or that she does not see that he desires her in the long run because he has no one else at his disposal. First, this situation suits her perfectly; second, she does not and will never know the true nature of male sexuality, which she identifies with her own—and which the man conceals from her with consummate artistry.

Here, masculine bad faith is limitless. All men, for example, know that practically *all* their fellows masturbate, whether or not they are having regular sexual relations with one or more women and that while they masturbate, they generally think about other women. Now, that is a thing almost *no* woman can bring herself to believe. It is useless for a woman to win wolf whistles on every streetcorner, patrol in front of pornographic cinemas bursting with male customers, stare at the illustrated objects of male sexual desire in hundreds of magazines, vicariously enjoy that desire herself, or learn that she can cause a raging fire with a single spark, and that if she is pretty she can seduce the most faithful lover into treason. All this can teach her nothing of interest to the man who interests her. And for a good reason: if she questions him, he replies as all liars do when asked if they are lying. He belongs to her, so he must be an exception. So his behaviour must be exceptional. In consequence, he must claim that he is the one man in a thousand who never masturbates (not since he met her), that he looks at pretty women in the street the way one looks at pretty flowers in a garden. *And she will believe it.* Doubtless he may half believe it himself; face to face with what appears to him to be feminine "innocence," his polygamy may fill him with guilt. One ends up imagining that one has become what one wishes to be, even though the whole world proclaims the truth from the housetops: that *every* man lies to *every* woman *every* time he pretends he desires her alone, and that if polygamy did not involve such a lot of trouble, no male in the world could imagine himself wanting anything else. To put it simply: a woman in love can only bring herself to "commit adultery" under compulsion, while a man—in love or not—refrains from the same act only if necessary and under a completely opposite compulsion. How can one not see that reconciling these almost absolutely opposite impulses is an almost perfect piece of trickery?

Thus, sexuality performs the miracle of being simultaneously tamed and wild, of becoming obligatory while remaining free, of having only reasonable reasons and overstepping them all, of serving as a sign and serving only itself, of being as practical as a mathematical calculation and as rhapsodic as an instinct. It is natural for a man to "make love" beyond the bounds of weariness; if he does not, the women believes that he no longer loves her or that he loves another woman since she ignores masculine sexuality's ability to make love without loving because she hates it so much. Or the man may approach his woman constantly because he must constantly reaffirm his presence and renew the pact, or because he has no other option anyway, or because he thinks it would be abnormal no longer to desire what he has had for the past five years.

A married man who consults a psychiatrist about sexual inadequacy is unlikely to be advised to commit adultery or even to hear that his reaction is natural. Likewise, it is regarded as normal for a woman to engage in sex so that her partner will not be tempted elsewhere, or because she believes in the genuineness of his desire, or by way of reward, or as a token of affection. And it is regarded as normal for her to respond *as though* in a physical ecstasy, during which the murmurings of "I love you" reveal, in the most logical way in the world, *where* love is situated. Her feminine cries and gasps enchant the man like a chorus of praise, making him think of Paradise, even though they may be interrupted, now and then, by thoughtful remarks about a position that might be adopted to advantage or even—why not—about the weekly shopping list. Marital sex is a tender, transparent dialogue between two souls, a dialogue that makes one lose one's head but not one's bearings, that is sometimes impossible without the partners' beating each other up. There is something admirable about a long-lasting fidelity that results in a human relationship needing sex in order to remain human and above all, to remain a relationship, even though the act has become hardly more than a comedy. Men have nothing to do with one another, apparently, apart from *sexual commerce*—a term like *appetite* that should not have been allowed to go out of fashion.

It is true that phrases like *the marriage bond, a ring through his nose,* and *the knot has been tied* are no longer used about married men except at village wedding suppers. But it is equally true that many more modern phrases reflect the way in which the institution of the couple, which enables one to escape individual solitude, recreates that solitude on the social scale. One is *already taken*, one is *no longer free*, one has *surrendered one's freedom*. The jargon is definitely akin to lying; it is more twisted than a nest of serpents, and one must abandon the literal meanings to see what lies beneath. The man loses not his friends—he usually has none—but his comrades, who now take a back seat or move right out of the picture. He makes acquaintances, to be sure, but they are carefully sterilized. A jealous prudence keeps an eye on potential rivals. The friends of one partner are well advised not to strike up too much of a friendship with the other if they are of the opposite sex—and even if they are not. Two wise partners steer very clear of any sort of friendly ties with their former lovers. The wife and the husband (or, in the language of modern "free" unions, the female companion and the male companion) each have imprescriptible and incontestable rights that inevitably fix schedules, set what free time is available, ward off intruders, designate which former friendships are suitable, and quickly arrange to kill off those they consider hostile. A third party cannot have a relationship—except a completely unimportant one—with just one member. It is the couple or nobody. The best and most frequent solution is for couples to stick to couples. "Each in his own place": the balance of taboos creates a symmetry of interests.

Of course, a married woman finds it easier than her husband to have private friendships and cozy little chats. First, there are purely practical reasons; for example, she has mornings and afternoons available, while her husband has only his evenings. More important, masculine friendship includes a subversive complicity—in other words, a threat—that is almost never found in feminine friendships. The male world, found in bars, clubs, and especially military canteens, is marked by ritual misogyny. A man who brought his partner into this world would feel ridiculous, timid, hampered as by a Siamese twin. Here the old complicity of prehistoric tribes is reborn, and the sexual lie is no longer necessary; in consequence, most drinking companions exchange confidences, generally veiled in jokes, that they would never address to their beloved wives—and with very good reason! Ah, the sublime transparency of love! The rustic ceremonies of not so long ago described as "the end of one's carefree boyhood days" or "farewell to liberty" have misogyny as their origin and tell all the essential truth. So too do the expressions *to be free*, meaning to be without a partner, or *sexual liberty* for polygamous sexuality. They all indicate that the couple's sexuality is imprisoned, like its existence, and imprisoning, like its ideal.

The mythology of love reaches its peak when it declares that marriage is an act of confidence—in other words, that it pledges the future in the name of the present, and that it pledges the souls of human beings under guarantee of their private parts. A fine confidence indeed that places love under the protection of the police, makes the sexual act the matter of a contract, and forces the contracting parties into cohabitation. Couples have never needed marriage—nor the now obsolete pretexts of the home or the family nest—to make a necessity of cohabitation. Yet the best friends in the world abstain from living together all the time. Even those who suffer isolation still refuse daily promiscuity for what should be obvious reasons: daily contact is wearisome; everyone needs a certain amount of solitude; ceaseless contact with the one person makes habitual what should remain rare (and precious) and imposes what should be a matter of choice. Throughout the world of human history, cohabitation only exists in cases of sexual "sharing." This is so true that in today's society two men who live together are immediately and justifiably accused of homosexuality, although two women can do the same thing without being suspected of anything.

But the couple is not susceptible to this logic. Jealousy makes up for the lack of any logical explanation. The partners never reach the point of having seen enough of each other because seeing each other is their only way of keeping an eye on each other. It is a tender surveillance but surveillance all the same. Try suggesting to a young couple that they live apart and see how worried they get. Their reaction gives an impression of insecurity that can be analyzed to reveal a threat—imaginary or not. It is all there is to find because it is the only threat that the couple know.

Marriage prolongs the couple's unformulated ideology: that the sexual act, already everlasting, does not become unpleasing simply because it has been made obligatory. It is the only case in which a pleasure can withstand a loss of spontaneity, just as it is the only case in which the *mono-* of *monogamy* accepts the inconvenience of the *mono-* of *monotony* for the immense advantage of the *mono-* of *monopoly*. What could once be broken asunder is now firmly cemented by the law. The prospect of a traditional jealous scene, with its power to create feelings of guilt, its paralyzing tears, and its potential for terrifying acts of violence, is enough to justify any renunciation, any withdrawals, and any act of contrition—especially since it has right on its side. It matters little that in the end this right kills every last illusion of liberty, that even the word *husband* has something emasculated and ridiculous about it, and that literature and the cinema, which live by the myth of love, are rarely interested in conjugal love and portray it only with irony and contempt. Juliet can be disturbing; Madame Romeo is merely dull. With marriage, what was familiar becomes familial. It promotes constitutional monarchy to a dictatorship that is confirmed when the first child appears.

At that point even the mask of the amorous fantasy begins to crumble. The man and the woman have become responsible, father and mother, asexual in each of these sexual roles. Henceforth the most effective constraint in the world drives them to discipline, to production, to regularity, to competition. When one was fighting only for oneself, one could allow oneself escapades and periods off. Now that one is responsible for a family, every failure to win is a tragedy, every promotion a victory. One must toe the line. There is no question now of risking one's job in a wildcat strike, or of choosing time off rather than money. (Of course, time off is no longer free time, and the hours one spends on the job would often be spent just as unsatisfactorily at home. Marriage and industrial life are made for each other.)

The child has the quite justified reputation of consolidating a couple. This widely held idea contains another: the being who should remain an objective or end is, at the beginning, only an instrument—and sometimes even an instrument of blackmail. "If you leave me, you'll never see him (or her or them) again"—a very common threat when a couple is at the point of divorce. "I'll stay because of the children"—an even more common reason when the first argument has struck home or not had to be invoked at all. A child is usually, if not always, brought into the world simply because married life has reached an impasse—an impasse that turns out to have been arranged for just that purpose. The child is a palliative for boredom, providing the woman with a diversion, a role to play, and sometimes with a *raison d'être*. So yet another human being is parachuted onto Earth for motives that have nothing to do with his or her own personal existence.

The law that says marriage is a prerequisite for the family claims to have the rearing and education of children as its primary concern. Certainly our legal arrangements serve the monogamous sexual couple (a double pleonasm there). This is most easily seen at separation and divorce proceedings. When judges decide on who should have custody of the children, they do not worry about the nurturing or educative talents of the father or the mother. All they want to find out is which of the two was the first to deceive the other. Any breach of the contract of sexual exclusivity takes precedence over all other considerations. The unfaithful husband is a bad father even if he is knowledgeable, cheerful, and friendly; a woman deceived is a worthy mother even if she is an illiterate and dull as ditchwater. Conversely, a wanton mother cannot make a child happy since she could not bring happiness to the wet blanket who married her.

IV

People often confuse two almost opposite things by calling both of them "instinct." The first is an unconscious, invariable, infallible, and automatic knowledge, the second a fund of impulse that motivates all behaviour and all knowledge, conscious or not, just as an ensemble of general ends justifies a succession of particular means. It is absurd to say that Humans dominate either kind of instinct. They are almost completely deprived of the first. As for the second, their ability to contain them has intensified them all so well that the human species distinguishes itself from the rest of creation by its capacity for every possible enjoyment—including, naturally, the most negative kinds. In Nature aggression between individuals of the same species leads only rarely to individual murder; among wolves, for example, it is strictly impossible, despite the Roman dictum "Man is a wolf for Man." Humanity, however, has brought the Human as far as genocide, while awaiting global suicide. In human beings the modest territoriality of the upper animals takes some dizzying forms—and profitably so. Simple animal appetite blossoms into billions of human gastronomic niceties, and all sources of sensation are exploited to exhaustion in the service of artistic expression or sumptuous display. Sexual bidding becomes crazy jealousy and amorous mythomania, and sexuality undergoes the most radical metamorphosis in ceasing to be seasonal and in joining forces with every known emotion.

One must remember, in fact, that neither the existence of "instincts" nor the need for their repression indicates their animal origin. The murder for vengeance from which a child must learn to abstain would not tempt a tiger; the cruelty and envy that fascinate us hold no interest for dogs. Expression and repression thus call for one another, just as the act of filling threatens to terminate in an overflow. When psychoanalysis sees in "sexual repression" the origin of the whole process of civilization, it is pretending to believe that, by nature, sexuality is too unbridled and too savage to allow the blossoming of conscience. In actual fact, conscience and sexuality blossomed together. The psychoanalytic view, in effect, defines "sexual repression" in terms of the prejudices that result from it. Implicit in this idea is an equation: continence equals strength. Thus, the rules imposed on sexuality gain in nobility and mystery by being linked directly with the laws of the species.

To return to the point at hand: the idea of equivalence between regulated sexuality and civilization contradicts everything suggested by the parallel developments of civilization and of Life. Only the animals have a naturally regulated sexuality, simultaneously periodic and selective; it gets nearer and nearer to automatism the lower one goes on the scale of species. Only in the Human Being is the sexual impulse unleashed, abolishing periodicity, selection, and rules more and more as civilization develops. The psychoanalytic view, following the common direction in this matter, makes a double error. First, it creates a point of departure and not a termination out of what one might well call the human sexual obsession—individuals contain themselves because they are obsessed, and not the obverse. Then it seeks for the origin of this drama in the unconscious. But the unconscious par excellence, which is the animal consciousness, contains no trace of it; it began with the appearance of consciousness, and nothing is more conscious than the simple balance of cupidity and hypersensitivity that results from it. In a society composed of couples (or at least of sexual proprietors, whether they are polygamous or not), the ban placed upon sex is the ban placed upon theft—with the notable difference that sexual theft tempts the whole world, that sexual property is maintained only through jealousy, and that reciprocal appurtenances, as twisted as any comedy could be, have every reason to see enemies everywhere. One does not talk about rope in the house of the person who was hanged, of gastronomy in the house of the starving, or of sex in the house of a monogamous couple. Sexual repression is anything but historically or evolutionarily necessary; it certainly does not resemble a civilizing force—provided that one does not class as necessities wars, commercialism, and wastage (without which it appears, quite clearly, that no civilization could ever have managed to develop).

We have already seen that if sexuality were not the couple's privilege, the couple would no longer have any privilege and would thus cease to exist. This is exactly what happens in a period of *lowering of moral standards* (as one terms, not the eras of military carnage, but brief periods of erotic carnival). Thus, to protect the couple, society must place an embargo on sexuality. Each individual learns to react to sex as either a threat or a temptation—and in both cases, as a danger. This tropism becomes so deeply rooted in each individual that it takes on all the characteristics of an instinct. The most elaborate sexual censorships still recall the most brutal jealousy, exemplified by voyeurism and impetuousness. All modestly preserve a property they are ashamed of. Jealousy always refuses to call itself jealousy, even when its mask serves as an emblem. Every time an animal catches its prey, its first action is to move away, to eat it in privacy. In the sphere of sexuality, this desire for privacy goes beyond the direct annexation that constitutes the couple to become the global dissimulation that constitutes modesty. Giving something to look at is already giving something away, and evoking is already giving something to look at. If one talks to a man about *his* girl friend in crudely sexual terms, one appears to be raping her under his very eyes. Thus one is forced into a thousand verbal detours, if not into silence, and since what concerns women in general also concerns this woman in particular, the sealed-lips approach must be extended to all the particular sexualities that make up sexuality in general. Thus, collective morals focus on an obsession, like a raging toothache reducing the whole body to a single tooth and the whole soul to a single raging ache.

There is no point dwelling here on the ravages of sexual repression, which run from the contortions of religious asceticism to results of censorship, passing through the absurdities of the Victorian era when two men hardly dared shake hands lest the contact be too carnal. The blushes of young girls, giggling, tortuous circumlocutions, double and triple entendres, the innumerable jokes—all these things mask sexuality to make it acceptable in conversation and the media. In the days of Louis XIV, one took offense at all breasts that were not termed *allurements,* at all desires not called *flames,* and later at all mirrors that were not *counsellors of the Graces,* and armchairs that were not *conversation conveniences.* Under Queen Victoria some English families dressed the *lower limbs* of their pianos, and one used phrases five lines long, of almost hermetic symbolism, to describe the buttocks, the vagina, or the penis. This nonsensical contagion turned into a horror of Nature and took over the language completely. Even today, when drugstores carry tens of thousands of different kinds of pills, we know what is meant by *The* Pill, and although medicine supports it (naturally), the dangers attributed to it are still more numerous than those another medical school of thought, no less authoritative, warned us about not so long ago on the subject of masturbation. (In very similar fashion, the absurd campaigns the world of alcohol wages against the innocent herb marijuana are also aimed at enjoyment.) The ban religious authorities place on abortion and contraception is said to involve "respect for life," which has failed to make them spurn the death penalty and military service.

The fact is that sexual censorship, like the jealousy from which it stems, is also mixed with a shame that drives it into lying. "Let them be" is a more honorable slogan than "Don't let them do it," and the censors must perpetually guard against allowing their agitation to be taken for emotion. Moreover, as we have already seen, the words *morals, immorality, good habits, intimacy, purity,* and so on are all degraded by the obsessive meaning to which usage limits them. We are only bodies. It is logical for us to locate morals in the same place that we locate love. (We even add mysticism; no religion exists that is not obsessed with sex, even when it makes it the object of erotic discipline.)

The many attempts at liberating sexuality, including pornography, resemble the grimace of a twisted face trying to smile. The appearance of a naked body on TV releases floods of wrath that would not be occasioned by a spectacle of carnage (as though a horror of flesh at least got something out of dead flesh), but a pornographic spectacle turns sex into exactly the monster that prudishness denounces. Sometimes, what reality definitely is cannot stand being definitely described. When Ovid was permanently exiled for writing libidinous verse, Rome was crawling with brothels and the Emperor Augustus surrounded by a drunken rout of whores and transvestites. Pornography takes good care not to present itself as practicable; its highly exaggerated sex is as far removed as possible from all simple human tenderness—and as close as possible to violence. It associates sex with blood, the suggestion being that one leads to the other. In de Sade's seedy dissertations, the least glimpse of nudity excites only torturers who dream drearily of new agonies amid impossible settings of impregnable châteaux and secret gar-

dens, while the Jesuitical periphrases of the narrator exude boredom, embarrassment, and hypocrisy. Black leather boots and gloves,
whips, pillories, and dungeons—all this Grand-Guignol paraphernalia seems to chorus, "See how wicked sex is!" If one wishes to
strengthen the police while appearing to resist them, all one has to
do is to preach banditry, having first taken care to blacken it.

The same remarks hold good for all group sexuality, whether it
take the form of bourgeois orgies, pseudopolitical protests, or
parareligious ceremonies. How can the couple who abhor adultery
"make love" in a group of six, eight, or even several dozen people? It
is because this kind of promiscuity allows them to continue their
mutual surveillance. What occurs before their eyes occurs, so to
speak, with their participation (more often than not, their active
participation). Meanwhile, "pure" (cold) sex excludes attachments,
confidences, and private conversations—in a word, freedom itself—
so one is freed in safe custody. Thus the amiable practice of swap-
ping partners even has the reputation, here and there, of
strengthening couples. What does not strengthen them, of course, is
true freedom, which would begin by doing away with all cohabitation, all rights of inspection, and all privilege. But what would love
become if it had to have the virtues of friendship? What could "I
love you" mean in a dialogue of souls when love consists of selling
one's soul to the devil who is within one's body?

Finally, there are the communes, which exist in theory by banning
couples. What actually happens, however, is that either the participants continue as couples and at each attempt at liberation jealousy
works to undo the work of the community, or the mechanism of the
commune itself contradicts its intent. Nudism makes all sexual con-
tacts dull under a show of making them direct; sartorial or bodily
cares are reduced to simple hygiene; the group invariably introduces
conventlike rules and sectarian regulations. Moreover, the women
and men alike make themselves ugly in an attempt to make sexuality
more attractive, and the group tries to solve problems of jealousy,
possessiveness, and property by conjuring tricks. How can one overcome a *moral* vice? By making it *materially* impossible. Are couples
isolating themselves, thereby creating universal social isolation? Is
sexual cohabitation repulsive, unjust, hypocritical? Very well, let us
remedy that by creating community isolation and sexual cohabita-

tion for thirty or forty. Change the manner in order not to alter the principle.

The true solution, of course, would be to realize that no true solidarity is possible except between Humans ready for solitude, that seeking a union in order not to be alone boils down to wanting a union from *interest*, and that Humans are not capable of loving one another while leaving themselves totally and radically free. A physical community, even though seen or desired as a community of the spirit, is a piece of nonsense, pure and simple, in which members continue to regard themselves as bodies and to give the word *love* the usurious meaning it has had till now.

If I ask Society to justify my existence, I am asking four billion other myselves to give me what I do not possess. My empty interior becomes that of a leech. I demand from the human community (which is not yet either human or a community) a spiritual supplement that I would first have to give to it, and, in consequence that I would have to acquire without or, if necessary, in spite of it. Human life has the same meaning for one individual as for ten thousand. Yet we cannot communicate freely so long as we do not live alone and so long as we cannot even create *interior* bonds in which sex neither plays a part nor is deliberately excluded (and thus does not yield to any desire of superior significance). Until we can do these things, earthly society will remain a jungle—which is naturally its objective.

V

Every time I used the words *sex* or *sexuality* in the previous section, I should have made it clear that I was referring primarily to masculine sexuality. Feminine sexuality remains a mystery, even to other women. The underlying nature of masculine sexuality, on the contrary, is so clearly evident to all men that when they are together they do not need to make do with half words and hardly ever allow themselves to sink into hypocrisy. A really desirable woman is desirable, with no ambiguity whatever, to every man around her (homosexuals excepted). But it is practically impossible to discover what constitutes a man who is desirable to women, or even to a particular woman.

History offers no example of pornography directed at women, and heterosexual male prostitution is extremely rare, partly because it is impractical for obvious physiological reasons, but partly for lack of demand. Now, in any given society, its pornography (or erotic imagery) and its prostitution are the only objective signs of its *pure* sexuality. A man who never buys a record and never goes to a concert may well "need" music in certain circumstances, but one can hardly say he loves it in itself. A pure pleasure has no conditions, either real or simulated. If women tried to find real sexuality for themselves, prostitution would be superfluous, rape almost inconceivable, and pornography and masculine tricks of conquest practically useless; men would be accosted in the streets and would submit to physical contact in all sorts of promiscuous ways. If, on the other hand, women were fond of sexual imagery, masculine nudity would fill women's magazines and be exploited by fashion in as suggestive a manner as possible. In actual fact, however, the few magazines that have tried this inverted eroticism have had no success except among *male* homosexuals, just as idiotic attempts at male striptease attract the same clientele, while causing well-deserved hilarity among women. The failure of these ventures is ascribable only in part to the uncomeliness of the male body (Apollo was perhaps quite handsome in the pose of a conqueror, but he was certainly quite ridiculous when he tried to rival Venus). Feminine sexuality is essentially introverted (or, to use a more positive term, narcissistic). It would waste itself if it were directed towards the exterior, for it is impossible to attract the source of attraction. Even lesbians do not usually have any taste for erotic feminine iconography, and the woman who is absurdly called a "nymphomaniac" desires only to *be* desired. The *sight* of another body is not of a nature to create the stimulus that the woman perforce directs first towards her own body. Women have never yet composed lewd songs or retailed dirty jokes about the male sex organs. Every public lavatory is covered with masculine homosexual graffiti, but even female homosexuals have never resorted to this method of expression.

In men, sexual desire is at its maximum during adolescence; in women—when it exists at all—it is very slow to reach its height. A young boy has a general inkling of the nature of sexual pleasure even before he begins masturbating; a woman, as long as she is a virgin and often still longer, has no idea what this pleasure can be like—not for a man, but for herself. The imperious character of male sexuality, the fact that it constitutes an end in itself, irritates nearly all women ("You only came here for *that!*") because it involves either a fund of violence aimed at themselves or a source of pleasure that remains mysterious to them—and that male society has done everything in its power to build up into a superiority that is primarily a *dependence.*

Most psychologists, out of an almost hypocritical and certainly misplaced desire for equality, hold that a woman gets by sexually by a general appreciation of her partner, an oriented affectivity. They do not seem to suspect that in making such a pronouncement they are saying that feminine sexuality can only "get by" by sex or call itself by some other name. Similarly, when one says that a woman can only make love with a partner she loves, one means that she is using the sexual act as a *sign* and that she is subordinating it to reasons that she finds strange in themselves. In short, sexual desire in the woman may well be a desire but it is not sexual. See how people try to prop up the equality of the sexes by equating their sexualities. . . .

The fact that the female orgasm has been and continues to be the subject of much research bears witness to the same obsession: the woman must get "as much" as the man, even when this quantitative "as much" presupposes a qualitative community that simply does not exist. One report reveals that half of all women are frigid; another goes as far as three quarters; yet another stresses the possibility of a woman's having up to twenty successive orgasms, whereas the man has difficulty in managing two (as though the word *orgasm* could be equally applicable to the two different realities). Students define the female orgasm variously as an indefinite ejaculation of uncertain origin, as a vaginal secretion of major intensity (while noting that this secretion also occurs in women who experience no physical sensation), as a psychological phenomenon (why not as an idea?), and as a succession of spasms. The *Hite Report* even talks about "emotional" orgasms (why not "abstract" orgasms?) and reveals that most women masturbate, whereas, thirty years ago, only 5 percent did and that they find real pleasure only in this solitary practice. Yet an only slightly earlier German study claimed that female masturbation almost never culminated in orgasm. If Shere Hite is to be believed, she has hit on another way in which the sexualities are reversed. A woman sees the sex act as a substitute for masturbation, while the man regards masturbation as a pallid substitute for the sex act. Similarly, having an orgasm seems to be the chief preoccupation of the woman, while not having one too quickly is the obsession of the man. Everywhere we find contradiction, equivocation, mystery, and mystification. Men know only one, universal kind of orgasm that almost always produces the same quality, if not the same quantity, of pleasure and have a single erogenous zone (facts verifiable beyond any need for verification), whereas women have an infinite variety of orgasms that are nearly always uncontrollable. They manage to cry out though, in fact, they feel nothing, to come ten times running without dying of exhaustion, and to find erogenous zones down to the soles of their feet, though they remain indifferent to masculine nudity and only reach these delights through the expedient of an affective choice or a general application that is of psychic and not sexual character. How could so many contradictory facts not remind one of low farce—especially since women themselves suspect each other of being imposters?

This suspicion is still further strengthened by the cries or gasping moans that most women utter while they are making love, which *cannot* be expressions of pleasure. If they were, we would have to admit, for a start, that the sexuality of women is much more intense than that of men. And if that were true, we would have to explain the absence of prostitution or illustrated eroticism for feminine use. Moreover, we would be hard put to understand why, from time immemorial, the man has had to earn each sexual act by conquest and why he has had to give this conquest a character normally *asexual*. From sonnets to madrigals, to the seductive maneuverings of Don Juan and Casanova, the man has always taken the greatest care to disguise his fleshly appetites as thirsts of the soul, while the woman, in inverse symmetry, uses her carnal powers of seduction with a view to still greater seduction.

That the feminine cries of "pleasure" form part of this seductive power is shown by the effect they have on the man in whom cries and sighs are extremely rare. Making a woman moan makes him feel he is the purveyor of unheard-of pleasures and nameless transports of delight—or is it that the spasms flatter male semisadism by their expression of semipainful sensations? How could a man be tempted to suspect that all this noise is a theatrical production so well done that the sound of it has an erotic effect on whoever hears it, even four floors away? To make her faint, to make her moan—could there be a more satisfying power trip? No matter that these exclamations are completely unauthentic: no pleasure or ecstasy exists that can express itself *at the same time* as it is taking place because the energy required for expression must be deducted from the energy required for the enjoyment of the sensation. On the contrary, does there not exist, in the whole animal kingdom, a single bodily pleasure that does not produce silence, call for immobility, and even induce a closing of the eyes. This is what a man normally does in the throes of orgasm, that is what a dog or a cat does when one strokes it, and this is what animals do when they are coupling. They may cry out before or after, in the grip of desire or in the ceremonial of triumph, but not during. Another, even more definite proof of the purely theatrical character of all these outbursts is the fact that nobody cries out while masturbating. If the function of a cry of pain is to reduce the pain, how can a cry of pleasure do anything other than reduce the pleasure? To ex-press is to ex-pel. However paradoxical it may appear, the only possible role of the cry of pleasure is to remove the effect of surprise, which interferes with pleasure, or the rare accidental overflow, which expands it. To imagine that love cries cannot be repressed would be to fail to understand that the man is not subject to them and that the woman can decide to end them, for contingent reasons, on the appearance of the first child.

The love cry is a collective manifestation by which, at most, one encourages oneself to enjoy. One cries out at a carnival, in a crowd, in a bar, when it is a matter of maintaining or creating an atmosphere that would not exist without the cry—in other words, one that cannot exist of itself. The more important such cries are, the more often they appear in these circumstances.

Naturally, anyone who is *interested* in a woman's love cries is likely to contest their falsity. For example a man considers that a woman "makes love beautifully" when she makes him believe that *he* makes love beautifully. She does this not by staying motionless and silent—as she would if she were alone, as he always does unless he is hysterical, as animals do—but by squirming and wriggling and gasping by way of stimulation and especially of stimulation, making herself simultaneously actor and audience, sound and echo, spectacle and applause. The very signs of frigidity are thus taken for those of orgasm, and vice versa—but who is quick to suspect a flattery? We see here a vicious circle in which History, Nature, and interest are accomplices, and completely tangled up. The less real pleasure the woman has, the less she has any objective other than pleasing and gratifying the man; the more firmly she has this as her objective, the more interest she has in feeling nothing lest the peak of her pleasure pass as nonexistent, void as it is of incontestable signs such as ejaculation. A few societies have placed voluntary shackles on feminine sexuality (for example, the clitoridectomies practiced among certain Moslem peoples), but it is generally masculine sexuality itself that precludes any reality in its feminine counterpart by demanding the pseudosigns of pleasure.

And yet, although the man is vain enough to allow himself to be taken in by simulated swoons, deep down he is not interested in the woman's sexual pleasure—if indeed he really believes in it at all. Otherwise it would be impossible for him to copulate with prostitutes, who are of necessity openly frigid, but always ready—of the same necessity—for stereotyped caresses. Each sex refers to the other in clichés that are thousands of years old and that are partly justified. The woman will never relinquish the idea that masculine sexuality is bestial because no sexuality, in itself, could ever be anything else. Meanwhile the man will always be firmly convinced that women are almost asexual. He is compelled to take all sorts of devious routes to seduce a woman, certain of offending her every time he speaks to her in openly sexual terms, conscious that she always subordinates sexuality to something else and that in simulating pleasure, she *can* do something of which he himself is physiologically incapable. Given this contrast, how can he help but condemn himself for his bestiality? This is another basic cause of the so-called blameworthiness of sex, in addition to those we have already discussed: the beast in him will have its rights—and it leaves him little choice between that and impotence.

Thus, whether a woman "makes love beautifully" or not is all the same to him, provided that she maintain certain appearances. What attracts a man to a woman, sexually speaking, is her beauty, and that alone. An average-looking woman who appears lascivious has no chance against a beautiful woman who appears cold; beauty is lascivious in itself by reason of the delights it promises, while lasciviousness, which is uncontrollable anyway, merely ridicules ugliness. Are there not many actresses, who are living images of frigidity and who sometimes make no effort to conceal their distaste for the world of sex, who have nevertheless become sexual idols? But, like the self-interest from which it stems, masculine blindness knows no limits, so most men imagine a woman has a sexual liking for fellatio and cunnilingus, to which, at best, she submits like a geisha. (Shere Hite reveals that women put up with these practices just as a minority of them put up with licking their partner's armpits or nibbling his testicles.)

The male world, which complains so freely about women's distaste for sexuality, has always done everything possible to ensure that this distaste does not lessen. *Chaste* was once a compliment. *Deflowered* means "having no more flowers"; in other words, sexual inexperience was considered flower-laden. Not so long ago, the cult of virgins and innocence went without saying, just as today there is contempt for women "of easy virtue" and in the terms *harlot* or *tart*. A woman who makes love too freely is a *bitch*, though a woman who refuses to make love is another kind of bitch. Today there is obvious contempt for virgins, but women of experience are viewed with considerably more suspicion. The woman who enjoys her power of attraction is a *flirt*, but a man loves to parade in front of as many eyes as possible with a conquered and captive flirt on his arm. Don Juan is a male hero, but the female version is a wanton. Even medicine gets into the act: the womanizing man is normal, but the man-chasing woman is a nymphomaniac. Men have a liking for the flesh, so they want it fresh; it is fresh not when it is sexually spontaneous, but when it is asexual and has not been used *by others*.

Men dream of a stronger feminine sexuality that would make conquests easier and potentially more numerous—but would allow itself to be tamed as soon as the conquests were achieved. Yet "stronger" implies "more active," and if one of the sexes is active, then the other must be passive to the same degree. A target that moves towards the bullet turns the bullet into a target; a sex that seeks out the other removes the initiative from the other. Now, a man would have a horror of playing, in however small a degree, the role he assigns to women; he could not stand to have them regard him primarily as a body, evaluate him in physical terms, be unable to make love to him except for pleasure, fall asleep or take their leave immediately afterwards, undress him with their eyes, dwelling overlong on his penis or his buttocks, and by taking the initiative away from him, make it impossible for him to see himself in the role of conqueror. So many spectres come close to representing Hell. Just a few would be needed to reduce the male universe to impotence or to make it topple over completely into pederasty.

Man suspects woman of duplicity that he is careful to maintain. Although he believes he is dreaming when a woman tells him, after half an hour of gasping and moaning, that she has had only limited pleasure, yet he wants her to tell him this, for otherwise he imagines he has given her unforgettable raptures. In brief, he regards her as a ghoul if she asks for more but as a monster if she forgets what she has had. Masculine desire begins before foreplay and is already at its peak at the start of the act, but feminine desire attains its maximum only during the act. The man desires *The* Woman, but the woman desires *a* man. The male body's gracefulness is questionable, but the female body is soft and tender. Despite all these differences, the verb *to desire* is supposed to have the same meaning in both cases, just as the noun *orgasm* is supposed to describe both something that is almost enough to exhaust a man and something that is not enough to lay a woman low, even if it is repeated four times over.

Taste, appetite, inclination, and desire are so fundamentally polygamous in orientation that introducing consideration of one particular person immediately tinges them with bad faith. Nobody can like *one* radish or *one* sonata exclusively. Even in art, where taste and desire are highly personalized, we call it snobbism when artists are able to raise the price of their work through the cult of the signature or respect for their name. Thus, the idea that one single subject raises the value of sexual appetite is either hypocritical or irrelevant; the hypocrisy is masculine and the irrelevancy feminine. But the man wishes that feminine sexuality were of the same nature as his own, while being neither polygamous (a state which is, as we have just seen, *complete* sexuality in itself), nor sexual (for he needs those looks, comments, declarations of love, oaths of allegiance, and sighs). He wants the woman to be simultaneously passive *and* desiring, as if "passive desire" did not boil down to a desire for desire, and, for the woman, the expectation of *being* desired. Now, how could she be pushed towards an exterior objective when it can only be a means, and the real objective is herself?

The woman no longer accepts this elementary logic. The repugnant animality she finds in male sexuality is also an object of envy, which she seems, in turn, to understand wonderfully and to ignore fundamentally. That the sight of her body is enough to excite men astonishes and sometimes scandalizes her, yet she brings this attraction into play whenever fashion gives her the opportunity, even while she complains about being considered a sexual object—exactly the quality that makes her appear most valuable. She sees male desire flaunted in the streets, supporting most advertising, barely bottled up by censorship, scarcely veiled by allusions, multiplied by the eroticism and pornography of the cinema—but persists nevertheless in believing that the man who "loves" her is primarily seeking her soul and miraculously desires no other body but hers. The brutality that horrifies her in the general run of men becomes a sign of love in one particular man, even though she knows enough not to give it any opportunity to appear except as a guarantee and thus a recompense of something else. Although she is not unaware that the masculine nature makes no correlation between physical "love" and moral love, when the impulse she considered bestial has just given out, she believes the man no longer *loves* her.

She thinks a man "makes love beautifully" when he can do it several times and for a long time, yet she never asks herself whether these Olympic coitions bear witness to effort or to enjoyment or whether the man has not simply *learnt* to hold himself back; what is beautiful must be lengthy since she sees it that way. In a spirit of competition, the men all chorus her opinion: an inability to make sex last for a long time is a matter for shame. Even the same psychologists who understand that conjugal coupling after fifteen years of marriage is clearly an erotic ideal, who treat the most justified sexual lassitude as impotence, use the label "premature ejaculation" for something that corresponds to the very nature of male sexuality. (This sexuality is also exemplified by masturbation, which rarely lasts more than a few minutes, and by almost all couplings in the animal kingdom.) Ejaculation is the result of an intense desire, and the sole means of avoiding "premature" ejaculation is to curb that desire. The techniques—all constraining, of course—that achieve this result lead to what is called "making love beautifully"; the more desire is fettered, delayed, and reasoned, the longer the sex act lasts, and the more the woman believes herself desired. It is as absurd as another myth that men have complacently allowed themselves to accept: the importance of the length and thickness of the penis—as though a vagina stretched to its maximum most closely approached fulfillment of its erotic possibilities (assuming that these themselves are not a myth).

The confusion on both sides is endless and always the same. What is merely a concession passes for an act of love, and what is a physical need gets taken for a spiritual quest. When the majority of men say they want "a woman in the house," what they actually want is a body at their disposal, though they pretend to be seeking a soul. How could women not believe them, since they too would really like a soul—for which a body must serve as a sole hostage? In the same way, women may consider it unjust to be judged by their beauty, but they do everything possible to make themselves beautiful and often use the same criterion to make judgements among themselves. And if their own choices of partners are really based on moral evaluations, it is hard to understand why the men who have success with women are so often imbeciles or men of wealth. Moreover, is it any more just to choose on a basis such as wealth than on the basis of beauty?

Since the man has well-defined sexual organs, the woman must have them too. Thus, it is sometimes said that the center of feminine sexuality is the vagina which is more or less nerveless and cannot be particularly sensitive, given the enormous expansion it undergoes during childbirth. (Not to mention that fact that sanitary tampons do not seem to give women any special pleasure.) Some people claim that only the clitoris is erogenous, which is doubtless true since female masturbation is usually confined to that organ. Yet the clitoris's dimensions are very insignificant, and its erection is not a constant or a distinct phenomenon in all women. Furthermore, if its role were really central, there would be no argument as to whether orgasms are vaginal or clitoral; neither would one read so often that a woman's real erogenous zone is her whole body. Our frigid grandmothers in their bourgeois houses had clitorises, though the voluptuous sultanas in their harems had none. And that is a typical example of the sort of clarity with which we view sex—even though it is, for the time being, the sole point of contact between men and women.

VI

What so-called feminists are unwilling to admit comes from Nature, they are quick to attribute to education (or to the environment, customs, and so on—they are all synonyms). Their objective is to arrange for the two sexualities to balance each other, as though the two sexes were not completely opposites, as though a less intense sexual drive constituted an inferiority, and as though "sexual liberation" depended on the strength of an instinct manipulated by jealousy (which takes instinct's place in its absence and grows as instinct becomes stronger). But as usual, blaming education is a subterfuge. Whatever interest, past or present, men have in extinguishing all feminine sexual desire, they do not hatch sinister plots to that end. What they sometimes seem to hope to extinguish is not a fire but themselves; so many repressions are rife within the male world that men have dreamed of castrating women far less often than they have dreamed of castrating each other. Given these repeated, insistent, and radical attacks against male sexuality, it would have disappeared long ago if education had any power against it. But it can neither disappear nor diminish; its only possible choice is between hypocrisy and deviation, between becoming clandestine or marginal. Nothing except real castration can stop an adolescent male's testicles from filling up with sperm; after that, whatever one does, his sexuality is present in its entirety. Thus, education cannot be used to explain the differences between men and women, even though it does produce in women the effect it cannot produce in men. Little boys show a sexual interest in little girls at an early age, but the reverse does not occur. Furthermore, in noting that female sexuality develops late and only through experience, one is saying that it is the reverse of an instinct. An instinct creates experience, it does not result from it, any more than hunger stems from the memory of having eaten.

Moreover, education cannot be the culprit because it is women who are responsible for it. What is called education is actually a whole stream of ideas and prohibitions in which children are steeped, originally within the family. Thus, from earliest childhood, it is the result of women's care. Would women really have tried to castrate themselves? Above all, would they have had the power to succeed in so doing? If the education theory were true, women would have had to be proselytizing, from generation to generation, an attitude that victimized them, that was imposed upon them by force, and that they never attempted to counteract by trickery. How can one not see the incoherence of such a theory?

The truth, of course, is to be found in Nature, and it dates from long before the emergence of Humans. Evolution had a basic need of the male orgasm, which is the reproductive act itself, but no need at all of the female orgasm, which is at most a luxury. In other words, from Nature's point of view, male sexuality is a question of life and death, while female sexuality is unimportant. Thus, amorous conquest is a male prerogative among nearly all animals; in many species, females do not couple except when forced to. This is what Darwin was expressing somewhat extravagantly when he said that the female animal does not choose the partner who pleases her most but the one who repels least. Notice, too, that the human species has stimulated sexuality by accentuating sexual characteristics. The physical differences between a man and a woman are infinitely more marked than those between the male and the female of lower species; this is true, *inter alia,* for height, voice, physical strength, hairiness, and cranial capacity. Psychic differences are no less important, if only on account of the maternal role, which *Homo sapiens* has expanded to the point of requiring almost exclusive specialization. If necessary, female anthropoid apes can hunt, defend a territory, attack an enemy; the women of prehistory and protohistory no longer did this. Sexuality does not escape the dizzying gulf that lies between Humans and the animal. The woman lacks the imperious sexual instinct that still exists in the female cat in heat, although the man is far more highly sexed than the tomcat. All the opposites that animals have in only a sketchy state are pushed to the absolute limit in the Human. Absolute virility and absolute femininity generate each other.

One would think, therefore, that if Humanity is to evolve any further, human sexual characteristics will become more highly differentiated. Nothing could be more logical since two categories of beings are most necessary to each other when each has what the other lacks. How then can feminists wish men and women to be equal, when they do not have the same physical potentials, the same turns of mind, the same aspirations, or the same sensitivities? Until very recently, they have never even been interested in each other except in the commercial (which here means sexual) sense of the word *interest*. When the word *equality* is used in reference to the sexes (and not to general human rights, which may be encroached upon on grounds of race, sex, religion, nationality, and so on), it has no real meaning. If feminism, which is largely an ideology of resentment, envy, and competition, were to succeed in the impossible and convince women to seek not equality but identity with men, defeat and disappointment would be assured. The arts, science, technology, law, and philosophy—the whole of civilization—are an absolute male monopoly. To rebel against this *fact* is absurd; to understand it would be intelligent.

Once woman considers herself in second place, she has allowed herself to enter a competition of masculine origin, in which her second place can only be confirmed. This competition begins in the sexual sphere, where a passive role has come to be seen as a matter of dishonour. Feminine sexuality must be *equally* as active as the male—but it must be repressed. We have just seen that this explanation is unacceptable. Even if the woman were somehow able to restrain the man, say through fear of pregnancy before the invention of contraceptives, she would have made him homosexual or onanist —but not temperate. Besides, male sexuality is already a lengthy series of repressions. The man must learn to live in a maze of images that stimulate his desire without offering him any way out; he can protect himself only very imperfectly and only by becoming accustomed to them. This repression, repeated several times daily, produces all masculine weakness.

The so-called "women's liberation" movements contradict their own theories in another way when they organize sex strikes against male tutelage. Such strikes would be unimaginable for men, partly because women could break them so easily by seduction, partly because their deprivative effect would be doubtful. The absurd campaigns against brassieres—"we are not mere objects"—and beauty contests—"we are not dolls"—are based on the idea that a woman who stops keeping up her physical attractions will automatically acquire others. Behind this idea is an even worse cliché: women wish to be desired for themselves and not for their bodies—as though they desired men for themselves and not for the sexual monopoly that serves both men and women.

That the woman cannot desire the man for his body is perfectly understandable, even apart from her lack of extroverted sexuality. Aesthetically speaking, every human being, man or woman, desires tenderness. Now, tenderness is feminine. In any street or café, one can observe that men always look mainly at the women, while the women look mainly at each other. They do this primarily not out of rivalry but narcissism, in a positive sense. With their square, knotty physiques and dull dress that usually resembles an undertaker's or a gardener's, men do not provide much of a spectacle for women, whereas other women do. If feminine sexuality did not contain a large proportion of narcissism, the woman would never know sexual pleasure, for it is herself—and rightly so—that she can enjoy as she feels herself manipulated, desired, penetrated, aimed at as the ultimate never-attained objective. It takes all the rancour of feminism to see this as a secondary role, to give advantage to the seeker over the sought, to raise the Beast over Beauty. In fact, one can readily believe that the pretended emancipation of women is of sly masculine inspiration. The nature of what should be the harmony of the sexes is best expressed in the name *viola d'amore*, which was given to an old musical instrument in which, when each string was touched by the bow, another vibrated without being touched, through a phenomenon called "sympathy."

When militant women object to beauty contests, because *they* are not dolls, when they feel *themselves* turned into objects because their bodies are objects of lust, when they publish books with titles like *Our Bodies, Ourselves*, or when they refuse the services of male gynecologists as a violation of their *persons*, they are saying exactly what they are defending themselves against: the idea that a woman is primarily a *body*. One cannot imagine men invading a stadium and shouting "We are not machines," protesting against a cultural festival, or refusing the attentions of hospital nurses who might touch their sexual organs. Likewise, feminist antirape campaigns seem to stem from the idea that male justice does not punish rape severely enough. In fact, rape is generally punished more stringently than other forms of physical aggression, although it is no less humiliating, serious, or traumatic for a man to be beaten black and blue and then left lying on the sidewalk than it is for a woman to be raped. Where is the difference? In the victim's sex, naturally; what touches sex touches the soul. And feminism seeks to *strengthen* this dishonouring line of thought, through which the human race has always located its honour below its belts (except when they were chastity belts). "Our Bodies, Ourselves": once again we see that feminism is the result of male inspiration; that women are bodies certainly does not disturb men, who have been thinking that very thing for millions of years.

The problem would not exist if only one half of a couple tended to consider the other as an object, but that is exactly what *both* men and women do. To exercise a monopoly over a body is really to transform it into an object, and in itself a body is actually nothing but an object. A woman takes over not only a man's body but also his name, social position, future, and freedom—in short, his soul. For his part, the man does the same, so a couple is never formed except from two objects. But as I have already pointed out, when one possesses real objects, one would generally prefer sharing their ownership to seeing them crumble away, whereas sharing a partner is so unthinkable for most people that they would prefer seeing an unfaithful spouse dead. Only possessiveness—as the very word implies —treats a person as an object. If women were not possessive themselves, they would be justified in complaining about being possessed. But what they are complaining about is masculine sexuality itself, which they welcome when it transforms them into *monogamic* objects. Hence, the women's magazines contain so much advice on the subjects of erotic positions, conjugal stripteases, and skillfully calculated states of undress, all of which is openly designed, like cooking recipes, to "keep a husband." It goes without saying that he also knows a thousand methods of "keeping his wife": financial dependence, blackmail, and even violent demonstrations. In love, the two sexes vie with each other in everything, even nobility.

And since the man and the woman live together, this rivalry can only end in a balance of deceits that is strengthened by the envy each feels for the sexuality of the other. The man would like to make himself as independent as the woman of purely physical criteria; being totally unable to do so, he lies, both because he is ashamed of the instincts he harbours within him and because he needs to divert his partner's rancour and jealousy: "X is very pretty, but I do not desire her, because she looks so stupid," "Y is physically perfect, but I could never sleep with her because of her personality," "Z is aesthetically superb but sexually, she does nothing to me," "You're the only one I want," "Other women only interest me as something to look at." The man is forced into this kind of affectation a thousand times a day, under pain of sulks and stormy scenes.

For her part, the woman would like to experience the intensity of the masculine sexual drive, which she regards as a power though it is actually more a subordination. Hence she offers the same lie in converse form, which the man is quick to believe, only too happy to be desired for his body and to feel himself the object of an erotic passion rather than of a taste for conquest—especially when his body is the only one she desires, and, by the same miracle, the erotic power emanates from him alone. Why this game of spin-the-bottle with lies (apart from the jealousy and falsification so typical of the couple)? Because human beings compete, and if the sexes are not alike, it follows that one must be superior to the other. Since left is not right, since north is not south, since low is not high, it is necessary to classify them in order of preference, of importance, of excellence. If one says that the woman has a sexually (or, even generally) passive role, people understand "passive" to mean "inferior" since to be passive is to do nothing. No one will try to see that passivity is what *creates* activity and vice versa, or that that which is sought is neither superior nor inferior to that which seeks. In short, in any sphere, if each of two opposed realities contains its exact opposite in its very essence, it is absurd to ask oneself which is more important than the other.

It only remains to say that sexuality could be a pleasure whether its source is psychological or instinctual. Thus this pleasure could be unleashed in woman as quickly as it is in men if it were not monopolized by love jealousy. After all, monogamy is not a feminine invention, but simply a human one. The idea that the woman is essentially more possessive than the man is a Freudian aberration or prejudice. One has to regard sex as enormously important to make it the pretext or object of an established jealousy. It is primarily, if not solely, to masculine jealousy that we owe all the faults that stem from obsessional sexuality, for sexuality is simply not an obsession of women.

One must also note that although the past half century has seen a very modest liberalization of sexual mores, this change has kept pace with a very modest emancipation of women. Since the phrase *sexual revolution* does not make sense unless it means the end of all couples, all monopolies, and all cases of possessiveness with sex as their foundation and their guarantee, we now find ourselves up against the wall. Here man and woman are, for once, equal.

VII

When we tackle the vast historical problem of the feminine condition, the most immediate and the most tempting interpretation centers on the forcible enslavement of women. Such an explanation, however, though clearly accurate, is inadequate. Certainly abduction, rape, forced marriage, exercising the power of life and death, incarceration, threats, isolation in virginity, reduction to silence, and all kinds of distorting educational processes are sprinkled throughout the history of Humankind, especially in its beginnings. Certainly even today, everything that could make women independent is shackled, sometimes with the assistance of women themselves, by the thousands of discriminations that are called "sexism" (a term all the more apposite in that, like the word "racism" from which it is copied, it can be employed in two contrary senses). Certainly masculine domination extends from scandalous inequalities in pay to restrictive job offers. And certainly men seem to have obtained domination by the use of physical force. But physical force has actually played only a minor role in this part of History. Today's reality depends on a much less controllable force, that of *things,* which gives men a cohesion that women could not have and did not wish to have until now.

No force is needed to compel a female to play her biological role, yet from any evolutionary viewpoint, it is this role that has ended up (and not begun) being constricting. Physical inferiority has never stopped a group of men from using other means to gain power. The slaves of antiquity used Christianity to free themselves: they had no physical preeminence at their disposal. Nearly all human elites have based their power on something other than muscular strength. If force were Humankind's only instrument of domination, matriarchy would never have been possible. In fact, the superiority of human frailness goes back for millennia; the animal species that would one day dominate the world could be called "the weak species" in imitation of a phrase applied to women not so long ago.

Among the mammals closest to the Human, the female is rarely as physically inferior to the male as in the case with *Homo sapiens*. The human female submits to the male (who very rarely uses force against her), but her submission ends and may even be reversed when it is a question of defending her young. It can be said that all sexual disequilibrium stems from this biological distribution.

During the earliest days of humanity, there was, on the one hand, the orderliness of family, cloister, stability, unity. On the other hand —the male hand—was the domain of the open, the exterior, instability, multiplicity. Hunting, harvesting, and fishing were already collective activities, so men were used to collaborating in a way for which women had no need. Little by little civilization was born from men's community; male activity developed indefinitely, while the female role remained stable, closed, perfected. Thus, it was the division of women from each other, in addition to their instinctive conservatism, that came to form part of what is meant by femininity, not only in the Human Being, but throughout the whole of creation. If, by some miracle, the women of Greek or Roman antiquity had wished to free themselves of male tutelage, their lack of solidarity would have prevented them from managing to do so.

The gigantic computer that constitutes the human brain requires lengthy programming. This programming is the work of the woman, and since human infancy lasts for some fourteen years, we find that the feminine condition, right from the start, coincided completely with the maternal condition. Since it is women who passed on the working knowledge from which every civilization developed, it is obvious that they have always had the same civilizing instinct as men. But in order to ensure simple survival of the species, they had to live withdrawn into the bosoms of their families, each isolated from her fellow women, each condemned to watch herself creating worlds in the most absolute passivity.

Now the game is over. All culture, all sciences, all arts, all philosophies, all religions are masculine creations. The more one tries to include women within these settings (which, fortunately, they do not recognize as their own), the more they are justified in saying that they are being allotted a secondary role. But on the other hand, women now know only too well that the importance of maternity, like that of the family, is continually shrinking, that motherhood is not true creation, and that their bodies are being used only as a relay through which Life passes of necessity. So today's woman is in a quandary. If she rejects everything masculine, she condemns herself to a return to prehistory, the very origin of her woes; if she accepts competition with the man, she brings the game's results into question at the very moment it is completed. For even supposing that from today onwards one scientist, one artist, one philosopher out of two were a woman, that every profession became female, the balance would not be reestablished. But the word *balance* is ridiculous here.

The conservatism and restrictiveness of the familial and maternal functions are necessarily doubled by financial bondage, which is all the more treacherous in that the woman is continually tempted to profit by it—hence the parasitism surrounding a rich husband, hence a thousand kinds of gilded cages, hence the way a woman can always play the role of spoilt child however much she may lack beauty. Moreover, for a woman to devote herself to a profession *and* maintain a family is to have two burdens instead of one, to be unable to bear either of them completely, and to have to be content with a double second place.

Furthermore, if it really is marriage and the family that enslave the woman, most real women regard their slavery as an ideal. What other sort of slavery is lived so well? And does the woman not consent to it, even seek it? From adolescence or even childhood, the woman values marriage and the couple much more highly than does the man. It is putting a false alternative to ask whether this is so because other paths are lacking or whether other paths are lacking because this is so. Here, education has been grafted onto Nature, and both now go in the same direction. Although monogamy is certainly not female in essence, the man who imposes it is incapable of treating it as an instinct, while the woman instinctively turns it to much better account. For him, monogamy is exteriorized; for her, it is interiorized. The two interests, exterior and interior, coincide.

Once again we see that sexual division is more logical than biological. But now we have reached the point where it is necessary to connect this division to the primary duality that governs both the material world and the universe of the mind.

We know that every concept has its opposite, by which it is defined. High/Low, Convex/Concave, Day/Night—it is impossible to think of one member of these couples (or pairs) without thinking of the other. One member is implicit in the other, the inverse being, on the whole, a mirror in which every reality rests on its exact opposite —its reflected image.

Now, when people think of the two couples High/Low and Convex/Concave, everyone connects High with Convex, and Low with Concave. The human mind perceives the relationship in outline before it is explained—if, indeed, a logical explanation exists. In what way does that which is concave relate to that which is low rather than high? If we arrange the two couples in columns:

Convex   Concave
High   Low

we can say that the linkages shown horizontally are *logical* relationships, while those shown vertically are *analogical*. Now, an analogical relationship is the result of concluding that because two things have *one* characteristic in common, they have *others* or are even completely identical. From the viewpoint of reasoned logic, this conclusion is false, an elementary error, a perfect example of hasty thinking. But this kind of conclusion is also the basis of all thought since the human mind works through resemblances; every idea and even every element of language is a general concept that assembles resemblances: *house, me, dog,* describe all houses, all me's, all dogs. Thus, the analogy (which is a synonym for resemblance in this context) forms the basis of thought, and thereby marks the genesis of the individual as much as that of the species.

But within the human mind, the analogy is not restricted to primitive or childish thought. It reappears when a reasoned explanation would be lengthy or impossible; it serves as a resource or shortcut, sometimes by virtue of its power of shock (which it owes to its very abridgement—hence the expression "a striking shortcut"). The savage or the child may think that the moon *is* the sun in another form while poetry says "the moon is the sun of the night"; what the former took for reason, the latter uses for perfectly valid, insightful comparison. In other words, analogy reigns where logic does not yet reign, then reigns again when logic can no longer reign—in the realms of art and mysticism.

It is the latter function that interests us here. The more couples we have that are logically opposed but analogically superimposed, the better the cumulative analogies help to express the richness of each term. Concepts that are apparently completely foreign to each other converge in relationships of resonance or harmony, just as a line gradually becomes a drawing, or as the separate notes of a chord justify themselves by one another.

Analogy operates from one end of our mental world to the other and consequently, throughout the actual world itself: from letters to figures, from colours to sounds. Our sibilant S is written in serpentine form; our O resembles a mouth articulating; our V, which resembles a pair of wings, functions almost like onomatopoeia in the words *Vivacious, Volatile, Volition;* M, which closes the mouth, plays the same analogical role in the words *Murder, Murky, Malediction.* The word *mama* vaguely recalls an act of sucking, like the word *mammary;* the word *papa* evokes the P of *Power.* In Arabic numerals, the zero and the one form respectively a hole and a figure standing upright, while the six and the nine, each the converse of the other, are associated by all the hermetic philosophies with the begetting of the universe in the shape of the number *sixty-nine,* which is also the symbol of the zodiacal Cancer. All this, of course, must be taken in the same poetic sense as Baudelaire's *Correspondences* (the italics are mine):

Nature is a temple in which living pillars
Sometimes allow *confused* words to escape.
Man walks there through forests of symbols
Which watch him with familiar eyes.

These multiple correspondences form a symbolism, with the same dangers but the same potential as analogies. The Greek *symbolos* means literally "with throw," or, going through the Latin, *conjecture*. The converse of the symbol in Greek is *diabolos* (the diabolic, the devil), which is that which unties or separates (the word, it must be added, has come to mean the "calumniator" or even the "liar"). Now, as we have seen, the function of *intelligence* (*intelligere* in Latin: "to bring together within") is to bring things together. And to bring things *back* together (which presupposes that they do go together even though they have been separated) is, in the most noble sense, the role of a *r*eligion (*religare*, Latin: "to retie"). The Roman emperor, head of the official Roman religion, was called *pontifex maximus* (Latin: "chief builder of bridges"), a term recalled today in the Roman Catholic Church's "pontiff." Thus, the universe is supposed to be a *text*—a *tissue* or *textile*. It is useless to try to explain these etymological connections; words themselves are symbols, and their source is all the more analogical because it is primitive.

The analogies for the couple Feminine/Masculine are what interests us here. It seems to me that one of the richest series of correspondences would be the following:

Feminine	Masculine
Left	Right
Orient (East)	Occident (West)
Soul	Matter
Liquid	Solid
Curving	Straight
Unity	Plurality
Passivity	Activity
Lunar	Solar
Time	Space
Zero	One
Even	Odd

Night	Day
Matter	Mind
Negative	Positive
Closed	Open
Interior	Exterior

Before examining this table, which one could spin out to the limit of one's vocabulary, it is important to state its use very precisely: the analogies shown in the vertical columns can only be enunciated by proportions; thus, Feminine is to Masculine *as* Matter is to Mind. The absurd idea that the woman is more material than the man is one of the numerous prejudices that stems from the perpetual analogical trap. Prejudices and analogy are so close as to be *almost* identical because historically analogy appeared before logic and thus before judgement (it pre-judges). Hence comes the idea that what is on the left is bad (sinister), the identification of the night with evil ("nocturnal," "noxious"), the feeling that the material is inferior to the spiritual, and so on. Each is an instance of taking similar poles in two different spheres and concluding that the spheres are identical—which is precisely what the table does not do. If it did, why should One, which appears in the righthand column in relation to Zero, turn up as Unity in the lefthand column in relation to Plurality? Why should Matter switch columns depending on whether it is in the couple Soul/Matter or Matter/Mind? How could Time appear on the left, in the same column as Matter, while Space is on the right, even though Matter appears to be more spatial than temporal? Thus, all value judgements based on such a table are necessarily false. To make a value judgement is to apply the criteria Bad/Good, Ugly/Handsome, or False/True horizontally—in other words, to allow the ethical, aesthetic, or logical domains to encroach upon territories that are foreign to them. If the lefthand column contains Ugly, Bad, or False, it is solely because *within its own couple*, each is the point from which one must start. But just as ethics, aesthetics, and logic do not allow either condition or limit, it is always tempting to extend their domain everywhere, to identify the night as ugly, bad, false, and so on and so forth. However, the slightest extension of this sort removes all value from the symbolism we are dealing with here.

It is also worth noting that the couples Left/Right and Orient/ Occident (or East/West) are more than merely relative (although my left is your right, my east your west). Kant marvelled at this: although left and right are impossible to define in space without reference to an observer, nevertheless they do have an objective, spatial existence; there are lefthanded spirals and righthanded spirals that cannot be superimposed one on top of the other. Like our two hands, they match only face to face so the universe has a left and a right independent of any subject, or as though it were a subject itself.

Likewise, it is curious that the ideas of east and west go beyond geographic rationality to function as almost universal symbols. The Chinese do not call the Americans "Orientals" or "Easterners," although geography gives them the right to do so, and we term ourselves "The West" or "Westerners" without any objective reason. Japan, as its flag signifies, is the "Land of the Rising Sun" though the sun does not rise there any more than it does anywhere else; Korea is the "Country of the Morning Calm"; Indian thinking frequently proclaims itself "oriental." Thus, East and West seem to be categories that are predominantly spiritual, so to speak.

The left is the side of what is new, still in a state of vagueness and unity; a child is "left," as is any other beginning. Soldiers always start their march with the left foot. Although the human heart is almost in the center of the thoracic cage, everyone feels it lies on the left side of the body, partly because everything that the heart feels is felt first on the left, partly because our regenerated blood shoots out to our left. The German word for left, *links*, is derived from a root meaning "vacillating, relaxed, languid," while the French *gauche* comes from *gauchir* ("to give way"), which is related in Old French to *quenchior* ("to swerve, to make detours, to curve"). Now the root of the word *orient* is related to that of the French verb *errer* ("to wander"): the languid, the relaxed, the curving, the indirect, are associated with what is "oriental," as they are with what is feminine. Likewise, the connotation of liquid is more "curving" than "straight," and we find liquid in the lefthand or feminine column. There, too, we find Unity, and liquid is not readily divisible because its parts melt into each other. (Solidity, on the other hand, is plural; solid parts lie side by side.)

The Temple of Solomon is a common symbol of the perfect Universe; the Templars, who had had it from the dark night of ages past, handed it on to the first Freemasons. It carries the letters B and J, which are considered to represent both Woman and Man (Boas and Jachin) and the prophecy: "I shall establish my reign." The B column is on the left. When the J column represents the Sun, the B column symbolizes the Moon: and when J relates to the Cosmos, B relates to Earth. Let us also note, with the same curiosity, this statement of Parmenides: "Girls are on the left, and boys are on the right."

The daily course of the sun starts in the east and ends in the west. History itself also begins in the Orient and ends in the Occident, achieving what Hegel calls the "Day of the Mind"; at the beginning, there is nothing but the mass, at the end nothing but the individual —just as the rising sun emerges as an ensemble, which then subdivides into infinity. Here we see the primary opposition of Eastern unity and Western plurality. Individualism, an attitude and an idea particularly Western in concept, leads to the West's conceiving solidarity as the result of an effort on the part of every human being—it is something secondary, something acquired by reflection, something as difficult to create as to uncreate. Thus, too, a solid is hard to break, but, once broken, it does not return spontaneously to its original state. Oriental unity is the converse, like the unity of liquid; it is primal, native, and natural. Thus the predisposition of the Chinese and Japanese for the communal life can easily be interpreted as a lack of taste or talent for individualism. The Greeks noticed this characteristic early on in Oriental armies (in particular, the Persians); they fought as though each soldier had no existence of his own but only followed the emperor, the unique (of course) image of the unity of the group, as a termite follows its queen blindly. Thus, Xenophon tells us, killing the emperor was enough to put the whole army to flight. The same rule holds good for the originally Oriental game of chess (*checkmate* is the Western form of the Arabic *Shah mata,* which means "The Shah is dead"): corner the King, and all is lost. Furthermore, in this game, it is the Queen that has the greatest power.

This tendency as a well-blended (or not yet disassociated) mass characterizes a number of Oriental languages that are called agglutinative (fusive) or *mono*syllabic (nondisassociative) as well as writing in ideograms, the ultimate blending of the symbol with the idea represented. It also appears in the major religions of the Orient. (All religions, in fact, are of Oriental ancestry, and the very essence of religion, which seeks to be all-inclusive, stable, foremost, and irremovable, reflects what I have just been saying about the Orient.) All is God, God is All, All is One: these three mottoes are almost enough to define pantheism, which still reigns over Asia. It was the Greeks who began to separate the gods; the differentiation of their powers immediately caused conflicts (whence comes the multitude of intimate stories in Classical mythology); finally comes the divinization of the Individual, which is the Christ. From its earliest days, this progression bore the stamp of the Occident, pending the time when analysis (division) would invade theology as it did everything else, culminating in Science and thus marking the rest of the world with the Occidental stamp. The West divides in order to rule.

We see here an act of authority or power. Now, all the connotations of Power are those of the Right, of the Masculine, of the Occidental. The words *rigour, direction, erection, right, rule, regime, royalty, rigidity* all concern the Male, and are all etymologically associated with *rea-*, the root of the Latin word for "right." The left, on the contrary, is original—*origin* and *orient* come from the same Latin verb *oriri* (to rise, to begin). Even in politics, the ideal of the left is fusion within the mass, the human unity (and equality) that is the theme of the Orient. The political senses of "left" and "right" may seem fortuitous (they reflect the distribution of the blocks of seats in the French Revolutionary assemblies), but in reality they are obeying the laws of analogy, just as language does. The right is perfected, and thus rigid, and thus conservative; the left is new, and thus revolutionary.

The relationships between the Orient and Woman are, of course, innumerable. The oldest eastern religions have a woman as their supreme deity; when Indian Hindus speak of the "Mother," they are discussing God. Oriental architecture insists on sinuosity, irregular curves, and convex walls. At first hearing, Western ears find Oriental music both *mono*tonous (or *uni*form) and languorous; it plays on imperceptible nuances and caressing modes and may seem vague ("left"), interminable, introverted, indefinite, and liquid. *Lascivious* was applied as often to the Orient as to women up to the time of the Renaissance; the Oriental woman still symbolizes absolute femininity, perhaps because one sees in her the passive gentleness, the inner mystery, the introversion, and the softness in which the symbolic Orient and the symbolic Feminine are united. (The Occident has never dreamed up women, mythicized or mythical, who resemble the houris, the almahs, or the odalisques.) The Oriental emphasis on the One in relation to the Multiple appears in the very biology of women: an ovum is a unique, stable, undifferentiated, closed cell that millions of spermatozoa approach until one—and only one—attains its objective, after which the ovum immediately closes itself to all the others. It would be impossible to find a more accurate analogy for the way males, animal and human alike, compete for the conquest of a single female. The spermatozoa behave as though they were in groups, while the solitary ovum awaits them; the ovum, like the woman, is the pole that is desired, while the spermatozoon is the pole that desires; the ovum is globular, the spermatozoon elongated. The ovum is passive, the spermatozoon active and thus, by definition, imbalanced, since it lacks that which it desires. In relation to the woman, the man is eternally in a state of need, of incompleteness, of lack because he desires her body as a body and the converse is not true.

One last analogous relationship between the Orient and the Feminine is their air of mystery, which glorifies them both. (Notice that both are in the Interior column; a mystery is something that does not reveal itself outwardly.) We find the Chinese mysterious and, in a general way, consider Orientals as "devious" people, as "dissimulators"—in short, as *doubles*. So, too, are women (who are in the Even—and thus double—column), even if what is mysterious about them is first and foremost their simplicity. If a woman is predominantly fascinated by another woman, it is primarily because feminine nature has a narcissistic component, a portion of shadow (column of the Closed and of Night). Then, too, this nature implies a certain amount of immobility, of conservatism, of self-sufficiency, which means that in a certain sense a woman sees a duplicate of herself in the other woman, from whom she can differentiate herself only by repelling her. Two beings who are complete do not really need one another; two beings who are equally reticent know that they are reticent without knowing about what, so their first relationship is one of suspicion. The fact that solidarity has no natural or historical support in the world of women does not negate its Oriental fusion of the individual within the mass. The relationship is between the Orient and the *Feminine,* not between the Orient and *women.*

Herein lies the justification for the presence of the Zero in the lefthand column and the One in the right. The written forms themselves are symbolic: 0 is a circle, or, more precisely, an oval, an egg shape representing the perfect closed figure, while 1 is a straight line. In a certain sense each woman, perfect in herself, represents all women; so Zeros add nothing to other numbers, whereas Ones add together to give all other numbers. In multiplication Zero is absorptive (the adjective has an obvious feminine connotation) since it reduces any multiplicand to itself, exactly like the Negative, which is located in the same column. (Notice, though, that neither is a nothing, since both do perform actions.)

This conglomeration of Ones is the Multiple, which, as we have seen, is associated with the Occident, the Right, and the Masculine. By the very fact of their incompleteness, males have been induced to units. Their solidity/solidarity is the basis of the masculine ideals of Friendship and Fraternity and extends from hunting to civilizing conquests (all the sphere of the Exterior, which is located in the righthand column, as is Space in relation to Time). Thus, it underlies all our social structures. Women are supposed to suffer from a castration complex (definitely one of the most platitudinous ideas of psychoanalysis—which, as we shall see, is not saying much). In fact, men's sexual organs leave them in such a state of imbalance that only by joining forces have they managed to achieve an exterior superiority that does not breech the feminine ideal, which is internal. The Eternal Masculine is eternally *seeking* what the Eternal Feminine already *is.* And Passivity is also in the lefthand column.

Sometimes clichés are revealing. When we say that intuition (from the Latin for "inward looking") is feminine and reasoning is masculine, we cannot really mean that women are more intuitive than men. The history of art suggests the contrary (which is equally false.) Women do, however, place more importance than do men on the world of singularity or subjectivity, in which reason plays no part. Sensation, which is the basis of the purely subjective, is absolutely incommunicable, in contrast to concepts, the kernel of the purely objective (or general), which are common or communicate to many minds. If you understand "ten" to be something different from what I understand, I shall be aware of it. But if the two of us see different colours under the *same* colour names, we may never realize the difference exists. Similarly, when I hear Rimbaud's "Sonnet of the Vowels"—"A black, E white, I red, O blue, U green"—it seems to me that the poet either did not see colours or hear sounds as I do. I see A as deep blue or violet, E beige, I white, O a deep red, U a pale yellow. The poet's associate exercise is an attempt to universalize singularity. Such is the object of intuition, the domain of the Feminine (the Arts, as opposed to the Sciences, lie in the left-hand column). And the incommunicability of the singular and the intuitive reinforces still further the unity of Woman and the lack of solidarity of women.

The opposition of Matter and Spirit (Mind) is so obvious as to need little explication. Matter is related to the Mother (material/maternal), while *spiritus* means a breath (in-spire, re-spire, etc.), and *animus* comes from the Greek *anemos* ("wind"). It is the air, masculine in relation to the earth as fire is in relation to water—and the spirit is often compared to air or fire. Likewise, the Spirit is "active," whereas matter is passive, closed, impenetrable, obscure. Sensations, which have matter as their object, are interior, concepts are exterior. To call matter the exterior world, the speakers must already be at the interior of the world. Spirit is the absolutely Open, the absolutely unfolded, while Matter is wrapped up, solid, lying *behind* its appearance or at the *interior* thereof.

The idea of unfolding brings us to Space ("opened out" or "unfolded") in the righthand column and in the left. Time is that which flows, like liquid (in fact, liquid would be impossible to distinguish from solid if movement—and thus Time—did not exist). Time is One in the sense of not having several dimensions. Finally it is primal, representing the basis of all reality—for although we know phenomena which, like thought, can reach outside Space, nothing can go outside Time. When theology wants to describe a divine truth, it calls it timeless (the "eternal verities"), not spaceless. Impossible to represent, except by spatial figures or metaphors, Time is the Interior par excellence. Among the Arts, the most mysterious, especially Music, use Time as their material, while the plastic Arts have their being in Space; it was the former that Nietzsche described, with justification, as Dionysian or nocturnal (and one may add, naturally, feminine) because they engender a drunkenness that has movement as its principle, while he called the latter solar, rigid, Apollonian. Fluid, sinuous, interior, Music brings craziness, dancing, irrepressible, pell-mell emotion; it is the Feminine art of Nature— and the registers that dominate its song are to be found nearly always in the feminine *tessitura*. It has a woman's voice. The Sirens could not have been men, any more than could the Muses. In the same way that Time logically precedes Space, hearing precedes sight. It is humanity's feminine dimension—nocturnal, irrational, primordial. A vision of the world must satisfy understanding, but understanding can do without vision. The deaf are more shut in than the blind, not because deafness is linked with mutism, but because the universe of the blind is a radio drama while that of the deaf is an uncaptioned silent film, something unbearable and, indeed, absurd. The auditive universe is like a bridge thrown between Spirit and Matter; it is already real even though it is still only internal. We carry Time, not Space, within us—that is why a deaf musician can become a Beethoven, while a blind painter cannot be a painter at all. For the living, hearing is essential. Life can put up with obscurity, which engulfs only the exterior world, better than it can silence, which would engulf Life itself. Light can blind, but sound can kill or send us mad. "The world of silence" is strangeness, "the silence of death," terror. Pascal did not say that sidereal distances terrified him, but that their "eternal silence" frightened him. Enigma hides itself, but mystery is silent.

Once again biology bears witness to reality in a fashion both real and symbolic (and hence more than real). It does so yet again in the distinctive chromosomes of the two sexes. Those of the women are labelled XX—in other words, the same unit duplicated—while the man has an XY pair, asymmetrical and thus unbalanced. If the Masculine desire the Feminine, the latter thereby desires itself. And since narcissism results from a splitting into two, the woman is double in her essence even more deeply than in such exterior signs as the two erogenous zones (the clitoral—physical—and the vaginal

—psychic), her twofold role of lover and mother, or the two hormones, estrogen and progesterone, that preside over the menstrual cycle. Not to mention the duplicity (literally "doubleness") so often attributed to the feminine character. The idea of splitting into two also relates to Even in the lefthand column. Even is that which engenders—for to engender there must be two. The words *pair, parallel, parent, viviparous, oviparous* are of the same family, and after an etymological detour, the word *part* appears again in *parturition.*

The couple Moon/Sun in my list may seem anecdotal, but it is none the less significant for that—after all, myths are anecdotes. (We could even add Cat/Dog, animals that appear in the oldest "sciences" of dreams as female and male symbols respectively. The Cat, physically handsome, unpredictable, anticollective, oriental, and nocturnal is opposed by the Dog, physically rather unattractive, inclined to social play, roughly demonstrative.) In fact, the relationships between the Female and the Moon are particularly fascinating because they seem to pass from analogy into biology. The Moon has a cycle of twenty-eight days; so does the female menstrual cycle on average. From time immemorial, being moonstruck has been associated with universal feminine characteristics. This association is not without foundation: the woman varies not with the moon but because she is influenced by two opposing hormones: estrogen, which is erotogenic, and progesterone, which prepares her for maternity. The Moon is stable—or constant in its cycles, but each is a succession of changes. Its indirect light is more a halo than a beam; its rays are caressing, pale, unobtrusive; its hidden face is merely the most obvious of its mysteries.

In brief, everything I have put in my lefthand column is primary. The Right is an amended Left, the Occident is a modified Orient, Plurality is Unity divided. Every beginning is the Negation of that which preceded it; the negative creates the positive, not the converse (a positive number combined with another positive can never give anything different, but two negatives multiplied together yield a positive). Nothing is more bizarre than the Biblical myth according to which woman was created from man and after him. Morphologically, the woman is younger than the man; she resembles the Child in her size, her voice, the smallness of her organs. Now, from the universal viewpoint, the oldest and the youngest are one (in the same way, for example, that the civilization of the Ancient Greeks is younger than ours). Symbolically, this means that fluidity, suppleness, interior abundance—which are the attributes of the Woman— are also those of Youth. A world that wishes to rejuvenate itself must first *feminize* itself, in the most noble sense of the word, if only by becoming receptive. Feminine nature, which is gentle and peaceful, execrates violence and rape, could play against wars, brawls, and competition the role that Aristophanes once assigned it as a joke. What we see today is the opposite; women know how to achieve solidarity *against* men and *like* men. Yet if solidarity could find a feminine meaning, it would be one of the greatest triumphs that a human community could achieve over its instincts—or rather over their absence. Rather than creating a mere exterior sharing, it would give birth to a warm and intimate society; it would no longer aim solely at communication but at communion.

In the absence of such communion, we must add the reciprocal rancour of the sexes to the mutual swindle called "love," to the cold war between couples, to the juxtaposition of sexual possessiveness, to the balance of the lie between the Woman and the Man. In our fascination with competition, we have refused the dualism of the universe as manifested by the sexes, which should be maintaining and even refining it. As a result of this refusal, we are headed for a world in which only masculine values will hold sway, a world that will be stiff, rigid, and conservative in all senses of the terms, a world that will have lost its own essence, and that will run for ever in neutral, far from its Orient—*disoriented.*

THE MUSEUM
OF THE FORGERS

I

To fight against a part of Leviathan is to fight for Leviathan as a whole. Whatever reigns by disorder and dispersion has nothing to fear from order dispersed. Thus, if one denounces psychiatric hospitals here, multinational corporations there, prostitution somewhere else, torture in *one* country and pollution in another, each time one is behaving as though, with the whole world flooded, nothing were more important than stopping the inundation in Chicago or Zambia alone. Every partial criticism of our world is an act of treason, even if global criticism is ineffective. Taking no action is better than collaborating with absolute Evil, preaching the impossible truth is preferable to trying to put a little truth into lies. Prolonging an agony is worse than doing nothing at all.

A society in which theft, swindling, competition, bluff, and egotism are already firmly rooted has little need of people planting them. The information given us and the culture imposed on us are more effects than causes, so it is not surprising that the facts themselves have refuted everything that has been written against them up till now. For example, demanding the suppression of schools is tantamount to calling for the individual sovereignty of the family. Establishments such as the British Summerhill schools give children a freedom that appears revolutionary, but, for this very reason, it has proved a ruse. In a mercantile, competitive, and police-oriented society, a school paradise merely prepares youngsters for yet another shock. What is the point of decorating a concentration camp entrance with flowers?

The schoolless society offers children the choice between home and the street; the society of the school appears to give them the means of escaping both while in reality it plunges them into both. The school incorporates both street and home in meaningful anticipation of the world of work: discipline, schedules, output. How can teachers do more than camouflage these principles, which govern their own existence? They are responsible for the bridge that leads from one jail to another; all they can hope to do is arrange a painless transfer of the prisoner. Family, Culture, Work represent a chronological cycle. *Culture* has the same etymological root as *agriculture*; it is a vegetable garden when it is oriented to vocational success, a flower garden when it is aimed at nonvocational achievement. In both cases, it must *produce*. Schools apply Bacon's "Knowledge is power" to the letter, and the letter is made to kill the mind.

Both the Platonic notion of the identity of evil and ignorance, and the nineteenth century illusion of Culture as a spontaneous creator of morals are at heart the same as our ideas, except Evil today consists in not succeeding and the morality that has success as its ultimate end uses Culture as its first means. Hugo's fine formula, "To open a school is to close a prison," is somewhat unfortunate. The only thing that a closed prison and an opened school have in common is leading to the opening of a factory or an unemployment office.

School imposes, even on the youngest children, what will be the rhythm of the adults' life. First, there are regular schedules; the children have to get used to them, so the sooner they start the better. Even nursery schools penalize late arrivals. Then there is discipline. The children must ask permission to go to the toilet, to get a pencil, to change places; they may not ask a question unless they first raise their hand. Classes are organized geometrically whenever possible, and pupils assemble in front of the main entrance, usually in ranks like soldiers. Sometimes the parallel goes so far as the wearing of uniforms. Again like soldiers, the children are led in group singing on every possible occasion. Any children who give in to urges to communicate are labelled on their report card as disrespectful, inattentive, and talkative. What a timely preparation for mutism and obedience, two cardinal virtues in the factory and office. Meanwhile the school allots good and bad marks: objects of competition and guarantees of later family punishments.

The kindergarten curriculum uses songs, counting-out rhymes, games, and picture books to teach the child to respect Daddy and Mommy—in other words, both Authority and the Couple. They also hear a lot of silly talk about Nature, family life (obviously), and society, all presented in infantile, aseptic, asexual form. In the days of Pascal and Mozart, one spoke to children seriously and treated them as adults as quickly as possible, with no fear that they would thereby lose their innocence; today, we find the idea of a child composing a symphony both monstrous and melancholy. The ideal of "letting the child blossom" is equated with play and freedom from care, but it scarcely veils a more Machiavellian motive: the child in full bloom is one kept longest from the reality of the world. We think it a pity for children to be overoccupied with serious problems, but we do not fear inculcating them with the things that make the serious aspect of the world so overwhelming. Primary school is too early for the Sciences, the Arts, or Philosophy, but not for schedules, grades, and discipline. By the time children are five or six years of age, recess and free-play periods have taught them how work and leisure are different and complementary. Even before they receive formal grades, they learn how to play their part in the great competition of Life. To win the approval of their teacher and their parents, they have to do better—in other words, conform better— than their neighbour. Thus, right from the start, school undermines any real mutual aid. Even in instances of apparent cooperation, such as painting collective murals or so-called group activities, the whole point is to learn how to distinguish oneself.

Next comes the only important part of the scholastic labyrinth: learning the methods of learning. Reading, writing, and arithmetic are the bases. The children who read poorly become ashamed in front of the others and read even more poorly. The ones who make an error at the blackboard and persist in starting their arithmetic problem afresh are the butt of enough gibes to ensure that they never again persist in anything. Nothing is worse than delaying a whole class and thereby getting all its attention—naturally malevolent. Gradually the sheep form one group, the goats another.

Whether the teacher uses labels or not, all children always know which they are. As long as the finish line exists, one cannot do away with the race by concealing the order of merit; even if it is not laid down from above, it appears quite spontaneously.

One of the early ambitions of mandatory public education was to remove the children from the influence of their family, especially from their social condition. The influence of families as financial powers has since become blurred, but not that of the Family in general, as is shown by the frequency with which parents intervene with teachers and by the power of parents' associations even in the realm of curricula. Collaboration between Family and School has never been closer; parents sometimes become substitute teachers, and teachers deputy parents.

And despite the ideal of public education, social classes always turn up in school classes. The rich children stand out by virtue of their dress, their speech, their common acquaintances, and so on, and they inevitably band together. I hardly need add that they succeed better than the other pupils, partly because they take special lessons and can allow themselves a series of failures without their families' urging them to choose professions immediately. Even more, it is because they bear the stamp of a milieu in which success calls for knowledge. They are the other face of the pedagogical axiom that knowledge brings success.

Of course, this knowledge contains some ideology; most frequently it is nothing but ideology. What begins as songs and nursery rhymes carries on into the most apparently neutral assignments: "A man buys 100 hectares of land at 2 dollars per square meter, then sells 50 of them at 8 dollars per square meter; what is his profit?" "The bank finances projects, the contractor carries them out." "Calculate the interest earned on X dollars deposited for Y years at a rate of Z%," etc. Pupils learn the purpose of courts, councils, legislatures, and laws (as though it were clear that they serve any purpose at all). Geography becomes political economy, and both are an introduction to the game of grab with its international competition for mineral resources, industry, and per capita income; History provides all the moral lessons the scholar needs: the decline of Rome can be linked to decadent morality rather than to Roman imperialism; the excesses of the French Revolution can be minimized or attributed to the maneuvers of the émigré nobility, and so on and so forth. What tells everything justifies everything.

Hypocrisy and shame reach their peak, naturally enough, in sex education courses. The simple fact that this education seems to be necessary shows that the matter is a serious one; here is the only source of pleasure that must be approached cautiously and that is not a matter of course. There are several approaches. The aim of one is to make children think that sexuality is nothing special, so it presents the sexual organs as being as interesting as the knee (the children, of course, establish straightway how many knees interest censorship or even themselves). Another treats children's curiosity about a forbidden pleasure as if that curiosity were anatomical and the mechanics of sex equivalent to those of the small intestine; this approach offers physiology courses complete with sectional drawings of oviducts, nipples, sperm-bearing canals, and Daddy and Mommy coupling mechanically strictly for purposes of procreation. A third approach diverts all the "mystery of life" (for it is through sex, not the reproduction of DNA, that Life is mysterious) onto innocent ducks or lambs, always monogamous naturally, that impregnate each other through affection and not for pleasure.

As this information—or any other—is dished out to twenty or thirty pupils, it crumbles under side comments, threats, questions, coughs, and general idleness. And since what the teacher says is rarely more than a poor rehash of what is already in the textbooks, the hours in class boil down to hours of copying, seasoned with disciplinary actions. Everyone learns infinitely better alone, following his or her own rhythms, than in a herd that is forced to follow the thread of an oral presentation that, even if is logical, would be more so in a textbook. Anyway, there is no question of *learning* in class, merely of noting what has to be learnt at home. But if the students were allowed to study alone, they might learn how to learn. All adults ought to be able to assimilate almost any material by themselves, but few can do so because they had no chance to develop this ability as children. Such autonomy would not be welcome in the classroom because it would be tantamount to originality; instead of thirty stereotypes delivered by thirty automatons, it would mean some thirty different types of scholarship, impossible to pass through the same sieve and thus uncontrollable. What one learns by oneself, one generally learns with pleasure and rarely forgets. The school is definitely no enemy of forgetfulness (which is almost obligatory, given the volume of "knowledge" that must be accumulated for each series of examinations), and it is quite pitiless towards pleasure. Yet it is not frightened by imagination—as long as it is the same for everybody.

From this point of view alone, education is an enormous exercise in time wasting that grows steadily worse from nursery school to university. Apart from a few hours of laboratory work in disciplines such as chemistry or physics, all the time spent in class seems to serve no purpose other than justifying the existence of teachers. One need only know how to read to complete all sorts of studies, and the modern tidal wave of specialized work and the standardization of scientific knowledge have removed the scholastic institution's last *raison d'être*. Teaching set theory on the blackboard is no more than an excuse to maintain obedience, perpetuate schedules, and treat students like stenotypists in the service of tedious repetition and mediocrity.

The secondary schools and colleges propound the value of a "well-rounded education" or "general culture." Its unity, as dished out by departments of bureaucrats, is exemplified by its fragmented methods. Students must be interested in the Greek philosophers at half-past eight, take a German test at ten, and enthuse over the chemistry of minerals about noon. They soon learn that what counts is one's grades, and that as the appearance of knowledge is sufficient (since knowledge must be an appearance), they must think less and memorize more. Every subject is best studied an hour before a test and forgotten an hour afterwards. If school is a preparation for living in society, it is because, like society, it encourages fraud, false pretenses, conformism, and baseness. The good students must be the very prototype of plodding cowards and competitive flunkeys, without tastes or distastes, objections or preferences. They must succeed everywhere, like everything, agree with everything. Above all, they must have no new ideas, for they can only spring from doubts and so must be paradoxical (in Greek, *para-dox* means "counteropinion"). A paradox is a fantasy, doubt comes from questioning, and questioning is a scholastic delay. Being a successful student boils down to doubting as little as possible—which is a definition of imbecility—and to playing the game of a penal institution—which is a characteristic of cowardice.

Everyone agrees, at least to some extent, that scholastic success equals intelligence. The word is used here in the same sense as in "intelligence test." In this definition, intelligence means knowing how to solve a given number of geometrical and logical problems in a minimum of time (thus artists are not intelligent, but all *idiots savants* are). When the students face their mountain of homework, it matters little that they have no wish to do it, that they are so distraught that their hands are clammy, or that they would prefer to take the time to study things thoroughly. The prime virtue of scholastic intelligence is superficiality; it is the virtue of computers, which also work on automatic memory. It uses all sorts of ridiculous but convenient rules. For example, the good student blithely says that if $a + b = c$, than $a = c - b$ *because* a term changes sign when it crosses the equal sign. The true explanation, that the same quantity has been subtracted from two equal quantities, is cumbersome. The good student therefore chooses the memory-jogger thousands upon thousands of times. School prompts one to think in stupid terms. Yet one must be prepared for surprise tests, held to outwit the automatism of routine preparation, that have the form, content, and spirit of a police raid.

Then come the examinations: timidity, funk, clumsiness, depression, exhaustion can mean nothing now. One must march in step and know how to present arms. Girls and boys aged sixteen, eighteen, or twenty (ages at which freedom would be dangerous) study up to ten hours a day, spend sleepless nights, anguish over a tenth of a mark—and are then required to give examples of Montaigne's serenity. This sort of thing seems quite normal to professors, who are themselves overworked. Under these conditions, they ask their students to become interested in what they are trying to drive into their heads, but the sort of conformism they take for interest is a carbon copy of their own recapitulation of the subject.

Even if school were abolished, some people claim, it would be necessary to retain examinations in order to regulate and record each young person's progress in knowledge. But why is it necessary to regulate knowledge? Teaching is aimed at filtering out the elite, and the only aim of the elite is money and hence power. If salaries for all kinds of jobs were equal, who would be interested in one for which he or she did not have the knowledge? Moreover, examinations would mean something only if teaching really imparted knowledge, which is not the case, and if the travesty of knowledge they test corresponded to professional competence, which is not the case either.

Here again is hypocrisy. It is useless for schools to dump hundreds of thousands of winners in the knowledge market out onto the employment market every year. People continue to entertain two contradictory ideas about education: that of its opening doors and that of its imparting an overall view of culture. One is as false as the other. Teaching does not open doors onto anything, and it does not impart any culture at all. Of course, when someone says that teaching is out of direct touch with the world, the usual retort is that the most important thing is to open minds. Opening minds by filling them up, teaching serenity as a drill, wooing converts to aesthetics by means of a questionnaire, inculcating familiarity with the sciences by intimidation: so many miracles, all of them—and school performs them all.

The idea is to teach the students a little biology, a little physics, a little mathematics so they will not be completely out of their depth when they have to deal with biologists, physicists, the mathematicians. Of course, the opposite happens. Learning a little mathematics leads only to awe (or fear) of mathematicians, just as playing the violin as an amateur makes one admire a virtuoso much more than if one knew nothing about the instrument. Thus, after a general education, the graduate knows enough of the sciences to respect them, enough of literature to think badly of it, and enough philosophy to be unable to understand a word of it. Which is better: to know nothing about astronomy or to think that shooting stars are indeed real stars?

General culture ("a liberal education") is so often compared to a sort of liberalism that one imagines it to be invested with a calming, even a sedative, power. Those who possess it should never be surprised at anything, and a little skepticism might even suit them well enough. In reality, it is more a matter of being spoiled. General education gives the impression of immensity only by the disconnectedness of its knowledge, of complexity only by its confusion. Years of Latin hardly leave enough traces to enable the graduate to glimpse a few vague or false etymologies, and it would be interesting to know how many B.A.s, one year after getting their degrees, can define a covalent bond. In brief, their cultural baggage is a nuisance, a souvenir of overwork, a collection of clichés born of intimidation; if they are capable of a moment's clear thinking, they know that the most intelligent course is to get rid of this clutter of rubbish as quickly as possible.

Specialized education, on the other hand, faces its students with the phenomenon of preselection. But since its methods are necessarily the same as those of general education, the final knowledge it produces is also nothing. Thus, this antilogical performance succeeds only in producing a nullity.

Thus, those who preach the educational value of ornamental disciplines such as history, philosophy, and literature lie as blatantly as those professors who are so anxious to politicize the schools that, in their desire to make scholarship subversive, they succeed only in making subversion scholarly. For teachers and students alike, the only interest in any subject lies in the teaching itself, because it results in grades or in promotion. One would say that secondary school or university should be something other than a preliminary to work—if work had not already begun in nursery school.

II

If the literature and philosophy that are taught in the schools had no faults other than being without practical application, teaching would be merely hypocritical—like teaching embroidery to police trainees. But the embroidery is hideous because the methods of teaching literature and philosophy suffer from much worse defects. Professors insist on trying to impart a taste for them, which is impossible, and to make summaries of them, which is absurd. Hence, it is inconceivable that students should garner any correct ideas from their study (if indeed there can be any ideas in literature).

The problem with teaching philosophy is simple: it is better to know nothing about a system than to have an incomplete or thereby false view of it. Students either recall the names of Kant and Hegel, along with some cloudy memories that serve them as reference points for an intellectual parade, or they have really been enriched by their thinking. The latter is possible only if they have read more or less their complete works, not once, but several times—which is frankly impossible at university. If summaries of Kantism and Hegelianism were possible, Kant and Hegel would have written them. (Both, in fact did something approaching that, Kant in *Prolegomena*, Hegel in *Propaedeutics;* but neither work, especially the second, is intelligible today to anyone who does not already know the man's other books).

Now, the Hegelian system is not only impossible to précis, it is also enormously difficult. Even Lévi-Strauss once told an interviewer that he had never been able to read much of Hegel and had understood nothing of the little he had read. Most philosophy professors are less intellectually gifted than Lévi-Strauss, but they do not share his modesty. As a result, they take a work such as *Logic,* one of the most important the West has produced, falsify it by incomprehension, and then summarize it by force. Their students make précis of these presentations, which they falsify again and then remember a quarter of them with difficulty. Then they study (still in summary) other philosophers, such as Russell, who are regarded as eminent and who claim that the Hegelian system has a thousand possible interpretations, an absurd idea that is reinforced by the existence of a thousand absurd commentaries. All in all, the student cannot help but form an impression of the Hegelian system that in *no* way corresponds with what the philosopher must actually have thought. Not even professors have the time or energy to read *Logic* six times (if they did, it would then appear to them as it really is—perfectly clear). But when authors seem so monstrously difficult, quoting their name or any of their ideas is a guarantee of intelligence. That is why one of the most profound thinkers of all time is often mentioned, seldom read, never understood—and transformed into an instrument of terror.

What goes for Hegel goes for others; Kant, Hume, Locke, and Leibnitz all call for long familiarity—several complete readings—which are worthless if they are imposed rather than voluntary. Why should I be interested in ultradifficult and hypothetical solutions to problems that have never entered my mind? The prerequisite of philosophy, even more than of Science, is astonishment and curiosity, while scholarly habit and conformity represent the exact opposite.

In former days philosophers taught their doctrines themselves, and they dealt with real questions. When Kant argued against Hume or Leibnitz against Locke, they were resisting truly current ideas, and the debate was public, even if elitist. Today, the traditionally metaphysical questions—causality, freedom, determinism, and so on—have been handed over to Science. Philosophy no longer *discusses;* it is a subject that has to be *learnt.* The discipline itself seems to admit that it no longer considers real problems, as if the philosophers had all been refuted. One reads in most textbooks that it is no longer possible to be Hegelian, that Schelling's vision of the world is outdated, or, still worse, that the way in which modern mathematics conceives space has destroyed Kant's old space (which has nothing to do with the number of its dimensions, at least as far as the essential of the transcendental aesthetic is concerned).

Philosophy has become a monument to the dead, of whom it is necessary only to present a panoramic view. Students hear an ensemble of caricatured commonplaces: Hegel's sempiternal dialectic of the Master and the Slave (which is merely a secondary episode in Hegelianism), Kant's categorical imperative, Fichte's Ego and Non-Ego: Plato's Cave, Aristotle's categories, Leibnitz's monad—all are presented as inexplicable chimaeras. So are several radically false ideas, such as Marx's reversed Hegelianism and Nietzsche's slaughter of metaphysics. Thus, philosophy appears as a series of reveries, each more disordered than the next. All the flabbergasted student has to do between roll calls, while thinking of a televised football match on his next date, is memorize the fact that an individual named de Malebranche, who is venerated for occult reasons, thought that we see everything in God, which ties him in—and why not?—with St. Augustine. After the bell rings, the same student goes to learn Boyle's law, as taught by an empirical physicist who is an agnostic like everyone else; during the following hour he has to write a paper on the multiple levels of the Unconscious according to Freud. All this scholarly tittle-tattle will amount to in the end is a series of calumnies, falsehoods, and misunderstandings, but the student will have learned to respect a collection of names, a ridiculous gallery of ancestors, and the disciplinary system that provided this opening of his mind.

I shall not linger here on modern philosophers, whose principal discoveries are either solemn trifles or speculations that border on the practical joke: the death of Man, Society and Language, libidinal economy, Aristotle's categories arising from syntactical structures, the responsibility of Fichte, Hegel, and Kant for the totalitarian society. The only thing worth noting is their quite predictable predilection for the so-called social sciences. Their favourite figures are Marx and Freud. Always those two are read and reread, fetishized, magnified, mummified. Characteristically, *no* philosophy has dared to unmask their almost total speculative incoherence, their philosophical emptiness, or their occasional intellectual dishonesty. (Both Marx and Freud will be examined in later chapters.)

If the teaching of philosophy is bad, the teaching of literature is, if possible, worse. What appeals at the start to sensitivity is attacked by knowledge, what incites to criticism or to revolt runs foul of conformism and is imposed by decree ("Rimbaud *is* a great poet"— and that's that), what appeals to solitude is stripped bare in groups. The older the language, the more exotic and thus the more difficult to understand: that is the only judgement invoked. In consequence, literary studies begin with medieval literature, the most unapproachable of all. Stumbling through a few hemistiches of Chrestien de Troyes or Arnoul Gréban is the imposition and thus the ideal. The same is true of more recent but "difficult" writers. When one knows what scholars believe Mallarmé means in a sonnet, when one has commented on every part of it syllable by syllable, then one has attained the objective of the poet. All creation is nothing but an enigma for scholarly dissection. Knowledge and analysis lead to emotion.

The study of languages itself is contaminated by this derisive ideology: spend three hours on a dozen verses of Sophocles or Propertius and one has *read* these poets in the original! Reading equals sweating, taking notes, beginning the same phrase over and over again till it throbs but is still enigmatic, becoming frustrated by the interminable declensions, aorists, and deponent verbs, and finally forgetting even the existence of what the poet may have wanted to say. But at the end of this Calvary, one may say one *knows* Virgil or Aristophanes. After eight years of German, students are generally as incapable of speaking the language as they are of understanding it, but as class assignments they have *read* Goethe's *Faust* and Novalis's poetry word for word and phrase for phrase—exactly as one would have *heard* a Bruckner symphony by spending a minute on each second of music. An American who has studied French probably cannot understand or be understood by a Parisian, but he has *read* Stendhal and Proust.

The same thing happens with the study of one's own literature. When French university students are assigned three stanzas of *Les Fleurs du Mal,* they soon have them cluttered up with notes, weighed down, shattered; in the slowing-down process the lines lose all the rhythm that gave them their poetry. Whatever remains is what they will retain of Baudelaire, and they are left wondering why they had to read this poet rather than someone else. Is this knowledge better than nothing? Only in the sense that it is more instructive to have seen an apple-green Mona Lisa with a mustache than never to have seen a Mona Lisa at all. Such treatment of literature can only be compared to describing some gastronomical delight as "Protein 43%, Albumen 37%, Carbohydrates 20%" and then demanding that the partaker show appreciation on demand.

Once the students have read the texts, they are asked to comment on them, on the assumption that what one does not know well enough to comment on, one does not know at all. The study of letters thus becomes the systematic exploration of all the possibilities of the gloss, the distinction, and the quibble. At a concert, those who pretend to love music ostentatiously unfold their scores and "listen" to them. True music lovers know that this is the antithesis of reacting to music; they prefer to let it make them dream.

Many methods are available to aid the literature students as they do the equivalent of unfolding their score. Textual criticism and psychoanalytical criticism are the most notable. For example, Chateaubriand's line "Rise up, ye wished-for storms" is a trite phrase in itself, but it becomes fascinating as soon as one learns that it is a personification, and that the wish for a storm refers to a subconscious demand for orgasm.

In order to function in the literary world, one must admit postulates: first, that evaluation of particular writers is not a question of liking or not liking them, but of knowing whether they are important (and they are, from the moment people start representing them as important); second, that the Oedipal structure and metonymy in

Balzac are more interesting than in most other writers simply because he is Balzac; third, that one gets to the bottom of a work by treating it as a palimpsest or conundrum (just as one might make a thorough study of a painting by taking X rays of it). From all these premises comes a mishmash of subphilosophy, psychoanalytic criticism, and textual commentary for which Culture is merely the pretext.

Authors who lend themselves to this sort of study become favourites (and vice versa). Mallarmé, who is obscure, takes precedence over Verlaine, and de Sade, who writes like a pedant but gives professors an opportunity to think themselves subversive, eclipses Vigny. Of course, university students have chosen what they do. But secondary school students have little choice, and they automatically identify with Authority everything they are taught on the subject of Art. One might say that it is a superficial reaction to dislike the *St. Matthew Passion* just because one was forced to listen to it at school. But only the very simple can believe that this kind of initiation serves any useful purpose. True lovers of Bach will always be extremely rare; let us allow them the pleasure of discovery and freedom to select their own preference.

The excuse for the widespread teaching of literature and philosophy, is that if certain works were not obligatory at given stages of the curriculum, no one would ever read Goethe, Racine, Shakespeare, and the other greats. The reality is even worse. No Latin or Greek author is read outside the world of scholarship, and modern poetry can count on a few hundred readers at the most. The universities themselves, even in France, almost totally ignore Victor Hugo's poetry, the richest ever born of human mind. Ronsard's sonnets have perhaps a dozen readers in all; Agrippa d'Aubigné has not a single one. The philosophers, as I have already noted, are almost never read (copies of the 1945 French editions of Schelling's works are still available today, suggesting that during more than thirty years they have attracted perhaps two hundred purchasers). Record companies say that the market for classical music is not much better. With a few exceptions, what we call our classical heritage is so neglected that it might as well be dead. How can one say that Horace's odes exist when they do not exist for anyone? Without a reader, a book is no more than some paper and a bit of binding.

Only someone living in never-never land can speak of the influence of great philosophers whom only ten people in a million have read vaguely and understood even more vaguely, of the message of great poets who might just as well never have existed since their work is not read anywhere. The few individuals whose works, barely comprehended, provide our literary culture are labelled "school authors," just as the syllables *em, Ur, ire* are classed as "crossword puzzle" words. The knowledge of which they form part is like a library in which every handsome volume conceals a bottle of whiskey. This travesty of learning culminates in the farce of the dissertation, which is not even worth discussing here since it is only an exercise of saying nothing at great length, of voicing ideas that are not the students' own about an obscure subject that does not inspire them.

Society's emphasis on education means that every real estate shark, every associate judge, and every alderman was at one time obliged to go into ecstasies, and very eloquently too, over the great writers. They all pondered human relationships, mystical desire, and the voices of Nature. And naturally they all found these matters laughable. Treating an author by the required methods means believing (or pretending to believe) in the importance of the former and the accuracy of the latter—in other words, superimposing two conformisms. This type of double hypocrisy is just what the school recommends.

The methods of psychoanalytic and textual criticism have the advantage of providing the immediate satisfaction that passes for the result of reflection in the matter of literature. As soon as one has made a simple but meticulous inventory, one has the pleasure of handing oneself a cultural good mark. An epic poem dealing with the return of a one-armed soldier? Immediately everything clicks into place: phallus, castration. . . . Don Juan enumerating his conquests? Here are desire for the Mother, misogyny, repressed homosexuality. . . . Why does Chateaubriand resort to prolepses so often? A weighty question. . . . One can draw diagrams showing the neat distribution of recurrent themes in Baudelaire or Nerval: the former was crazy about clocks and corpses, the latter about voices that sang. Either one knows from that what these writers wished to say (since it was exactly what they did say), or one thinks that they were basically expressing something quite different; in the latter case, what has become famous under their name is merely the work of another. It is the same story with Shakespeare, whose works are not authentic, seeing that they were written by another man who was *also* called Shakespeare.

A noted psychiatrist recently stated that it is impossible to say what psychosis did for Nerval or anguish for Baudelaire. It is not enough that *Aurélia* is the semiliteral story of Nerval's manic-depressive psychosis or that *Les Fleurs du Mal* expresses anguish; one must still find out how all this came about. Perhaps one could also measure the influence of joy in Beethoven's *Ode to Joy* (maybe it amounts to repressed sadness?), the part played by real sadness in Chopin's work, or the archetypal image of Christ in Bach's cantatas.

The reaches of textual criticism can be adequately illustrated by showing how Roland Barthes, who has gone so far as to write a, treatise on sociology, sees the language, which he must have pondered for twenty years. Words, he says, are exchanged for ideas, as money is for goods (a fascinating parallel between economy and ethnology). The comparison is quite fruitful, if one forgets that: (1) a word generally corresponds to a single idea, while a sum of money corresponds to an infinity of objects; (2) a sum of money does not permit identification of the goods it serves to purchase, whereas a word is the identification of the idea it expresses; (3) a sum of money divided is still money, but a word divided is no longer a word; (4) several different words can represent the same idea simultaneously, but several different sums of money cannot represent a single good simultaneously; (5) two sums of money can be compared quantitively, but words are not quantities; (6) strictly speaking, words cannot be exchanged for ideas, since words have their place and ideas theirs—rather, ideas are exchanged by the exchange of words. No doubt Roland Barthes was thinking about Language; apparently, for him, the noun *language* and the verb *to think* tend to get exchanged for ideas that are not worthy of them.

The obscurity of the work is what is important. When one acquires knowledge, one is cultured, and culture pays off in prestige, especially if the effort to acquire it had to be immense and the knowledge is of doubtful value. The more the dice are loaded, the more successful the game. Authors can almost be graded in order of obliqueness, with the highest points for the least approachable.

Being able to drop one of their sibylline names intimidates half the public but allows the other half to give itself airs. Thus, culture becomes an item of capital, a territory, an investment property. Any individuals who believe they lack knowledge, which is a possession, feel themselves poor, and this poverty prompts them to be ashamed of themselves as much as to show respect for riches. A degree is a castle keep; the slightest cultural merit is almost a promotion to a higher social class. Correspondence courses owe much of their success to the fact that half the purchasers dared not go into a library for fear of the questions the librarian might ask them. Only pornography inspires a similar sense of shame—as if cultural paranoia could be compared to taboos of sex.

People are too afraid to think that an abstruse author may be nothing but a charlatan. Just as we allow fear of Science to condemn us to respect for all the nonsense that has a scientific origin, so we say only that we do not "understand" an art form. The university has imposed its ideology: sensitivity comes from knowledge and not the converse; people will like music more if they have studied an instrument or musicology, a degree in alimentary physiology will open the door to gastronomy. No one believes that ten years of study may give doctors no more than a rudimentary theoretical knowledge and that pharmaceutical firms (for whom he is scarcely more than an unpaid distributor), must explain to them how to use their drugs. Anyone who has a degree must know something, even an amnesiac. Television seeks to dignify itself by staging debates between academicians.

Yet because the traditional forms of culture are venerated to the point of fetishism, people cannot pass for educated if they get their information from TV. Only reading is regarded as a serious approach. (On the other hand, it is "cultural" to watch programs that could be about a movie star and her manager, provided the protagonists are called Henri IV and Gabrielle d'Estrées or possibly Balzac and Mme. Hanska—even if one will never read Balzac and has no idea what part Henri IV played in history.) In Bach's day no peasants would have venerated a piece of music they found unpleasing on the pretext that their lack of education did not allow them to understand it. Today, those who dislike twelve-tone music prefer to blame themselves by respectfully admitting their own incompetence.

III

And so we come to Art through education. This triumph of pedantry and insincerity, this morally and logically specious enterprise, this religion of bad faith resulted in modern art, a phenomenon whose noun and adjective are each as barefacedly usurped as the other. It is a false offshoot of real Art, which died, roughly speaking, around 1920.

The idea of the absolute death of Art horrifies even people who are not concerned with aesthetics. For Humanity neither to express nor to create anything any longer is seen as a dishonour for the past and a matter for distress for the future. So artists continue to produce a dizzying plethora of the eternal. When the world's forests have all fallen to our quintillions of literary masterpieces, we shall have to read a book a minute to achieve a global culture; the past must die continuously in order to keep Art alive.

The problem is that in a world in which durability is impossible, aesthetic creation, which has durability *inter alia* as a principle, is also impossible. Since the nineteenth century our literary heritage has dwindled away. Romanticism and Symbolism still have at least twenty known heroes, though the Renaissance has no more than five or six, the Middle Ages are already in darkness, and Antiquity is but legend. Like an aging individual, Humankind is losing its memory. Today a century seems to flash by in a decade because there have never been so many new books, paintings, films, and musical compositions. Even though a work can still live on unbeknown to the whole world, the eternity in store for works of art is death itself, and Parnassus is a potter's field. The world produces tens of thousands of novels each year; all are imperishable works in the sense that they exist. But durability is merely *one* of the conditions of Art, and to prolong the artistic image, we are compelled today to reverse all those conditions. Thus, the field of Art is inexhaustible only if we admit that everything that has not yet been produced *can* be produced. Thus the art of the past was wrong to choose to be Art—in other words, wrong to be Art—since, in the end, *everything* must be chosen.

The idea of collective art is no less absurd, since it plays on the meaning of the word. "Art" owes its prestige to its individual creation, without which it would be "skill," which is what the word meant up to the age of Romanticism. Moreover, this skill in the works of the past, even in so-called collective works, was such an individual matter that it could remain anonymous, protected by a cloak of secrecy and initiations. But today the idea of Art disappearing is terrifying simply because it seems to condemn the world to anonymity.

If collective art were not a contradiction in terms, it would be difficult to see why pastiches and counterfeits—which are the pure expression of collective art—should have been greeted with horror from the earliest days of Antiquity. If there were ever an era opposed to this form of creation, it is definitely ours, in which a painter can give value to a piece of canvas covered in solid blue by simply adding his or her signature. This impulse is nothing new. When craftsmen building cathedrals felt they were doing better than their fellows, they put their names to their work. Likewise, the Ancient Greeks wanted Homer, who had perhaps been several different authors, to be only one. A Roman crowd can teach us less about Rome than a single Roman; the crowd merely produces crowd noises, but the individual speaks. The most beautiful letter means nothing to me as long as it remains unsigned. Yet the dancers of Bali and Tahiti do not claim to be either artists nor collective; they dance—nothing more. The idea of Black art is not a Black idea; the authors of the Bible or the Bhagavad Gita had no intention of creating what we call Art; an anonymous work, even the Angkor Wat or the Taj Mahal, is admired for the same reasons as a painting by Velasquez or a sonata by Scarlatti. In aesthetics, those who have too complete a grasp of what they are doing are fakes—a studied sadness or a prearranged joy are ridiculous. Art, especially when it is collective (in other words, folklore), demands an absence of prearrangement, a first impulse, a naïveté. What we have is the reverse—namely craftiness —and the whole pseudoartistic production of this century bears its mark.

The most common first reaction to contemporary works of art, especially the pictorial, is, "Why I could do as well." It is unbelievable that patient training should have succeeded in convincing the public that this spontaneous judgement has no value. But no form of art is possible without public admiration. I cannot really admire something that *seems* to be within my own scope. Even the cave paintings of prehistory admit no infraction of this law. As soon as I notice a trick, a system, a prejudice, a gratuitousness, a piece of luck, an insignificance, it is pointless to tell me that this merely *appears* to be so. In fact, it is impossible to say anything worse about a work than that it *appears* to be so. What is Art except an organization of appearances? There is no meaning to the statement, "This music is not really ugly—it just *appears* to be."

If I believe I could have done something as good as a work by Klee, Hartung, or Arp, it is not their technique I am thinking of. Although the technique of these three painters is apparently non-existent, that of Vasarely is evident; nevertheless, I find his work facile, in the same way that I can find a piece of music facile though I am incapable of composing it, much less scoring it, myself. Brilliant technique applied to a commonplace idea—that is a definition of bad taste, such as crops up sometimes, very faintly, in Lizst or Paganini. Art exists only when technique and its effect are fused and both are beyond my scope, thus allowing me to glimpse the source that justifies them. In its day, Art was simply an expression; the more indescribable its object, the more expressive the Art. The posthumous art of today seeks to move its beholder by what it does *not* express. The viewers of an abstract canvas find themselves in a situation of total bad faith; sunk in an uneasy reverie (generally one as public as possible), they seek emotion at the end of an enigma—and thus play one of the most serious games of society.

The fact is that no true pleasure, aesthetic or otherwise, is compatible with doubt—with even the possibility of doubt. Awareness cannot simultaneously blossom into joy and strain itself in a search, since the joy comes from that which is *already* perceived, while the search is aimed at that which is yet to be achieved and may never be. Neither can awareness prevent itself from searching when it perceives something whose interpretation is not obvious. For example, when patients contemplate the antifigures of the Rorschach test (which are, after all, abstract works of art), they draw not the slightest pleasure from them because they know that these images contain no message, that they alone must create their meaning. So Art disappears at each equivocation, each ambiguity, just as a message is reduced to nothing when half its words become garbled.

Awareness expects answers, but in today's works it finds only questions.

Moreover, what is not intentional cannot be artistic. We say art "wishes to say"; the phrase contains not only the verb *to say* but also the verb *to wish*. When we perceive crystals or pebbles as beautiful, their beauty exists only by virtue of *simulated* intentions—colours, evocative forms, or symmetries—and Art is absent simply because simulation is not reality. Notice too that Art requires *both* the absence of equivocation and the presence of intentions; one alone is not sufficient. This double requirement restrains Art's field and the size of its stake. In the past, dying Art tried the long shots of brushing against the arbitrary without ever actually touching it and of expressing its intentions at the very limit of perception. It was soon clear that it could push these limits no further without producing music that could be mistaken for the noise of traffic, poems that could have had pure Chance as their author, pictures to which stains could have made no difference. Beyond paroxysm there is nothing, and it is in that nothingness that we find ourselves.

Another major point: Art today has lost practically everything that served it as social support in the past. What was an integral part of life in days gone by is now no more than a ritual commemoration. Art sprang from the sacred—and it did not *spring* from it for nothing—and has returned to it to die, to be embalmed there in order to retain the appearance of being alive. In brief, Art has become a cult to Culture. The most gloomy of magics reigns when three lines on a canvas or any unlikely cluster of notes acquire the property of making people think, just because they emanate from the intentions of an Artist. These intentions cannot be just anything at all *because* it is a question of Art, and the Artists cannot be just anyone at all *because* they are called John Doe. No one can see all the artists wanted to do in what they have done because Art is a sacrament whose objective is not to say something but to conceal nothing. It is always contrary to appearances, which, in the last resort, are only there to deceive and would thus do better not to be there at all. The John Does are both artist and metaphysician; their metaphysics are too lofty to express except by expressing something else.

During the twentieth century the languages of pictures, sculpture, poetry, and even the theatre and music have become artistic conventions without popular foundation, for internal use only. Sculpture was eloquent for the Greeks even though (or because) its subject matter was restricted to the human body, its material cold but everlasting, its aspect votive and propitiary. It had something to say to these people because it was their only means of representing a figure lifesize and in three dimensions; when the industrial age introduced giant concrete structures, all that was left was an empty mould. Likewise, before photography, painting was the only means of reproducing a person, a landscape, or a series of objects in colour; it was precisely when photography began spreading that painting abandoned strict representation. Before the invention of motion pictures, the theatre was the only way of presenting a living story to a multiple audience; it was on the appearance of the first films that the theatre began to become symbolic. The novel reached its peak at a time when there was nothing to replace it, when the printed page was the only means of transmitting words. Likewise poetry, which originated in the laisses, rhymes, and rhythms inherent in spoken scansion or musical prosody (the ancient epics were chanted) reached its highest point in the silent, solitary world that depended on writing. It presupposed slow reading and even visual rhymes (for example, although the French words *feinte* and *peintes* sound exactly the same except for the initial consonant, the rules of classical poesie did not permit their use as rhymes).

Most of all, it is what Art expressed up to the time of Romanticism and even afterwards that is now foreign to us. We are no longer able to speak a solemn, ritual language whose form is bound by rules; the sole exception is in song, a convention that is still popular—but not for long. Now, some people may say that the failure of the arts to speak to the people is not decisive proof of their death. It is, however, as decisive a proof as the other. An art that speaks a dead language finds it hard to stay alive; all the languages of art are now dead—and some of them have been dead for a very long time.

In addition to the failure of language, there is the matter of themes. It is not hard to show that here too the arts—even the cinema—are being driven into ever-narrowing corners. Sometimes the art form itself calls for restrictions; sculpture, for example, has always revolted quite spontaneously against embellishments, over-anecdotal scenes, or even landscapes (although it is technically possible to portray fine lacework in marble, doing so is regarded as a display of bad taste). More often, it is our world that imposes restrictions. The transistor radio and the refrigerator are simply not fit subjects for still lifes, nor can one include freeways and service stations in landscapes. It is not that these things are commonplace— Vermeer could take a kitchen as his theme and his contemporaries found inspiration in towns, villages, suburbs, ports, countrysides— but the fact is that practically nothing that forms part of our daily life could be immortalized by today's art, even if Art wished it. Thus the artist's choice is between a few strips of countryside (with the cars, telephone wires, and asphalt roads carefully omitted), and the abstract or the imaginary (both slanted towards the past). In other words, the choice is between useless repetition and any old rubbish at all.

Likewise, in poetry, the technical world has reached that forbidden point at which the words rarely bring poetry to mind since they act essentially as provocations. The vocabulary and syntax of writers as recent as Claudel and St. John Perse seem to date from as long ago as the Hellenistic age. Unless novelists adopt the current style of writing, they can no longer say anything without seeming to be hallucinating for the fun of it—like Lowry and his school. The broad sweep of *War and Peace* or *The Human Comedy* is debarred from the New Novel—a landscape cannot be examined under a microscope.

Twelve-tone music that tries to express joy or simply to reproduce a dance beat inevitably brings to mind an old maid bubbling with enthusiasm; since it excludes the minor and major scales to which Western sensitivity clings, as well as the more restrictive modes that belong to the Orient, it is necessarily neuter and by analogy sexless. Bach, Beethoven, and Schubert could write peasant wedding dances worthy of their names; Bartok, Honegger, and Kodály could still claim, here and there, to have written popular pieces of music; Maderna, Varèse, and Webern are reduced to works that scarcely command polite attention at an official UNESCO concert. The Impressionists did lifelike portraits and realistic landscapes for bourgeois clients who were insensitive to art but fond of coloured images; today's painting retains nothing of this iconographic function. Not too long ago a novel such as *Toilers of the Sea,* an opera such as *Tannhäuser,* or a ballet such as *Rite of Spring* could shake a whole city; today even a film could not cause such a stir, although producers have attempted the worst kinds of provocation.

Certainly the cinema killed neither the novel nor the theatre, any more than photography killed painting directly. Each new medium merely obliged the older one to specialize in its specialty, nothing being better defined than by its complement. Painting and the theatre especially were never so pure as at the moment photography and the cinema freed them from their utilitarian function. The problem is that one can only come down from a peak. The beginnings of decadence are often exhilarating and the death throes known as swan songs are often the ultimate in exaltation, but there is always the sequel, which is an ending. The art of today is heir to the art of the past, as a dead man is the heir of a dying man.

The initial pleasure of dissonance in music, of odd associations in poetry, or of nonconformism in painting exists only in reference, however fleeting, to the rules that have been broken. The ninth chord has considerably more effect in Bach's work, where it is rare, than it has in Wagner's, where it is quite common. Rembrandt's famous "Flayed Ox" has a power of shock infinitely superior to that of Soutine's work. Ernst Fuchs and the Surrealists are technically more meticulous than Hieronymus Bosch, but they cannot equal his apocalyptic visions because they can only say what he has already said. Verlaine's nine-foot, eleven-foot, or thirteen-foot verses created an effect of novelty that others such as Verhaeren can no longer obtain. When the violation of the rule becomes the rule, it can only be violated in its turn by the restoration of the original rule (thus, we hear tonality from composers such as Hindemith, Stravinsky, and especially Honegger, who is without doubt this century's most inspired composer of symphonies. What is a tickle at first becomes, as it goes on, an irritation, then a discomfort. For the same elementary reason, dissonance, nonrepresentation, and nonsignificance, cannot be prolonged without resulting in a uniformity infinitely worse than the one the artist was trying to avoid. The fact that this law is simple—and restrictive—does not stop it from being true. The fact that $a = b$ and $a = c$ lead to $b = c$ is equally simple—and equally restrictive.

Because modern art is unwilling to admit this kind of evidence, it denies laws that go beyond psychology to biology (if not, quite simply, to logic). The twelve-tone scale ought to enlarge the field of music by making possible some 480 million tunes—in somewhat the same way as the field of poetry might be enlarged by including all possible combinations of the words in the dictionary, including, of course, such phrases as "We remain, gentlemen, yours very truly" and "The discount rate will be reduced by 1 percent."

When the disciples of Schönberg forbid tonality in the series or the repetition of any of the twelve semitones, they do even more than slam the doors they are trying to open; they also mandate countless scholarly recitatives whose differences are quite undetectable to our ears. Now, some may say that distinguishing forms—any forms—are a question of culture, but cultures *are* matters of awareness; a Chinese of the Ming era, a Frenchman of Louix XV's time, or a modern Westerner encounters many more forms that, despite dissimilarities, seem identical than those that can be recognized as different. If this were not so, the human mind could never have formed a single concept. Two things are never exactly the same in any respect. Living matter is distinguished from inert by the rules of repetition and homology; living awareness is sensitive to only a very restricted number of forms; and children begin to outstrip the anthropoid ape the moment they begin to take an interest in *symmetries*, which leave the chimpanzee uninterested.

Thus, each twelve-tone melody is worth no more and no less than all the others—even when Berg or Webern respect the canonical form of the melody. If all forms are possible, why bother to write *one* of them? Rigorous formality led to monotony, but discarding all form results in even worse monotony. Everything seems as similar as two moments of boredom; the freedom to do anything one pleases produces nothing that pleases anybody. There were many more real differences between Chopin and Schumann than there are between Nono and Berio, and there are more differences between Nono and Berio, than between two computers. The words *brighten* and *frighten* differ only by one letter, but because they have different meanings they are less easy to confuse than the words *xankalu* and *orimep*, which have not a single sound in common but are both nonsense words. The cretinism of contemporary art shows up very clearly in improvised productions; awareness, which is the supreme form of anti-Chance, is expected to show an interest in something that, by its very nature, cannot possibly mean anything to it. Artists have not yet realized that the phrase "It could be anything," which is a precise definition of Chance, is one of the most disparaging ways of describing ugliness. Moreover, aesthetics, being the reality of appearances, admits no difference between the apparent and the real—saying that something appears improvised but is not—boils down to saying that the artist intended what was produced but did not produce what was intended. In other words, a picture is meant to conceal the painter's art, or a symphony is composed so that one does not take it to be the work of its composer. In this way, too, the same geniuses who ostentatiously sign almost empty canvases cloak their better works under the chaste veil of Chance—doubtless through modesty.

All the other alibis that serve modern art are equally naïve. First is the idea that a work of art should leave the imagination or the mind free. In fact, because freedom is the very essence of imagination and thought, there is no better way of praising a work than by saying the exact opposite—that is *captivating, eyecatching, arresting, fascinating*, and so on. Second is the idea of "expressing one's period." This is absurd even beyond its Boy Scoutish flavour. The art of the past never sought such expression, even if it achieved it; moreover, it affects us only when it extends beyond the time of its birth, ideally beyond Time itself. Cherubini expresses his era better than Beethoven, and Telemann, who was much admired by his contemporaries, bears better witness to his times than the unappreciated Bach. Only the mode gains by being dated; by definition, Art begins only when dates disappear. Finally, there is the idea of an inexhaustible artistic field. This is a corollary of freedom of the imagination and is also fundamentally contradictory. Art is choice, choice is exclusion, exclusion is a limit, a limit is finitude.

Why does modern art need all these innovations? Because of *traditionalism*. Anyone who says that the history of Art stops around 1920 is behind the times. To believe that the cult of Apis is past is to belong to the past; a modern attitude is to belong to this cult and struggle to keep it alive. The myth of Art must be perpetuated, even if the world suffocates under a heap of lies. It is essential that I have something to say and that I be the only one to have said it. The fatal moment must never come when all artists are obliged to admit that everything is over in their lifetime, and that nothing will ever begin again. Such is the epilogue against which all the creators of the last half-century's anticreation are struggling ever more absurdly.

It would matter little if this grotesque drama were not taking place in the midst of the greatest publicity campaign for all forms of art—pictorial, musical, and verbal—the world has ever known. Schubert heard Beethoven's Fifth Symphony perhaps four times in his entire life. Which of us today has not heard it at least twenty? What had to be searched out in the past is today so widespread that one almost has to run away from it. A modern radio station broadcasts as much music in one day as all nineteenth century Europe heard in a year. Recordings of symphony orchestras blare away in supermarkets, cafés, and cars. Art reproductions abound. Michelangelo's work appears in advertisements for a brand of jeans; Chopin and Bach provide catchy tunes for hit songs, form the subject of televised documentaries, and are listed in the credits for background music in films. All the media dish out drama by the kilogram and poetry by the kilometer. The lifespan of a book is that of a magazine. Schools succeed each other at a rate that will soon be monthly: op art, pop art, crude art, kinetic art, naïve art, committed art, recommitted art, Realism, Surrealism, Hyporealism, Hyperrealism, Literalism, Dadaism, Futurism, Pastism, Formalism, Informalism, New Romance, New Critique (and then their negations), abstract painting, concrete music (curiously enough the last two do not clash). All these titles are necessary, of course, to cover up uniformity and distinguish lack of distinction.

In former days artists used to borrow ideas and formulas from each other; the ensemble could characterize a school, even though it was not aware of itself. Ruysdael was close to Rembrandt, Mozart broke very little new ground compared to Haydn. Today, however, artists feel they must refashion Art as though it had not existed before them, and the emptier their work is, the more necessary it is for them to launch it with manifestos. The intentions that Art expresses, without which it has no reason to exist at all, are now so clear that the public must be warned about them. Since there can be no admiration without astonishment, and since people cannot be astonished at something they believe they are able to conceive themselves, cultural intimidation is called for. The work, which used to be a key, has become a lock.

There could scarcely be a better testimony to our times. Once Art tried to give an inkling of ideas by appearances, then the appearance itself tried to make itself felt; today the aim is to make us grasp appearances through ideas. Happily, one is worth the other: The fundamental idea of Surrealism, for example, is that the real is that which can be seen. One cannot appreciate Giacometti's threadlike men or Moore's thick rotundities without knowing their whys and wherefores—explained, naturally, by a shoddy metaphysics in which there is an endless alternation between the thousand and one structures of Space and Time, the dereliction of modern man, the meaningful shape, and so on and so forth.

Art is becoming the receptacle of thoughts, as though Tapiès used painting as another method of writing his treatise on knowledge. Once upon a time sensitivities formed (or rather deformed) by knowledge were precisely those that resisted innovators. Schumann, Beethoven, Wagner, Bizet, and so many others moved the public, but more often than not they had to push criticism aside. Nowadays the so-called cultured public obeys only the dictates of criticism, and the innovators have discovered that the way to win over the critics is to become even more pedantic and false than the critics themselves —or to become one of them.

IV

The image of the artist as the enemy of the establishment has never been more robust than it is today, when the establishment is flying to the assistance of Art and most of its creators are subsidized by or work for governments, industries, rich patrons, and other oppressed minorities. Artists cry "Death to the bourgeois!" and the bourgeois revel in it; they demonstrate against the police under the protection of the police forces themselves; they roast Society in general beneath the delighted gaze of some society in particular; they hack false culture to pieces—other people's culture—in front of a public that has gathered with them to perfect its own.

The revolutionary school of painting gives cocktail parties; outspoken sculptors model pathetic cries of revolt in scrap iron or polyester and sell them to Argentinian torturers in exile. Nietzsche, Gide, and Artaud in succession call for all books to be burnt; while they are waiting, they write some more themselves. It is absolutely essential that Art be subversive. If shock and scandal prove impossible, if all the artistic dynamite is damp—as is the case in the West—all one can do is condemn censorship in the U.S.S.R., where abstract painting and surrealist poetry, by virtue of being banned, have at least won that most indispensable of characteristics: being admitted to exist.

In brief, the idea of all art containing revolutionary leaven is an empty commonplace. When Art was anonymous, it contained not a single ounce of subversion; in fact, it played a generally conservative role, glorifying official cults, state religions, military victories, national heroes, and the sacred Family. Artists began wanting to be political revolutionaries only around the middle of the nineteenth century when, as Art began to falter and Society to stir, the latter gave the former a guilty conscience. There is, of course, evidence that the content and revelations of Art can incite people to revolt against all forms of established order. But *anything* can produce that effect (or its opposite), not only artistic works. If Hugo, Zola, and Vallès did not upset the world of politics, despite the way in which all of them both spoke a clear artistic language of belief in the Revolution and engaged in concrete political activities, how could André Breton, that master of bad faith, and the countless narcissistic poseurs who served him as disciples, have subverted anything at all? They had already betrayed everything, they all talked rubbish, and their Revolution embraced, among other novelties, the cult of monogamy, which they rechristened wanton love. During the last part of the century, Zola's novels and *Les Misérables* were in great demand, making their readers either grind their teeth or break out sobbing; people talked about them at the table. But *Nadja* was soon discarded as the bible of a minority who considered themselves, naturally, an elite. What could be more pointless than all those sects excommunicating themselves from one end of the Latin Quarter to the other in the name of the masses, who had never even suspected their existence?

Human sensitivity is stubborn. Despite abstract painting, people continue to show an interest in semirealistic images. The songs they sing, the tunes they remember, and the music they like instinctively are based entirely on themes that date, at the latest, from the early days of Richard Strauss. It is a waste of time for public-spirited leftist dramatic groups to play the theatre of the absurd in factories; the TV soap operas know enough to stick to the intrigues and ideals of the nineteenth century. The ex-New Novel, which relates the everlasting story of The Gentleman and The Lady in tones of orphic mystery, has not changed the taste of the reading public by one iota. Most people would rather give up the arts altogether than imagine them in different forms.

From the naïveté that the masses understand, Art has retained only enough conventions to ensure its anachronism. For example, one finds nymphs in Picasso's work, gods in Matisse's, ancient towns in Delvaux's paintings, Christs, virgins, and halos in Rouault, satyrs, centaurs, dryads, and minotaurs everywhere. What is the famous innovator Le Corbusier doing? Chapels. Today's Artists also use conventions to classify themselves, thereby delighting the public, which loves mnemonotechnic abbreviation. There is no Miró without little birds, no Chagall without flying moths and blue donkeys, no Tanguy without deserts and gravel, no Klee without squares and irregular triangles. This tendency is not entirely new. Earlier on, Van Gogh was recognizable by his obstinacy of line, Seurat by his system of dots. Even then the themes themselves had become stereotyped: for still life studies, endless bowls of fruit and indefatigable tobacco pipes lying beside newspapers; for nudes, the eternal woman, eternally ugly; for landscapes, indispensable Provençal farmhouses; for compositions, the inevitably sad Pierrot (for all clowns are sad, of course). Today, artists have reached the stage of using gimmicks to differentiate themselves: Christo gets enthusiastic about valleys, César compresses his cars, Tinguely builds Tinguely machines, Calder has invented a gadget, Duchamp is celebrated for his laundry iron, Bacon has become established as *the* painter of hideousness. Salvador Dali, the virtuoso of the working drawing and the geometrical projection, is the very image of the Artist as envisaged by a bourgeoisie that, for half a century, has been alternating between being ticklish and swooning away. Sick humour with no jokes, the honesty of an armaments salesman, and the soul of a court jester. Just the sort of subversion needed in a world in which the oceans are dying! The acclaimed Dokumenta VI exhibition at Kassel in 1977 included W. Maria's hole, D. Pacilio's kitchen stove, Morris's site, the Poiriers' house of gold, and Warhol's hammers and sickles; all that was lacking were some Oerlikon shells and Westinghouse nuclear power stations.

Meanwhile, Art also claims the right to be above morality, to exhibit an ideal from which it itself escapes. Dali, for example, can dissemble, do anything for money, and support Franco—but what counts is his work. Unfortunately, there is no escape from the rule that says that a work reflects its author, and Dali's smells of lies, cash, and reaction. Some people hold that there is no relationship between artists' morals and their aesthetics. I would ask them to quote me a good racist poem, a fine piece of music glorifying murder, a splendid Nazi work, or a romantic masterpiece produced within the guidelines of Stalin's socialist realism.

If artists have serious defects of character, these defects are present in their work. Berlioz was conceited—and so is his music. Haydn was conservative—it shows in his music. Wagner was arrogant and at times calculating—his operas tell you as much, here by their extravagance, there by their guile, despite (or perhaps because of) the immense genius of the composer. Voltaire's novels and especially his short treatises make it unnecessary for me to know the man. All that was annoying in Rousseau shows up in his *Confessions*. I have no need to read biographies of Hugo, Beethoven, or Bach to be convinced that the mixture of strength and goodness that makes their work sublime was part of their *personas*. In the final analysis, when one likes a work, has one become attached to some*one* or to some*thing*—to a mind or to a computer? When one describes a style as uninspired, stilted, precious, vulgar, aggressive, ironic, or whatever, one is not using adjectives that denote formal style (as when describing a line of verse as iambic); rather, the words refer directly to the stylist personally and are consequently moral judgements.

Attempts to separate form and substance in art are the result of the same confusion. The stories authors relate define them just as much as does their style of writing. Not a comma is without significance. Let us examine two trite sentences that are very similar:

1. On horseback, he went through the forest to get back home.
2. To get back home, he went through the forest on horseback.

The difference in form is, in fact, a difference in substance. The first statement tells us the man was already on horseback before he went through the forest, while in the second, his only reason for going through the forest on horseback seems to be to get back home. The first also suggests that other solutions were available to the man than going through the forest on horseback, but the second says nothing about this. And so on. There are never two different ways of saying *exactly* the same thing. If there were, the forms of etiquette and diplomacy would be pointless; all languages have these forms precisely because, for example, "frank and cordial exchange of views" does not *say* "disagreement," even though it can be taken to mean it. Thus, too, one style does not say the same thing as another. Everything that is inherent in artists' existence also appears in what they create; a real swine has never produced a masterpiece, and all the world's beauty is but another facet of its goodness.

This convergence of the ethical and the aesthetic is so striking that Kant, in his *Critique of Judgement,* made one symbolic of the other. The Good and the Beautiful, quite indefinable though they are (and even because they are) lay claim to (and thus tend to receive) universal approbation. No Art would ever have been possible without artists' certainty that Beauty is *communicable,* and that it is, in consequence, *common* to all minds. It does not matter that all minds may not realize this; the universality of ethical, aesthetic, and logical criteria does not need to be recognized in order to exist. The logarithm of one *is* zero, even if the whole world thinks otherwise. True art was based on the prodigious wager that beyond conceptual truth, which cannot be denied, there exists another truth which must (or should) meet and be met by all human souls, which are but one. The ideal of modern art is the converse: everyone has his own world, everyone has his own tastes—everyone for himself. According to this theory, I must admit that what appears to me to be a pebble stirs the emotions of my neighbour, who has acquired a special pair of antennae through a surfeit of studying. In other words, the separation of men equals the separation of Art and Morality. I am sincere in my belief that Dubuffet is acting in bad faith, but he is equally sincere in putting together his fiftieth Hourloupe, imagining all the while that he is overthrowing culture and quite convinced that I do not understand him. Others are perfectly sincere when they say that Dubuffet's work is ugly, but Soulages's is inspired. Everybody is sincere—as though sincerity guaranteed anything other than itself, as though such-and-such an artist who committed suicide or so-and-so who went mad were not a crazy fake and a suicidal charlatan. It is as though Hitler did not commit suicide and Caligula did not go mad, as though dying for a false ideal makes that ideal less false and one's death less commonplace.

The usual objection here is that it is works that are on trial, not persons, and that a work, by definition, does not express anyone; artists, when all is said and done, create for themselves. This argument ignores reality; it tries to eliminate the "common" part of the verb *to communicate* and ignores the separation of types. There is not a single aesthetic dislike that is not simultaneously a moral dislike. A style persists in being an attitude, and an attitude persists in stylizing a being. When I see the slightest appearance of affectation in a work, I cannot help seeing the pursed mouth of an unlikeable man; when I hear the slightest overloudness from an orchestra, I get irritated. If I like Verdi *in person* when I like his music, isn't it normal for me to get exasperated at someone else *in person* when his music exasperates me? If a very close friend hates a work I like, I can probably rise above our disagreement, but only by regarding it as a hiatus as intimate as the friendship itself; a few more hiatuses of this sort and the friendship disappears.

Unfortunately, speaking of the fusion of the moral and the aesthetic makes many people shudder as if at a piece of bad taste, especially since they inevitably dislike the word *moral*, seeing in it connotations that it should not have. Our century has been the century both of Dadaism and of the new morality, a shoddy affair that goes from the bolsheviks to the Nazis via the Zarathustrian zealots (a description that fits it like a glove). Just as modern art contradicts itself by pretending to demystify a myth that it in fact prolongs and to revolutionize a tradition that is in fact dead, so mere immorality is brought to nought in the face of the unshakable evidence of evil. *Thief, liar, assassin, coward,* do not become terms of praise in the mouth of Nietzsche or Goering. They never can, because they summarize the negatives of universal morality. In ten thousand years' time, cruelty, hardness, pride, slavery, and censorship will still be excluded from the category of the Good.

For the same reasons, no civilization has ever admired anything all members believed they could create, or found beauty in excreta, graffiti, shapelessness, filth, rusty iron, or anything that stems from Chance (unless, of course, it seems not to, like tree trunks and pebbles shaped like humans). None has ever shown those "sensitivities different from our own" that people like to evoke when it comes to modern art. The most advanced non-Western civilizations, those of India, China, Japan, and the Maghreb of the Middle Ages, never even raised Art to the level of an independent and individual entity. One reason is that what we think of as Oriental arts are almost entirely the work of privileged classes or castes, who are out of touch with the people and have been able to produce only elitest rites.

Today the Indian sitar, the No theatre, and Chinese engravings have scarcely made more than a brief tour of the Occident, but Japan is plunging headlong into a frenzied cult of European music and painting, and the Chinese are composing cantatas that sound (alas!) like Gershwin's work. It is pointless to talk of the effects of Western imperialism. When the Romans invaded Greece, Greece Hellenized them all; Rome latinized the Goths; no Chinese, Indian, or Japanese institutions have been destroyed from outside. Historically, Oriental arts have been nothing but decorative supplements governed by protocol. Concerts, exhibitions, recitals, signatures, Art conceived as an end in itself—all these are Western creations. This divergence between East and West goes back to the days of the Roman republic, of Phidias, or even of Hesiod, when neither pole knew of the existence of the other.

To believe that each race lives its culture as we feel ourselves obliged to live our own is to take a somewhat touristic view of the world. The average Japanese are just as bored by the No theatre as we are, find nothing metaphysical in haiku, are no more interested in *Stories of the Shadowy Moon* than we are in the *Song of Roland*, and they read Kawabata (who writes in the Western style) as we read Graham Greene. The Chinese do not whistle in quarter tones and do not put their own prints on a par with museum paintings. The background music in Indian films is generally not that of raga but standard Western symphonic film music. Even if all these cultures did regard Art as the West does, they would spurn the forms of contemporary art even more fiercely, in the name of stricter rules, than they ever have been in the Occident.

One can find more justifiable examples of "sensitivities different from our own" in our own past, saying, for example, that Bach would have abhorred Beethoven, who would have hated Debussy. But it is Beethoven who follows and thus derives from Bach, Debussy who presupposes Beethoven, and not the converse. Each of these composers is conceivable only as deriving from those who preceded him. Why would people not be shocked at what takes place two or three generations after their lifetime? Knowing nothing of the history that separates me from the year 2100, I obviously cannot know who I would be if I lived then or what I would be doing. Similarly, it is impossible to say who Bach would have been if he had lived in Debussy's day. (It is, however, certain that neither of them would be composers now—unless one is prepared to admit that Stanley, today, would be running safaris and Livingstone organizing tours.) No one can judge his future state of mind as long as he is deprived of the history of events that will produce that state of mind. But contemporary art has not sprung from the future, and I do not see how the "different sensitivities" that supposedly give access to that future have been able to advance centuries ahead of my own sensitivity, especially since Art had already become a masquerade fifty years ago.

Moreover, insofar as Art is a language (and if it is not a language, it is nothing), it is spoken in accordance with certain conventions, whose simplest examples are the word and the sign. In the same way, every sensitivity is a selectivity that absorbs only an infinitesimal part of what passes across it, and it makes its election in accordance with rules. (Some of these rules are merely physiological, such as those imposed by the retinal cells.) If the musical framework is essentially diatonic in the West, it is even more restrictive everywhere else; Indian, Turkish, and Chinese music is based on precise frames of reference, and there has never been any question of these cultures reshaping or going beyond these frames.

In brief, there may be different sensitivities—although their differences, as I have just suggested, are largely illusory—but there can be no sensitivities that are inarticulate, without models, without framework, without rules. In music, for example, memory always plays an enormous part, and a music that cannot be memorized at least vaguely has no chance of moving anybody. Likewise, the idea of a perfectly abstract painting is absurd; whatever does not portray the world merely adds itself thereto and thenceforth is of no more interest than any other part of the visual field. Hence, the importance in modern art of the signature, the advertisement, the commentary, and the exhortation. Nobody would take a Rembrandt for anything but a picture, but a sculpture by Brancusi runs the risk of being taken, at first sight, for a millstone, a stovepipe, or nothing at all.

De gustibus non est disputandum. This maxim (which criticism quotes often yet condemns by its very existence) applies to everything except Art; what is based on nothing common cannot be communicated. This means that gastronomy and sexuality, to which the maxim applies, cannot be artistic; if they were, they would be in conflict with themselves. Both are, in fact, based on interest, which by definition seeks to keep itself to itself, while Art is disinterested by nature and seeks, on the contrary, to spread out. Art is a centrifugal enjoyment, while pure enjoyment is centripetal.

In point of fact, this is why a language cannot be aesthetic if its components are not neutrals. Colours, signs, words, and lines play the role of intermediaries in Art because, being neither good nor bad in themselves, they can conduct every current that passes through them. Odours, touches, and tastes, on the other hand, are fundamentally incapable of fulfilling this function, since they already have their own positive or negative values that prevent them from transmitting any others. In this sphere, and this alone, the concept of "Each man has his own tastes" is applicable. In other words, "Every man for himself" is the ideal here as it is for industries, for nations, for sport, for couples, for the pollutionary game of grab, and for modern art.

V

The majority of the public today is simply not interested in modern art. The rest can be divided into three categories: those who turn away because they realize there is nothing to understand, those who understand nothing but do not want anyone to realize it, and those who have never understood anything but have not yet realized it. The artist is usually in this last category: the popular myth of the fraudulent painters who have discovered a trick to make their fortune while thumbing their nose at the world is without foundation—although it explains a great deal about the popularity of modern painting.

For the first time in History, the masses suspect artists of deliberate swindling, and for the first time, they are wrong—to the benefit of those they suspect. Most people simply cannot believe that before hoaxing others a person must be able to hoax himself. Moreover, most people are reluctant to bring their suspicions to bear on the origins of the evil, which have become sacred because they are historic. And yet what justifies their mystification in the cases of Pollock, Bissières, and so many other contemporaries is also present in certain of Van Gogh's and Modigliani's works, which are absolutely hideous and inconsequential despite their signatures. Similarly, Picasso's blue period was his only really approachable one (which accounts for its popularity—it allows one to say that one likes Piccaso), but it was already stamped with the same bad taste as the cold, episodic "Guernica" and the cellulitic naiads and other Cyclopean females for whom the painter became famous. The seeds of the bad faith that would spread out over half a century of problematical poetry are to be found in Mallarmé, who, despite his brilliance, sometimes indulged in lugubrious pseudometaphysical solemnities, triteness of thought cloaked in a formal obscurity, clumsiness, inner emptiness, and Baudelairean pastiche. In the same way, Rimbaud's genius did not always save him from arbitrariness and ineptitude, and Verlaine's work was sometimes nothing but the flourish of a pen at the end of an ostentatious display. As soon as Art begins to cudgel its brains, first affectation, then comedy, and finally imposture are not very far away. It matters little that the artist may previously have been authentic or inspired; after his Fifth Symphony, Mahler himself knew this temptation, even though he refused to give in to it. After the post-Debussy pullulations of jets of water, waves, Pan's pipes, and other such nonsenses, atonalism began simultaneously with Stravinsky in France and Schönberg in Germany; it soon gave free rein to arbitrariness.

The worst feature of all these transitions was that they were hardly perceptible; the same artists were able to produce masterpieces *and* empty nothings with the same material. In one way, it is fortunate that this confusion is no longer possible today, even though the public does not take advantage of the clues offered it. In its anxiety not to repeat the blunders of the past, such as the outlawing of Monet and Toulouse-Lautrec, it swallows everything (though with reservations); it believes itself finally proof against errors—at the very moment when it is doing practically nothing but making them. What people more or less forgive in Cézanne makes them afraid of in Derain, Braque, Gromaine, and Fernand Léger. Rodin's liberties are obstructive in retrospect because of all the concessions they justify today, and Henri Rousseau's genuine naïveté now excuses thousands of false imitations, thereby producing a distaste for all general unities without excusing naïveté, false or not, for being stupid.

In the same way, successful poetic metaphors pass into unsuccessful literary obscurity. When Claudel wrote "in the salt of the clattering fire" or Fargue said "the sea was blazing black," the shock was legitimate in both senses of the word, but the professorial body could still stand aloof. But when Mallarmé wrote:

> All Pride smokes of an evening
> Like a torch quenched with a hasty swing
> Without the imperishable puff of smoke
> Being able to delay its surrender

not only did this ultrapurist not realize that his French was ungrammatical (the original translates as "without . . . not being able"); he also pretended not to know that reader-students were going to end up sweating away over his message and would consequently receive it as though it came from some narrow-minded pedant. They were going to remain in doubt—in other words, be the slaves of Chance—and in order not to feel Chance for what it really is, they would take the bourgeois Mallarmé for what he dreamt of being: an oracle.

Given the abundance of material, a label has never been more indispensable. A literary work gains from being an apologue. Kafka's *The Trial* equals the human condition: absurdity and pointless death. Ionesco's *Rhinoceros* equals the rise of Nazism. Beckett's *Waiting for Godot* equals waiting for God. Each key makes a good literary point. Explicative literature is more and more necessary, first as an introduction, then as a ratification; once approved by Malraux or Apollinaire, a work is no longer contestable under pain of outrage against authority. Today literature itself would be nothing without Philosophy; Rembrandt needed no support from Spinoza, but Calder needs Sartre in order not to be mistaken for the decorator of Scandinavian living rooms that he appears to be. And Art needs Science even more than Philosophy, so we have musical *laboratories,* centers of sound *research,* graphic *patterns, Gestalt Theory,* and, as a source of inspiration, the *structuralist* objectivity that eliminates all nonscientific judgement and chooses to direct its purely objective gaze at Baudelaire and not at some anonymous writer in *The Monitor.* Naturally, titles and initials follow: *Octahedron VI, Monomer-Alpha, Galactic Strata, Hypophysis, Density 3.5,* and others that sound like names for food dyes.

It is not surprising that public manifestations of art could now win prizes for pomp and scholarly ritual. At a concert, the empty, unpleasing spectacle of the orchestra, the soloist, and the conductor overshadows the music, a cough seems like intentional interference, each member of the audience tries to attain the peak and posture of ecstasy by adopting the posture of constipation. Beethoven's call for brotherhood is sung by a choir of ladies dressed like nuns; a stand-offish look never leaves the faces of the singers during Bach's *"Der Himmel lacht"* ("Heaven laughs"); painted women encased in furs and men dressed like undertakers sit in their boxes and watch the gesticulations of a conductor whose costume dates from the nineteenth century who is there only for show. At an art exhibition, all must display the depth of their soul to their neighbour by spending five minutes in front of a canvas that would not bring three ideas into their head if they were alone. Then we have the theatre with its eternal creaky floors, its bad lighting, and its ridiculous sets; the actors converse with each other in shouts and sometimes come down into the auditorium like anarchist firebrands so that the public can become participating revolutionaries before leaving for home in their evening dress and their fine cars. And finally, there is the opera. In past centuries it was almost as popular as the cinema today; now it is no more than the rite of rites, followed by an elegant ball at which all the big shots in oil (and sometimes torture) get together in a Wotan cult organized by Pierre Boulez.

Now we come to the popular arts, the chief of which is the cinema. Logically, an art that started much later than the others should be holding out better. But this proportional rule has never been true. Sculpture is older than painting; music, as an individual creation, is of much more recent origin than either of them is; in historical times, however, all three have developed on more or less parallel lines and have been faced with the same crises at the same time.

Between 1920 and 1935, the development of the film industry proceeded at a pace reminiscent of the Gold Rush in the American West, and the pioneers took only a few years to sweep the board. Even in the days of the silent screen, Dziga Vertov and Ruttmann explored *cinéma vérité*, Lang, Murnau, Pudovkin expressionism, Eisenstein and von Stroheim dramaturgy on the grand scale. By World War II all the Western masterpieces—those directed by Ford, Hawks, Walsh, and a score of others—had gone from the studios to the world's screens and thence to the film libraries. In the sixties, the New Cinema appeared along with the New Novel, although, strictly speaking, their romantic style was already some two thousand years old. At the moment both are bogged down, searching for a new language on either side of the same roadblock. Yet both remain prosperous precisely because they can speak a traditional language, with reality supplying them subjects that are always new. There is no need to outdo or even to equal Octave Mirbeau or Max Ophüls in formal audacity; real life offers plenty of new subjects. Gide, Mauriac, Malraux, and even Sartre would not have shocked Stendhal by their style, but by their subject matter. The same holds true for filmmakers. Painting and music can only renew themselves by formal research; if this were the case with the novel and the film, they would be no less academic today. The fact that one can still talk of these two media as popular arts is no thanks to Butor or Godard, but to Böll and Solzhenitsyn in the one case, to Schlesinger and Kubrick in the other. Words and images are part of both the utilitarian and the artistic lexicons; although they are quite distinct, they are always confused. Thus the novel and the cinema are the only present-day arts that participate in Art; their participation in everyday life guarantees their survival, for better or worse, even though it earns them mistrust. In this way, current practice defends itself against something that is constantly threatening to force its way into it: we say disparagingly "That's only a novel" (or a movie), whereas we use "That's painting" (or music) as a term of praise.

Television (which after all is merely films shown in our homes) proves that the cinema is the most modern and vivid of the expressive media. But an expressive medium becomes an art if—and only if—an individual—and only an individual—manages to express him- or herself through it. Now, the cinema does not create its reality but borrows it from Reality itself. Moreover, it is so essentially collective that no one can specify the exact contribution of a director such as Losey when Pinter is his scriptwriter. Even in Fellini's films, it is impossible to say whether the beautiful shots should be credited to the cinematographer, the brand of film used in the cameras, pure chance, or Nature—in short, whether they are intentional or not. The most godlike of directors are dependent on their producers, on favourable reviews, and on achieving commercial successes (a striking crowd scene may simply be a matter of dollars). Eisenstein is at the mercy of Prokofiev; Bergman and Buñuel must have their actors and set designers; most of the others rely on their scriptwriters and adapters. Since there is no film without scenes or words, the medium's principle is that of the theatre (though its possibilities are increased tenfold). So despite its dimensions, the cinema can cover only a part of what used to be the literary domain; an essay cannot possibly become a film, and poetry is out of the question. An audience comprehends the spoken word at least twice as slowly as the written word. The cinema must produce a concentrated image to compensate for this defect. Even when dealing with a well-described object, this compensation is a change of level. There is no relationship between the description of a quay and its photographic image; the former guides the imagination; the latter makes imagination unnecessary.

The major disadvantage of the film is that its definitive character makes it provisional. Nothing goes out of date more quickly than literalness. The work carries its setting with it; it is complete, but it is no longer adaptable. Imagine that it were impossible to read Calderón and Goldoni; no doubt one would still find many points of interest in them, but *Devotion to the Cross* delivered in a shout or mumbled at the footlights by mountebanks in a puppet-stage setting would not attract the public in vast numbers. It might fascinate us once as a piece of historical testimony, but it would concern us all the less for being a museum piece. Today a silent film of the 1920s generally seems more old-fashioned than a poem of the 1300s. Antiquity, on the other hand, has no more age.

The photographic image offers the possibility of retouching (which is close to faking, and thus to the system) but not of creation (the difference between creation and choice being the same as that between a person of genius and one of taste). It is also an incitement to realism, though the cinema responds only rarely to this possibility. For example, until Bergman's most recent films, the cinema showed death in a manner as conventionally insipid as the theatre does; in reality, of course, the sight of persons in their death throes is nearly unbearable. Screen lovers never lisp. A man talking to himself gives a theatrical soliloquy that is far too coherent for reality and, above all, far too slow; if the spoken word is twice as slow as the written word being read, the word thought in the mind is infinitely faster and more multiform than the latter. Impossible music accompanies sentimental effusions; lapses of memory become like mist in a landscape; sudden awarenesses has the brutality of a receding dolly shot; memories are automatically sustained visual flashbacks whereas real memories are never *true* images, and they fly over or zigzag through the past in no fixed sequence. (Any who doubt this should try shutting their eyes and bringing some memory to mind. Blackness remains for a memory, even a visual memory, is not a hallucination.)

To these fundamental conventions must be added others that are more technical. People never look as though they were working, doors slam loudly, traffic and other background noises are softened or disappear, trains have a tendency to pass always overhead; voices on the telephone sound as though they were coming from beyond the tomb; and it is always light enough to be able to see an actor on a dark night. Clichés are innumerable: the Bedroom Scene, the First Kiss, the Return-Twenty-Years-Later, the Family Meal, the Car Chase, the Final Showdown, the Sunset-over-the-Sea, the Nazis'-Fury-after-Guerrilla-Attack, the Face-of-the-Enemy-Appearing-in-the-Mirror, and so on and so forth. All this has no importance in itself but shows that cinemagraphic "art" reached its limits long ago, even if only through overconsumption.

Moreover, it is striking that almost all the famous novels brought to the screen have been miserable failures, that the cinema has not succeeded in creating a single one of the great character types that appear so frequently in literature and drama; Jean Valjean, Julien Sorel, Rastignac, Werther, Othello, Hamlet, Don Quixote, and Tartuffe have no equivalents on the screen. Film characters are paraliterary in origin. Three languages of expression—words, pictures, and music—may fuse to form yet another, but it is more restrained in its principle than any of the three taken separately, a little like the way Nature has more red, blue, and white objects than objects that contain all three colours at once.

Be that as it may, the exhaustion from which all repertories are suffering today is increasing even in the realm of the cinema, where it affects themes as well as forms. The media use expressive human resources much as Humanity uses its energy resources; in both cases, they seem to believe blindly and in the face of the evidence that they are drawing on an inexhaustible source. Here too the defenders of modern art have the same ideology as industrialists. The Beaubourg Palace is a factory planted in the heart of Old Paris as the legacy of a president who was the image of reaction and consequently supported the Art of his day; behind it real chimneys belch forth real sulphur dioxide. The director of a British TV station said recently, "We've interviewed the whole island—there's nothing for it but to start again." That need be no obstacle: we shall start again. . . .

So we shall continue to turn to Art like a prayer wheel—revived, pastiched, disparaged, commented on—with no end in sight. Our age thus expresses itself in two ways: future centuries will inherit a tainted atmosphere *and* will know what Andy Warhol thought about it. Both forms of expression will be understood, the one through the other. Each polluted forest is the collective work of art on which individual art comments. While sculptors wrap up mountains in plastic, the industries that make much of them coat the seas with fuel oil. The creators of the past dreamed of a world; so long as Art goes on, it can't be helped if we are turning their dream upside down. Better the end of the world than the end of the dream. . . . What does it mean to "move with one's times": to modernize a liturgy or to declare it completed? Apart from its industrial wastes, our age salvages everything: false sadness, false revolt, pseudo-curses, revolution for nothing, and subversion for nobody. Behind all this the most conservative of cults endure and worsen. It is the cult of the signature, of the edict of genius, of initiation in the enigma that protects class division, of the separation of people by the very thing that formerly sought to unite them, of arrogance, of bluff, of arbitrariness, of imposture, of incitement to hypocrisy, of knowledge as a way of sensitivity, of sensitivity as a cultural attainment, and of culture as a juxtaposition of conformities.

Orwell imagined a novel-writing Department that produced stories on an assembly-line basis. There is no need for such a department: novelists exist. A lot of Art is being expended, and the stock must be renewed. To achieve the nine-hundred-ninety-ninth interpretation of the same sonata, radio stations steal freely from past interpretations for the benefit of the new. To each his own: to each book its week of fame, to each writer his or her hour (soon, literally) of glory. We have no need for song-writing computers: our pop music only uses about fifteen chords and imbues the whole thing with empty frenzy, fabricated anguish, fraternity, pacifism, and interstellar peace at a discount. Like free jazz, whose liberty is Chance, the popular catchy tune still uses the harmonic and melodic resources of the nineteenth century. People croon endlessly about love, liberty, and peace, while torture, the armaments industry, hate, and pollution croon away too and make their fortune with (or through) contemporary art. This upstart, perverter that it is, is already in the process of losing the schoolboy iconoclasm that once masked its subsidized conservatism. If henceforth it is permitted everything, it is because it can no longer do anything. The fear of silence and of death dwells within it. It is better to be nothing than to appear to be nothing. For a myth revolutionized so many times that it has lost even the power to support itself, what could be more beautiful than a revolution supported by power?

THE OBSERVATORY
OF BABEL

I

The current meaning of the word "culture" implies gratuitousness. One is "cultured" if one has a merely literary skill, but "scholarly" if one has a mathematical skill. The two are traditionally opposed to each other and communicate in only one direction: a scholar can, without preparation, read a writer's work, but the converse is not true. Incapable of solving problems posed in a language it does not know, nonscientific culture is all the more terrified of the other because scientific authority is inevitably based on technical success. Philosophy today consists largely of historical and literary commentaries, whereas the contributions of Science are accepted without discussion as advances in Knowledge—even if they come from one of the pseudosciences, such as psychoanalysis. Moreover, Science, without having the slightest right to do so, manipulates subjects that formerly belonged to metaphysics: space, time, causality, determinism, chance, the origin of ideas, and so forth.

It is not my intention here to elaborate my own philosophy of science, only to show that Science cannot provide one; that it is totally incapable of assessing the real nature of time, space, or causality; that it cannot examine these or the other concepts it has borrowed ready-made from common sense except by putting its own postulates back into the melting pot. This happens when, for example, Physics disputes the principle of causality—without which there can be no Physics. Gödel's famous Incompleteness Theorem illustrates the problem. One cannot use geometry to demonstrate the truth or falsity of the axioms that make geometry possible, or speculate on the nature of numbers only with the aid of numbers, or, generally speaking, examine any system of knowledge in the light of that knowledge alone. Within the limits of any system, certain truths must be accepted without proof.

Any science may seem limitless at its peak; but it is nevertheless restricted at its base—and that base does not belong to it, but to something outside it. Moreover, it is not difficult to show that every scientific explanation boils down to a tautology (a truism that Wittgenstein was not the first to point out), to the explanation of a fact by itself ("He is talented *because* he is gifted," "I find it hard to sleep *because* I am an insomniac"). Thus crystallization is "explained" by a molecular arrangement that is merely crystallization *described in another way*; a predisposition to diabetes is "caused" by physiological attributes that merely define this predisposition; the colours in a prism "provide" refractive indices, which are in fact nothing but the colours of the prism expressed in quantitative terms; the innumerable particles of modern subatomic research are, properly speaking, mathematical necessities hypostasized into objects. One says that bodies are attracted to each other "because" of gravitation—which simply means that bodies are attracted to each other. The Law of Inertia states that a body that is not subjected to any force is in uniform rectilinear motion, which means that a body does not spontaneously change either speed or direction, but a force is defined as something capable of changing the speed or direction of a body, so what the Law really says is that a body not subjected to any force is not subjected to any force.

Far from being merely a matter of thought marking time, tautology constitutes both the end and the means of human knowledge. To solve a problem is to see everything that its statement implies (and hence *is*), then to see what is implied by these implications, and then—always by a series of equivalences, and thus of tautologies—to arrive at the final implication, which is the answer. Now, either a law is empirical and so is not a real law (the fact that a phenomenon has appeared billions of times in the same conditions does not necessitate its reappearance), or it is logical—and only then is its necessity absolute. It is infinitely *probable* that the sun will rise tomorrow, but it is absolutely *necessary* that an event have a cause, for "to be an event" and "to have a cause" have the same meaning. If Fact A must of necessity produce Fact B, it is either because A is identical with B or because A contains B. Anything that is logical is merely identity, and Science is a progressive *identification* of the Universe. The equal sign, without which no Science would be possible, is tautology par excellence, since it states that two things of different form are actually one. The scientists use, with rigorous logic, an inexhaustible well of "or in other words" that allow them to explain the implicit—nothing more. Their observations and experiments only enrich the material or verify without ever justifying—which is to say that it merely confirms the fact instead of explaining it. Logic follows the phenomenon instead of the phenomenon conforming to logic.

This point will, perhaps, become more clear if we consider an example cited by Hegel in both *Logic* and *Encyclopaedia*; it deals with the Newtonian interpretation of Kepler's First Law. Centrifugal force is considered to increase the distance between a planet and its sun. However, before this force can fling the planet into space, a centripetal force gains the upper hand and pulls it back towards the sun. The result is an equilibrium that sustains the planet in an elliptical orbit. Yet having invoked these forces, we are no nearer to understanding why planets have elliptical orbits. We have merely found another way of expressing the phenomenon, without providing the slightest shadow of an explanation for it.

Newton's Law itself is simply an identity derived from the statement: "bodies are attracted to each other." If they are attracted to each other, then the greater the distance between them, the less the attraction. For if the reverse were true or if the attraction remained equal at all distances, there would be no reason for the distance between them to alter. Let us suppose that one of the masses is X times greater than the other: then its power of attraction must be X times stronger, for attraction is proportional to the mass even as it is inversely proportional to the distance. If we call the mass m, and the distance d, then the attraction of one body for the other is m/d. But since each body attracts the other, we get the product of the two masses divided by the product of their mutual distance, i.e., mm'/d^2 —Newton's formula, which is a tautology and means only that bodies attract each other. This statement is itself tautological, for since every portion of matter is necessarily infinitely divisible, any body can be considered a conglomeration of material points—and hence a result of attraction.

Science reaches it limits, however, when, in order to account for a reality, it resorts to creations that are valuable as tools but conceptually void. If I cannot understand a phenomenon except by admitting the existence of $\sqrt{-1}$, I am exchanging an enigma for something that has no meaning. The Theory of Relativity is much the same: useful as a tool but barren of real content. Relativity claims to have legislative powers in philosophy and to overthrow traditional notions of space and time, yet it begins by restricting the meaning of these terms, calling the material Universe "space" and "time" the ensemble of speeds—including, of course, the speed of clocks.

When Physics plays around with the speed of light, it can only put its own foundations into question; this speed is the speed of images, on which Physics depends entirely since the physical world is nothing but images and without images nothing can be observed. Relativity is laden with paradox because physicists consider light one phenomenon of the visible world, whereas it is the *condition* of that world. No experiments were necessary to prove that the speed of light cannot be exceeded or that it is constant and isotropic (i.e., independent of the motion of the luminous source), properties demonstrable by reasoning alone. All three, but especially the last ("demonstrated experimentally by Michelson and Morley), are central to the Einsteinian revolution.

Why is it impossible to exceed the speed of light? A moving body that did exceed it could only be indicated by points of light or by electromagnetic waves (whose speed we know to be the same as that of light); this body would have to have a luminous or electromagnetic trajectory—implying that the light points or the electromagnetic waves were travelling faster than themselves.

It is equally logical that the speed of light must be constant. It is the speed of transmission of all visual images. Now, an image emitted once per second would still be emitted and recorded once per second even if the speed of delivery were suddenly reduced. If you send me one letter per day and if postal service suddenly slows down to half speed, I shall nevertheless continue to receive one letter per day, after a certain delay. In the case of light this delay would be imperceptible, for all images, and hence everything that can possibly be observed (including brain waves, the hands of a watch, etc.), would suffer the same delay. No measuring apparatus, not even Fizeau's, would detect the slightest lapse, for a luminous emission is an image just like any other. Since it is absurd to imagine a single unobservable variation in speed unless all other speeds varied to exactly the same extent, to say that the speed of light is constant boils down to a pleonasm, if not to a meaningless preciseness.

There remains the third property, isotropy: the speed of light is independent of the motion of the luminous source. However in reality this source is *never in motion*. In classical Physics, as in common sense, a body A shot from a moving body B acquires their added velocities; a man running at 10 km/h in a train doing 100 km/h in the same direction is running at 110 km/h in relation to the ground; two cars going in opposite directions from the same point at 60 km/h move away from each other at 120 km/h, and so on. Light contradicts this Galilean Law of Added Velocities. To observers on an asteroid rushing towards the Sun, the rays of light coming towards them should appear to be travelling faster than those going in the same direction as the asteroid. But this is not the case. Why not? Relativity's answer is that the motion of the asteroid distorts the observers' time and space, and thus their measurement of speed. Now, from the observers' point of view, it is the Sun that is coming closer—the asteroid itself is immobile. But one cannot talk, as Relativity does, of the motion of a luminous source. It is simply incorrect to say that light is *coming from* the Sun, or that the observer sees the Sun moving. The Sun is an *image* consisting of luminous points in space, and its motion is merely the succession of these points. Each point is at a given distance from the observers, and a distance is a fixed quantity. So from the observers' point of view, the light of the sun comes from an infinite series of fixed points. Thus the speed of the asteroid cannot be added to that of the light represented by these points; the asteroid's progress merely serves to reveal them. To claim that a star emits light (strictly speaking, it is light that emits a star) is to believe that the image of a body at a given moment emanates from this same body an instant later—in other words, that the image is emitted by another body that is different from it.

But let us suppose that a solar eruption takes place. The inhabitants of the asteroid will see it occur at whatever distance away from them the Sun happens to be at the time. Now observers elsewhere in space who take the Sun for a fixed point (accounting for the speed of light) will not put the Sun in the same spot as the inhabitants of the asteroid have put it, nor will time on the asteroid elapse in the same way as it does for them. Every body in motion takes its own space with it and hence its own time—they are necessarily linked because the human measurement of time is always spatial. It depends, in fact, on speed and it is impossible to say, for example, whether two speeds measured in kilometers per hour are the same when the word *kilometer* does not mean the same thing in both cases.

Let me remark in passing that astronomy is in error when it supposed that galaxies moving away from us faster than light can travel could not be perceived. The image of a galaxy does not depend on the galaxy itself, but on the point in space where it was emitted; this point is fixed in relation to any given observers, and consequently it must reach them at the speed of light, whatever the speed of recession of the galaxies may be.

All the innumerable paralogisms that Physics countenances with regard to light are based on the same false concept of a luminous source in motion—for example, the proposition that two rays of light will move away from each other at the speed of only one of them. To establish the contrary, it is only necessary to measure the speed of propagation of the same light in two different directions. But a false concept derived from observation is readily confirmed by observation—like Newton's centrifugal and centripetal forces.

Now let us imagine two planets, one equidistant from two stars A and B, the other rushing towards B. If A and B explode at the same time, the two explosion images will reach the inhabitants of the first planet simultaneously; but the inhabitants of the second planet will see B's explosion first because they are approaching it. Thus, from the viewpoint of Relativity, the simultaneity of two events in the Universe is a fiction. It can exist for some, but not for others. In fact, even knowing the relevant distances and the speed of light, the inhabitants of the two planets would not end up with the same results from their measurements of the situation, for their clocks could not be keeping the same time. When a body is moving away from another body, the light of the messages they exchange takes

progressively longer to reach them; there is thus a general, reciprocal slowing down.

By itself, this slowing down could be corrected for, but there is a
second discrepancy for which no correction can be made: it derives
from the fact that nothing can exceed the speed of light. Let us
suppose that the planets are moving away from each other at a
speed less than the speed of light—say, at only 2,000 km/sec (the
speed of light is 300,000 km/sec). This 2,000 km/sec then represents
the maximum conceivable speed for each planet *in the eyes of the
other*. Now, this maximum conceivable speed is precisely that of
light, which *must* be constant. In consequence, the 2,000 km/sec
must *represent,* in fact, for the inhabitants of these planets, 300,000
km/sec—and all other speeds, including the speed of clocks, must
obviously be reduced in the same ratio. The problem would be the
same if a speed of 60 km/h had to stay at that figure when it had
really fallen to 1 km/h. One would have to deduce either that one
hour had "become" one minute—for 60 km/h is 1 km/min—or that 1
kilometer was now *equivalent to* 60. There is the origin of the
famous contraction of time. If all speeds contracted, Physics would
say that time had contracted.

This gives rise to the well-known Langevin's paradox. An as-
tronaut who left Earth at a speed approaching that of light would
find, on returning after two years of "his" (or "her") time, that Earth
had aged two centuries. The reciprocal would be true if we had
clocks that ran at "our" speed, and if, as far as the human organism
were concerned, there were no biological clock working at "Earth"
speed. Atomic clocks launched into space have "verified" this paradox: they slow down in conformity with Relativity. But on the one
hand, Langevin's traveller would be strictly equivalent to a human
in hibernation—of whom one would never say that his or her time
had contracted; on the other hand the experiment with the atomic
clocks demonstrates that time does *not* really contract: only speeds
are affected, including the speed of clocks. The confusion arises
again from the fact that physicists are compelled to give the name
time to an ensemble of speeds.

Imagine a time contracted in the ratio of 60 to 1. A one-minute
speech would be the same (otherwise it would not be contracted,
but shortened: whereas time, if it contracts, does so over the whole
of its "length"), but it would only last for a second. Now, during this

second, for the same reason, the clock would show one minute. The speech would thus have lasted a minute; neither the watch nor the calendar of Langevin's traveller would differ in any way from ours. Every imaginable measuring device would show the same amount of time elapsed as would have elapsed on our planet if he had spoken—or thought or acted—here. We would be able to pass from our universe to his without detecting the slightest change. Now, a change that is radically undetectable is a contradiction in terms: thus, in "contracting," *time is not really contracting at all.* The same thing happens if one tries to add the contraction of space to that of time; 60 km/h would become 1 km/min—i.e., the same speed—but during this minute the clock would show one hour had elapsed, while the 1 km would be the equivalent of 60: here again, *nothing* would be altered. The atomic clock launched into the cosmos would not go any slower if time contracted; if it ran slower and if the term *slower* had any meaning, it would be in relation to a time that did not change. The whole thing boils down to a contraction of speeds, and nothing more.

All the Relativity experiments on the slowing down of clocks or the contraction of lengths apply only to speed. Scientists persistently forget that so-called variations in time or space refer to a time and to a space that are supposed to be invariable; that the speed of light, on which the whole of Relativity is based, is everywhere and always the same—which implies that *second* and *kilometer* mean the same thing everywhere and always. In other words, the bases of Relativity are the absolute space and the absolute time that it seeks to deny.

The same thing can be said about simultaneity. The Relativist dogma says there is no absolute simultaneity, alluding to the fact that the same event cannot be perceived simultaneously by any two observers. (But if there are two observers, on what grounds can one talk about the "same" event?) Nevertheless, Relativism, like all physics, does and must posit absolute simultaneity—which is nothing other than absolute time. If simultaneity, which refers only to time, were not absolute, it could be said that the rest of the Universe is, at this precise moment, either past or future. But if it is not yet, or is no longer, in being, then it does not exist. On the other hand, this past and future are *simultaneous* with our present down here, and therefore they are neither past nor future.

When the astronomers say that Alpha Centauri, which lies about four light years away, appears to us as it was four years ago, they are saying that four years ago the present aspect of this star and our then-present were simultaneous. Likewise, Langevin says that two years pass for his traveller *while* two centuries pass on Earth, and that in consequence these two durations are simultaneous. In the statement that the light emitted by a star will reach one planet later than it will another, this "later" postulates a universal elapsing of time, and hence an absolute simultaneity. The same can be said about space. Time is an ensemble of speeds, space is an ensemble of distances. The idea of a curvature of space (or of space time, which is merely a simple amalgam of four coordinates) is applicable only to the material universe *within* space. We know that light does not travel in a straight line in the neighbourhood of a star, but what could we know about it if we could not calculate what trajectory the light would have to follow to be travelling in a straight line and therefore know that this line does not exist in space? This knowledge is neither Euclidean nor non-Euclidean, but common sense. To apply to time and space notions like "contraction" or "curvature," which are borrowed specifically from time and space, is to beg the question. When scientists say "we are beyond the old space of Kant," they give us an idea of what Relativity can bring to Philosophy. Kant's space is defined essentially as the a priori framework of exterior phenomena; it would be interesting to know if Science sees it differently. Einstein's theory is regarded as having introduced geometry into physics—for example, by making gravitation a property of space; in fact it has introduced (with purely practical intentions) physics into geometry. Fundamentally, there has been no effect on the concepts of time, space, simultaneity, and even cause, which Relativity is said to have overthrown. Science continues to use them, following the example of the common sense from which it stems.

II

It must be added that Bergson was right, and at Einstein's expense. Science cannot understand time, but it is compelled to use it, and to do so it perforce changes time into space. An idea is an image, an image is visual, and the visual is spatial. The moment we *see* time, we picture an arrowed line, reversible and infinitely divisible but motionless. In order to consider motion, we have to see it as a succession of points or stops. This obligation alone makes time and motion the opposite of what they are. The former becomes an immobility, the latter a succession of immobilities.

It is always a question of past time and past motion, but the past, being fixed, is no longer either time or motion; it has only *been* time or motion. Zeno's arrow never reaches its target because it first covers half the distance, then half of the remaining half, and so on ad infinitum, since space is infinitely divisible (whereas time is not in the least divisible). But the arrow is never *located* at one of these points; it merely *passes through* each of them in succession. The whole of Bergsonism stems from this observation.

Everything used to measure time really measures space. Clocks, sundials, hourglasses, using the position of the stars, and so forth are all based on the principle that traversal of a given space means an equivalent lapse of time. When we say that one minute has passed, we are merely saying that the secondhand of a watch has completed one circuit of the watch face. If we were condemned to speak of time in purely temporal terms, no precision would be possible. Saying, for example, that an instant is equivalent to three moments and that a moment is equivalent to two ticks is sufficient to show the absurdity of a language of time in which there are no spatial implications. To be sure, we have an intuition of the equality of durations; the existence of rhythm proves that. But if several people start together on the same rhythm and are then required to carry it on individually in isolation, it very soon ceases to be the same rhythm. Physicists would doubtless say that this is a question of "psychological time," but what they mean by "time" here is a group of speeds and a journey through space. Moreover, they might invoke Langevin's traveller and come up with "the contraction of time," meaning the slowing down of brain waves, a preeminently physiological and psychological process.

However, the adjective *psychological* is ridiculous. Numbers are at least as objective as any physical object, yet we realize their existence only in our minds. Can one say therefore that they are psychological? If so, there would exist, as Frege has more or less said, ten vagues, ten sads, ten forgottens, and so on—and several different people could each conceive the number ten in a slightly different way. Pure time is not psychological, but it is irrational in one sense, and one sense only: *that a science of time is impossible.* The spatial treatment we force time to undergo certainly has no practical scientific importance, but my purpose, once again, is to examine the theory rather than the practice of Science.

Nothing brings out the nature of time more clearly than another myth—one that is parascientific to which Physics (especially Relativist Physics—cf. the "temporal inversion" in the "black holes" of astrophysics) lends itself: the myth of reversibility. Wells's time machine is a perfect absurdity. It "goes back in time" to its date of manufacture and changes the past so that what has been never takes place. If time could go backwards, musical notes could pour out of my ears and go back into the piano; I could know less at the end of a sentence than at the beginning, and so on. The very images are false, for they liken the regression of time to what happens when a film is run backwards. Now, in order to watch time go backwards (or a film run the wrong way), I need some time—time that is not going backwards. For if the time I were in was itself going backwards, I would see the film running the right way—and at once time would no longer be going backwards. It is impossible to picture a reversible time, because time is always irreversible. Neither is it possible to imagine time standing still; as soon as one tries, the question arises: for how long a *time* would time stand still? Even the expression *past time* is radically wrong. Time cannot be that which passes; rather it is the relationship between that which passes and that which does not pass. If everything, including myself, passed with time, how could I know that something was passing? And *before what* would time pass? A car is not in motion in relation to me if I am moving at the same speed and in the same direction as the car; nothing moves if everything around me moves with me.

Direction is at the root of the matter. The apparent direction of time, as represented by Science and by common sense, is the reverse of its real direction (if indeed one can talk of a direction). The traditional representation of time is the simple arrow:

Past ————————————————→ Present

The present, shown here at the head of the arrow, *is changing position*. When it changes position, it does so in relation to the past, which is regarded as fixed. The arrow starts at an instant in past time, in relation to which all other instants are located and which is thus their point of reference. Now, here we have a practical convention that is a logical absurdity. A past date can never be a true temporal reference. It has no meaning unless I know at what date we are *now*. This *now*, however, does not in any way depend on the past and is consequently the only criterion possible. The question "What time *is* it?" calls for an immediate answer; the question "What time *was* it?" merely calls for another question: "When?" The answer is meaningless unless it says: "One hour (one day, etc.) *ago from now*." The past is defined by the present, not the present by the past, and thus the present is the fixed point. Furthermore, time does not elapse in the direction past-to-present, but in the direction present-to-past, for the very simple reason that *every event is present before it is past*. Thus the time arrow is properly drawn as:

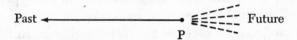

It is from point P (the present) that the past *recedes*. Only the present always precedes everything that happens and is, strictly speaking, the cause of it. Apart from the fact that there never has been and never will be anything but the present, saying that the past produces the present (as the current concept of "cause" tends to do) is tantamount to saying that a ship is propelled by its wake or that what *is no more* produces what *is*. Only the converse is true, of course: only that which *is* can produce that which *will be no more*. In other words, only the present produces the past.

One should not be surprised to find the present described as a fixed point. Granted that the present, by definition, is never the same. But it is at the point of the present that two things coincide: the motion of that which passes and the fixity of that which does not pass. Real time, once again, is nothing but the *relationship* between these two realities. But the fact that the direction of time is not past-to-present-to-future but future-to-present-to-past (or rather, still-to-pass-passing-past) does not constitute a reversal of time itself. Our change of perspective does not change the order of succession of the phenomena; in practice, saying that the present advances or saying that the past recedes amounts to the same thing. In practice, but not as of right: causality, as hitherto understood by scholars, philosophers, and the human mind in general, is no longer valid. We shall see presently that it has never been valid.

Why have we always been wrong about the direction of time? Two philosophers, Maine de Biran and Schopenhauer, do have at least an inkling of the reason. We have no option but to await the outcome of both our actions and our thoughts. Our awareness can do nothing but turn towards the future. When it believes it is turning itself towards the past, by recalling a memory, it forgets that this memory, like its own remembering of it, is unfolding in the direction present-to-future, or—what comes to the same thing—past-to-present, thus following the classical temporal arrow. Everything that one's awareness does is intentional, in the sense that whether one is looking ahead, remembering, acting, or thinking, that which *is* must (or desires to) produce that which *will be*. Thus, my present produces my future. Therefore, how can one doubt that the Universe's past has produced its present? So in the traditional assignment of our time arrow to the world, we are merely projecting onto the world our own orientation, which is finalist. In other words, our notion of universal causality is a disguised version of our own bias towards finality.

We apply this conception of causality to our only possible field of action, which is our experience—i.e., the past. As Berkeley noted some time ago, we have learned that the appearance of a given phenomenon is the *signal* for the appearance of another phenomenon; since all we need do to obtain the phenomenon is to produce the signal, we say that the signal creates the phenomenon. In fact, it only ushers it in, and it does so because it is already part of it.

Under close examination, causality dissolves into identity. What we call the cause of a phenomenon is not that which immediately precedes it (the whole world can precede a phenomenon without being the cause of it), but the ensemble of the conditions that enable it to appear. Now, in the absolute sense (and there can be no other), the ensemble of conditions required for this appearance constitutes the appearance itself. In fact, there can be no time, however short, between a cause and its effect; if there were, the latter would not start *as a result* of the former, and the words "cause" and "effect" would no longer have any meaning. Now, two states of the same thing between which no interval of time can be observed are simultaneous—i.e., identical. Thus, if the complete fulfillment of the conditions of x do not produce x (this fulfillment being identical with x), we would have $x \neq x$—a violation of the principle of identity. This law of causality could be violated only if a thing could not be itself. Let us suppose that a number of events, n, is required to obtain an event, m: then there is *no difference* between the n events taken together and the event m.

The drawback to this law is that it is based on simultaneity and thus excludes time, with the result that causality has no validity in the sole sphere in which it interests us, namely in the sequence of time. On the other hand, if one insists that a cause immediately precedes its effect, the cause of any event is easy to define: it is the event that was present immediately before it became past. Yet this definition is useless, for if one were to pursue a demonstration that the present state of the world "is the result of" all the states that preceded it, one would never stop going back through the succession of past "causes," with the result that the present state would never be correctly determined. Or else one would stop and pick some "prime cause," which, since it was present before it became past, could not be determined either. In either case, the result is indeterminacy.

Since cause and effect are strictly identical, predicting the latter when one knows the former boils down to predicting something one already knows. Furthermore, the simultaneity effect-cause (or cause-effect) is that of the present with itself; the present can have no duration, however infinitesimal, since a duration is a succession and thus includes a past. A duration composed of presents without duration is a contradiction—but time is this very contradiction. That which passes is the reverse of that which does not pass, and the present—and hence time—is only, as we have just seen, the relationship between these two poles, the obverse and the reverse of a figure. Now, a relationship does not exist outside its terms: it *contains* them—that is, it holds them together. An effect must "follow" its cause, because there can be no violation at any point of the principle of identity, which requires that a thing be itself. Indeed, there are no points, except for time arrested, for the past, like water frozen into ice, has no more direction; ice is no longer water, and time arrested is no longer time. The past is determinate because it has been determined and thus ended. It is precisely because there are no points, because time is indivisible, that one cannot find anything after the event except the identity of the present with itself. Take two points on the temporal line: however close they are to one another, one will find that the change from one to the other takes place *between* the two, just as real time (which is impossible to grasp, since to grasp it is to stop it) lies *between* the presents.

The principle that "the same causes always produce the same effects" is another tautology. If we can establish that two causes are exactly the same but do not produce the same effects, we have to conclude that the same two causes are not actually involved. Even if a stone dropped from the top of the same tower sometimes falls upwards and sometimes downwards, nevertheless the Universe continues to obey the above-mentioned principle, and I can never say that this rising and falling have the same causes, since all the causes that I can find for either also produce a rise or a fall themselves.

The same can be said about Leibnitz's Principle of Sufficient Reason, which holds that every event has one or more reasons that explain it in its totality. We have just seen that the conjection of the conditions of an event *is* that event. Suppose the event lacks one of its conditions (in other words, one of its reasons); it would then be lacking a part of itself and would not be what, in fact, *is*. This would violate the principle of identity and hence is impossible.

Since the coincidence of cause and effect is nothing but simultaneity and thus instantaneity, and since the latter is nothing but an abstraction performed on temporal *points* and hence on time arrested or negated, the concept of cause applies to everything except duration. Respecting duration, unfortunately, it means nothing. The present Universe only "determines" the Universe as it will be one second from now as the *basis* for the changes that will take place. How can there be any change if everything is merely a series of linked identities with no possible failure or ending? The answer is at least threefold. First, the concept of change presupposes that of identity; the former is able to exist only on the basis of the latter and in relation to it. Second, either one considers identity, which can be grasped but has nothing to do with time, or one considers succession, which does relate to time but cannot be grasped. Finally, change and identity, the two poles of time, are totally irreconcilable, even though duration achieves their synthesis. A phonograph needle can be placed at any number of points on a record, but unless the record turns, no music will result. One is welcome to thinking of the movement of the record as a very rapid succession of needle positions, but it is precisely because it is *something else* that the music does come out. In any case, "very rapid succession" is a double begging of the question: succession implies time, and rapidity implies movement. The needle plays the role of the present, of perpetual instantaneity, of the fixed point; if it were to turn with the record, there would be no music. A river cannot be said to flow if its banks flow along with it; neither does the hour change if the sundial turns with the sun.

All that we know about time is that it is a perpetual production of the past *by* the present, and that everything always unfolds in this order—*first* the present, *then* the past. Thus, free action is not only possible but the only thing that ever takes place. Yet freedom cannot violate the law of causality; however free an action may be, *after the event* it will always be found that it could not have been other than free—which simply means that it could not have failed to take place. Even if the inert Universe were unfolding only in accordance with divine intentions, it would seem no more mechanical or determinist than it does. If the present "wishes" to do something, it is obliged to begin by producing the conditions for that thing—either its causes or, finally, the thing itself. Can one speak of a *law* that requires me to attain my objective in order for me to attain my objective? The "law" of causality is nothing other than this. A series of instantaneities would show that my cerebral states are necessarily linked together. Determinism would deduce from this that I am not free to think what I wanted. In fact, to think what it thinks, my mind (and thus also my cerebral states) has to be directed to this end, an end realized being nothing other than a result whose means are, *after* the event, its causes.

That it is possible, locally and approximately, to foresee that a cause x will have an effect y, results solely from the facts that x *is* already y, and that it is always foreseeable that a thing will be itself. If I drop a stone, I am certain that it will fall, but my certainty is absolute only because a dropped stone already *is* a falling stone. Strictly speaking, the physical Universe considered in time offers probabilities (some of which—for example, that Gauss's Law will still be valid in two minutes' time—are infinite) but no certainties unless one is dealing with laws that yield identities. This is the case in mathematics, in physics, and in every discipline in which the word "law" retains a precise meaning. All Science is, as we have already seen, merely an identification of the Universe. The present ceaselessly alters what already is; this alteration is always partial, and all we can predict is that which will *not* be modified. Every scientific expression involving time has the form $y = f(t)$. The independent variable t represents time, but it varies only in proportions that must not vary themselves. For Science, time is thus a duration without change—a nonduration. It remains to show that, since this is the case, the law of causality loses all heuristic validity and Science all explicative validity.

III

No doubt the reader is familiar with the thinking of Laplace, the putative father of scientific determinism. Give me a complete description of the Universe at the present moment, he said, give me the ensemble of existing laws, and I shall deduce the state of the Universe at any future moment. It is not difficult to show that what this proposal really means is: "Give me the world completely foreseen, and I shall foresee the world completely."

To simplify matters, let us suppose that the Universe consists of a single material point. Given its position, direction, and speed, I can in fact say what the position of the point will be at any future moment. But I have already been told that; giving me the position, direction, and speed of the point was only an indirect way of telling me where it would be at any given moment—exactly as the equation $2x + 2x = 4x$ is another way, general and therefore indirect, of saying that $2 + 2 = 4$, that $4 + 4 = 8$, and so on. To suppose that laws exist permitting one to foresee what an event will be with absolute precision (for merely relative precision already excludes determinism) is to suppose that determinism is true—which is precisely what one was trying to demonstrate. Laplace's dictum thus becomes: If determinism is true, there are laws that make it possible to foresee the whole future of the Universe; give me the ensemble of these laws, and I shall show that determinism is true.

In any case, such laws do not exist. I have already remarked that a law can be necessary only if it is logical. Empirical "laws" are not logical: their basis is simple repetition, and so their violation would not involve a contradiction. That a phenomenon has recurred since the beginning of the world is not a reason for it to *have* to occur again. Now, real laws are necessary only because they are expressions of identities, either in the form x equals y (x is identical to y) or in the form "if x, then y" (y is identical to or included in x). Given the totality of laws and facts, not even God could not deduce from them anything but the present, since every law expresses an identity and the only constant law in the Universe is causality. A "given moment" is without motion and thus outside of time: from a set of immobilities that constitute a state and a set of equivalencies that constitute laws, nothing can be deduced other than this state, motionless and identical to itself. But even if God insisted, by reasoning ad absurdum, that deducing the future is logically possible, He could not count on constant speed, force, direction, or mass; He would have to verify these at every instant. At best, these verifications and therefore the deduction itself would be instantaneous. *But the passage from one instant to another is also instantaneous.* In other words, deduction could never do more than keep pace with the present. Determinism is thus not valid for either the Universe as a whole or its most infinitesimal component.

That foreknowledge is unthinkable even for God merely brings God into closer alliance with Life, which is improvised rather than providential. Creation is continuous in the sense that it has been *present* since the beginning of the world, which was the first present. The future, in conformity with the real time arrow as I have drawn it, may be considered to flow continuously into the present and then become the past. The origin of the very first present— which is our most distant past—lies at the end of the future; the beginning of the world is at its end. Yet one should think not just of a circle, but of a circle growing continuously larger. Time is final by definition, since causality is, in fact, merely intemporal.

This does not mean that "everything"—namely anything whatever —is possible. It is impossible for what *is* not to *be,* and time acts on what *is.* The miracle of Life is not an inexplicable mechanism but a graspable objective.

Logicians used to distinguish between efficient causes and final causes—in modern language, between causes and objectives. The expression *final cause* is preferable to *objective* because an objective can be *either* a motive or a result, whereas the concept of finality equates the two. A finality is a cause that is also its own effect. I light a cigarette. The lit cigarette is the result of my action, but the cause of this action was an objective—the lit cigarette itself. Of course, an unlit cigarette and a lit cigarette are not the same thing, so in this and equivalent instances cause and effect are not strictly identical. This is why Science, which admits only identity, cannot use final causes to explain events without abandoning logical precision. If someone throws himself out of a window, his action evidently has a final cause, namely an intention to commit suicide. But a strictly scientific explanation can only use efficient causes: he threw himself out of the window because his cerebral chemistry produced a certain state, which followed from a certain other state, and so on. According to Science, the cause precedes the action; objectives that a phenomenon *appears* to manifest after the fact can only be conjectural.

Efficient causes characteristically lose their verisimilitude as one goes higher up the scale of the living. The inert world appears to obey the old maxim *post hoc ergo propter hoc* ("after this, therefore because of this), although we have seen that this saying is fallacious. Even the behaviour of a plant permits mechanical interpretations: the bud grows "because of" the sun's rays and not "with a view to" becoming a leaf. In the case of animal behaviour, however, efficient causality carries little conviction: one finds it hard to believe that a cat heads for a bowl of milk *because of* cerebral mechanisms or that the *objective* of drinking plays a merely ornamental role in the process. Finally, when it comes to human actions, efficient causes become truisms. Thus physics and chemistry can make shift, more or less, with traditional "causality." But physiology and even biology cannot say anything at all without resorting to the concept of *function* and hence of objective. And psychology and linguistics can deal only with final causes; a behaviour can be explained only by its objective, and the cause of the beginning of a sentence, as well as of its whole, is its meaning, which is only discovered at the end.

However, there is more to the idea of finality than this. It is intimately connected with the concept of chance, and this connection is referred to increasingly by both biology and cybernetics in their efforts to interpret the vital processes. Chance is often contrasted with causality, as if an event produced by Chance had no cause—whereas it would be more accurate to say it has no objective: the expression *by chance* simply means "without design." Thus *chance* and *finality* each provide a negative definition of the other; their connection is reciprocal, and as one advances, the other must recede. The finalist element in any given instance of this connection can be expressed as a probability. In tossing a die, one can never say that a given number will turn up, but one can say that a given number has one chance in six of coming up. In other words, it is impossible to predict a number but possible to *expect* one, and an expectation is simply a passive objective. Now, such an expectation is simply a passive finality. Chance, like time, is a relationship. It is the relationship between what one expects and what actually happens—that is, between our own finality and the unknowable finality (and hence, in practice, the nonfinality) of the world. As for probability, Pascal defines it as "the relationship between the number of favourable cases and the number of possible cases—all cases being equally possible." Note the adjective "favourable," which refers to the objective being sought (or expected), and especially note the precision of the phrase "all cases being equally possible."

Science, for all its determinist rigour, inevitably becomes probabilist when it has to deal with the very large or the very small. Thus it uses two contradictory principles. Probability supposes that a single event can result in one of several equally possible events, but that it is false to say the same causes always produce the same effects. Determinism says that if the die comes up five, no other number was possible *because* no other number came up. Science is probabilist before the event and determinist after. It thus makes two statements simultaneously: through causality, that the world could not be other than it is; through probabilities, that the world could be other than it will be.

Here the important scientific concept of entropy comes in. The stars die, matter decays, heat trickles away, arrangements—whatever they are—go awry, every machine (living or not) consumes more energy than it produces. In short, entropy is the universal law of degradation—indeed, the whole interest of this law is its universality, that is, its mathematical and logical character. If I put five thousand white beads on top of five thousand black beads in a big jar, the more I shake the jar, the more thoroughly the colours mix, and the more improbable it becomes that the original two-layer arrangement will appear. Any material system can be considered as an initial arrangement of this sort. The shaking is equivalent to the work of time, and the game rules, if one can use that phrase, are those of pure chance. Any portion of the Universe, indeed the Universe itself, is moving inevitably towards deterioration, towards the undifferentiated, towards a zero state. The concept of entropy, before becoming universalized, was called the Second Law of Thermodynamics and concerned only problems of heat. Carnot's formulation of the Second Law noted that it is impossible to wholly convert a given quantity of heat into other forms of energy (or into "useful work"). This implies an *absolute* loss, an irreversible devolution of matter or energy (which, as we know, are the same thing).

Every state of any part of the Universe can be considered as a given arrangement—but this arrangement changes, if only to an infinitesimal degree, even as I start to observe it, for if there were no change, there would be no such thing as time. Any finite collection of atoms, cells, or other objects is equivalent, in other words, to a mosaic whose elements form one arrangement out of x possible arrangements—all of which, according to the Law of Chance, are *equally* possible. The moment I consider such a mosaic, I accept it as the arrangement that will serve me as a reference (without which no probabilist evaluation is imaginable). In the following instant this arrangement has $1/x$ chance of remaining as it is, and in the instant following that, $1/x$ chance multiplied by $1/x$, that is, $1/x^2$, etc.,—just as in roulette one has $1/36$ chance of one's number coming up, but $1/36^2$ of it coming up twice running. The more time goes by, the more improbable it is that the initial arrangement will be restored. Thus, every material system moves towards absolute disorder, in the same way that universal energy travels, with no return, towards thermal death. This process annihilates even the crude consolation that atheism or agnosticism sometimes tries to draw from the eternity of matter; matter dies like everything else, and one day nothing will remain of the starry sky itself.

One cannot say that, because the Universe is infinite, entropy cannot apply to it. Even an infinite Universe is a single arrangement or system, and entropy applies equally and universally to all systems and parts of systems. If it is in the nature of a certain fuel to be consumed in two minutes, and if the process of consumption is applied to it universally, then any volume of that fuel, from a cubic centimeter to an infinity of cubic centimeters, would be consumed in two minutes. If the material Universe had begun at an infinitely remote time in the past, it would have had infinite time in which to die and would therefore already be dead—or, to carry strictness and paradox to the limit: if the Universe had *never* begun, it would have been finished since *always*. Consequently, either the Universe had a beginning, a moment at which all matter was created out of nothing, or it has existed eternally, in which case its continued existence can only be explained by a continuous creation of matter—again out of nothing. In either case, all matter is *created*. Thus, the Second Law of Thermodynamics contradicts the First, which states that energy and matter do not arise *ex nihilo*.

But mathematics expresses the implications of entropy far more simply and generally than does thermodynamics. No less certainly than thermodynamics, mathematical entropy condemns the material Universe to a ceaseless movement from order to disorder, but it departs from the arbitrary convention that the word *order* must be applied to the first arrangement one chooses to consider and *disorder* to those that follow it, thus equating *all* change with disorder.

It has long been said that Life does not conform to entropy because it proceeds from disorder to increasing order, from primitive organizations to superorganizations, from the probable to the improbable. This observation lacked precision until a new science, cybernetics, defined *information* as the reverse of entropy. If I want to draw the word *O–R* at random out of a bag containing the letters of the alphabet, I have one chance in twenty-six of drawing an *O*, multiplied by one chance in twenty-six of drawing an R. In other words, the chances of drawing both are 1 in 676. Clearly the odds against bringing out a word of five or six letters would be staggering, for the addition of extra letters results in the multiplication of the odds. Now, when addition in one series produces multiplication in another, the former is known as the *logarithm* of the latter; in the present instance, the logarithm is negative because the mutiplicands are fractions. Drawing the word *O R* is a datum (it can also be called a "negentropy"), and the more time passes, the less likely it is that the data will increase. Thus entropy and data are each the inverse measure of the other. But data, which are the epitome of order, decay as all orders do in conformity with entropy; they diminish as they are transmitted. Thus, every message contains errors, redundancies, and omissions, and the messages carried by the cells of organisms are no exception—hence the aging process.

Cybernetics, the theory of machines, is rightly assuming an ever larger role in biology. However, it will never be able to explain fully even the one aspect of Life with which it is equipped to deal—functions. This is because Life has, for three billion years, constituted a sphere of determination in which data pass ceaselessly from one living machine to another and nevertheless ceaselessly increase. Individuals undergo entropy and die; the messages they emit decay; civilizations, races, and species perish. But the hereditary "message" lives and is enriched. We are leaves on a great genealogical tree: as leaves, we die; but as parts of the tree, we contain its principle, which grows younger with the passage of time. A bacterium is far more ancient than a human, but contains far less data. *Where* these self-creating data come from, no science can say; for the spontaneous creation of data, like the creation *ex nihilo* of matter and like everything that is, strictly speaking, without cause, contradicts the very foundations of scientific knowledge. *Die Rose ist ohne Warum*, said Angelus Silesius, *Sie blühet weil sie blühet* ("The rose has no 'why': it blooms because it blooms"). Yet one cannot imagine a more absolute *why* than this. The creation that produces every *raison d'être* has no need of any.

On the other hand, many scientists believe that cybernetics "exorcises finality." They are wrong. Their usual model is that a machine provided with a thermostat shuts itself off when the desired degree of heat is attained. This action involves a simple process known as retroaction or feedback, and they suggest that processes of this sort might account for every kind of behaviour—in which case there would be no need to explain behaviour in terms of objectives or final causes. Several things can be said about this theory. First, it is true that if one denies finality, finality will inevitably *look like* a series of retroactions. Second, retroactions are possible only in organized structures—structures informed by objective or intent (nothing could be more intentional than the construction of a thermostat). And third, every retroaction reestablishes a broken equilibrium (homeostasis); now, an equilibrium is an organization, and hence a product of finality.

Another objection is even more fundamental. Indeed, cybernetics necessarily assumes the very finalism it claims to exorcise. If all data are not correct, or, rather, if everything is not data, this is by virtue of a criterion that, once again, marks an expectation and thus an objective. When I wish to draw out the word $O R$, the appearance of the O is a datum. But if I had wished to draw out ART, the O would not be a datum. Data exist only by bringing about finality, just like Chance—which, as we have seen, represents the reverse of finality. Furthermore, cybernetics is the science of machines, artificial or natural, and the very concept of the machine depends on the finalist concept of function.

Not only finality, but the purest subjectivity is presupposed by every aspect of cybernetics. Any bond between any two phenomena is either logical or functional. In the first case, it is subjective; in the second, final. In mathematics, anything at all can become an order provided one has a rule—but this rule, like an objective, can only stem from a subject. A message, cybernetic or not, must have a meaning—and the concept of meaning is the qualitative absolute (on principle Science does not have to worry about pure qualities, which are not quantifiable). Symmetries and repetitions, like order, are also fundamentally qualitative. Forces and speeds are applied to us directly, and we can apply them likewise to inert objects, whereas symmetries and repetitions need our intervention in order to exist. We receive them indirectly, piecemeal; we assemble them by comparison, aided by memory *inter alia*. That is why they shock us when they appear whole in inert Nature—we instinctively feel it impossible for them to come from that source. Bees, however negligible as subjects, nevertheless justify the symmetries of the honeycomb. If we saw their plans executed on a larger scale in rock, our first reaction would be to wonder *who* had done such work.

The impossibility, for Humans, of ever producing life or awareness (unless by borrowing from what both of them already are) is a *logical* and thus an *absolute* possibility. The cyberneticists define data by means of a criterion that is not only an objective, an anticipation, but already—and especially—a datum. If they expect the word *ART*, they will not suddenly start making do with the word *ARE*. But Life ceaselessly modifies both datum and criterion, and the latter is always both indefinite and infinite. Cybernetics decides in advance what shall or shall not be data, and thus optimal or maximal data. Life decides progressively what is or is not data and knows no maximum. That which is fixed can only decrease; only that which *fixes itself* increases. When the quantity of data circulating between machines (living or not) is calculated, it is calculated by an exterior awareness—which cannot apply its calculations to itself without rising above itself. Now, it is in Life itself that the principle of Life is to be found. When there were only single cells on Earth, the maximum degree of information, as fixed by cyberneticists (or biologists) would have corresponded only to the data necessary for the perfect reproduction of these cells without variation. Thus, Life could never have moved on to multicellular organisms.

In any case it is useless to talk of data when one is dealing with living things. The concept of datum includes the concept of chance, which in this context becomes mere preconception. When there is one bacterium in the water, it is mathematically improbable there will be two—whereas in reality the second bacterium is almost inevitable. If we already have the letter *O*, then the probability of the word *O R* is not 1 in 676, but 1 in 26—as was that of *O* alone. In denying the persistence of data in the presence of chance, cybernetics rejects its own basis—for there can be no data at all without a durable criterion and an awareness to maintain it. The letter *R* would not be a datum after the letter *O*, if the criterion *O R* had not been maintained from one letter to the other.

To say that Life appeared by chance is like saying that if a dice player put aside all the sixes he or she threw, then this ensemble of sixes drawn *from* Chance was drawn *by* chance—which is to confuse the material that a finality uses with the finality itself. Besides, what is the good of denying finality in the Universe, since one has no choice but to confront one's own human awareness—which exists, forms for this reason part of the Universe, and is *only* final? Science cannot only do nothing against finality; it can do nothing without it. The human brain is a pure machine, like all brains and all organs. But to what end was this machine built, and *who* uses it?

IV

In Science, materialism is the first working hypothesis. For the rest, it is merely a subphilosophy in which all the most ill-assorted prejudices come together. Since the days of Epicurus, it has been supported only by amateurs (Gassendi, La Mettrie, D'Holbach, Marx, Lenin, and so on) who have nearly always been motivated by a desire foreign to knowledge: that of putting religion (and thus the established order) in the wrong. From its earliest expressions, materialism has called for a bad faith considerably worse than that of the beliefs it seeks to fight (which, however, as we shall see later on, are really nothing but disguised materialism themselves).

I see a blue point. Either this blue point is nowhere, in which case it is immaterial, or it is material, in which case it is somewhere. In the latter case, it must be outside or inside my body. If it is on the outside, what I call blue is simply a vibration of a certain frequency; if it is on the inside (naturally, within my brain), it is merely a nervous impulse of a certain form. The blue point itself occupies no space. Similarly, for five hundred people in a room, their "image" of that room is the room lifesize. If this image were within their brains, the lifesize room would contain itself five hundred times. To say that the image is reduced or coded is absurd; *who* enlarges it or decodes it, and *where* does the lifesize image exist? If the materialists answer "nowhere," they are saying it does not exist, since only matter exists and something that is nowhere is not matter. Materialism cannot admit that awareness is immaterial without contradicting itself. It is a pointless subterfuge for it to describe awareness as "an epiphenomenon"—an appearance—for here too it contradicts itself; there can be no appearance without awareness, and it is difficult to prove that awareness is not real by postulating that it *is* real.

Thus, I am outside space and time. I am outside space because space is defined as the lifesize image of everything that surrounds me and includes me, and a whole cannot be contained in one of its parts (the brain). I am outside time because, as we have seen, nothing can pass except in relation to what does not pass; there is no change without stability, no movement without immobility. This is what is lacking in Kant's Transcendental Aesthetic: time and space are, a priori, prerequisites for every experience, but experience is possible only because we find ourselves fundamentally outside them. All awareness is submerged in the spatiotemporal, all life is merely its exploration, but this medium can be explored only if the explorer is not part of it.

To speak of time one must also speak of memory. Every duration implies that the first of two successive instants is retained into the present. There could be no melody if, at each note, all the preceding notes were totally forgotten; there could be no time, no passage from one instant to the next, if at each instant the one before it completely disappeared. Every type of perception endures and thus implies memory. Now, if one of the poles of time is the fixed point, the "intemporal," one of the poles of memory is the *integral survival of all the past,* whatever awareness has lived this past. It is not the image of past reality but *the reality itself.* All of us agree that the past exists once and for all, eternally—that it would exist even if the Universe were destroyed. The fact that it will exist forever in this manner, yet no longer exists absolutely, is not a contradiction but a tautology: we say it no longer "exists" because it is no longer present —which is the definition of the past.

The fallibility of our contingent memories, which invent false recollections and fail to recognize true ones, is obviously not at issue here. It is a question of principle: one *defines* a memory as "an image *of* a past event." Now, to be recognized, this image must have a model more precise than the memory itself. If this model were another image, the secondary image would necessarily have a model, and so on back to the final model that is the past itself, an absolute reality, *present,* unaltered. I judge the accuracy of a memory by its agreement with a criterion that my memory does not know, since it is searching for it, but that I myself recognize once my memory has found it, because in reality it has always been there. Otherwise how could I recall a forgotten word precisely for the reason that I *have* forgotten it? We are not talking here about the "total preservation of memories" (as images) of Freud or Bergson. What we are talking about is reality as experienced, which, although past, still *is,* just as it is forever, independent of my brain, of my present awareness, and finally of my life. Nothing is more stupendous or more contradictory than this fact; I confine myself here to recording it, precisely as it derives from the very principle of the memory. Its explanation would call for a complete philosophical study.

How can the awareness "see" this eternal past—this absolute present and why is it unable to attain it? It has access to it because this past is one of its foundations; it cannot attain it because, in order for it to do so, time would have to stop. As it is, the smallest precise memory forces me into a great, if momentary, distraction or abstraction, and I must close my eyes to remove the screen formed by my present perceptions. Likewise, when I "see" a landscape in my imagination behind my closed eyelids, in reality I am *seeing* only my closed eyelids; if I were really to *perceive* what I imagine, I would not be mistaken about it for an instant, and I would be afraid. During sleep, when real perceptions approach zero, images from the imagination can profit from this void and attain a persuasive power almost equal to that of perceived reality. But only almost —from the first perceptions on waking, all persuasion is utterly lost. In sleep, it is only spatial conceptions that cease thwarting the imaginative awareness; for it to gain access to the real past embodied in the absolute present that serves as the basis for my every memory, it would have to encounter a sleep capable of suppressing the temporal flow as well. What the dream almost obtains by the abolition of space, only death can obtain absolutely by the abolition of time.

Of course, memory almost never provides images that are really close to their models. If it did, memories would be visionary and would paralyze action. Real memory aims, modestly enough, at the contrary. Its objective is to make action or thought more effective, for like all aspects of awareness, it addresses itself to the future, not the past. From ten thousand views of the same face, it forms *one* image only. From myriad occurrences, it instantly extracts a single meaning. Memory uses abbreviations, not from weakness, but from necessity. Any perfect replication of the past through memory would be not only undesirable but absurd, for it would abolish time. As we have seen, time would not flow without the absolute memory that makes memories possible, but neither would it flow if we had perfect access to this absolute. Each minute would be spent in remembering—actually in reliving—the preceding minute. And that could not in fact occur because each second of that minute would have had to be remembered during the whole of the succeeding second, and so on ad infinitum. Absolute memory can only exist outside of time. It coincides exactly with that fixed point before which—and hence *by means* of which—time "passes."

When materialism says that awareness is an "epiphenomenon," it is saying that awareness is a thing that presupposes awareness (since no phenomenon is possible except for awareness). Moreover, it is saying that thought unfolds *within* the brain. If this "within" is a metaphor, so much the better—but where then is materialism? If it is not a metaphor, then images, sensations, ideas, truths, concepts are cerebral secretions—or, if one prefers, waves and vibrations, phenomena fully as material as any liquid secretion but not quite so vulgarly tangible. In this view, matter attenuates into mind, and cerebral electricity, which is invisible, is nearer to thought than the cerebral cortex itself. The materialist attitude corresponds to the infantile aspect of the human mind: because one thinks to a great extent in images and hence in terms of space, it is difficult not to sense a paradox in the simple truth that the interior of one's own brain is part of the exterior world. In addition to this bad habit, human intelligence has another that is indispensable in practice but dangerous for knowledge. Grammarians call this habit of language —and hence of thought—*metonymy*. We say "let's share a bottle" whereas we share the contents of the bottle; we say "see a film," though what we see are the images that the film makes it possible to project onto a screen; we say "listen to the radio," when in fact we listen to the sounds the radio emits. Metonymy here consists in describing the container (bottle, film, radio) in order to talk about the contents (alcohol, images, music).

But language and thought *must* be metonymic—otherwise a sentence could go on forever. "To listen to the radio" is a metonym, but so is "to listen to the music coming from the radio." In fact, only waves are coming out—and not from a radio but from a radio receiving set; the music is my auditive apprehension of these sound waves . . . and so on. "This computer contains information" is a metonym; the apparatus contains electricity and electronic relays that are capable, after a thousand detours, of becoming the medium for information for my awareness. It would be easy, though tiresome, to show that these precisions are themselves metonyms; the point is that a computer contains information only in the same sense that a magnetic tape contains my voice. Similarly, a brain contains absolutely nothing other than nerve cells and nervous impulses. When specialized medicine talks of "cortical zones of vision" or "zones of memory," it does so simply as a form of shorthand, to avoid saying, for example, "zones of material media permitting the awareness to visualize (or to remember)." Similarly, when we call the brain the seat of thought, we are describing it as an instrument and then by a final metonym we confuse the instrument with the instrumentalist. The temptation is so strong that Descartes, an out-and-out spiritualist, insisted on locating within his "pineal gland" a soul that he incessantly proclaimed as being unextended—and thus unlocatable.

Because the brain is a machine, it cannot be anything other than an instrument; at best, thought "comes from" it in the way music comes from a piano. Nobody has ever called the piano "the seat of music," but if pianists were invisible, no doubt someone would. This comparison is misleading only on one point; when pianists play, their bodies move other bodies (the keys of the piano), whereas the mind that moves the brain does not touch it physically. The difference is unimportant here. Without the brain, there is no thought, without the piano no music. But it is not the piano that plays nor the brain that thinks. Damage the brain, intoxicate it, alter it—awareness will be lessened or distorted; put the piano out of tune, remove the strings—and the music will become unrecognizable. Suppress the brain, annihilate the piano—awareness and music will become impossible, but no harm will be done to the pianist who was producing the music or to the Mind that was producing the awareness.

How can the mind, which is nonspatial and nontemporal, influence matter? How is it that Mind and Matter march in parallel as though their harmony were preestablished (as Leibnitz believed)? This question is too enormous to tackle here. My intention is only to disclose the false philosophy the sciences sanction or strengthen. In any case, the difficulty of the question lies in the fact that it is badly put. Mind and Matter are merely particular expressions of the opposed pair Subject/Object. Not all objects are material; numbers, for example, are immaterial, and yet they are objects, for they exist whether we think of them or not, and they are alike, by definition, for all Subjects—that is, for ourselves.

And we ourselves are double proof that Subject and Object—and thus Mind and Matter—can only be one. First, I am both spiritual and material. Second, in the very interior of my awareness, I am both subject and object. When I think of "me," I am describing myself—but "I" is not "me," even though it is. I am both describer and the described, perfectly distinct and perfectly united. Reflected awareness is thus its own mirror of itself; it is simultaneously that which thinks, that which it thinks, and that by which it and its mirror image are but one. Subject and Object, opposite in principle because the former is *only* whatever is not the latter, mutually condition each other *in that very opposition*. If matter is thus the image of the mind, inverted by a mirror effect, then the harmony of which we are one of the chords needs no explanation. I need not touch a mirror for it to show my reflection.

Perhaps the best image we can have of the relationship Matter/Mind, as we ourselves live it, is of a single sheet of paper. Its back represents the sphere of human awareness and the front the sphere of the body. Now, if I tear this sheet, both sides tear simultaneously, and it is not the tearing of the back that causes the tearing of the front, or vice versa. Similarly, when I think or act, nervous impulse and awareness move simultaneously and at the same pace, without any causal relationship. If I cause a nervous impulse, the front of the sheet tears—and also the back; if it is my awareness acting, my nervous impulse changes, and the tearing of the back seems to "produce" the tearing of the front. We can test the action of countless substances on the psyche, whereas a converse testing is impossible; this is the origin of our ineradicable prejudice in favour of a nonreciprocal Matter/Mind determinism. In reality, to alter one of the two sides is to alter the other. When awareness alters, its psychic "back" and its cerebral "front" *belong* to the same action and are one. Yet this alone does not explain why such correspondences are possible. In order to find an answer to that enigma, we must first accept that our idea of Matter and of the objective world is false, that *both* of them boil down strictly to pure *concepts*. The relationship of Matter to Mind becomes that of the concept to the conceiver: Subject and Object are an identity. The Mind/Object of itself is the World.

V

Space and time, causality and finality, determinism and chance: all these subjects, as we have seen, reduce the exact sciences to self-contradiction. At least the empirical sciences, the sciences of observation, can claim credit for a ceaseless flow of thought-provoking material. In the Theory of Evolution, for example, zoology and paleontology have put forward one of the greatest philosophical ideas of all time. But the closer Science approaches the psychic, and the more it applies itself to observing behaviours and evaluating their objectives, the further it drifts into ideology and mere chitchat. Modern linguistics and psychology are promoted as visions of the world; they are really nothing but colossal examples of begging the question.

Linguistics could lay claim to philosophy if it were true that language produces or at least influences thought. That this is the case at the level of the individual is a truism: one cannot say the same things in German as in Vietnamese; thus a German thinks differently from a Vietnamese. But the tongue imposed on one is a manner of thinking; the question is whether this manner of thinking is or is not the result of formal constraints.

When linguists attribute Aristotle's categories to Greek syntax, they are pretending not to see that this syntax results from a thought that contained the categories in question. In the most general way, the meaning precedes the signal, both logically and chronologically: chronologically, because the first signal ever transmitted was transmitted by a meaning; logically, because it was a signal (and not a simple sensation) only by virtue of this meaning. The "arbitrariness of the signal" that Saussure noted is a tautology; a nonarbitrary signal would necessarily have a meaning, which it would have to lose to become *merely* a signal. If the meaning could not exist without the signal, languages would not be enriched (signals that signify nothing are not a source of richness) and children would not learn to talk. On the other hand, if the signal produced meaning on its own, each human being would know all languages. Hence it is true that language influences ideas, but only insofar as language is formed of concepts (or monemes—that is, units of meaning). That a concept composed of conceptual units should be influenced by its components is not in the least surprising.

However, one can only speak of components with reference to the final composition. Now, the final meaning of any sentence only takes shape in order to culminate in a meaning as close as possible to the meaning that motivated the start of the sentence. This is the very definition of finality: the cause of an event is its objective. The meaning that makes me speak is not exactly that which results from my words; it always goes further with respect to objective, but falls short with respect to origin—which is in fact the same as the objective. We find this circular course, this Alpha that is Omega yet seeks nevertheless to become what it already is, everywhere that Life is involved.

Because the meaning precedes the signal of which it is creator, animator, and end, Chomsky's generative grammar is a fiction. A grammar is made up of rules, which are not signals but concepts. It is ridiculous to wonder how children can form an infinity of expressions though they have not actually heard them all: once I know *hang* and *hanging*, I can imagine *banging* if I hear *bang*. What is operating here is a rule of symmetry that Saussure calls the "fourth proportional." This rule, observed consciously or not, is a *concept*, which implies that there are other, more general concepts; thus a grammar would not be generative if it were not the simple manifestation of a logic that is generative of itself, and that alone is generative.

Thus, Carnap and the preeminent Wittgenstein were running in a circle when they sought to replace philosophy with an analysis of language. The analysis of language *is* the analysis of concepts— which is philosophy. I can counter the false philosophical question

"Does the world exist?" by observing that "the world" here means "that which exists." But in linguistics the word *world* has plenty of other meanings ("the world of the theatre," "a world of good," etc.), and nothing allows me to prefer any one of them to the others.

The logical analysis of propositions also rests, like any science, on identity—i.e., tautology. Therefore, it too is powerless in the face of notions such as time, final cause, and chance, and even space, matter, and mind are outside its competency. "I am" is not metaphysical as a proposition but as a fact, and in *formal* logic it is no more contradictory to say "I think, therefore I am not" than to say "I think, therefore I am." As for etymology, it makes for thought but does not think itself—which is why only Heidegger can make it think for him (see *The Sentence from the Ground Up* or *What is Called Thinking?*). He sets about it with his customary Greek and his habitual honesty. According to him the fundamental question of metaphysics is "Why is there Being, rather than Nothing?" The eminent philosopher would find it vulgar to consider: (1) that Being is what there is; (2) that when there *is* something, it is necessarily "rather than nothing"—just as, if there were nothing, it would necessarily be "rather than something"; (3) that "why?" means "what cause *is there?*" His question is thus "What cause is there for what there is to be what there is?"; this cause, once found, would be a cause that *there was*, and the question would have to be put again. Thus, one would know why Being is on the same day that one found out why Nothing is not, why water is wet, why circles are round, and why the Heideggerian comedy is a Heideggerian comedy.

The real generative grammar would be one that explained the genesis of concepts. Science persists in trying to derive the general from the particular, though, properly speaking, it can only be done the other way around. Just as the meaning precedes the signal, generality precedes singularity in awareness itself, both logically and chronologically. The precedence is logical because a definable idea can only be defined by others that are more general. (For example, the idea of whole number derives from the ideas of number and entirety, both of which are more general than it is itself; the idea of number is defined by the more general idea of the ensemble, and the idea of entirety is defined by the ideas of the whole, of the part, of unity, and so forth.) The precedence is chronological because the most primitive animal is that which distinguishes least, and thus generalizes most. To grasp an idea is to enclose it as if within concentric circles, moving closer and closer—moving, in other words, from the most enclosing to the most enclosed, from the most general to the most particular.

When Science pretends to explain ideas of concepts, it inevitably takes its cue from Hume (or Locke). For Hume, as for all the empiricists, general ideas result from the assembly of particular ideas or even perceptions, which can be connected in three ways: (1) by resemblance (I see many trees, and they give me the general idea of Tree); (2) by contiguity in space or in time (light and heat become identified because they accompany each other, lightning and thunder because one follows the other); (3) by the relationship between cause and effect (the shock that produces the rolling of a ball becomes indissociable from that rolling). Now resemblance, contiguity, time, space, and cause and effect are all ideas; thus, in Hume's scheme, general ideas cannot come into being without the aid of general ideas. But even if we ignore this absurdity, we find that empiricist criteria cannot explain the existence of general ideas or perceptions.

Consider resemblance: A resembles B if they have a common component C—and, by definition, every component precedes that which it composes. Resemblance precedes dissemblance; before being distinguished from each other, many things are only one. Hence, it is not the particular idea or perception that forms the general idea or perception, but the reverse. The mind evolves like Life, proceeding from the one to the many by successive divisions.

Contiguity is merely a resemblance of position (temporal or spatial). This leaves cause and effect. Hume states that we give the name *cause* to what we have always seen preceding a phenomenon. But a cause can only be a logical necessity—an identity—whereas a regular succession of phenomena does not logically necessitate the continuation of this succession. As a basis for general notions of causality, succession is neither sufficient (night always precedes the dawn without being mistaken for its cause) nor necessary (gravity is the "cause" of bodies falling, yet the falling and the exertion of gravity are by definition simultaneous). Furthermore, if the idea of cause did stem from experience, that would be a means of explaining it; but an explanation is already a search for a cause.

The "formation of general ideas" is thus absurd. What forms are ideas that are always more particular than the ideas from which they spring. But while these particulars cannot precede the general, they inevitably return to it. In fact, every explanation reduces what it is explaining to more general principles. It does this in one of two ways. The first consists in deriving from one concept the more general concepts embodied therein (e.g., "triangle" and "right angle" from "right-angled triangle"); this is *deduction*. The second consists in establishing the particular and then generalizing from it (I have seen bodies falling, and from that I infer that all bodies fall), in other words, "posing" the general "under" the particular (*sup-pose*); this is *induction*. The more general is already there, whether it is already within the concept or one supposes it to be so. Since all thought is either deductive or inductive, we can say about awareness what we say about language: it tends towards its points of departure. Notions such as effect, cause, time, and so on are both the bases of thought *and* its supreme objectives, towards which the whole of Philosophy is directed. The cause seeks itself as its objective; that which aims is that which is aimed at. And since thought that aims itself in this way is by definition further away than any stage of its search, it always has its cause before it. Circular course, pure finality, Alpha and Omega.

The number of concepts one can form is infinite, but the objective of every science is to reduce them to general laws; thus absolute generality, prior to all thought, is also absolutely subsequent to it. The parallel with machines, artificial or living, is obvious: simple organisms and machines are constructed of simple or general elements, and their function is very particular; as they become particularized (or more complex), their objective becomes more general. The descendants of a machine that could only add can carry out *all* numerical operations; the descendants of an animal that could perceive only some movements of a certain nature can perceive them all. Note too the infinite interlocking of the increasingly *particular* concepts of a philosophy that aims at the greatest possible *generality*. The notion of Objective, which is indispensable for the comprehension of Life, of machines, of languages, or of concepts, can only be of an *infinite* generality, for any objective can justify itself only by another even vaster objective, such as causality. Objective *per se* and Cause *per se* are the same thing.

Like Hume's explanation of general ideas in terms of perceptions, the explanations of those psychologies that describe ideas as the result of stimuli, "gestalts," or conditioned reflexes are completely worthless. We have seen that fundamental concepts *cannot* derive from experience—on the contrary, they are the conditions of experience. Moreover, the explanation of concepts is itself necessarily conceptual and therefore presupposes the existence of the very thing whose origins it seeks to establish (for example, the explanation of the idea of cause is the explanation of the idea of explanation). Nor can the science known as genetic epistemology, which deals with "the formation of ideas," enrich Philosophy. The word "concept" is already sufficiently explicit in itself. In the realm of ideas, as in the sphere of Life, *conception* precedes every *genesis*; it cannot, in consequence, be the result of any genesis.

Just as a body is made up of its present cells and not of its past states, so the other, more general concepts that a given concept contains will enable one to analyze its makeup only as it is *now*. For this reason, even Saussure is obliged to insist that linguistics must deal only with the present state of languages and not with their evolution, that what a word has meant in the past tells nothing of its present meaning. The fact that *spite* used to mean "contempt" gives me no information about the meaning of this word today. Likewise, a concept is no more made up of its past than a clear image is made up of the fuzzy images that preceded it in the process of resolution. To say that a thing is formed of the stages of its formation is to say that it is formed of the fact that it is formed—which is not very revealing. A monument is easier to see close up than from afar; the concepts that Science uses and assumes to be true are not so by virtue of their avatars; $3 + 2$ does not equal $2 + 3$ merely because one learns that this is so at such-and-such an age.

Much learning consists of readjusting concepts that are too general. Piaget demonstrates this despite himself. When a child says there is more matter in a square lump of dough than there is in the same lump pulled out into a long stringy shape before his eyes, he is confusing matter with size, which is a more general concept. When he makes time depend on speed, he is combining time and speed into a single too-inclusive concept. When he refuses to believe that $3 + 2$ equals $2 + 3$, he is extending the notion of quantitative equality to include that of formal identity. In all these instances, childish confusion is in fact generalization.

It is clear from all this that concepts exist before our awareness of them. To assign concepts a historical origin would be to say that one day 2 + 2 *began to* equal 4. The genealogical tree of concepts, like every such tree, is really a matter not of branches but of roots. When we go from its more complex to its more simple components, we come finally to concepts, such as cause, object, and time, that cannot be broken down any further. These elementary concepts have nothing in common other than the fact that they are concepts, but this common ground is itself a single, all-enclosing concept, the most general concept possible—that is, *the concept of Concept,* the concept of itself, the concept that conceives itself, or the universal Ego, *for that which is both conceiving and conceived is an Ego.* If concepts existed only in the human mind, they might be said to constitute a sort of collective (or intersubjective) Ego. But since the very foundation of the exterior world is conceptual, the universe becomes the Absolute Object of the Absolute Subject—which is to say it becomes itself, reflected and reflecting, for Subject and Object are the poles of a single unity.

It is not difficult to show that everything that is objective is necessarily conceptual, and that, far from being abstract, a concept is the most tangible thing possible, as well as the most immediate and the most real (the last adjective in the sense of "thinglike"). In its first response to a stimulus, the first organism made use of the concept of duality and therefore those of cause, time, and space. There were *two* distinguishable situations in *time* and *space*; the stimulus was the *cause* of a given reaction that came *after* it. To say that the first organism did not have these concepts merely means that it was not aware of them. I do not need to *have* a road in order to *make use of* it. Likewise, to say that the inert universe is subject to laws is to say that it is subject to concepts. Now, a concept can only "subject" another concept. Concepts exist *outside* of us—and this is the definition of objects. The concept of space is real space; the concept of matter is real matter. Indeed, the expression "concept of (cause, matter, number, angle, etc.)" is tautological, for these realities are concepts in themselves.

The common error is to believe that a concept, because it can only be thought, *is* a thought. In that case, an exterior object, which can only be sensed, would have to *be* a sensation. We say that numbers are "abstractions"—by which we generally mean that they are unreal because they do not address our senses. As though the fingers on our hands were not objective five in number! The objective concept five and the number five in thought are the same thing. On the other hand, the "idea" that forms in our minds when we perceive the colour yellow derives not from concept, but from sensation; it consists of nothing but imagistic sense-memories. Yet the exterior source of this perception of yellow is a congeries of objective concepts: the waves to which Physics reduces colours are themselves composed of conceptual data—space, time, number, and so forth. Thus, the sensible world is real—objectively real—in precisely the same way that numbers are real: not insofar as it is sensible, but insofar as it is conceptual. In any case, we must distinguish between our ideas of concepts (that is, the realities in which our minds participate) and our "ideas" of sensations; the former constitute the thinkable insofar as we are able to sense it, and the latter constitute the sensible insofar as we are able to think of it—or rather to remember it in the form of images.

We assume that space, time, matter, and so forth are independent of the way we perceive them—that, of our sensations. But what is not sensation is concept, and only a concept is the same for everybody. Inserting a third term—namely matter—between sensation and concept is contradictory, since the insertion implies, however vaguely, the *concept,* of what it inserts. When we give the name of *objective world* to what our sensations reveal to us and *subjective world* to the universe of ideas, we reverse reality. Sensations are fundamentally incommunicable, while concepts do not need to be communicated because they are already common property. Let us consider two examples. If someone brings me two pears when I have asked him for two, it is impossible for me to think that this person's idea of the number two is different from mine. If "two" meant "three" to him, he would have brought me three pears. But if the same person brings me a blue pencil when I have asked him for one, I can easily imagine that he sees blue as I see red. He brings me the pencil he calls blue, as I do—but it is *impossible* for me to know what he means by this name. When I read Rimbaud's "Sonnet of the

Vowels," I doubt that Rimbaud saw colours as I see them (or that he heard sounds as I hear them). "A black, E white, I red, O blue, U green" seems to me a catalogue of errors; for me, A is deep blue or violet, but E is beige, I white, O deep red, and U pale yellow.

Notice that the difference between sensation and concept that we are discussing here is not related to the confusion of someone who suffers from colour blindness. His confusion lies in seeing *one* colour where others see *two*—and it is impossible to confuse the numbers one and two *without* its becoming a known fact. It is also impossible, using all the concepts or all the connotations you like, to give someone blind from birth an "idea" of the colour blue. But it is just as impossible for persons blind from birth not to form the same ideas as I do about number, causality, time, or space; their image of time, for example, will perhaps be different from mine, but they will not call temporal what I call spatial. In short, *concepts have only the meaning in common, and sensations have only the signal in common.*

The greater part of our vocabulary, apart from names, contains only general ideas, and hence concepts. Most are what can be called "concepts" of sensations (blue, sonority, hardness, etc.). This demonstrates that beyond what is literally our Common Sense—the objective concepts that are imposed on all of us—we have imagined a community very much closer still: a community of the subjective. Sensation, born of the living, is the antithesis of concept. Concept is always general and always included in something still more general, but sensation is always absolutely singular and exclusive. Like everything singular, it can be designated, but never defined.

For example, suppose I want to identify a certain cat without resorting to mere designation, such as proper names, place names, and dates. I can describe it as minutely as I can; I can envelop it in concepts running from the most general to the most particular (cat —brown—tabby—in a street with such-and-such characteristics— and so on and so forth). Yet my description is always applicable to other *possible* cats. In the end I can only say *"This* cat," pointing to it, and thus abandoning concept for sensation. Similarly, none of my states of awareness can be described in a set number of words; even if such a description were possible, it would give only an idea of this state, not the state itself. Everything that a living being can be, do, feel, or think is absolutely unique, and the singular absolute of this singularity, its kernel, is the Ego—not the universal Ego in this case, but the individual Ego. Concept makes us part of the first, sensation gives us the second, and the whole of our existence is spent in trying to make the two coincide. In the beginning was the Word, but the Word has a Meaning, the end of which is to rediscover itself: that is the Story of the Universe.

Through language, we have generalized sensations, affections, and states of mind. If there is a miracle of language, it is that. "Red, sadness, nostalgia" are concepts projected onto the singular but constructed in the same way as the others: first "colour," then "dark" and "light," next "blue," "yellow," and so on. In short, the existence of pure concepts proves that we come from the One; the existence of sensations proves that we are unique; and the existence of concepts of sensations proves that we are returning to the One. At the end of the chain is an Ego; at the other end, an Ego. There the Indivisible, here the Individual.

What we call matter has been defined as "the substratum of our sensations." We conceive of this substratum as necessarily independent of those sensations—and this independence is, once again, the attribute of the single concept. There are, in fact, sensations without a substratum and to those sensations must be added implicit judgements, preorganized forms or gestalts, schemas, etc., but all this is of no importance here. We can say generally that we suppose an exterior, objective base for everything we perceive; what we *suppose* we call matter. Take a mountain covered in grass and snow; remove from it all sensation and every representation that might be forcibly derived from it. What is left are laws combining space, time, number, and so on—that is, concepts; the substratum of our sensations— also a concept; and, finally, Matter itself—the concept par excellence. Everything that can be said about Matter boils down to *qualifying* it. It is the x, indefinite in itself, that serves as a subject for attributes—or, if you prefer, for predicates. *It* is undulatory, vibratory, atomic, chemical, coloured, moving, but *it* is *it*: x is x. It is not Kant's noumenon. Matter is not unknowable, but ultimate. It is the concept that defines itself by itself, that itself defines *itself*. It is thus the Concept of Concept, that is to say an Ego, or rather the other face of the Absolute Ego of which·I have just been speaking, the reflection object of this pure subject. *Duo in deo*. Everything that we do is thus merely a way for the One that is ourselves to enrich the original One with perpetual newness. By virtue of being absolutely unique *and* absolutely united, we are ourselves this One of the origins and of the ending, as the drops of water in the sea are the sea itself.

VI

As I have already said, my purpose in this book is not to criticize the sciences (which would be a ridiculous undertaking), but to lay low the myth of scientism. It would be better to let Philosophy die than to have scientists take the place of philosophers. (Unfortunately, the former result would only guarantee the latter.) Scientists can only teach Science. Thus, Piaget's genetic epistemology constitutes the most useful guide offered to education, but it tells us nothing about the nature or value of concepts. Science does not so much enrich our knowledge of the world as renew the world itself, and in this endless renewal awareness finds its progress.

Even if the identification of the world can never be complete, it can still be accurate. Following the example of many other authors, I must now denounce a pseudoscience: psychoanalysis. No more remarkable for its intellectual dishonesty than for the infinite indulgence with which it is still welcomed and cultivated (especially among the literati), psychoanalysis is a fake from A to Z, from its first principle to its final conclusions. Determinant prejudices, the quantification of quality, the unwarranted extension of terms, reasoning by analogy, question begging, pleonasm—all the defects possible in a theory are in it. Various and innumerable as these defects are, it is unnecessary to attack them methodically. If the fragmentary criticisms that follow are not enough to bring the whole structure crashing to the ground, it is because one cannot refute faith. From the start psychoanalysis has been a sect rather than a science.

Let us start—the choice is random—with the Oedipus complex. Freud announced that small boys desire their mother sexually, a circumstance that determines the behaviour of grown men. But he immediately specified that "sexual desire" must not be understood in its commonly accepted sense, but as meaning pleasure in general. Moreover, the word *mother* does not necessarily mean the real mother, but the mother concept in general—that is, Woman (otherwise motherless children would never go through the "Oedipal stage"). Thus men tend to desire women, and male children take pleasure (sometimes) in the company of their mothers; here we have—somewhat to our amazement—the sum total of what psychoanalysis teaches us. Similarly, when we consider the father, we must take care not to understand "real father," but Father in general; that is, Authority. Otherwise fatherless children, never having known who they should want to kill, would have no Superego. Our moral behaviour, then, is determined by an internalized (paternal) compulsion—an ingenious way of explaining the remarkable fact that one can do neither good nor evil without wishing it.

We have the same word game with penis envy. A little girl is traumatized for life when she discovers she has no penis (whence women's tendency to jealousy, asserts Freud; Othello, of course, was a woman . . .). It doesn't matter if she does not discover it or that it is not a real penis that is at issue. There are, in fact, little girls who have not found out that little boys are made differently from themselves. Their penis envy is thus directed towards the Penis in general —that is, towards the status of the male. Now, who would have expected a stunning piece of news like that?

Freud obtains some rhetorical success by describing everything that has any bearing on pleasure as "sexual." To quote him: "Since the need to suck [in the child] tends to give rise to pleasure, it can and should be described as sexual." This is both easy to understand and obviously useful; everything changes when one speaks of the sexual pleasure of smoking, of the sexual pleasure of listening to music, and finally, though incidentally, of the sexual pleasure of taking pleasure in sex. The infant's desire to suck is called oral sexuality, which, after many avatars, *becomes* genital sexuality. Thus, when I admire a painting, I am a visual music lover, and when I listen to a record I am an audient music lover; in both cases I am a music lover. If I read to distract my hunger, however, my desire to eat has *become* a desire to read. One desire becomes another desire but nevertheless remains the same. In what respect? In that it is still a desire. How we go from revelation to revelation!

Freud explains these metamorphoses by analogy. In chemistry, the term *sublimation* describes the transition from the solid state to the gaseous. The sexual instinct might thus *sublimate* itself in artistic inspiration or creation. If the analogy were justifiable, if "the economy of the libido" were not mere word play, then one would find in great artists a diminution of the sexual instinct corresponding to the "quantity" of inspiration so obtained. There is no need to remark that one finds just the opposite (e.g., Hugo). If anything is "transformed" into the creative impulse, it is *not* sexuality. Apart from that, the word *sublimation* is certainly completely appropriate. Freud's analysis of the origins of the Fifth Symphony was prodigious; it is fascinating to contemplate the sexual impulse bereft in the end of both its nature and its attributes, like Lichtenberg's knife without a blade or a handle. We can read about Freud's concept of sublimation in his *Leonardo da Vinci*; his *Gradiva de Jensen* shows us how he understood what he had conceived. From an unsatisfied harlot's remark to Rousseau, "Leave women and study mathematics," Freud intelligently concluded: "Mathematics enjoys great renown as a sexual derivative." Here we have a renown that is scarcely known, and a derivation that derives a great deal.

Psychoanalysis has about fifteen meanings for tens of thousands of symbols. Why are there so many symbols, since they all say more or less the same thing? Why are two myths or two images—e.g., a tunnel and a cave—more significant for their resemblance (they are both cavities) than for their dissimilarity (one is a tunnel, the other is a cave)? Finally, how did Freud decide what is symbolic, what is not, and what a symbol means? Actually, since the Freudian method consists essentially in assuming the truth of what it wishes to establish (*if* I describe as sexual that which is pleasure, then all pleasure is sexual), its symbology is easily understood. Thus when Oedipus plucked out his eyes, the deed was a symbolic substitute for castration. But when Origen actually castrated himself, his action was not a symbol for putting out his eyes. We read in *The Intepretation of Dreams* that a distaste for the skin on milk stems from a taboo against the maternal breast; that a child who dreams about a wasp is symbolizing his fear of tigers (for who could be afraid of a wasp?); that most of the snakes that terrify us in our dreams symbolize the phallus (for who could not be afraid of phallus bites?); and that by virtue of the old German phrase *Sich einem ausreissen* ("to pull one off oneself"), used for "to masturbate," the dream of having teeth pulled is masturbatory (which would explain why dentists are so well off). In *A Demonic Neurosis in the XVIIIth Century*, the Devil is a substitute for the Father, a role formerly played by God, so that Satan, for a change, looks enough like God to be His brother. Again, a little girl's doll is a symbolic substitute for the baby she wishes (subconsciously) to have had from the father's penis. Moreover, the doll is her baby, and hence her penis, since every mother regards her child as a surrogate penis. This is the reason for maternal possessiveness: a cat who protects her kittens is in *reality* protecting her penises. Of course, all this goes on without our knowing it—i.e., subconsciously. We shall see that this "subconscious," which has passed into our everyday vocabulary, is one of the emptiest ideas ever accepted by a culture—and that the idea owes its success, as always, to its flattering character.

In psychoanalysis, all equivalences are valid. A smoker is returning to the "oral stage"—his cigarette is the maternal breast. Yet if a symbol is subconscious, if it is not grasped, how can it be a symbol? Moreover, a cigarette is white and not brown, contains nicotine and not vitamin C, burns rather than flows, is made of paper and not of skin, gives off a gas and not a liquid, stimulates rather than soothes, and so on. But *apart* from all that, cigarette and maternal breast are the same thing. Compare the well-known gag: "What's the difference between Louis XIV and Napoleon?" "None: they both wear wigs, except Napoleon."

There are even better ones in the relevant "literature." An example from Melanie Klein: "For little boys, a car in motion represents masturbation and coition. Two cars meeting also represent coition, while comparison between two different cars expresses rivalry with the Father and his penis." In other words, everything "represents" masturbation, coition, and the penis—not for the little boy himself, but for his subconscious, which, since it knows everything, scarcely deserves its name. Properly, of course, "representation" refers to the act of *awareness*, intense or feeble, clear or fuzzy, by which a subject illustrates or symbolizes ideas, sentiments, states of mind, and so forth. A representation that is not conscious is equivalent to an image that is not seen: zero—and even zero in Roman numerals.

Everything is possible to the empty, the contradictory, and the unverifiable. So it can be said, for example, a homosexual's attraction to buttocks is a prolongation of the infants' attraction to their mothers' breasts—even though one knows that when children were feeding from those breasts, they could not even *perceive* them and cannot, *a fortiori,* remember them, deprived as they were at that time of any notion of shapes. No matter: the subconscious has done the rest, and the madness can continue unabated. A young boy can thus identify (subconsciously, always subconsciously) the penis with the vagina, the vagina with the mouth, semen with milk. A man suffering from premature ejaculation is spilling milk before it reaches the mouth (for when a man makes love to a woman he is suckling her, of course). Bulls, who are noted for premature ejaculation, are very obviously affected by this complex. By the same token, impotence is a refusal to suckle one's partner.

But let us scan the peaks, though we cannot hope to scale them. In Gérard Mendel's *Atomic Agony,* we read that our fear of fissionable material may be rooted in the gigantic chimneys of the atomic generating stations, so that we "may well ask whether it is really a question of paternal penises . . . or of huge maternal phalluses." Mothers have a subconscious phallus, and plutonium is a simple rationalization of Oedipal anxieties. For my part, I would summarize the matter thus: an atomic bomb is a penis that, in the process of making a gash (incestuous rape) in the Earth (mother), immolates with nuclear fire (semen) the population it kills (castrates) or blinds (castrates) in a symbolic punishment for the desire (repressed) to kill the Father (eternal). Hence the totemic character of disarmament conferences. . . .

If, in dreams, the subconscious chooses to appeal to the conscious only in symbols, it must do so in order not to rub the conscious the wrong way. In order to know what would rub it the wrong way, the subconscious must contain what the conscious contains, plus other elements. So the subconscious equals the conscious plus what the conscious does not know, plus all the tact necessary to make the conscious know it without the conscious actually knowing that it knows it. But what the conscious knows without knowing that it knows is precisely what the subconscious is supposed to be. Thus the subconscious appeals to itself, an operation of problematical usefulness.

Furthermore, if instead of expressing itself in symbols, dreams were to say in so many words what the subconscious really thinks, the sleepers would presumably wake themselves up—because, argued Freud, the "real meaning" of the dream would frighten or scandalize their conscious. Now, can one imagine a worse terror than that of a nightmare, and a more reassuring banality than its psychoanalytical interpretation? Whatever horror I may have of incest, I would rather find out that I had desired my mother than be burnt alive—the sort of thing that happens in dreams when inner conflicts are pleasantly symbolized. It is not in order to reassure me that a dream scares me. As for the therapeutic value of interpretation: a man is screaming; when he understands why he is screaming, he will stop. Of course he will. That was what he was shouting for.

Since the Freudian subconscious is partly formed from what the conscious "represses," and since the repressed material is the sole matter of dreams, then what do animals dream about? *They* never repress anything. And what about babies? They repress nothing as yet. The function of the Freudian dream, tricked out in symbolistic fancy dress, is to maintain sleep by sheltering the sleeper from direct revelations. But no man ever woke up because he became aware of something—whereas one is happy to escape the veiled suggestions of the subconscious offered in nightmares, not because of the suggestions, but because of the veils. Besides, we really must be dreaming when we read (in *The Interpretation of Dreams*) that Freud asked the analyst to consider "the morality of the dreamer." Apparently, morality acts in dreams as it does in waking hours; thus the oneiric subconscious frees itself simply by not freeing itself at all. Finally, to say that a dream is the manifestation (symbolic, and hence not manifest) of desire or fear is not a very risky statement; all awareness is always expecting something, and if this expectation is not a desire, it is necessarily a fear.

But, of course, the idea of repression is a misconception. If the conscious represses what it cannot tolerate, it must obviously know the thing it represses. Therefore, either the thing repressed exists in the conscious (otherwise what grounds would the conscious have for repressing it?) but then it is not repressed, since it is conscious. Or the thing repressed remains in the subconscious—and then what need is there for the conscious to repress it? In any case, the power to repress would amount to an ability to forget at will. Now, willful amnesia runs counter not only to our experience but to logic itself, for to want to forget something is to take an interest in it, and interest and forgetting run in opposite directions. We never forget anything voluntarily, especially anything traumatic. I can be guilty of a really major act of forgetfulness and thereby compromise what generally interests me most, but at the moment of forgetting I am no less captivated by something else—perhaps I am a prisoner of sleep. Of necessity, we forget 999 thousandths of what we live through; our conscious chooses what is useful to it and lets the rest go.

So forgetfulness is synonymous with inaction. Indeed, the idea of an active subconscious is a contradiction in terms. What could a subconscious act on if not *on* the conscious. But by definition the subconscious is whatever the conscious is not, and vice versa; how then could the latter be touched by something that was part of it? What affects my conscious to a given degree is itself conscious to the same degree. I can trace my wild irritability to a hitherto unsuspected toothache; because the ache is only a slight one, it disturbs my conscious in no less slight a fashion. A wholly subconscious toothache would be quite simply nothing.

All the same, there are three functions that we must call subconscious, although the first two barely merit the adjective *psychological*. The first are all acquired mechanisms, such as methods of calculation, the fingering of musicians, and so on. Automatisms of this sort permit my conscious to go beyond the letters and encompass words and even complete sentences when I read. Obviously these processes are abbreviated, rendered automatic, and relegated to the subconscious, so that the conscious can rise above them. They have no significance in themselves.

Second, all the tasks carried out by the automatic nervous system (cardiac rhythms, intestinal peristalsis, and so forth) are subconscious and, as far as we know, not subject to voluntary control. At any given moment, one is unconscious of one's ears, one's molars, and often one's whole body, just as one is unconscious of what is going on in the rest of the terrestrial globe. This aspect of the subconscious is the sum of what one does not know and cannot desire. The subconscious of psychoanalysis, which never stops knowing, desiring, and remembering, must be something quite different—but what?

In fact, *subconscious memory* is an oxymoron. The third aspect of the subconscious is its function as a repository for our experience. The proportion of past circumstance that the average memory can recall does not amount to more than a hundredth part of the whole; the remainder is present in the subconscious. It is not memories (which are selected views of experience taken *by* the conscious) but the past itself that is the model for this buried experience, and the past has *no activity* (for the past could only change by the absurd process of ceasing to have been what it incontrovertibly was). Because the subconscious is not memory but the past itself, and because this past is altogether inert, the subconscious has no power to influence our conscious minds. Therefore, any initiative respecting this past must come from the conscious itself. And in fact however hazy, obscure, or phantasmal a fragment of the past may be, the conscious will find it—often without expressly looking for it (this is what happens in association). The subconscious can thus *be* thought and wished—but it does not *think* and it does not *wish*.

Either we call subconscious that which has none of the characteristics of the conscious, or we pervert the word and the idea with it—as constantly happens in psychoanalysis, where sexuality equals pleasure, mother equals woman, castration equals loss, and so on. That which is intemporal, inanimate, and inaudible has nothing of that which is temporal, animate, and audible. Nevertheless, psychoanalysis attributes to the subconscious the two principal (and exclusive) characteristics of the conscious: will and thought. The subconscious of the psychoanalysts is an anticonscious, superior to the conscious in that it takes care—as we have seen—to handle the conscious gently, and is much more docile in that it escapes all verification.

It is an abuse of language to say that animals have no conscious. If they were unconscious in the strict sense of the word (and any other sense would make the term meaningless), they would be dead. Their consciousness is not reflected, as ours is, and its intensity varies according to species, but it is consciousness all the same. Similarly, consciousness in a human being under hypnosis is weak, not reflected, and capable for this reason of slipping the memory, but it is still consciousness. As it happens, "proof" of an active subconscious could only be provided by hypnotism. The suggestion is made to the subject to open a door; on wakening, he opens it, and the motives he attributes to his action are only conscious alibis— they have no basis in his real experience. Therefore the initiative came from the subconscious. In fact save for comedy (and this "save" does not save anything very important), what has happened? The subject's conscious has been inoculated with false memories, and it has taken them for its own. (This is also the principle of subliminal advertising.) The subject simply opens the door in a state of irreflection; it is not a buried memory working in his conscious, it is his conscious working through the memory.

As for dreams, if they were not an activity of the conscious, how could the conscious remember them, given that one cannot remember something one has not actually experienced? Furthermore, we dream in the waking state, for our conscious has several levels, and we are always thinking a host of different things at the same time. Dreams manifest that madness that Schelling said, correctly, is the basis of intelligence. Tunes, images, and words "run through" our minds (in reality it is the mind that runs through them); the main thought we are pursuing makes it difficult for us to see the satellite or parasite thoughts that surround it like a fringe. If we do focus our attention on them, they seem of problematical origin, since the conscious cannot simultaneously explore its field, its methods of exploration, and the reason for these methods. If the main thought becomes woolly and slack, we are in an "uncertain" state of exploration—a dream state; indeed, if we were not kept alert by our perceptions, we would dream perpetually.

The dream is a compromised consciousness, and incoherence is its rule. The brain still imposes its order, but this is now organic and not deliberate. When I lose the thread of an idea, my mind searches in every direction, examining, hopefully and fearfully, amid the disorder of its memories and its precepts the shapes that most closely resemble what it is seeking. Suppose I am trying to remember a name—say, Mirabeau. I draw up a list of everything that comes into my mind, and I find: Dorval, Octave, Rivarol, minaret, etc. Once I have found the name *Mirabeau* again, I realize that the "Dorval" Airport was an allusion to the "Mirabelle" Airport (substitution), that "Octave" was meant to lead me to "Octave Mirbeau" (assonance), that "Rivarol" offered a parallelism no longer nominal but historical (connotation: French Revolution, royalism, etc.), and that "minaret" was a phonetic analogy.

Thus, in the case of such a search, the conscious uses all the devices that psychoanalysis attributes to the subconscious: substitution, word play, allusion, symbolism, misunderstanding, parody. They all manifest themselves in dreams, in which the sought-for idea is my complete waking life, in which the fears and hopes of the search are wonders and terrors, in which the disorder of memories and precepts is what the wavering light of my conscious discovers in its erratic progress towards morning. How can the conscious proceed when it is no longer subject to the strict limitations of perceptible reality—when, in fact, it perceives precisely nothing—if not through profusion and confusion, fantasy and hallucination, the remembered and the improvised? And how can the dream not be unrecognizable when its creator is a mind that no longer recognizes itself? How can this creation not be strange and arbitrary when the mind is a stranger to itself and cannot allow itself a meaning that is not an allusion or an allusion that is not the beginning of awakening and thus the dissolution of the dream? Psychoanalysis, unable to admit the existence of oneiric images, which would necessarily be *immaterial,* here again contradicts itself. If there are a thousand possible symbols for the phallus or the Mother, the choice of one symbol rather than another has to be made, no matter how. The dreamer's conscious is like a person going along a dark corridor to a far-off well-lit room. The door of the room is the awakening; the passage through the corridor is the dream. In the corridor the person sees monsters, deformed shapes, and broken-down foundations, then enters the room itself. If a dream can turn a single match into a raging fire, why can it not turn a commonplace little worry into a nightmare? The dream is thus a reflection and a forerunner of the awakening. Psychoanalysis is not far from thinking the opposite. . . .

What projects into the moving obscurity of a dream is not symbols by which the subconscious communicates to the conscious what is obsessing it but misshapen images of what lies within the consciousness itself. Even granting the existence of the premonitory or divinatory dream, warning and prophecy alike would nevertheless refer back to the conscious. Mysterious, certainly—if one believes in them—but no more so than thought itself.

When one speaks of the meaning of dreams, one thinks of their objectives, not their causes. It is significant that oneiromancy captivates the very people who are not interested in the meaning of the awakened mind, of concepts, or of the real world. Certainly, human awareness, which is essentially finalist, looks everywhere for intentions and reacts against the mere gratuitousness that victimizes it in dreams. But the mystery and even the terror of dreams, like those of hypnotism or so-called subconscious thought, are primarily facile and pleasing. Faith does not require any reflection, recourse to the nocturnal calls only for a little sleep, unveiling the secrets of the "supernatural" rids one of the obligation to wonder endlessly before the veils of Nature. And when one is banality in human guise, nothing is more stupendous than to have within oneself—and unknown to oneself—thousands of swallowed enigmas and accumulated mythologies. It is to *this* quest for knowledge that psychoanalysis addresses itself.

VII

If I could remember the traumatic episodes of my period as an embryo and a newborn babe, it could only be as I lived them. But I lived them on a level of awareness so infinitesimal that my present awareness has no precise perception of it. Psychoanalysis proposes not only to bring light into this inherently shadowy area—just as one might colour a green leaf white in order to preserve its colour. It also claims to demonstrate that experiences that cannot influence one's awareness even if fully "relived" can orient that awareness when they are not relived at all. Hence it puts such enormous importance on the oral, anal, and sadist phases, on the mother's breast, on Oedipus, and so on. The past produces the present, that which is no longer creates that which is, that which is most intense is subject to that which is least intense, the subconscious directs the conscious (which is nothing but passivity or the embroidering of alibis). Moreover, dreams have a meaning other than that given to them by the conscious; thus, they emanate from an unknown intention—from an awareness—and so the subconscious is no longer what one said it was at the beginning, and so on and so forth. . . .

If two interconnected vessels contain a liquid that is heated to 20°

C in one and to 90° C in the other, psychoanalysis says that the heat of the second vessel *comes from* the heat of the first, and not the reverse. Similarly, what I think *comes from* what I do not think. The old scientistic causality reappears here in its most absurd aspect. Moreover, it links up with the popular prejudice of the "theory" of repression: that everyone has an equal *quantity* of hate, aggressiveness, jealousy, and so on, and spends it in different *forms,* in bulk or in detail, even if these forms apparently contain no hate, aggression, or jealousy. The disciples of Reich and the champions of psychodrama are persuaded that by daily shouting and stamping they can rid themselves of their repressions. Even supposing the efficacy of this technique, one would like to know why the irascible members of these groups, despite all their expressed "repressions," continue to be more irascible than other people. It is as though their share of anger renewed itself with expression, ceaselessly and spontaneously.

Clearly we have not yet exhausted the subconscious of the psychoanalysts. In addition to everything else, it is the receptacle of the "instincts." Freud and his school, including the deviants Jung, Rank, and Ferenczi, pretend to believe (or actually do believe, which is worse) that we have within our souls immense cesspools, caverns, oceans of instinct, which our animal past has bequeathed to us and of whose particular contents we can have no idea. Now what can this be all about? They are certainly known to us. They stare us in the face.

Sexuality, aggressiveness, territoriality, property, possessiveness— we are told these have grown out of all proportion as our awareness and our thirst for self-aggrandizement have increased, the one through the other. To believe in the occult character of appetites promoted into institutions is as stupid as overestimating their importance. Both amount to the same thing: namely, a belief in the antagonism of instincts and the civilized world, which, born of all the passions, secretes them all a hundredfold. There is more instinct in New York than in Tahiti, in the heart of Paris than in the villages of Brittany, in the Rome of the year 1 than in the Patagonia of today. Of course, psychoanalysis alludes to instinctual drives that civilization compels us to control: murderous desires, incestuous desires, possibly desires to rob and to rape. But in the first place these temptations are much stronger in our heavily policed urban world than in any "primitive" community, so clearly civilization is not born of repression of the instincts. Furthermore, the repressed is nothing more than a pure, simple matter of reserve. If one has ever felt like raping a woman or stealing or killing an old man getting off the bus too slowly, one remembers it and *knows* it. As for any wish toddlers may have to kill their father or to sleep with their mother, we have seen that this is merely a play on words; the children who desire their mother have no genital sexuality, and they want to kill their father simply because they wish him to go away. Psychoanalysis insists on searching for dark interpretations, but the public at large has adopted the word *repression* in its only reasonable (and perfectly trite) sense: what a person deliberately conceals and the wholly conscious desires the person keeps down. That these desires show through from time to time in dreams is entirely possible— provided they show up even more clearly in his waking state.

Psychoanalysis starts from the principle that if one can recall the traumatizing scenes of infancy, the ailment will be cured. Here it is reasoning by analogy, as though the scene in question were a thorn in the psyche that in time becomes infected. As we have seen, such feats of recall are impossible, unless one invents them, and infant memories would pass unnoticed even if their recollection were perfect. Besides, since when has the fact of remembering the origin of an ailment—much less what one merely *believes* to have been its origin—cured the ailment itself? If the memory of watching a fatal accident has given me insomnia for the past two years, reliving the scene in my imagination will surely not help me find sleep. Talking about it, however, would no doubt bring me relief. Reason is cold, and thus refreshing; in enveloping the brutality of the images within its fabric, it would warp them—and time would do the rest. It is not memory that cures, but oblivion.

Freud "established" the existence of the subconscious by presupposing it not only in dreams and in hypnosis, but also in slips of the tongue. This last "proof" is even weaker, if possible, than the others. We have seen that the idea of the conscious censoring the subconscious is absurd, since the conscious can censor only what it knows— and by definition it knows only itself. Freud imagines that when we commit a *lapsus linguae* and say one word instead of another, the subconscious is taking advantage of a temporary lifting of censorship to transmit its message. Instead of the last word, I have just typed *massage*. Without any doubt, to a psychiatrist this would mean that my subconscious was speaking. On analyzing this typing error, I see that the *a* lies quite close to the *e*. I note that the word *message* contains both these vowels and conclude that I hit the wrong key. Since my lapse has no obvious meaning, I can put it aside. The slips that interest Freud are not of this nature. *Visage* for *village, bear* for *pear,* or *bean* for *dean* are merely linguistic slips. The subconscious chooses its moments, and psychoanalysis chooses them for it. Freud quoted the example of a Viennese student who asked a girl to go out with him; instead of the word *begleiten* (to accompany) he said *beleidigen* (to show lack of respect). Apart from the odd fact that only one lapse in a thousand has any signifi-cance, the strange thing is that Freud attributed this shift in mean-ing to the *subconscious,* apparently under the impression that the student was completely unaware of something that, on the contrary, he must have been burning to do. . . . If you read *screw* for *skew,* is the preference you are giving to the subject matter of the first verb over that of the second highly *subconscious?* The theory of the verbal lapse is thus one of the most striking examples of Freudian strictness.

It is not surprising that the subconscious wins in the interpretation of neuroses. With their ceremonials and their superstitions, they are products of pure anguish or hysteria. The latter is a species of men-tal attack so specifically feminine that the word derives from the Greek for "uterus" and that organ was long considered the ailment's source. It must be added that names—hysteria or neurosis—matter little. The only thing that matters is the role—and only fear plays it. Now, anguish has no cause, and it is this *acausality* that produces it from start to finish; acausality also brings it relief once it finds the motives it was looking for, however false they may be. Human nature not only *has* a horror of emptiness; it *is* that horror. In our very natures, as in dreams, we seek meaning in signals that—as signals—are quite arbitrary. Psychoanalysis, which wants to see meaning everywhere, naturally denies the arbitrary, and here again it draws strength from the *vox populi.* A particular dream *cannot* be just anything at all, since it is *this* dream—a prejudice that extends to manifestations of pure chance: I purchase a number for the lottery, but this number is not just any number, since it is *the* number 223,556. Nothing is chance after the event, since then everything is defined. Anyone who has ever gambled or awaited an outcome knows that the conscious, in its anxiety, invents ceremonials, ordeals, exorcisms—and invents them literally out of anything at all. Intention has meaning; signals do not. Nearly all of us have avoided stepping on the cracks in the sidewalks, counted the steps in a staircase, or practiced momentary—and spontaneous—exorcisms: scratching our heads, crossing our fingers, saying some word or phrase very quickly, and so on. To ask ourselves why these rituals take *this* form rather than another is to forget that *some* form is necessarily chosen rather than another.

Insofar as neurotic rituals do have meaning, that meaning is not subconscious but unconsidered. If it were subconscious, no symbol could have any meaning for the conscious—and in consequence there would be no symbols. The parallels sex/fire, woman/water, earth/mother, and sea/mother do not date from the intrauterine or early infancy periods or from any collective unconscious. They come from analogical thought, which certainly preceded reflective thought, though we still use it every day. When we call an action "low," we are generally incapable of justifying the analogy between "low" and "bad"; nevertheless, it seems quite obvious. We can grasp relationships by analogy before they are explained to us, though, as I have shown in a previous chapter, an explanation is always rationally possible. It is unbelievable, moreover, that psychoanalysis attributes to the subconscious symbols whose meanings should be glaringly apparent to any conscious whatever; who could not see the phallic plough in the vaginal furrow or the resemblance, explicit even in biology, between the marine environment and the amniotic fluid.

Besides, are neuroses anything more than the exaggeration of ordinary tendencies? Who does not have some fear or other: of being shut in (claustrophobia), of wide open spaces (agoraphobia), or of cancer (oncophobia)? Who does not have anguishes, tics, habits, rituals? Who is not just a little paranoid? Why some people are neurotic and others not is a question of no theoretic interest. Discovering the causes of influenza would be by no means useless, since it would mean discovering what influenza is *equivalent* to, and then medicine could act on those equivalents. But we have seen that, strictly speaking, the cause of an objective occurrence is that occurrence itself. When one asks why certain individuals are predisposed to certain maladies, the answer must be that they have physiological characteristics x, y, or z—in other words, that they are predisposed to certain maladies. But if causality has no explicative value in the physical world, it has still less in the psychological world, which is completely finalist. When a neurosis is attributed to traumatizations that have predisposed the patient to a particular malady, it follows that he or she has reacted to these traumatizations in this manner, and not in another, because of a predisposition to it, and so on and so forth. If the problem is pushed back to the birth of the patient, his or her life becomes a set of determinisms. We are thus computers. . . . If psychiatrists admit that in the face of the same event, two individuals may react in different fashions, and if they admit that certain individuals can choose their reactions to particular circumstances, even if only to a slight degree, then they are admitting first, that the same causes do not always produce the same effects, and second, that the essence of the human mind is spontaneity. Now, these two statements constitute the negation of all causal reasoning; therefore, psychoanalysis cannot be what it claims to have become—a science.

Every time one says that a characteristic, an obsession, a phobia, or any other psychological trait "comes from" such-and-such an event, one could say with equal authority that it does *not* come from it. If it is possible for phenomenon B not to follow phenomenon A, A *cannot* be the cause of B. But psychoanalysis rests entirely on this noncausal causality, which we see triumphant in the criticism of literature and the plastic arts. We pretend to explain the works of Da Vinci or Michelangelo on the basis of circumstances found in hundreds of thousands of lives that never produced a single watercolour. We detect in the works of Baudelaire or Nietzsche the aftereffects of their infancies; since countless unknowns have lived through similar infancies, this amounts to explaining everything *except* the works of Baudelaire and Nietzsche.

We have no right to attribute a cause to any mental illness if this cause is not unfailingly and universally followed by the same illness. In these conditions, the only more or less honest psychiatry would be chemotherapy; LSD, mescaline, even alcohol provoke uncontrollable deliriums that differ from one subject to another only as much as the subjects themselves differ. Wisely, psychoanalysis has never risked interpreting the major deliriums that are lumped together under the name of madness, which is divided almost arbitrarily into three categories—schizophrenia, paranoia, and manic depression. It would be difficult, to say the least, to use symbols to tackle the symbolic floods that are the psychoses, to interpret what is already nothing but endless interpretations, or to consider as the subconscious what is merely the conscious gone astray.

The theorists are less inclined to smile at the idea of a purely chemical, organic, or even hereditary origin for mental maladies now that the drugs I have just mentioned have become popular. Psychoanalysis counts for *nothing* in the very slow transformation of psychiatric prisons into hospitals; without modern neuroleptic medications, we would still be using cold baths and straitjackets. Nothing *subconscious* appears in the most intense maniac delirium, and nothing *conscious* disappears. To lose consciousness is to faint, not to go mad. Even the idea of madness as a loss of reason is faulty. Madness reasons from false premises, but it reasons perfectly; the very rigour of its logic produces its delirium. The psychotics who ramble or shout are perhaps more conscious than I am, but they are conscious of other things; if one seeks the reason for what they experience, it must be found in what they experience—just as the reason for one of Mozart's symphonies is that symphony itself, or at least that symphony is what comes closest to being the reason. Once again, mental life is made up of intentions and objectives; and there is no possible science for intentions and objectives.

When psychoanalysis tackles myths, it reduces them all to the same value—or lack of value. Each myth is explained by what *does not form* its special feature. The Mount Caucasus of Prometheus and the Cross of Jesus are equivalent, except for the fact that they are not equivalent. The Sistine Chapel and the pyramid at Gizeh are both built of stone in honour of a god—and little more. Noah and Deucalion, Icarus and Baron Munchausen, Aphrodite and Freya, Diana and the Virgin Mary, Mithras and Christ have still more obvious points in common, but above all they have differences, and these alone give them their interest. Psychoanalysis deals with myth as it deals with art, invoking the lesser to explain the greater. It claims to justify the birth of mythologies by *mechanisms*, but in fact it only reveals that the same fabricating causes never produce the same confabulated effects. It insists that nothing is born spontaneously—in which case nothing can be born at all, much less explained.

No matter. Kronos castrated his father Uranus, Oedipus plucked out his eyes—hence Oedipus and Uranus are castrated. According to Freud (*Totem and Taboo*), human society begins with the "murder of the Father"—which gives all sons the solidarity of guilt. How has this secret spread all over the world and yet remained a secret? Freud's *Metapsychology* explains the marvel: the conscious communicates with the subconscious, but without knowing it, having recourse to a sort of screen called the *preconscious*, whose name— and naturally that alone—signifies by decree that this communication is possible. No doubt the systematic killing of fathers by their sons since the beginning of real History would have created an amazing solidarity among men, but of course, this slaughter is a matter of only symbolic—i.e., imaginary—History. It nevertheless enabled Freud to explain the origin of culture (*Civilization and Its Discontents*); the first men were accustomed to piss on the fire, in a homosexual, incestual contest against the flame, which represented the phallus of the Father (if the connection seems obscure, this is because it is subconscious—in other words, it does not exist). The first man to restrain this universal instinct and spare the fire enjoyed the benefit of the first hearth and was thus the first civilizer.

An explanation hardly less ingenious deals with the "prohibition of incest"—an expression that in itself embodies a complete judgement. For an act to be prohibited, it must first constitute a temptation. Psychoanalysis supposes (and we have seen on what grounds) that we have all wanted to have sexual congress with one of our parents. What else could a one-year-old boy want to do when he is taken into his mother's bed? After all, the child is merely an adult in miniature, even when his sexuality is centered on the mouth or the anus. By the same token, it is obvious that without stringent taboos against necrophilia and coprophagy we would all be irresistibly drawn to making love to corpses and to feasting on excrement. The horror inspired nearly everywhere by incest indicates forceful disapproval and *hence* forceful repression.

Freud and his successors will never agree that incest may simply inspire disgust—disgust similar, in kind, if not in degree, to the revulsion that makes us flee the stench of charnel houses. Yet at the bottom of this disgust, there is elementary biological wisdom. Exogamy multiplies the chances of genetic variation, endogamy reduces them; that is a sufficient basis for an instinct. A monkey born in captivity reacts violently to a rubber snake and tries to chase it from the cage. The man who discovered the genetic ravages of incestuous union no doubt saw them as a curse from heaven—and biologically he was right. In any case, for parents to be desired, they must be desirable; a child could not develop incestuous longings unless he were insensitive to the rancid close-quarters smell that is the invariable product of family intimacy.

Of course, the chimera of incestuous impulses has provided psychoanalysis with an excellent opportunity to uphold the holy institution of the Family (a child has to be able to "do his Oedipus thing," and so on . . .). Psychoanalysis is the theoretical expression of the Victorian morality that flourished at the time of its initial development; this "morality" explained it in the same way that an obsession explains increasing extravagance. Taking the spectre of sexual liberation as a reality, Lacan, followed by the whole of the subversive intelligentsia of Paris, dubbed it a "cunt trap." These revolutionaries, who had never had a hard word for marriage, suddenly discovered that Desire is Power, that Eros and Thanatos are brothers, and that the libido drags the death wish in its train. The equation of sexual repression with civilization enabled the former to be preached in the name of the latter, while the identification of sexual repression as the cause of jealousy conveniently veiled the fact that jealousy is the cause of all repressions. The only evidence of incestuous passion is the existence of homosexuals. One becomes a homosexual through having loved one's mother too much (unless one loved one's mother too much because one was already a homosexual). As for a homosexual who did not love his mother, the case is simple: he has a repressed love for her.

Thus, psychoanalysis is merely an enormous good conduct certificate handed over to the Humble. They have never done anything, wanted anything, known anything, or been capable of anything. The past has produced their present; they are not what they are because of what they no longer are. And since this past is merely the unbroken series of choices that *they* have made, it must be that their subconsciouses and their educations rigged everything in advance. What could be more convenient than being possessed by pandemoniums, interesting to a medical specialist four times a week, and being merely the humble result of Oedipal necessity. The man who dare not thumb through an album of nudes in front of his wife is relieved to find the reasons for his sexual hang-up in his early infancy. His virtues are always to his credit, but his vices are not his fault. Psychoanalysis knows no cowards, no hypocrites, no dirty swine. Its patients are merely sick patients.

Perhaps no one would be harmed if psychoanalysis could cure these patients. But when outside investigators suggest that psychoanalysis cures about as much as fortune-telling does—and with more or less the same degree of good faith—its practitioners answer that nobody really knows what a cure is or what normality consists of. They are rather like the students who are asked what sodium bisulphite is and reply, "It all depends on what you mean by sodium bisulphite." The difference is that they will probably never become chemists, while the psychiatrists, too honest to dare define the adjective "normal," make their fortunes from the treatment of anomalies. Moreover, *honest* is not the right adjective, given the Freudian theory of "resistance." The analyst tells you, "You are thus and thus." Say no, and you are resisting—which proves he or she is right; say yes, and you are confirming—which proves the same thing. Moreover, when Freud discussed cures, he took a last precaution by declaring that a psychoanalysis is never finished. Armed with such knowledge, psychiatry is not afraid to come to the aid of Justice, which (as we shall see presently) is based on an idea the reverse of psychiatry's. This matters little, however, since in the realm of vagueness all ideas are alike.

But while we are on the subject of vagueness, we must mention the man to whom we owe all the precision that is lacking in the Freudian theory—Jacques Lacan. Determined to spread light everywhere, Lacan adopted an impervious style (which he owed not to Mallarmé but to senility) and defined his concepts in terms of themselves: "The subconscious is that part of the discourse . . . that is lacking in the subject for the continuity of its conscious discourse."

Lacan's subconscious is "structured like a Language"—which, for an entity supposed to express itself in symbols, is not surprising. But this comparison means (says Lacan) that within us there is Another that makes us a signal; the subconscious "is the discourse of the Other." It speaks, and it speaks even of the time when it did not know how to speak; the children can scarcely babble a couple of onomatopoeias before the Other within them is devoting itself to metaphor and metonymy.

Thus, to speak means to use significants, a concept that must be defined, like the others, with relentless rigour. The definition, hammered out after many tries, is as follows: "The significant is that which represents a subject for another significant." And the master adds that no other possible wording exists. If I had to define Smirgelia in this fashion—the pivot of my theory of the Alcibiades Complex—I would say that Smirgelia is that which represents a subject for another Smirgelia.

But there is more to come. When Lacan had to say what constitutes desire, he wrote: "Desire is neither an appetite for satisfaction nor a demand for love, but the difference that remains after the subtraction of the former from the latter." An admirable ellipsis! In other words, desire is a demand for love that does not wish to be satisfied and that in consequence demands nothing; from which it follows that desire is neither a demand for love, nor an appetite for satisfaction, nor a desire.

As regards love, M. Safouan, a disciple of Lacan, stated firmly—like Lacan himself, but with more ingenuity—that in the last analysis all love is a love of a name: "Everyone knows that the moment in which the name of the person to whom our love is directed is pronounced indicates that an important threshold has just been crossed." Eureka! The mysteries of intimacy, hitherto opaque, are brought to light. The name evokes the loved one! Thus, it is not the person who is loved; it is the name. The same logic could be used to prove that I turn around when someone calls me not because I am called, but because my name is called. This is why, in Lacan's illuminating work, the role of the Father, which is already outstandingly clear, becomes that of the name of the Father.

This discovery, whose intellectual force contends with its novelty, is like the idea that constitutes the virtual essence of the Lacanian doctrine: the Mirror Stage. At a given moment in their history, children discover their image in the mirror or perhaps in water. An inner voice then says to them, "That is you"—a decisive event in the formation of the Ego. Naturally the Egos of those born blind are deprived of shape—not because they cannot see, but because they have missed the Mirror Stage. That individuals can be influenced by the physical aspect they discover in themselves is, of course, something nobody knew until now. . . . But my irony is unfair and even ridiculous, since the Mirror Stage is not only a matter of real mirrors, but of the mirror concept in general. This changes everything, for then the stage spotlighted by Lacan becomes the moment of adherence to the reflective conscious—whose existence nobody suspected before the master thought of it.

Lacan also excels in the art of making distinctions. Two examples suffice. First, the child Oedipus did not want "to have the Phallus," but "to be the Phallus." The difference is noteworthy: to have the Phallus is to be a consciousness that has the Phallus, while to be the Phallus is (necessarily) to know that one is the Phallus—in other words, to be a consciousness that has the Phallus. We have, of course, glimpsed the meaning of this symbolic Phallus of the symbolic Father above. Let those who would believe that the Phallus is a phallus disabuse themselves of the idea: the Lacanian Phallus is Law, Power, Authority, and so on. The children enter a family of adults; they discover that they are not the Phallus, therefore they discover they are not Law, Power, Authority, etc.—and it is Lacan who has discovered this discovery. Our second example of Lacanian distinctions is this: Lacan insists that one should not confuse *privation* (defined as "the real lack of a symbolic [imaginary] object") with *frustration* (defined as "the imaginary lack of a real object"). The readers may claim that the object of a fictitious loss is of necessity also fictitious, and hence that the loss of a fictitious object is equally fictitious. In this case they have also failed to grasp the subtle but important difference between persons who are really suffering from an imaginary illness and persons who only imagine themselves to be suffering from a real illness.

There remains but one of Lacan's ideas to disclose: that the subconscious exists "only in the speaking being." What then becomes of the various subconscious-inspired stages of the infant, stages that Freud said begin before the infant learns to talk? The answer is simple: when the children begin to talk, they will have lived through these stages (including the Lacanian Mirror Stage), but if by accident they never learn to talk, their ex-future future will replace this more-than-past. Tomorrow I shall have lived through events yesterday that have not yet happened to me today; and we have nearly all not remembered subconsciously what would have happened to us afterwards without our knowing why.

When we reach conclusions like this, it is prudent to reason as little as possible and quote as much as we can. To be fair, it must be said that Lacan possesses both style and humour. When he wanted to say that an author was close to his "thought," he said, "Borges, in his work that is so harmonic to the phylum of our subject. . . ." When he wanted to speak of the Here and Now, mark his words: ". . . this Hic-Nunc pair, the twin croaking of which not only ironically mocks our long-lost Latin, but also gives us a whiff of good-quality humanism by resurrecting the stars at which we find ourselves gaping once again, without our having to draw our auspices from the impudence of their oblique fitting and from the sly shutter of our wink, any more than from the itchings of our counter-transference." If the master was talking about an exercise that may produce knowledge and awareness, he said (being doubtless extremely well-practiced in that sort of thing) that it is an "epistemogenic and noophoric ascesis." But what is lacanophanic and lacanophantic becomes lacanotropic or even lacanoclastic when Lacan pushes his autoadmiration as far as lacanomimesis. Baudelaire spoke of "the green paradise of infantile loves"; the master, despite his magnificent erudition, allowed this to appear in the following garbled version: "the paradise of infantile loves, in which holy Baudelaire does without green ones." The awareness that slips away behind the Other became "The politics of the Ostrich." We are born from an ovule: "Breaking the egg produces Homo—but also the Homelette." Dogs and cats are "animals badly in need of Man, and for this reason we call them "man-ageable."

VIII

From the peak of psychoanalysis one can only come down—and about time too! So I will pass rapidly over a number of its aspects that are lesser but still contribute to its status as perhaps the most afflicting avatar of modern scientific thought. Fortunately, such secondary psychoanalytical heresies as the death wish, the repetition compulsion, and the repressed aggression/sexuality identity can be dealt with briskly. Everything that lives must die, so it must necessarily be pushed towards death by an instinct (obviously a machine that gives out through normal wear and tear has done so by instinct). As for compulsive repetition, human beings are driven to rediscover similar situations (although they do not always rediscover them and they are never really similar) not because they are always the same being, but because the human subconscious is grooved like a record. Finally, aggressiveness is repressed sexuality (even though, everywhere in the animal kingdom, it attains its maximum when the sexual instinct and aggressiveness are in touch with each other). Let me also mention in passing the theory of transference, which shows that patients who are put into the confessional every other day invariably become attached to their confessor (unless they turn against him).

Psychosomatic medicine, as conceived by its founder Groddeck, merits the same total rejection as psychoanalysis itself, for it holds the same views about the *subconscious*. Everyone knows that the conscious and the body are in constant interaction, and all our jargon tells us so ("I've no stomach for that," "I can't swallow that," "you make me sick," "it gave me a lump in my throat," "my heart was beating wildly," and so on). Nearly all nervous disorders have immediate organic repercussions, and one may even ask if there is a single idea, a single state of mind that does not have some physiological result in addition to the cerebral chemistry itself. Our attitudes mould our very skeletons, our faces reflect our efforts to hide all traces of what they show, and all our organs adapt themselves to us better than musicians adapt to their instrument. Our hearts, our stomachs, our intestines, and our glands run with us through the psychological life that runs through them. We can even appear to achieve the miraculous: an ecstatic can walk over hot coals without being burnt, faith can heal rheumatism, and the desire for motherhood can produce false pregnancies. But ecstasy, faith, and the desire for motherhood are not subconscious. At most, they are not reflective. The mechanism that leads from distress to a heart attack is perfectly clear, but distress is not subconscious either—and to say that it originates there is to assert, as we have seen, that the lesser produces the greater, that a conscious state of weak intensity produces a conscious state of greater intensity. In which case, *where* does this additional intensity come from? As for asking why some people are distressed and others are not, this is equivalent (as we have also seen) to wondering why some people are albinos and others are not or why individuals are not all exactly the same.

Psychosomatic medicine states that the body expresses through illness matters of which the conscious is unaware. The Id is speaking, not the Ego. But if the Id is not understood, why does it bother to speak? What is the purpose of such a monologue? Moreover, why do some Egos give the Id free rein and others not—given that all Egos have precisely the same Id?

Psychosomatic medicine fully admits the influence of chemistry on the mind, but it does not take this influence into account—which reduces to not admitting it. If some people resist influenza and others do not, say the practitioners, this difference is by virtue of psychological, not physical, predispositions. Asthma is thus always the result of emotional distress—a doctrinaire conclusion that ignores the equal or superior plausibility of the opposite hypothesis, namely, that emotional distress is the invariable result of asthma. Does being nervous turn a person into a heart case—or is it being a heart case that makes this person nervous? This question would get an answer if it deserved one, as would the question from which it derives: Is it the body that influences the mind or the mind that influences the body? How can one know, since they always act at exactly the same time? In either case, to say that allergies are psychosomatic is totally unfounded, because the victims react to substances of whose proximity they are unaware. Moreover, it is hard to imagine what negative connotations aluminum or pollen could have (or symbolize) for the mind, much less radically new chemical compounds (unless the subconscious keeps itself up to date on additions to the pharmacopeia).

The idea that the body uses analogies as symbols of which the patient remains ignorant (the knee means the genitalia, the legs the penis, and so on) merits psychoanalysis itself. Somehow animals, whose conscious is sufficiently inadequate for them to have a right to a subconscious, never symbolize in this manner. Other ideas advanced by psychosomatic medicine have the immense advantage of being unverifiable, such as the one that considers every accident to be the equivalent of a verbal lapse. When an accident happens, one merely has to look for the reason in the victim's past. Groddeck goes further: according to him, a woman giving birth experiences the acme of pleasure, even though she *thinks* she is in agony. So female animals who cry out in pain as they are giving birth are *deceiving themselves.* No doubt there is a very great difference between hating a food and *believing* that one hates it; all the subtlety of the subconscious lies in this distinction.

Finally, psychosomatic medicine would not be what it is without this axiom: locate the origin (obviously psychological) of a disease, and you will cure it. Of course, just knowing why my car won't start is not enough to get it running again, but my body is a miraculous machine; when I understand what my Id was symbolizing when it opened the gates of my body to a rival invasion, the viruses, conquered by my conscious, will let themselves be slaughtered on the spot. Obviously psychosomatic medicine is as powerless against infectious disease as psychoanalysis is against mental illness. All that either of them can command is a clientèle of hysterics or fakers— and when all is said and done, treating fakery by lies is merely an honourable form of homeopathy.

But psychiatry also has some public functions, and it would be a pity not to mention them. Everyone remembers the affair of the XYY chromosome. Statistics seemed to show that this abnormal chromosome was found more often in criminals than in law-abiding citizens. If it drove one to murder, said the psychiatrists, this new biological element was an extenuating circumstance. The courts could not accept this without being asked how they knew a chromosome could be the *cause* of a crime, and they could not reject it without being asked why they were ignoring this particular extenuating circumstance and not others, such as environment. All sorts of people can come from a given childhood environment; if I am innocent as a result of my chromosomes, why should I not be innocent in view of a series of events that constitute me since they constitute *my* past?

In any case, the statistics were questionable, and for the same reason that psychiatry and Justice itself are questionable. Even if

the dubious chromosome had appeared more frequently in murderers than in other people, this would not have meant that the majority of criminals had abnormal chromosomes or that the majority
of XYY-carriers had ever carried out a murder. In fact, even if *all*
the XYY-carriers *had* been gangsters, the scientific thesis would still
have been false. A statistical relationship between two phenomena
may be causal, but only a logical relationship is *necessarily* causal
(otherwise, knowing that among the nations of the world, Hungary
has both the highest suicide rate *and* the largest per capita consumption of paprika, we could infer that paprika leads to suicide).
Now, the relationship between mind and body *cannot* be causal,
because the mind and the body are, by definition, heterogeneous,
whereas cause and effect are also by definition, identical. Moreover,
strictly speaking, even proof that a certain organic state always goes
hand in hand with a certain state of mind would demand that a
state of mind be observable and describable; but only the Ego can
observe states of mind and not even the Ego can describe them.

Furthermore, if one accepts the existence of one "criminogenic"
substance, one has grounds for suspecting the existence of others—
perhaps a substance specific to each individual, which Science, limited in this situation to the statistical route, could never discover.
In these circumstances, there would be as many judicial errors as
there were people on trial—for Justice would hold them responsible
for what were really matters of chemistry.

Even without this complication, Justice and its handmaiden, psychiatry, manage to find themselves in a perpetual dilemma trying to
choose between two views. In the first, Humans are entirely the
product of their past, of their body, of their brain, and of circumstances. In that case, cause and effect lead unfailingly to determined
states of mind and everyone is totally irresponsible. Justice, which
would appear to be put out of business by this conclusion, in fact
need only maintain that since Humans are the ensemble of these
mechanisms and *nothing* else, it is the ensemble that must be held
responsible. Result: total irresponsibility equals total responsibility.
In other words, to be declared not guilty by virtue of "diminished
responsibility" does not exempt even an ensemble of mechanisms
from accountability, and a mental hospital is only another jail.

According to the other view, Humans act freely, and material influences, cerebral and otherwise, only appear to determine them, when in fact it is they who determine them. In this case, freedom equals total responsibility.

Justice and common sense claim to reconcile these alternatives; in reality they alternate between them—an arrangement reminiscent of Science's equivocation between the determinist and the probabilist points of view. The statement "sometimes my action results from my cerebral state and sometimes it does not" is just as scientific and honest as "Bodies are *usually* attracted to each other in accordance with Newton's Law." When psychiatrists give evidence in a court of law, they have by definition strayed from their sphere of competence—which is understandable in view of that sphere's small size. There is no psychiatry without determinism, no Justice without liberty. Now, when psychiatrists declare a murderer responsible, they draw their authority as a witness from a pseudoscience that they betray by that very declaration—for if responsibility is conceivable, then psychiatry is not. Yet psychiatry in a courtroom has recourse to more than one self-contradiction. Psychiatry is quite capable of describing as normal someone who has hacked a little girl to pieces and holed up in an attic with the corpse, murdered three men from jealousy, or stabbed an old woman for no reason at all. Only appearances count. A criminal has to foam at the mouth, scream, rave, kill twenty people instead of one to escape execution or a mental hospital. If I put myself in the place of the "normal" criminals, I realize at once that I would have to be completely mad to commit half their crimes. In other words, what I cannot do without being mad, another can do while in a state of normality. There are thus *many* normalities—a statement that contradicts the very definition of this term without in the slightest way upsetting psychiatry, which has seen other normalities. . . .

Justice is no less logical. When it condemns a murderer to death, it does so because he is beyond rehabilitation. One must conclude from this that the true madman who shoots down half a village from the top of a tower is better material for therapy—at any rate no court of law would have the heart to order the death of a being who is so "irresponsible."

Morever, if we accept the absurd proposition that we are sometimes responsible and sometimes determined, it becomes impossible to say when we are in one state and when we are in the other. If it were otherwise, we would have a rule allowing us to "reveal" freedom, and hence a definition of freedom—which is a contradictory phrase since a freedom defined and involving rules is merely a mechanism. This problem does not arise for Science; it does not have to define what it will not admit (except when the "science" is psychiatry, which admits everything because it defines nothing).

Meanwhile, Justice tries to look like a venture in rehabilitation. No matter that the prisons turn amateur criminals into professionals, that gangs form or meet again in jail, or that the individuals who are fifty when they get out of the cell they entered when they were twenty do not really look rehabilitated. No matter either that it is easier to rehabilitate a responsible person than an "irresponsible" one, and that by imposing heavier penalties on the former, judges do exactly the reverse of what they claim. In the last resort, Justice admits that it is content with punishing, but this admission does not get it anywhere, for either a punishment is rehabilitative, or it is not, and in the latter case it is nothing more than *vengeance*.

Who has not at some time or another wished that the perpetrator of a particularly gruesome murder would die? It is this, and this alone, that Justice accomplishes. It makes pronouncements, with the blessing of that imposter psychiatry, on responsibilities about which it can know no more than anyone else; it makes monsters out of responsible people; it admits that the "norm" varies from one person to another like a standard measure that continually changes size; it considers extenuating or aggravating circumstances without knowing whether they have extenuated or aggravated the action in question, and without considering that they can neither extenuate nor aggravate the action committed; it pretends to punish in order to rehabilitate, while it does exactly the opposite; it mounts incredible productions based on special effects—flowing sleeves, ritual costumes, and archaic jargon; it embroiders its proceedings with quibbles that were stale and pointless in the days of the First Crusade. In short, it absolutely coruscates with bad comedy, bad logic, and bad faith—all in a vain effort to sustain an illusion of order and procedure in the face of the most primitive passions and superstitions. Here, at last, psychoanalysis provides some veritable experts.

There are, in fact, only two ways in which Justice could be truly logical—and we could accept neither. Either Justice would function like a refuse dump, and we would eliminate all vermin without ceremony—the Nazi method. Or we would devise a penal system that involved no penance and was truly rehabilitative. But our shameful societies would have some difficulty in putting themselves forward as rehabilitators. Moreover, the man in the street would not go along, for they want anyone who makes them suffer to suffer as much—or a bit more—in return. In practice, Justice can only confirm lynchings: the function of the judge is to dignify the bigotry of a jury. The murder of a child will always be more severely punished than the killing of an adult—as though an adult at gunpoint were at less of a disadvantage than a child, and as though I were less innocent today, and therefore more deserving of violent death, than when I was four years old.

Jealousy will always be an extenuating circumstance and sometimes even an exonerating one. We have some self-understanding. Rape will always be considered quasimurder, but multiple fraud will merely incur censure. The idea of real theft will never arouse any uneasiness; although stealing means appropriating something that belongs to another, I will not be given the opportunity to say what I consider mine if someone buys my land at a modest price and then resells it overnight at a profit of three or four million francs.

I will pass over the matter of drugs, but not without revealing the name of one—alcohol—that causes several hundred times more deaths than heroin. Almost half of all road accidents can be laid at its door; it is rapidly habit-forming; its toxicity makes it a "hard" drug. But while the whole scientific world is beating its brains out trying to prove the harmful effects of hashish and finding proofs to the contrary, the sale of alcohol is open, authorized, encouraged, legal, legitimate. For what *reason?* But the heart has its reasons, and psychiatry is not at variance with them.

The incoherencies of the courts seem less whimsical when they result in the final agony. Even knowing that the death penalty does not deter and sometimes fascinates murderers, some people hold that it serves as an example—although the example serves only the victims, and only once they are dead. The idea of killing a person to warn *others* would seem curious if it did not date back to the time when gibbets decorated the entrance to towns. But what do examples matter when the French public wants its guillotine? In July 1976, the liberal Giscard d'Estaing signed an order for the execution of Christian Ranucci, aged nineteen, who had been pronounced normal by a psychiatrist. (Other executions have followed.) Giscard authorized the executioner to carry out his task, and slept well. Towards dawn, men leapt on the terrified Ranucci, read him texts of which he understood nothing, and led him with great ceremony to the guillotine while a priest recited prayers for the dying. The blade fell, putting an end to the condemned man's cries. Death was not his punishment: when death came, he was no longer there. His punishment was fear, physical suffering, and agony—otherwise known as *torture*. Vengeance and torture are the two truths of Justice, the two scales of its balance. That Justice should be blindfolded is the most logical thing in the world; that everyone closes his eyes when these things are done is the most normal thing in the world. Hatred and shame call for the same darkness—the one so that it may be blind, the other so that it is not blinding.

IX

Let us recapitulate. Science has dethroned neither absolute time nor absolute space, but uses both of them. The duration it envisages is spatial and runs the wrong way. The movement it deals with is merely a succession of stops. Its universe goes from the past to the present, as though everything were not present before it is past. Its causality is mere identity and cannot, therefore, take into consideration that which changes. Obliged to exclude finality, Science implies it in the idea of chance, which is inconsistent with determinism. Because of this inconsistency, cybernetics is powerless before the principle of Life—as are all the biological sciences, deductive or inductive, theoretical or experimental. Yet Sciences cannot better explain the conscious by means of language, nor of concepts through their genesis, nor of ideas through perceptions. Thus, the whole possible body of Science gives us a better *picture* of the world, but not a better *understanding*—even though this improved picture can and must alone become the foundation of a better understanding.

Anchored forever in identity—in tautology—scientific knowledge identifies and does not justify. With psychoanalysis we fall into verbal confusion, unconsidered plots, and lies; while with psychiatry giving assistance to the Justice we have a false science meeting a pseudofaith. All we have to do now is to examine how all forms of lies culminate in all forms of faith.

INCANTATION
TO THE MUMMIES

I

Pascal was right when he said that nobody ever loved the God of the philosophers, and that all our prayers go to the manifested God of Abraham and Jacob. The God of the philosophers is the supreme Ego, while the God of the religions is the absolute Other. We call the God of the religions to our aid, while the God of the philosophers calls us to his. The Creation of the God of the philosophers is here and now, aimed through Matter at the future. The Creation of the God of religions is past and aims only at passing; Matter is only an appendix to it. The God of the philosophers wants everything, but he holds strictly to the script of the drama he has set in motion. The God of the religions can do everything; though he stays aloof from the drama, he manifests his power by breaking rules through revelations, miracles, and visions. The God of the religions is an indulgent judge who loves his creatures over and above their faults. The God of the philosophers is neither tender nor merciful: all lives, all deaths are his life and his death, all the past is his memory, he has had no pity on *his* weaknesses and does not cherish *his* bad memories. The God of the religions has foreseen everything and knows how the Universe will end (Fatality or Providence); the God of the philosophers *is* that Universe and knows nothing in advance (Vitality and Improvisation). The God of the religions is love of his subjects. The God of the philosophers is love of Matter, which he constantly penetrates, awakens, reanimates; it is by means of Matter that he sets his course, it is to Matter that he clings, and it is

325

in Matter that he tries to attain the ideal that he is. Nothing is guaranteed, nothing is given, at any moment everything may return to the abyss. The God of the religions is perfect; the God of the philosophers is infinite—and all perfections are shattered in advance by the infinite. To supplicate, to beseech, to praise the God of the religions is to please him, but to call the God of the philosophers by another name than theirs is to betray him.

All religions everywhere entail being small, being forgiven, heaping unending praise on an authority who exempts one from reflection and on an omnipotence who preserves one from the dangers of action, piling up good deeds like an advance payment and sacrifices like the rent money, pretending to see the salvation of others as a means of realizing one's own salvation, imagining salvation as happening after death so that one can create a living death for oneself during life. Such are all religions, and such is the *ideology* of humility, which we have already encountered in a more blatantly materialistic guise.

Agnostic or religious, all the humble are materialists, but the latter call materialism spirituality. God manifests himself—in other words, he *materializes*—in miracles, laws, and biographies. Life is not a miracle, but the changing of water into wine is one. Because the humble person is religious, he or she is above reason; he trusts only his senses. To understand divinity is nothing, but to *see* it is everything. The mystics are superior to the philosophers because they *feel* what the latter merely reveal. Religions abhor determinism because it excludes free will, but they worship it as Providence, as All-Powerfulness, as Omniscience. They baptize as a mystery the ancient contradiction: "If God has willed evil, he is not good; if he has not willed it, he is not all-powerful; in either case he is not God."

God overflows with love for the personal souls of the humble—thanks to whom his oceans, earth, and air are becoming poisoned. A Pope in an automobile brings cancer to men's lungs as he blesses their souls. Three billion years of life are merely a pretext to put the humble to the test; religions from East to West know Life only as something quite different from living. "I am the Way, the Truth, and the Life" means: "I am the rut, the dogma, and the hereafter." The true life is death. Paradise means Garden, but only a heavenly garden. Flowers, forests, animals are only illusions or allusions. The

Lord Most High, seated in his empyrean of pearls and emeralds, knowing the beginning and the end of this interlude called the world, praised unceasingly by cohorts of spirits marshalled in hierarchies—it is he who looks out for the humble as they choke in their death rattles, loves the death that Life detests, detests the sex by which Life remains in existence, and dotes on offerings, sacrifices, prayer wheels, sufferings patiently endured, contritions and contortions, ecstasies, eyes raised to heaven, bended knees, and ceremonials. Hindu military gymnastics, which run from the Lotus Position to the Cobra to prostrations, are equivalent to the suffocation of the Dervishes, the fasts of Ramadan, the ritual prohibitions of the Sabbath, the false sorrow of Lent. God with his death's head can bring to life only by putting to death. As symbol of the most firmly established power possible, how could he not have sanctified all forms of established power? And where is the humble person who would not say "I love you" to any form of power whatever? Everywhere, all that the humble person considers sacred puts him or her into a state of *representation*: he curries favour, speaks politely, solemnizes; the comedy is all the more sinister in that it is serious. There is no believer who does not speak of God as though with his finger to his lips, nothing sacred that does not stem from fear, nothing fearful that does not lead to hypocrisy, nothing hypocritical that is not found in the religious mind.

Religions never have any relationship with the powers they support (and sometimes found). Mohammed was innocent of the *jihads*, the Gospels counted for nothing during the Inquisition, St. Dominic burnt the Albigenses but not on purpose. Calvin tortured Servetus inadvertently, the Russian Orthodox hierarchy was not responsible for the Tsars, whose feet they kissed. The Hindus have nothing to do with the caste system, the sacred cows, or the famines; eyes turned devoutly towards the sun, how could these love-filled men be responsible for the corpses beneath their sandals? The Brahmanic *Laws of Manu*, which sanctions the most abject social system in History, was contemporary with the highest Indian mystical theology. Sages who have known the truth of Shiva, Krishna, and Vishnu have learned a supplementary certainty as to the excellence of a political organization that condemned the Untouchables to an existence as bestial as that of the Spartan helots—the hierarchy of castes being merely a reflection of the hierarchy of souls. Medieval mysticism reached its peak in a world crackling with the funeral pyres of witches. The Synods that celebrated the hierarchy of angels had no interest in the condition of the serf. The great poems of Sufism rose above a universe of seraglios, castration, impalements, murder, and legalized theft that pious souls disdained to notice. The world is vanity; that God should have created this vanity is a mystery.

Of course, mysticism does not exclude order. For example, Yoga is divided into three categories: the highest is *royal* Yoga ("Raja Yoga"), and the lowest requires the presence of a Guru. Immediately we have an upper category and a lower, a king and disciples, masters and exercises. There are grades, stages, obligations, privileges. Certain special souls can even attain the highest level without passing through the normally requisite stages. The supreme objective is to reach *Samadhi*—"transported." Let the world go hang; I, I, I, I am in contact with my God. The Schoolmen proclaimed that God is unknowable even as they wrote about him, producing tomes as thick as dictionaries, building Heaven into a hierarchy (Hell, Limbo, Purgatory, Paradise) much as ineffable Hindu wisdom reproduces the caste system in metempsychosis or reincarnation, which classes animals in order of merit. After my death *I* shall become another, but this other will have nothing of what is called "I." Nirvana, like Paradise, is a resting place; God's objective is a *stop*. It is not at all surprising that when Ramakrishna heard the word "revolution," he retorted, "It can only take place within us." Thus absolved from carrying it out elsewhere, he entered into *Samadhi*—and half Calcutta died of hunger. Sri Aurobindo announced in every key that terrestrial life is not an ideal, then mentioned Yogis who have lived for more than three hundred years. Knowledge of God does not come from reasoning, which it vaporizes, but from physical training and alimentary hygiene. Transcendental meditation consists of not thinking; thought is close to matter, but the visual and material tricks of mandalas approach ecstasy. Gandhi said, "If the railroads disappeared, we would not weep over their loss." In a country so backwards that railroads are the only method of distributing supplies and medicines, who indeed would weep over the loss of mere technological process? The same great reformer slept beside a naked girl "to test himself"; one has to admire the Hindu mystic for having gone so far beyond the obsessions of Christian morality.

All religions revile sex as rigorously as they denigrate common sense and the human intellect. Japanese Zen may substitute *Satori* and The Drawing of the Bow for the Indian *Samadhi* and Yoga, but it includes the same ecstasies. Krishnamurti recommends not thinking—and practices what he preaches. He opposes thought with observation and adds that the former is the root of wars; he manifestly disdains study of the animal world, in which he would have noticed the presence of wars and the absence of thought. But observation without thought is doubtless an occult art.

The adjective "spiritual" applied to religions is a fraud, clear and simple. Every religion aims at manifest—and thus material—results. Every religion is based on tangible and precise—and thus material—practices. Every religion relies on guarantees that are historic and thus material—or revealed—and thus materialized. Every religion directs itself towards individual—and thus egotistical and thus material—hopes. That every religion also requires a show of contempt for the material merely adds to the hypocrisy of the whole thing.

Every sect cries out for itself and the coming of its own God. Judaism prays for the Jews, Islam pleads for Mohammedans, Christianity seeks the reign of Christ the king, Buddhist spirituality works only for itself. "If Christ be not risen," said St. Paul, "our hopes are in vain." If this miracle (material, like all miracles) had not occurred, the apostle would not have believed; it mattered little to him that even if Jesus had been resurrrected, he would have to die a second death. The absurd is real if it is *visible*. Thomas wished to touch the Master's wounds. Christianity dies without the historicity —and thus the materiality— of Christ, who makes himself believable by his miracles. The thaumaturges and buffoons of the vulgar world of the Gospels and the Acts of the Apostles find it natural that the dead no longer speak of themselves after their reawakening. We have no idea what Lazarus could actually *do* after he was raised from the dead.

Every religion, no matter how spiritual, also has its liturgies— material acts that are conditions and not symbols. There is no such thing as abstract baptism, communion, or extreme unction. One is not washed free of original sin by thought, but by water; one does not receive Christ by the mind, but by bread and wine. God is "truly present" in the host—which implies he would not be elsewhere. The soul is deemed to "leave the body"—as though it had been located there. Though it alone exists, we must bless corpses and bow down over tombs; though it alone can be saved, the Creed insists on the resurrection of the body. Faith can work miracles—provided it is based on magic.

When it comes to theology, faith uses reason as long as it serves a purpose, then discards it when the winds of the mind begin to change. *Credo quia absurdum*—I believe because it is absurd. But since the number of possible absurdities is infinite, I am careful to choose those that suit me. Faith is respected like property and monogamous possession. One says "I respect your convictions" when one distrusts them, just as one says "Every man to his own opinion" when there is no advantage in fighting for one's own proposals. Faith is a gift, a received privilege, a charisma that one spreads around or lays aside. It is impossible to shake one of the Elect by rational arguments, but what faith is not sure about, it uses argument to affirm with a desperate certainty. "Increase our faith," demanded the Apostles, but there is no need to have faith in the existence of the Sun, and surely the existence of the anti-God of the religions is even more certain. Though faith is more encompassing than the whole of metaphysics, it totters on its brazen bases whenever a Church changes a minor tradition, as when an ecclesiastical bureaucrat orders the clergy to use the vernacular, to say "Lift up your hearts" instead of *sursum corda,* or to face the faithful when introducing God into a piece of unleavened bread. Preserved, faith makes one fear eternal damnation and gives one a contrite air after each act of provisional contrition; resuscitated, it has a funereal look; life giving, it petrifies; revolutionary, it preserves; sincere, it restrains itself; ransomed from original sin by Christ, it shows no surprise that orginal sin still exists and that Hell, which was merely Limbo before the appearance of the Saviour, becomes through him the biggest torture chamber ever imagined by a spiritualism that knows only matter, by a mysticism that dreams only of pardon.

The God of the Old Testament intervened in the military operations of Israel; the evangelic God recommends abstention from worldly affairs. Caesar on one hand, God on the other; thus I shall

not displease anybody, especially not Caesar, whose kingdom is not
God's. The central theme of the First Epistle of St. Peter is obedience to authority in general and the emperor in particular. When
Celsus accused Christians of anarchism, he slandered them; under
Marcus Aurelius, the invincible Fulminata Legion was made up
entirely of Christians. The fact that the *idea* of Christianity, treated
as a mythology, can be gripping—singularly so in the stories of the
Passion and the martyrs—does not prevent Christianity from wishing to be something quite different from a myth. Neither does it
prevent the great figure of Christ from having to be invented in
spite of his story. The Gospels are irritating in their specificity: Jesus
changed water into wine, multiplied the loaves and fishes, cursed a
fig tree that then withered up incontinently on the spot, sent seven
demons into a herd of swine, urged all individuals to work for the
salvation of *their* personal soul, declared that the poor will be with
us always, announced that his Kingdom is not of this world, demanded that his followers burn out and reject everything hurtful,
doomed the ungodly to everlasting torment, decreed that whosoever
offends children (the offense being only sexual in nature) deserves
the death penalty and that desiring a woman is equivalent to com-
mitting adultery with her. The word *adultery* occurs frequently in
the evangelic texts. A miracle being worth more than a sexual act,
Jesus's mother was a virgin, and though the Scriptures speak of the
brothers of Christ, official interpreters tell us that the word *brother*
is to be taken in a symbolic sense. When Jesus preached goodness,
even in the Beatitudes, he promised it a reward. Two millennia of
bigotry, selfish motives, and ferocity are rooted here. Between two
major oil spills in 1976, the Pope reemphasized his exhortations
against masturbation, homosexuality, and premarital sex; he was
acting in the purest of evangelic tradition, for it is in the Scriptures
themselves that prudishness makes its obscene face of disgust. But
the Sermon on the Mount is now covered by a mountain of sermons,
and it was with little reference to the Scriptures that the Valentines,
the Marcions, the Makaires, the Cappadocian gnostics, the Samarian
stylites, and the hermits of the Thebaid achieved their salvation—all
for themselves, all according to themselves, all in their own sphere—
and then anathematized, cursed, and excommunicated each other.

Some people try to rationalize or excuse elements of religion, though none are really separable. For example, the attempt to separate morality and religion is absurd; Allah, Jupiter, and Krishna are distinguishable only by their prescriptions and prohibitions. Claiming to separate morality and politics, however, is merely hypocrisy; every religious obligation imposes a policy upon us. If we can condemn abortion, contraception, Marxism, divorce, conscientious objection and *not* condemn the death penalty, Fascism, and nuclear weapons—all without politicking—what then constitutes politics? Similarly, to say that religions *are* allegories is to take them for what they refuse to be. If the stories of the seven demons and the cursed fig tree are merely symbolic, what do they symbolize and why should the rest of the evangelic story be regarded as literal? If the Old Testament forbids all images of God—even going so far as to refuse to name him—why does it write his biography? As for the great works of art that religions have inspired, it is, on the contrary, these that have given the religious sermon all its inspiration. St. Matthew and Luther did not improve Bach; Bach transfigured them. Finally, there is the claim that religions at least preach love. But this love, like all the others offered us, is offered cheap. In fact, the word *cheap* is doubly justified here; I love my neighbour only for the ulterior motive of my own salvation, and this love is possible without its conditions being necessary. On the human level every disagreement or inequality reduces love to a stage production. But for religious reasons, I can love beings whom the whole of my own being detests because I see their souls—and behind them, my own. I pardon my brothers who exploit, who spy, and who torture, even if they do not stop being what they are. In this market, evil always wins—and yet religion says nothing is more lofty than this charity. Similarly, not even the ecstasies of St. John of the Cross or St. Theresa of Avila are not higher than *my* personal encounter with *my* personal God.

Clearly, religions had an important historical role to play in the enclosed world of yesterday, but so did profit, and pollution. They still do, and they are increasingly more important than religion. For more than two centuries the attacks of reason, men such as Voltaire, and scientism failed to shake the established credos; in today's Western world they are giving way before TV, the good life, and erotic imagery. No other fact gives a clearer explanation of just *where* the spirituality of the humble was anchored. Vulgarity, materialism, concealed egotism, reverse determinism, the cult of Chance under the name of Providence and of Death under the name of Life—religious craving was an answer to all these. There is no need for it to abandon its foundations in order to follow new paths today.

Mystery today lies not in the world's objectives but in its methods —and only when scientists have not yet explained the technique. Fascination does not come from the thinkable, but from the visible; the conscious is not something to wonder at, but telepathy, telekinesis, and premonition are. Thought crossing space must itself be spatial—and thus material. That a mind can move distant objects is miraculous, but that I can move my body is not, for my thought is *within* my body. If one event out of billions has been glimpsed in advance, neither chance nor intuition enter the picture, though it is the future of the universe that is already settled. Vanished civilizations and occult societies are worth more than plain History and difficult human research; jealously guarded secrets are better than would be the disappearance of the jealousy that guards them. Humankind is alone in the universe, but if extraterrestrials joined us, we could be so in greater numbers. A properly initiated mind could *leave* its body and travel elsewhere—because, once again, it is normally found *within*. Myers, James, Tyrrell make mediums speak with the dead; what the dead say may be atrociously trite, but at least they do say something.

What need is there for me to lengthen the inventory of all the nullities? They only make one nullity, whose whole can never be any greater, any more than three times zero can yield a product.

II

If religion holds no answers, neither does revolution in the usual, leftist sense of the word. Although revolutionaries realize that no religious faith can be compatible with their wish to change the world, their Marxist philosophy retains the essential features of religions: the love of cults, materialism, and the ideology of humility.

Actually, to speak of a Marxist philosophy is as much a misuse of the word *philosophy* as is religions' appropriation of the word *spirituality*. Apart from the fact that materialism, which only Engels has defended in two indefensible works, has no right to the title of philosophical doctrine, the materialism called "dialectic" is a verbal parade. Every dialectic presupposes opposites and thus comparisons and thus thought; thus, making thought stem from a material dialectic boils down to making it stem from itself. Both Marx and Engels referred to Hegel *via* Feuerbach, almost in the manner of a pastiche; in his *The German Ideology*, *The Holy Family*, and *Manuscripts*, Marx poked clumsy fun at a Hegel whom he had made unrecognizable, without ever stating precisely what he thought could put Hegelianism back on the track. In the postscript to *Das Kapital*, he wrote that though Hegel believed thought creates reality (actually Hegel did not speak of thought, but of Mind), "for me, on the contrary, the movement of thought is merely the reflection of real [sic] movement transported and transposed in the brain [sic] of Man." That single sentence contains the immemorial prejudice of the antiphilosophy: the contrast between thought and "the real" (as though thought were not real); the designation of the brain as the *location* of thought, which is thus made spatial; the then-logical transposition of the whole exterior world into the brain (which means that the part contains the whole, or the lesser encompasses the greater); the creation of truth by material processes; the idea that concepts of cause, effect, time, and space come from experience (although experience merely assumes them). In other words, since a human being cannot think "$2 + 2 = 4$" without serotonin in his hypothalamus, this chemical process becomes a logical condition of truth. Nothing more trivial can be imagined.

Engels himself did not get down to tackling the problem of the conscious—a problem materialists always find nullifying. The world had to wait for Lenin, creator of "the supreme philosophy of our time" (as Sartre described Marxism) to give this question a shining answer: the conscious is an "epiphenomenon"— i.e., an overappearance. To whom does this appearance appear? To itself, so it becomes an appearance itself, and so on. A typical Hegelian "bad infinity." . . . Whatever the cortexes of Marxist exegetes can secrete (or possibly irradiate) on this subject, Marx's "reverse Hegelianism" necessarily *thinks* (even if, through an understandable modesty, he abstains from saying so or even thinking about it).

Every untenable tenet of past and present philosophies—materialism, empiricism, determinism—is concentrated by Marxist ideology, even though its ulterior antireligious stance has no need of the materialist catechism that is both the whole world's "natural philosophy" and the implicit philosophy of all religions. The complete works of Marx and Engels contain so little and such poor philosophy that only a few more examples need be quoted. Thus: "The materialist concept of the world signifies only the concept of Nature as it is, with no additions from outside" (*Ludwig Feuerbach*). Engels was doubtless unaware that measurement and perception are "additions from outside" without which Nature is nothing, and that it is in no way "the same" for physics as it is for chemistry, painting, or the law. The elimination of all distinctions "with no additions from outside" leads finally to the celebrated Kantian "thing in itself," to which, Engels said, Science gave birth by synthesis (*Utopian Socialism and Scientific Socialism*). What urea is when we eliminate perception, time, and space, we can discover by this simple method: make some.

Elsewhere in *Ludwig Feuerbach* Engels declared that thought is a *product* of matter, that "intellectual objects are reflections of the real world," that "the world as experienced" is a product of the human brain, which, after all, is itself merely a product of this world—platitudes that Lenin repeated in *Materialism and Empirio-Criticism*. The number ten is a reflection—in what?—of real tens, as though it were not real itself, and so on. In *Dialectic of Nature* Engels attacked induction, in opposition to Haeckel, but in *Anti-Dühring* he defended the empirical genesis of ideas which all materialism must do of necessity; yet what is empiricism if not induction systematized? Hegel's dialectic is caricatured as: deny the death of the seed, then the negation of this negation would give birth to flowers. The same type of "dialectic" runs from start to finish through *Das Kapital*. It is dialectic reversed in fact—as Hegel or Kant are reversed by one who understands them not at all.

Marxist thought pretends to be a science in the actual sense, not Fichte's. Marx and Engels got away with it because they wrote for (and are still read by) a world that devotes itself entirely to Utopia and the oracle. Rather than wistfully describing a society of the future or inveighing against contemporary society, they outdid the dreamers they held in contempt—Saint-Simon, Fourier, Owen, Proudhon, and so on—by formulating a complete and logical revolutionary theory. Revolution must be foreseeable and scientifically explainable; when it takes place, there must be preestablished methods for obtaining its prime objectives. Thus, the difference between Marx and other socialists is not one of nuance but of nature. Without this fatal and demonstrable character of Revolution, Marxism would have become a dream of Utopia like the others.

Das Kapital is nothing other than an unbelievably meticulous study of the mechanism Marx believed would produce revolution everywhere. Its pivot is the impoverishment of the proletariat, an idea that Marx never abandoned, whatever his innumerable commentators may claim, for one very simple reason: without it, his Revolution would no longer be inescapable. It required salaried workers to become progressively poorer and more numerous, the owners to become progressively fewer and richer; a general—and violent—strike would then allow the proletarians to establish the dictatorship of the proletariat (whose image Marx saw in the Paris Commune) and then to pass progressively from socialism to communism, from the victory of one class to a society without classes.

As we all know, no Marxist revolution has ever taken place. Marx's basic premise was wrong. The proletariat did not become impoverished. Rather, beginning in the late nineteenth century, it became progressively allied with the bourgeoisie. Strikes ended in negotiations. Marx had forecast that the first revolution would take place in Germany or England, the most industrialized countries of his day. Rather, the first unrest broke out in Russia, a country that Marx had doomed to the role of ultrareactionary policeman. The peasant masses and the soldiers, whom Marx had not classed as proletarians, came onto the scene; from October 1917, right from the start, the Russian Revolution has had nothing to do with Marxism as an economic theory. And what has happened all over the world since then is the exact opposite of what this theory forecast. In fact we now see that the more industrial a country is, the less poor its proletariat and the more its wealth is shared; hence, the less chance it has of staging a revolution.

According to Marx, history was exclusively the history of class warfare, with the proletarian class, deprived, rootless, estranged, cast in the role of the historic saviour—a collective Christ attracted to the Resurrection. He refused to see that a class is composed of individuals and that its history is primarily that of the struggle of these individuals among themselves. A class is not a community of function; it is hard to see how a French, a Swedish, and a Moroccan welder could form part of the same class. Neither is a class a category of salary; the going wage for a plumber and a professor may be the same, but they clearly come from two different classes. Besides, the idea of International solidarity clashes with deep-rooted nationalism; it was a terrible letdown for the theorists when the events of 1914 made it clear that the Prussian working man felt closer to his Prussian boss than to his French counterpart. The international ideal is also bound to encounter racism (which both Marx and Bakunin practiced—one against the other, since Marx detested Slavs and Bakunin hated Jews). In brief, class consciousness and solidarity depend only on self-interest. It is easy for the ruling class to divide and rule when all the divisions are already present, ready to be exchanged for all the fiefdoms.

Every time Marxist theory makes itself out to be complex, it is because it is covering up enormous simplifications. Thus, the call to abolish the class of salaried professionals and managers became the unbelievably ingenuous (and idiotic) proposals of Marx's *Value, Price, and Profit, Critique of the Gotha Program, Das Kapital,* and the polemics against Lassalle and Bakunin. Work that is not explicitly productive must nevertheless be rewarded. But who would validate the services performed? Above all, how could one define the value of an hour's work by a bandleader, a diplomat, a journalist, or a writer in relation to the value of an hour's work by a tinsmith? Marxist justice put off solving the problem to the day when work would "become a need" and all goods would "spring forth in abundance" (all revolutionary grandeur lies, perhaps, in that last word); thus it did not aim at the abolition of work as a means, but at the absolute proportionality of profits and the effort expended to produce them. In doing so, it provided the ideal human of tomorrow with the possibility of practicing every profession at once—which is technically impossible and humanly meaningless. There can be no question of total equality and a priori equality of incomes. Let society coast along in neutral, let it treat its products as pretexts—but to each his due. Do we really need *Das Kapital*'s dreary bookkeeping, with its stipulation of production reports and overtime as a provider of extra wages, to realize that no society is possible as long as one person earns more money than another or holds a greater share of social power? Why bother to prove the existence of theft whenever the slightest inequality exists?

The problem is that Marxist principles are simply not egalitarian. The mind boggles at the feebleness of Marx's theory in this respect. Not only does it never tell us what a class actually consists in; it also implies that the simple collective appropriation of the means of production is sufficient to turn social cacophony into the beginnings of an obvious harmony. What actually happens is exemplified in the U.S.S.R. today, where the range of incomes is wider than in most Western countries (not to mention the range of powers, which is frightening), and in China, which tolerates salary differentials of 400 percent or even more. These are not deviations from Marxist theory; from the start, all the so-called socialist societies have been nonegalitarian in conformity with the ideas of Marx and Lenin. Can any individuals consider themselves the equal of someone who earns four times as much as they do? Can they even feel they belong to the same "class"?

When the Soviet government expropriated lands, factories, banks, and all the country's natural resources, it labelled as Communism what was actually a form of state capitalism. It turned the U.S.S.R. into a huge company with the same goals as any company—profits and profitability. It is, however, much less efficient than most companies. U.S.S.R., Ltd., had to *produce*, so in order to participate in a game that it denied formally, the government stripped the play of its only possible attractions: the opportunity to make money and accumulate private property. To obtain this laughable result, it was necessary to invoke the idea of the "dictatorship of the proletariat," and here Marxist naïveté became deadly. Lenin, for all his Marxist "realism," never speculated overmuch about what he would find himself speculating about once Revolution was an accomplished fact. On the very eve of the event itself he harked back to the absurd theory of the "decline of the State" (as though hundreds of thousands of State functionaries had any intention of "declining"), announcing in *Pravda* on April 16, 1917, that the first priority of a

Bolshevik regime would be the dismantling of the police, the regular army, and the omnipotent bureaucracy. Lenin noted elsewhere that the Bolsheviks could indeed be accused of authoritarianism—nothing being more authoritarian than a rifle. Predictably, within a few years, the U.S.S.R. became a paradise for the police, the regular army, and upstart bureaucrats—and has remained so for over sixty years. During this time the Soviet state has only slightly overused the rifle—without which, it is true, it might well have declined before its time.

In short, Marx counted on an absolute human cynicism to bring on the revolution and on its reverse to prevent the dictatorship from becoming a straight dictatorship. The ulterior motive is quite clear: the ideology of humility. The oppressed have better intentions than anyone else because they are oppressed. The proletarian condition purifies the soul. We know what forbearance and gentle complicity these intentions call forth in any so-called socialist country: forty million dead in the labour camps, hundreds of thousands of dissenters in psychiatric hospitals, censorship, police rule, boredom, enforced silence, and false information everywhere. Yet clouds of vapid subphilosophical intellectuals closed their eyes to these things for half a century, during which they mumbled tirelessly about the New Man, the historic vision of the Concrete, revolutionary praxis, social contradictions, and objective dialectic. When they finally looked, they discovered a military-industrial complex, just like all the others, and lyricism exploded into platitudes. All they can say for themselves is that they have been deceived, and all they can do is change their ideas—for the dictatorship of the proletariat will not change its system. But the intellectuals persist in believing—even if they must now use the Chinese pattern rather than the Soviet model—that there are two ways of life in the world and that the value of one of them justifies or excuses crimes that would be infamous in the other. They set ten horrors committed by the Right against ten horrors committed by the Left and announce a tied game. No one adds them together to give, quite simply, twenty horrors.

Revolutionary awareness, which seeks a free society, peaceful, colourful, and joyful, expresses itself, curiously enough, only in warlike fashion. When it sings, it seems always to be marching. When it speaks, it sounds as though it were barking out orders. When it writes, it announces the arrival of the Revolution in terms of menace: socialist and capitalist camps, social strife, class struggle, battles joined, victories, heroes, pioneers, strategies, guerrilla warfare, encircled cities, multiple fronts, tactical phases, proletarian dictatorship, mass mobilization, militants, militiamen, military units, parties, partisans, partisan warfare, resistance, chiefs, directors, allies, class enemies, traitors, saboteurs, shattered morale, serried ranks, order, discipline, vigilance. Reading the texts, one wonders whether the chorus leaders of the Revolution have ever used a single word that does not belong to the vocabulary current in a military headquarters. Now, using a word is using an idea. . . .

Nothing pleases the ideology of humility as much as rancour and authority. Marxism offers the two together and elevates them into methods of conquest. The humble man has only to bow to the orders of his superiors, who will plan the Revolution in his place; the struggle will not be directed against him but against others who possess what he does not. The Marxist exegesis is so fundamentally humble that it is always loath to detach individuals from their context (historical, political, and especially economic)—except in the case of Stalin. Hitler or Franco were merely puppets of the ruling class, but Stalin succeeded in falsifying thirty years of Soviet Marxism all by himself. He alone was neither a puppet nor a class emanation, but an individual. The whole German people may seem accountable for the six million dead in Nazi concentration camps, but the responsibility for ten times more victims in the Soviet prisons will never be laid on the heads of the Russian people. In the end the whole of the blame devolves on Hegel and Fichte. Skoundrelovski, Bastardin, and Humblovitch, illiterate warders all, were never there at all, and as for the intellectuals around at the time of the drama—Lukacs, Ehrenburg, or Althusser—why, they were all at a conference. . . .

No Marxist has ever realized that violence, which so easily fulfills all their basest instincts, contains its own ideology, and does not let itself be mastered by anyone. The word *revolution* itself owes its prestige to violence; the U.S.S.R. and China have an almost magical influence because they are authoritarian; Communism fascinates because of its prison camps, purges, censorship, and armed brutality, not in spite of them—if it were peaceful, it would inspire only boredom. Aggressive, menacing, vengeful, Communism serves as aggression, menace, and vengeance. History is exciting only when it resembles a Western film.

The militant Westerners of the 1950s sometimes took a secret delight in dreaming of herding their oppressive fellow countrymen into Soviet work camps; the spirit of revolt, tired of remaining merely verbal, had a revolution to brandish. The spectre of Communism that, according to Marx's prognostications, would haunt Europe was doing so much more effectively with the aid of the Red Army than through the proletariat alone; it was enough to mistake fear of the former for fear of the latter. In any case, it was better to go along with repression in the East than to join the bourgeois in crying out against it. After all one had the comfort of a "philosophy" with broad historical views —among them, the dogma that the word *liberty* is part of "bourgeois thinking" (as though proletarian thinking were not exactly the same, as though all the humble of the whole world dreamt of anything other than enjoyment, possession, profit, monogamy, and power). In the extreme case, not to be born the son of a working man constituted a definite defect.

Moreover, it would be pointless to get worked up over a revolution, that is if revolutions did not have several ways of being over— the simplest of which is never to have started. How can a takeover of power be organized without the help of a powerful army and a police force? How can they be dismantled without the help of a another police force and another army? How can one imagine a real revolution that reeks of the military and the police, yet how can one carry out a revolution that does not? Only insurrections of unimaginable violence could shake the Soviet, Chinese, and even Cuban regimes today, yet as late as 1970 Marcuse and many others declared that the U.S.S.R. must consent, despite itself, to vast military expenditures and cannot get rid of its bureaucracy. Since the U.S.S.R. *is* this military machine and bureaucracy, what we seem to have is a whole ruling class burning with the impatience to suppress itself. One must admire the shrewdness of Marxist realism, which contradicts itself all the more in the advanced industrial countries of the West; the revolution it defends is also the revolution against which it defends itself, since nobody wants real violence or civil war.

The material, ultraconservative ideal of the masses could be attained today if it were not for the ecological threat, which no revolutionary program ever seriously envisaged. The conclusion of the *Communist Manifesto* that proletarians have nothing to lose but their chains, that they have a world to win, no longer applies except to the inhabitants of the Third World (and perhaps the Communist countries of the East). Western proletarians know that they have the beginning of a world to lose by violent revolution and that they would win only chains. In consequence, Marxism is no longer more than an old social heresy coupled with philosophical impostures. It has been taken for Christianity's successor, but it is merely its bastard. It has been dressed up in a set of morals and metaphysics it has never possessed; it has been seen as the ideal of masses who have accepted it only under compulsion; its success has depended entirely on the number, military prestige, and importance of the populations whose rulers quote it as their authority. A Marxist government in Albania or Hungary, even if it had transformed them into a Paradise, would never have made Marxism a subject of conversation anywhere; the works of Marx and Engels would be no better known than those of Proudhon or Fourier if it were not for the existence of the U.S.S.R. and China and the peril they are deemed to represent.

The only thing left to do is to draw up a global balance sheet. Thanks to Marxism, equality is lost in vagueness. Thanks to Marxism, fraternity means nothing to anyone; it will result automatically from social mutations and is meanwhile merely a pure strategic alliance. Thanks to Marxism, liberty is becoming, for the first time in History, a rightwing argument. Thanks to Marxism, since 1917 we have seen just one spontaneous, unanimous, and popular uprising against a regime of oppression; that was the Hungarian revolt of 1956, and it was crushed by Soviet tanks. Thanks to Marxism, the humble have switched from their secular rancour, one religion to another. The Catholic faith and the Communist credo manage to flourish side by side in backwards Latin countries because both include the idea that evil comes from the Others, that the first shall be last, that the smallest are the best, and that the safety of the world stems from the simple judgement of God or (the same thing in other words) from a simple collective act of vengeance. Both include the same cult of discipline with authority, the same prudishness, the same sly materialism, the same vulgar messianism, the same cheap exaltation. Marx thundered against prostitution, which he saw as the "sisterhood of women"; Engels put the advent of *true* monogamy after the Revolution, and was admired for the idea by Breton, who advocated wanton love (out of jealousy); Lenin took Clara Zetkin to task for daring to speak to him of sexuality; Reich was thrown out of the Communist Party for immorality; "socialist" countries place the family, modesty, and the chaste, productive couple under police surveillance. Workers of the world do not unite in groups of more than two!

Thanks to Marxism as practiced, we know that theoretical Marxism was wrong not only on the subject of violence—and thus of revolution—but also on the subject of nationalism. Trotsky justifiably but uselessly denounced revolution within a single country; it could produce nothing but militarized supercompanies such as the U.S.S.R. and China. In terms of economics, Marxism as applied has produced ten different economies whose only points in common are scarcity and stagnation. In terms of social science, it has produced and defended closed, unequal, and disciplinarian societies. In terms of technology, it has paralyzed cybernetics and clapped a ban on relativist physics; as a result, among the innumerable technical inventions of the twentieth century, not a single one has come from a Marxist country. Some say that Marx has been betrayed, but how can a science be betrayed, and what sort of science rejects experimental verification?

Thanks to Marxism, the past fifty years has seen the most unbelievable outpouring of lies. Science, philosophy, literature—everything has been forced to participate. Lysenko found a Marxist method of getting around the laws of genetics, promised to make giant potatoes grow, had biologists thrown into jail—and Arago intoned a hymn. Soviet science used Heisenberg and Einstein even as it abused them. Budapest burned under a barrage of phosphorus shells, and *L'Humanité* wrote: "The U.S.S.R. is sending supplies and medicine into Hungary." A few years earlier, Sartre returned from Moscow persuaded that the New Man was about to be born; although all Stalin's old friends, disoriented by Pentothal, confessed to being American agents, Western dialectic materialism went to work and explained everything. As an explicative method, this science of sciences strongly resembles psychoanalysis in its justification of the greater by the lesser (Dostoevsky was a pure product of his politicosocial and historical context—although that context was shared by millions who were not Dostoevsky), its unbeatable self-defense (to criticize Marxism is to prove that it is right; for Marx anticipated that criticism, its reign of suspicion (all unorthodox behaviour conceals deliberate material intentions), its opportune use of the unverifiable (just as a heterosexual can be an *unconscious* homosexual, an anti-Fascist can be an objective Fascist), its absolute evasion of proof (just as psychoanalysis is never finished, it is never the right time to move on to the classless society). Marxism describes as complicity with the Right any attack on the regimes it defends, no matter how justified the attacks may be, because only facts, not intentions count. But it also condones sixty years of horrors and lies because they are directed towards a social objective, because only intentions count, not facts.

When Brecht returned to East Berlin, he suddenly lost all his critical faculties; he did not see the police in the streets, and the faked trials did not arouse his suspicions. In 1915 talk of Soviet prison camps classed one as a Rightist; it might earn one a trial and at best deserved laughter. In 1954 the Soviet government denied the existence of these camps; the faithful agreed; in 1959 it acknowledged some of them; again the faithful agreed. Stalin was a genius when he was Authority, and when Authority decided he was merely a traitor, he was a traitor. The intellectuals had seen nothing and were too humble to have lied; *They* had betrayed them. Those shining luminaries of our time had been led astray by will-o'-the-wisps, which they suddenly and in unison pricked like balloons—without ever accusing themselves of having been windbags too.

Thanks to Marxism, the "revolutionary" party in every country became the equivalent of a fifth column. Thanks to Marxism, it became clear yet again that a universal morality that forbids killing and lying refuses, like violence and lying themselves, to be manipulated by any interest, and that it is a contradiction in terms to make this morality one's objective and use methods of achieving it that do not conform with its requirements. If revolution cannot be brought about without cynicism, it cannot be brought about at all. Now, violence is cynical in itself. The Western pro-Communist intelligentsia has lost its honour and its time for the edification of a pollutant industry coupled with a galaxy of police; such is the "objective" truth they keep quoting as authority. Besides, their talk of great hopes betrayed is merely hypocrisy; Communist hopes were anything but great. What can be expected from a doctrine founded on philosophical bad faith and social myopia, a doctrine whose objective for human societies is fair shares of the terrestrial cake for these *things* called people?

Thanks to Marxism, we now know that all Marx's plans for calculated revolutions were wrong in every respect and on all points. Materialism is a nothing; materialistic dialectic is a formal clause. The proletariat is not being impoverished; the proletarian revolution is impossible in industrial countries and ends up elsewhere in one variety or another of Fascism. The rifle lies at the end of Power every time that Power comes into being at the end of a rifle. A society of equals (which has never been achieved) would remain a society of egos. Human collectivity cannot be its own objective. The dictatorship of the proletariat is more immoveable than all the others. The masses do not put class consciousness before their national, linguistic, and racial adherences. The supreme ideal remains the Ego. The law of the majority is still baseness. The antidote for the capitalism of monopolies is merely capitalism monopolized. No industrial nation ever responds to Nature in any way. Communists, like everyone else, are in favour of the atomic bomb; like everyone else, they set out to exploit Matter and get caught in its trap. Threatened by a utopia a hundred times more radical than those they fantasize, they are forced, like everyone else, to realize that this paradise is costing them too much, that they want none of it, and that, in consequence, the word "revolution" was a lie, for there is no way to attain something nobody wants.

All that is left is the dialectic passage from the same to the same. Emanations of the universal mediocrity, as alike as Scylla and Charybdis, statesmen world over have come from the same ruts defined by the same boozy meetings, the same electoral beer gardens, the same combines, the same contests of personal ambitions. Shoe salesmen, peanut farmers, or industrial managers, they are perfectly average people, admired for the sole reason that they are in power. They have generally acquired that power merely by dint of being able to ponder without disgust, indeed even with complacency, everything that turns politics into the image of prosaic human reality, like a business without greatness. Just look at them all in their three-piece suits, taking the salute as the soldiers march past, going from reception to banquet, from charity fête to conference; praised if they find time to read a book, but even more if they watch a football game. Superficial and hence vulgar, quick to lie, no longer able to think of anything but financial problems and strategic computations, they are perfect delegates to the ideology of humility, perfect salesmen of the veiled apocalypse. In the face of this gigantic equivalence, which no longer offers either a possible set purpose or a decision to be made, the worst temptation is still to resign oneself to the inevitable.

Each country has its ruling classes: here, to the right of the Right, there to the left of the Left. The more one recognizes the differences in shades, the more one is struck by the similarities. The comedy of the ambidextrous world is not yet over; we shall refuse, to the bitter end, to admit that the most fundamental opposition is only a mirror effect, that an active complicity unites the tough militants of the egalitarian forces and the simple soldiery of the law-and-order battalions.

The militants do not seek the abolition of the family, of the couple, of censorship, of military order, of profitability. They do not work for real, absolute equality. They do not struggle for a nonhierarchical society, for nondisciplinary education, for nonlunatic work, for nonconformist philosophy. It is only the remainder that revolution looks to change, and it lacks the wit to see that this remainder consists of *nothing*. Hence, there are rightist barracks and leftist barracks, bourgeois nuclear bombs and progressive nuclear bombs. On one hand, the Humans exploit other humans, on the other they oppose them. Here the interests of individuals clash; there they fight each other. On some occasions pollution occurs because the state heads business, on others the environment is mortally contaminated because the heads of business have supreme control over the state; in one case monogamy and modesty are the rule because sexuality demobilizes, in another modesty and monogamy are the rule because sex demoralizes. Capitalist tolerance is repressive,

Communist repression is waiting patiently to be able to be tolerant. The consumer society reduces all utopias to fashions, the short-supply society reduces utopia to silence in order to reach the stage of conspicuous consumption. The Communists are patriots and racists in the expectation of better things; their adversaries are racists and patriots because they expect the worst. Should one wish a little variety in the farce, it is easy to turn it into a comedy.

III

Religion and Communism are the most widespread lies offered as answers to Humanity's dilemma, but they are by *no* means the only deceptions available to us today. A thousand varieties of anarchism, pacifism, mind-altering methods, and the return to nature are advocated as *the* answer. All are so patently false that we need examine them only briefly.

Anarchism is a decorative mythology that predates Marx. Its successes can be counted on the fingers of one hand—Kronstadt, the Asturias, and one or two others—and all were temporary. It has only two ideas: syndicalism and terrorism. Now, syndicalism has two possible outcomes. Either it spreads over the whole world, which then changes from the game of grab to a vaguely collectivist free-for-all in which the self-interests of the employers are replaced by the enhanced self-interests of the employees, or it remains localized and is thus incorporated into the world of haggling and competition, in which case it is not worth talking about. Like any other business undertaking, a syndicalist cement works must aim at producing a maximum amount of cement, regardless of the real measure of need for it or for the ecological damage it causes. Forecasting the likely outcome of a given case, however, is probably a pointless exercise. Historically, anarchist cooperatives have always turned sour (never, so their defenders say, through any fault of the anarchists themselves, but always through the machinations of the Communists or the bourgeoisie).

The public identifies anarchism with terrorism, even though most anarchists have been pacifists. One reason for this association is that the word *anarchy* has connotations of disorder, panic, and hence terror. Moreover, only a few scholars can define the doctrines of

Proudhon, Bakunin, Kropotkin, Voline, Makhno, and so on. On the other hand, the outrages of Netchaiev, Caserio, Bonnot, Emile Henry, and Ravachol are well known.

Anarchism also has a well-deserved reputation as a visceral attitude. Its ideas are even more feeble and more contradictory than those of Marxism; their sole merit is coherence to the point of absurdity. Its hypocrisy is threefold. First, it demands the impracticable, as though it wished to be relieved of the necessity for any practicability, in the name of an infinitely platitudinous ideal; Proudhon's vague mysticism is the equivalent of Bakunin's materialism, which is essentially identical with that of Marx. Second, when it resorts to violence, it pretends to see it as a means, whereas its adepts, of course, regard it as an end. Third, it authorizes anyone and everyone to claim allegiance to the black flag (which is a perfect symbol for illustrating both anarchy's intention of instilling fear cheaply and the absolute nullity of its program); this laxity provides every type of political dilettantism, especially those of the Right, with a gratifying image.

Anarchist outrages have multiplied rapidly since the beginning of the century. Changing the social order with bombs seems simple, especially when one has no intention of changing anything at all, merely of throwing bombs. Vengeance, blood, and murder are even more savoury when they are disguised as justice—as Justice well knows. Hating the present for love of the future is a marvellous bargain—provided that one can begin by hating. No matter that "propaganda of the dead" ended up discrediting the anarchist ideology entirely; people were treated to a few "deeds"—and the publicity never materialized. No wave of outrage has ever advanced a cause unless it was already won. Any society that is harassed by violent amateurs ends up calling for professionals, who are always of the Right. Baader served only German reaction; the Palestinians did not gain access to the U.N. by hijacking planes, but as a result of the pressure of the Arab oil embargo.

Anyway, what use is crime as a political weapon in a world in which the major cities have become dangerous after dark? Terrorist violence not only duplicates organized crime; more often than not it stems from it. Moreover, it is worse than useless; it is antipathetic, the reverse of persuasion. Authoritarian in itself, intimidating, Fascist, it appeals ultimately to the most facile, the most vulgar, and the worst of human impulses—the one that puts pictures of earthquake victims on the front page of newspapers and makes the inquisitive gather around car accidents. Political crime cannot be unaware that its only special value is as crime and not as politics. Therefore, its sole justification lies, once again, in the ideology of humility: by killing the managers one frees the managed, because the latter, always so numerous and always so passive, were under the thumbs of a handful of individuals. No doubt terrorism would be effective if it were practiced on a large enough scale. To do that, of course, Revolution needs a police force and an army. Return to the dictatorship of the proletariat....

Like all the other specious ideologies, anarchism runs out of steam and comes to a halt at the very moment of its triumph; what will happen *afterwards* is too far removed for it to cope with. When we acknowledge neither God nor master, we will still need to know what to do; when society becomes games minded, it will still need to know what game to play; when self-administration becomes general, it will still need to know what to produce and why; when society consists entirely of free individuals, it will break up into an equal number of unrestrained egotisms, and when barter replaces money, we shall return to primitive exchanges—in other words, to the origins of theft.

If violence as a method can only end with violence as an institution, all peace-loving revolutionaries can do is to practice what they preach. This is what all the recent pacifist movements have tried— without success, although some, such as the Hippie movement of the 1960s, were supported by hundreds of schools or sects, adored by a complete generation of youths, boosted by successive fashions, swept along by the overall economic situation, and buttressed by an impressive number of thinkers (more impressive, incidentally, for their number than for their thinking).

The Hippies, like some of their younger brothers and sisters today, preached only three ideas: recourse to drugs as a means of understanding; return to Nature as a means of liberation; sexual liberty as a means of fraternity. The first two were both absurd and facile; if the third failed, it was because it never tried to succeed.

Inevitably, the proponents of the drugs pretentiously labelled psychedelic ("Soul-revealing") mixed them with religions, especially Oriental religions. The disciples of both described a series of visions or sensations as awareness—and thus equated the material with the Soul. Psychedelics did have an advantage here; they offered the whole religious rigmarole, already cheap in itself, with a supplement of delirium and a rebate of exercise. Yoga disciplines are rigorous even if their objectives are the same as all the humble prejudices: suffering to achieve salvation, reducing one's stature to increase it, losing oneself to find oneself, dying to encounter the source of life. Although these sacrifices were as vulgar as other religious practices, they were difficult; taking psychedelic drugs was not. The presupposition, however, was the same: that which goes beyond perception is not intelligence but *another* perception. The senses are above reason because they are more immediate, more generally accessible, less critical—in short, more humble. Philosophy was boring and led to a headache, but LSD, mescaline, and psilocybin offered adventures in Technicolor. But these products came with no guarantee against distress, so it was not surprising that the infallible, soothing comfort of hard drugs was usually preferred in the end. God for a pill is as good as Happiness for a cigarette, and the humble inertia of the heroin addict, who willingly searches for every possible pretext without ever finding an excuse, bears perfect witness to the truth of psychedelics, which found everything without ever having looked for anything.

Those who tried to push this type of knowledge even further were soon engulfed in real madness. Anyone who touches this nameless chaos is obsessed by the thought of one day finding himself there again. *Nothing* can be drawn from the state of unspeakable terror that follows the certitude of reliving the universe's history and awakening the dead while cosmogonies and visions fall foul of one another. Human beings under the influence of psychedelics shout like the devil while convinced that they are talking like an angel; then they awaken slowly, stupefied with sedatives till they can hardly speak with fear giving way to shame deep in an empty cell. Madness offers only one experience: itself; similarly, the psychedelics offer, in the form of an expurgated psychosis or a miniature madness, only one awareness: that of the psychedelia. The pity of it is that in order to know this, one has to have lived it.

I spoke of the counterculture's return to Nature in an earlier chapter. As a rule, such removals were to a slice of countryside subsidized by the tourist industry. Urged to make progress, the seekers
responded with regression. The reign of God having been systematically retarded by millions of prayers and ecstasies, they went into
ecstasies and prayed. Nature never having stopped advancing, they
retreated towards it. Human technology being ahead of natural
technologies, they set the two against each other and were thereby
able to cheat business, which alone had been guilty of falsification.
Revolutionary ideas having miscarried through lack of depth, they
replaced them with bizarre hairstyles and clothing. After a few days'
vacation punctuated by music, with "Love" and "Peace" sown everywhere in armfuls of flowers, world fraternity was at hand. . . .

The communes of the 1960s also preached sexual liberty, but indefatigable jealousy always beat it without a fight, reducing it to
monogamy plus nudism. America of the sects emerged from its
multifaceted Buddhism neither richer nor less sectarian. The anti-
establishment movement that considered itself as Oriental as the
dawn had proved Oriental all right—just like Attila. The new fraternity did not stop hospitals from getting a growing number of
unfortunates who had injected themselves with detergent purchased
at enormous cost; heroin, the most antipsychedelic of drugs, had
appeared on the scene, starting its ravages on the musicians' plat-
forms and resulting in the ominous victory of heroin over heroes.
Equality and sharing fared scarcely better. The spaced-out middlemen disguised as Christs had not received enough fraternal love
from their cosmic ecstasies to spare their brothers a hashish made
from henna and raw opium, especially since it earned them profits
large enough to make the profiteers of the System look like amateurs.

Empty frenzies, raptures to order, commercial mysticism—everything, after all, had been only make-believe, affectation, emptiness,
pliancy. The public's idols got married at city halls, the preachers
were all millionaires, record store owners were doing marvellously,
and the impresarios were rubbing their hands with joy. Communication stopped at the exact limit of its language, a hybrid
rehash of American imperialism and Asiatic parochialism. Since
then, emptiness has grown hollow, but the wheel still turns, casting
off fashions one after the other: Satan after God, red meat after

macrobiotic cuisine, the tarot deck after the horoscope, the dilapidation pose after the defiance pose, the comedy of hatred after the comedy of love. Women, Blacks, Palestinians, the ecology minded, the fringe, homosexuals—all have the same struggle, but each group struggles on its own account and then stops. A show with no spectators is a lost cause, a world with hazy ideas has no liking for fixed ideas, and nothing is less rewarding than solitary, nonconforming certainty. A fashion, however, is a piece of nonconformity that offers the undeniable advantage of being able to be practiced by everyone simultaneously, and in the same manner.

IV

Every question that calls for a single correct answer is susceptible to an infinity of wrong answers. The saraband of human grimaces would thus be literally interminable if the Sphinx that questions us did not sanction each of our lies with a turn of the screw, if the revolutionary role that Marx assigned to the proletariat did not have to be fulfilled by Matter itself—this time with no possibility of failure, compromise, or negotiation. What all revolutions have aimed at up till now is nothing in comparison with what has always attracted Evolution.

What must we achieve to answer the riddle of the Sphinx? The answer is perfectly clear: the abolition of all forms of profit, the total and absolute equalization of all salaries, the disappearance of all national boundaries and a world government, the end of the family and the couple, sexual freedom with the word *love* reserved to a disinterested exchange between two or more souls, collective education, general disarmament, and the welding of the human race into the same global idea, stronger than any religion has ever been. Every item in this list is a utopia in itself. Clearly, *we shall achieve nothing* by ourselves, but anything else we might be able to do henceforth is also nothing.

Once again—once and for all—let us stop pretending that even the smallest of these utopias is impossible for lack of method. And let us stop looking for answers under the guise of prescriptions. *There are no methods* capable of abolishing jealousy, religious fanaticism, love of comfort, or nationalism; there are no ways of changing bad faith into sincerity or the old man into the new man. There are no techniques for getting people to accept even a single idea if they reject it just because it comes from another; saying "What do you want?" or "What do you suggest?" is just another form of hypocrisy. No one has ever needed to propose tactics for achieving the society of profit; Humanity knows how to go about that all by itself, and it achieves its aim without ideologies. In short, no program or strategy will ever allow us to attain objectives that we reject.

Property must disappear, not to give way to a society of equitable exchanges but to allow us to stop deceiving each other and to let the word *Humanity* acquire a meaning at last. Technically, this is possible: for thousands of years, small, self-contained communities have practiced giving without receiving anything in return. Morally, it is impossible. Nations must efface themselves, not as linguistic entities, of course, but as political powers. Technically, this is possible: alliances have gone so far. Morally, it is not. All forms of power and competition must be abolished so that Humanity can achieve not disorganization or dispersal but the superorganization displayed by all living organisms that is Organism itself. Technically, this is possible: animal communities, despite their perfection, are only a rough sketch of what we could do, for instinct is no more than the petrified face of free conscious activity. Morally, it is not possible: animal societies have common objectives that go beyond them and embody them; we have nothing, and we *want* nothing that could outdo our Ego. Hierarchies must disappear, which would require universal acceptance of a certain amount of work, while we wait for all laborious and repetitive work to be transferred from men to machines. Both stages are technically possible, but morally impossible: we want our work and our hierarchies. Science, snatched away from its military diversion, delivered from the secrets that hold it prisoner and from the dizzying wastefulness that enfeebles it, would be capable of prodigies worthy at last of the Nature from which it came. But this would mean abolition of profit and national boundaries and so it is impossible.

We can do nothing but work tirelessly to discredit the counter-ideals that prevent the ideal from coming into being. We must work so that the ideology of the family is unable to defend itself any longer; so that religious thinking becomes ashamed of the treason, the baseness, and the materialism that are united in it; so that jealous monogamous passion no longer dares to appropriate the name of love; so that profit suffers from an increasingly guilty conscience; so that wealth becomes obscene and political revolution atrophied; so that education falls into errors too obvious to overlook; so that the most blatant forms of pollution, starting with the automobile, fall into disrepute.

But my spontaneous allusion to the automobile suggests the real problem. The readers probably each own a car, and in spite of all arguments, proofs, and injunctions, they are not going to get rid of it either today or tomorrow. What more can be said? As soon as pollution concerns *me*, I start looking for evasions and pretexts. I invoke technological remedies that have not yet appeared, I put myself into the hands of Science and governments, I talk of vital necessities, I object that my sacrifice would be useless given the number of other types of pollution. In short, I stifle the voice inside me that says "Give up your car." I am pollution personified, and there are four billion of us polluting individuals to insist that a general wound is not the sum of particular injuries.

I do not want to be singled out, but pesticides, power plants, fertilizers, industrial chemicals, armaments, and additives are also *I*'s. So are profit, social lies, useless repetitions, and wastefulness. An atomic generating plant is *no* different from the cars of its shareholders. Rich or poor, winners or losers, oppressive nations or oppressed, we form a single group of malefactors that is nearing senile decay and ruin. The very principle of its existence means the end of the world, and a principle cannot be altered. 2 + 2 do not make 6 any *more* than they make 987. There is no part of society for whom the protection of Nature does not represent a dead loss, and the reduction of profits to the barest minimum would not alter that fact in any way; cleaning up the oceans, even if possible, would not make them any more profitable.

The very term *protection of Nature* is a matter for shame. Why should Evolution be obliged to safeguard its nutritive environment against itself? Who are we to go on believing that something that lies beyond us on all sides must serve as a source of food and not as a guide? How can we imagine that the politics of theft and bluff can dominate the immense success of symbiosis, which is the politics of sharing and openness? Either Nature will be not protected but prolonged or it will cease to exist. That is what is at stake for it—and hence for us. Meanwhile, we have turned against Nature—and hence against ourselves—in a struggle to the death. On the day when our interests are one with Nature's, death will be on hand to impose upon us the identity that, despite all the speeches, we have renounced *sine die*. The proof of our repudiation is *our* automobile.

The great mistake political ideologists have made is their failure to see that History is simply the conduct of the world, and that, like it or not, its moral law is cut from the same stuff by which (or rather by *whom*) we judge our own conduct. If the Ideal applies to society as it does to a single person, it is because its first desire is a society that is unified, like a person. We must move towards the Good. This is neither an inevitability nor a certainty, for one individual or for many. It is an *unconditional order*, and what is unconditional offers no method, since a method, being precisely what an objective is not, cannot be conditioned by it.

What I have just said means that what has been wrong in every revolution has been not the means, but the ends. The wrong means is an error; the wrong end is a lie. Human baseness thought itself free at last of the moral law. For us to rediscover it in the heart of Matter, in the kernel of that *dura mater* that tirelessly answers the same ruses with the same *NO*, letting nothing go, discussing nothing, never making the slightest concession—well, nothing is more admirable. And perhaps nothing could demonstrate more clearly or implement more firmly (even at the price of unimaginable horrors) the convergence of the material Absolute and the spiritual Absolute.

True and false, in the sphere of logic; good and evil, in the sphere of ethics; handsome and ugly, in the sphere of aesthetics—these cannot *have* criterion, condition, or definition, since that is what they *are*. A criterion of the truth must already be true; a definition of handsome must produce all beauty (and mechanically so, which is contradictory); a condition of goodness must be good—and by that very fact it would already have goodness as a condition. Kant's arguments on this subject are irrefutable, although his *Critique of Practical Reason* is incomplete. Good and evil are not subordinate to anything, no parameter can determine them, no formula can contain them. Consequently, it is impossible to argue about them. The good is not the useful, or the pleasant, or the necessary. It is not Bentham's "greatest happiness for the greatest number." If need be, it runs counter to all collective or individual interests: saving a drowning person may be of no use, refusing to lie may be displeasing or even fatal. If killing a human being, even in the case of legitimate self-defense, were not fundamentally evil, there would be no need to claim self-defense. For persons being tortured, telling the torturer the truth would be evil; thus, it is their duty to lie. But in so doing they feel a great need to justify their lie to their own conscience. All those who have lied of necessity (which means everybody) know how they hated doing it at the time—how much they hated the major evil that made them commit this minor evil and saddled them with a disgrace that went beyond their suffering or was itself another suffering for them to bear. Good and evil *demand* assessment without criteria because they *are* the supreme criteria, and one does not assess that which assesses everything. Utilitarianism contradicts itself by making morality the result of a reasoning process. If this were so, morality would be interested (which is an absolute contradiction) and *calculating;* Good would only exist because it is useful (the implied question is "useful to what?"; the answer is "to Good"). This confusion of moral law with its accidental content is as hypocritical as the way civilizations have passed their prejudices and their interests off as morals (as is the case every time the word "morality" has a sexual meaning). Pretending to redefine good and evil, which are absolutely undefinable, is a charade. Asking what good and evil consist in is asking Pilate's question, "What is truth?" while pretending not to see that an answer is impossible, not because the question is a trap, but because it is meaningless. If I say what truth is, my answer must *be true;* if I say what characterizes good, these characteristics must already be part of it. The words *traitor, assassin, coward, thief, liar, egotist,* and so on never have been and never will be terms of praise in any civilization, despite social differences or passages of corruption. Morality calls upon every human being to make the same choices and hold the same opinions without criteria, without logical reasons, without interest. In its own sphere morality is like aesthetics, in which indefinable beauty can and must be fundamentally the same for all. Thus, morality makes the most sublime revelation of human history: *we are One*. Becoming more and more what we are has been the object of Evolution as far back as we can see.

The existence of absolute morality confirms the existence of absolute freedom. There is no guarantee, no prescription, no method for making our choices. A method would be a model of Good, making every choice a calculation and every false calculation an error, not an evil. The mathematicians who make a mistake are not liars because their objective was the truth; liars are swine because their objective was error. Good and evil affect only objectives; they do not recognize means. Every action is an objective in itself. The choice between good and evil admits of no compromise, and dissymmetry is absolute. There can be no question of doing good with the intention of doing evil, nor of doing evil with the intention of doing good. In the first case the intention was bad, and the result is merely apparent; in the second, the intention was merely apparent and hence bad, and the result was too. Moral law does not say that necessary evil does not exist; it says only that it wants none of it. Using evil means for good ends is a lie on top of an evil; the means is a calculation, and moral law does not calculate. It does not say that it is bad to lie *because* of x and y—but that it is bad to lie, period. If we were infallibly oriented towards fixed objectives that reason could justify, if we could not choose from objectives (including good and evil), we would be computers and the idea of freedom would be without foundation—as *a fortiori* would be those of good and evil. But with what could we replace the notion of freedom of action? As I have adequately demonstrated, determinism is unacceptable, and causality, strictly speaking, does not apply to anything that unfolds in Time and hence to anything that performs actions. It is absurd to see morality as an exterior restraint; human beings' own consciences accept responsibility (a fact that is enough to make the word "restraint" inappropriate). In the first place, *every* morality demands freedom as its a priori condition, rejecting the results of restraint and of the exterior from the categories of Good and Evil. Second, if morality were merely a legacy, one could not explain the fact that it has evolved in an increasingly global sense; therefore the origin of morality, like that of Life, lies in the future. Besides, writing the word *morals* in the plural is an undue concession, since morality cannot be, like ethics, a phenomenon of History. As we have seen, no civilization has ever argued that murder, lying, theft are not evil in *themselves;* all ethical differences of opinion relate to the manner in which these evils can be excused as *means* (and the necessity for excuse is the very proof of evil).

What then are individuals responsible or not responsible for? They alone know—and know in only an approximate manner. First of all, there is the question of whether I can call my body, my chromosomes, and my brain "me." We are all ambivalent about our bodies: their achievements are "ours," but their failures belong to them alone. Of course, the body is merely an instrument, but if this instrument is not mine, it is even less someone else's. If Mozart does not get the credit for being what he is, to *whom* does the credit belong? If it belongs to nobody, why do we see it as belonging to somebody—and to somebody in particular? All the same, morality does not demand that we be Mozart; our abilities and talents are received, but there is no morality except in intentions, and intentions cannot be received. Consequently, it is impossible to attribute evil to habit, for to acquire the habit of evil is to practice it. Neither can one confuse freedom and possibility. Here, grammar recognizes something that philosophy overlooks: the verb "to be able to" has no imperative.

The same reasoning applies to the results of birth, education, language, and so on. Our ambivalence about these things is very obvious; it is the same as that of Science in relation to the world in general. At every instant I can choose between several courses of action, but once I have made those choices, I am no longer free to "unchoose" them retroactively—thus I make myself a victim of my past, as if the Ego *who* results from it were not the same as the Ego *from whom* it results. Thus, it is doubly futile to ask whether another person would have done what I have done if he or she had been placed in the same circumstances as myself. In the first place, when these circumstances were the present, I was conscious of facing several choices and of being free in this respect. Second, a person placed *exactly* in the same circumstances as myself must have been me. A brain, glands, a past: these are circumstances.

One last point is important to remember. When one says that moral law rests on the principle that Good and Evil *must* be recognized as such by the whole world, one is not saying that they *are* so recognized effectively. Although differences among various societies' and individuals' morals have been exaggerated, differences do exist. But they prove nothing. A truth is not variable because it is understood in varying ways, and the laws of logic have never *begun* to exist; the cause *is* identical with the effect—even if no one is there to know it. Suppose that all human consciences had not, since time immemorial, put lying and murder in the category of evil; moral law would still be exactly what it is. If human beings cannot agree to admit that any given act is evil, our disagreement itself rests on a previous argument: the meaning of the adjective "bad." The idea must have *the same meaning* on both sides for the interpretations, which are its contents, to be different.

In summary, to demand programs for utopia is to find oneself face to face with the universal, collective moral law, demanding of it methods for Good, criteria for Truth, and definitions for Beauty. Yet we have never needed methods, criteria, or definitions to admit that competition, profit, and jealousy are objectives in themselves. We thus find that we are contradicting ourselves, standing alone against our own bad consciences, floundering in our own bad faith, unable to respond to a nightmare except by sleep, slowly losing our reason because we would not hearken to it, clutching feverishly at a few shadowy ideals that soon nobody will be able to accept as worth pursuing. Our heads are down, absorbed in the purring note of our engines—which has the double advantage of covering our silence and of replying in our stead.

V

A mood of pessimism or optimism is about as important as being lefthanded or righthanded. We are not required to strike a pose before History. Moreover both pessimism and optimism are complicity; a pessimist is a traitor, an optimist a coward. Imagine a ship steered so badly as to be in the path of a hurricane. The crew is divided into three groups: the pessimists, who think that shipwreck is inevitable and so will do nothing to avoid it; the optimists, who do not even believe that the hurricane is coming and so will do nothing either; and finally those who bestir themselves because they believe the danger is real *and* think the ship can escape it. When the last group sounds the alarm, shouting, "We'll all die if we do nothing!" the optimists regard them as pessimists because of the first half of their cry, and the pessimists regard them as optimists because of the second half. The hurricane strikes, and the third group manages to save the ship, but some twenty sailors lose their lives. Then the optimists, who never lifted a finger, say, "We kept telling you everything would turn out all right!" And the pessimists, who never left their bunks, say, "We kept telling you there'd be a typhoon, and people would be killed!" This is the way optimists and pessimists are and always have been; both refuse to move, to see, to act. The group that saves the ship cannot be classified as either; they wish for Good, so they are optimists; they fear and see Evil, so they are pessimists. In fact, since one cannot wish for Good without seeing and fearing Evil, the only possible attitude that is human and vital is *optimism through pessimism*. My choice is made, and the better I understand the Universe's divine purpose, the more afraid I am of its failure because I know this failure is *possible*; if it were not, then we— Humanity and God incarnated with difficulty, painfully and fanatically—would all be playing a meretricious comedy.

The revolution we face is completely different from anything that Life has known since the beginning of its enormously long history. The only possible comparison is with the Human's obtaining of reflective consciousness, and it is a superreflective consciousness that is now on our horizon. Never have the stake, the risk, or the possible gain been so large, never has the change been so total, never has the price been so high. The value (and doubtless the only value) of Teilhard de Chardin was that he saw (rather than showed) the sort of conflagration Evolution is headed for and how Humanity is speeding up its pace. But Teilhard was satisfied with the anti-God of Christianity, the use of technology to bring humans together, and an abuse of History that stayed abstract. He did not foresee the presentation of a concrete alternative between absolute good and absolute horror.

Human violence has always been ambiguous, its objectives mere pretexts and its effects mere provocations to revolt against the malevolence of others. The violence of things—pitiless, neutral, unconditional—shows us our own likeness, and only this violence can make us change our ways. We shall do nothing against nuclear

energy until large populations have been exposed to radiation or
the entire Earth has been contaminated by plutonium. Real revolution may require any number of disasters; a complete climatic up-
heaval that brings famine even to industrial societies and ravages
entire nations elsewhere; a threat to the very seeds of Life by ultraviolet radiation; the atmosphere of cities becoming intolerable because of noise, lack of oxygen, and foul odours; the countryside
becoming hideous; the atomic powder keg threatening to explode.
At that point the craftiness of the lie will lead our souls gently to the
edge of the void, and the demoralization of the human race will
become complete, as Hesiod forecast almost three thousand years
ago in describing the Age of Iron:

> They will be tormented by weariness throughout the day, by distress
> throughout the night. Zeus will bring to naught this race of mortal
> men, born with white temples. Then oaths, justice, goodness will no
> longer mean anything. They will respect only crime and excess,
> their sole right will be force, their consciences will disappear, and
> against this evil there will be no recourse.

As Hesiod suspected, our moral violence is worse than all the
other kinds. A human society that could use unheard-of technological miracles to halt the death of Nature without abandoning its old,
traitorous laws of profit and competition might still be unable to
prevent its own downfall. Criminal and partisan violence will continue to rage everywhere, despite its outcome in nothingness. Fewer
and fewer reasons will be found to stop the spread of hard drugs (if
indeed mere reasons could stop it). Suicide and murder will become
more common; the incidence of mental illness will increase much
more than the 400 or 500 percent it has over the past twenty years.
It will be useless to cling to the ideals whose inanity and hypocrisy I
have partially shown in this book; nothing can stop them from disturbing our conscience, and nothing will replace them. The time is
not far off when nobody will understand anything any more, when
nobody will be interested in anything any more, when all individuals will be forced to play out their little comedy for themselves,
and when human beings' reasons for living will be no more than
alibis.

Starting right now, all over the world, Humanity is being put to the question, and each false answer tightens the garrote we have constructed. Yet what chokes us *can* and *will* deliver us! Like everyone else, I feel this garrote and nevertheless I say *it is a boon.* Without it we should die. No human violence could have achieved what it may achieve, and yet nothing except violence can take it away from us because collectively we have no soul, and that which has no soul learns only by force. The material and moral agony ahead are necessary; this double death is a double birth. Lying, murder, bad faith, jealousy, and egotism have lasted long enough. Provisional eternity has served its time. Our nonsense is a blemish on the pure, noble universe of the galaxies and the mysterious grandeur of the animal world. *Unanimity or nothing.* The impasse at which we find ourselves cannot be absolute; it is a door, though a terribly narrow one. The contraction that is beginning is a token of the expansion that will follow—and it is, naturally, proportional to it. Nothing resembles a narrow door so closely as the neck of the womb, and nothing has so much in common with a death agony as the moment that precedes birth. We are not in the world—but we can be. Like a fetus in the ninth month, Humanity has amassed toxic wastes that make inevitable its emergence into life-giving air—or its death.

No doubt we really want universal love and world brotherhood, but the Sphinx questioning us demands the absolute, material, unconditional equality of humans first. No doubt we want peace and the status quo, but the Sphinx demands justice first—and if it does not get it, it wants war. No doubt we want the peaceful coexistence of different opinions in every sphere, but the Sphinx wants the same opinion in each sphere—or defiance unto death. No doubt we want agreement between Egos that are side by side yet distinct, but the Sphinx wants the fusion of the Egos—or their mutual destruction. Before we can hope to build anything, we must reason out everything, agree on everything, renounce every idea at whose heart lies self-interest, convince the whole world, and reach the point of sharing the same ideas and the same morality. It is no use hoping that bad faith, even in the least of its forms, will give up and turn to confession. Lying, by its nature, admits nothing. We must wait for lies either to die with those who spread them or to be thrown into confusion on the spot by the crushing, uncontrollable force of things.

We have no choice between this gigantic, enormous, terribly difficult series of conversions and the end of the world. The only part of our awareness that may be absolutely and immediately collective is, as we have seen, formed of pure concepts and constitutes understanding. The *understanding of understandings* will form the basis of the Super-Ego that we are called upon to become. While ecological violence is preparing the greatest turning point in history, the only ideas that we cannot regard as personal are the most general of concepts, the only voice that can speak to us in a peaceful vein is that of Reason. The old, hypocritical belief in certainties or realities beyond Reason has interests, in the lowest sense of the word. Nothing goes beyond Reason a priori (if anything escapes it, it is still Reason that determines the fact); in consequence, everything can and must be discussed. Only Reason opens the door to awareness; only Reason is communicable because only Reason is common to us all; only Reason can provide an alternative to the natural violence that, bereft of intentions, is endowed with the same disarming power.

DEATH OR TRANSFIGURATION

I

What I have said so far in this book is not just what I believe, but what I *know*. Although the limited scope of the work has led me to avoid metaphysics, each idea has been supported by adequate argument. This final chapter is part of the same certainty. Either Earth is doomed to death, or the era of Awareness will begin with the present era. Then, after the long plutonium-ridden night of anguish in the tomb lit by sinister holy candles, the Sun will rise forever, more beautiful, more radiant than dreamed of by any philosophy. The word "Apocalypse" does not mean "catastrophe," even though catastrophes encompass it. It means "Revelation."

All real discrimination between Nature and artifice is subjective. Whenever and wherever awareness recognizes order, symmetry, and repetition, it recognizes itself. These characteristics simply do not exist without awareness, whether they are in a vegetable cell or in an integrated circuit. Of course, a living entity reproduces *itself* because doing so is both its end and its means, whereas a machine is made for a purpose but has none of its own. But distinctions between human fabrications and those of Nature are possible only in terms of quality and energy yield; beyond that level, the criteria that permit the identification of a dead tissue are the same as those that make it immediately evident that the ruins of a church are not of the same nature as some scattered rocks, and that the menhirs of Stonehenge are too well aligned to be erratics.

A corolla and a solar furnace are machines with related functions;

the natural and the artificial are technologies with closely connected origins. To put it simply, the techniques we have invented resemble those that invented us, the way a child's drawing recalls a Michelangelo. They are two aspects of the same Spirit, one of which tries to prolong the other. Both aim only at enlivening themselves, but the more Science progresses, the easier it is for us to see how wide we are of the mark. It is not only that we cannot provide a rational explanation for Nature's machinery (for such an explanation is beyond the competence of scientific reason); we do not even understand its methods.

If bats are taken in sealed containers 700 kilometers from the cave in which they were born, they can find their way back home. We know they use the technique of sonar: emitting ultrasonic waves, picking up their reflected echoes from obstacles ahead, and then "unscrambling" the resulting signals. As used by Nature, this system is so accurate that it enables a bat to fly through a spinning fan and to zigzag through a totally darkened room strung with nets. A similar artificial system, using present-day technical knowledge and electronic equipment, would just barely succeed in helping a large plane navigate. Similarly, electronics experts have long been baffled by Nature's model for the perfect antiaircraft gun: frogs' eyes, which perceive only effective movements but perceive them without fault or fumbling. The human eye is also capable of this kind of performance (it takes only six-thousandths of a second to foresee the end of any change of position). Cybernetics can duplicate these results—given sophisticated equipment to make a vast quantity of very-high-speed calculations. But Nature performs these calculations (if they are performed at all) without the cerebral computer playing any part in the process; the service terminal in humans, as in frogs, is situated not in the brain but in the eye itself.

Certain insects have eyes composed of an incredible number of ocelli or facets (a bee's eyes, for example, have some 2,500); each covers only a fraction of the field of vision. The human electronic equipment needed to integrate that much data would today take up several cubic meters, even with the greatest miniaturization presently possible; Nature makes do with a few rows of cells so microscopic that several hundred would fit into one cubic millimeter. Between the facets of the insect's eye are hairs, each of which gives information about the direction of the wind; again, a vast amount of information is coordinated in an immensely restricted space. Bees can see polarized light and so "know" precisely where the sun is, even if the sky is overcast. A dancing bee is telling the swarm, in a language akin to that of analytical geometry, the angle between the solar point of reference and particular flowers—flowers that might be 30 kilometers from the hive (this distance corresponds for a bee to the distance between Chicago and Paris for us).

Bees can also perceive ultraviolet rays, a phenomenon that takes us into the myterious field of symbiosis. Through a bee's eye, a meadow that seems quite uniform to us must be the equivalent of the Champs-Élysées on a Saturday evening. The flowers literally compete for the bees' attention with bursts of scintillation, showers of sparks, luminous cascades, phosphorescence, and fluorescence. The more a flower needs bees to pollinate it, the more it glows with ultraviolet whimsies. Many would not survive without this expedient. Yet the technique is all the more enigmatic in that plants evolved earlier than insects and therefore must have originally been able to live without them.

One can thus speak of a symbiotic understanding that extends over the whole range of insects and flowers. Certain birthworts can only be fertilized by a kind of carrion fly; they start smelling like decaying flesh as soon as their stamens are ready to receive pollen. One orchid's labella assume the appearance of a certain sort of female wasp when real wasps of that species are about to emerge from the ground. The *Ophrys insectifera* of the South American jungle emits an odour so like that of a local butterfly that a mistake could easily be made—and the butterfly makes it. In the last two cases, the same extraordinary comedy unfolds: an insect ready to impregnate a female with its sexual organ seeds a flower with its feet.

Other species live by devices of no less incredible subtlety. Certain deep-sea fish have a photogenic organ composed of a multitude of bacteria irrigated—i.e., nourished—by another organ that operates with greater or lesser intensity according to the need for light. Ants assume responsibility for the upkeep of stables of aphids from which they obtain sugar, "milking" them by stroking their backs; this example of husbandry is by no means unique in the insect world. When most butterflies unfold their wings, they reveal two "eyes" so like those of the owl that few predators dare attack them. Some butterflies and American grasshoppers also carry on their folded wings the exact replica of a particular species of leaf, very accurately defined, including the veins and stalk; the pseudoleaf may even have pseudo insect bites, a pseudo bird's dropping, and pseudo mould of a type that actually exists. Certain other butterflies that would make a perfect snack for their enemies emit the odour of a poison specifically deadly to the predators in question. Owlet moths have wings fringed with special little bristles that absorb only the particular variety of ultrasound emitted by a species of bats that hunts owlet moths; thus cheated, the bats' sonar no longer works. And if need be, the moth can go beyond this passive defense to a series of ultrasonic cries that their enemy never fails to take for those of bats of another species—this puts it to flight immediately.

A deep-sea fish, *Gigantactis macronema*, goes fishing with the aid of a "lamp" hung from its forehead; when it lights up suddenly, everything in the vicinity is paralyzed with surprise. *Chauliodus*, another fish, has 350 spots that shine like rubies deep down in its mouth, which it opens as its victims swim by; the small fry are attracted to this Ali Baba's cave lit by candelabra, and the cave snaps shut on them. Now, about 5 percent of the energy used by a humanmade lamp goes to producing light; the rest is wasted on heat. Animal lamps function at almost 100 percent efficiency, using two chemical fuels, luciferin and luciferase (names more picturesque than instructive). Thanks to these chemicals, the darkness of the marine depths is lit with fireworks of all shapes and colours and entire forests in the Antilles blaze with swarms of luminescent beetles. Nature makes no attempt to save energy here; it merely uses it without waste. Yet there is nothing miraculous about this use: it results from cellular cooperation—clear, absolute, and unconditional.

A further example: the golden plover travels 3,600 kilometers on a kilo of fat, which is the equivalent of flying a passenger plane from Geneva to Paris on—dare I say it?—four liters of fuel. The whole structure of the bird, including its hollow-boned skeleton, is aimed at this fantastic economy. Nature's technology is almost unbelievably efficient. The teal can fly eight hours a day, often at close to 110 kilometers per hour, with absurdly low reserves of energy; the tern can cover 19,000 kilometers (almost halfway round the world) twice a year; the plover can do 5,200 kilometers nonstop. Electric rays, mormyrids, and electric eels can produce two hundred discharges of 750-volt, 1-ampere current, which is strong enough to light a forty-watt neon tube 1.2 meters long. The frog can go without food for a year, the boa constrictor more than two, and the scorpion three; it is hopeless to try to compare organisms that can keep going for such long periods deprived of outside sources of energy with the most sophisticated, economical machines of present human technology. The baleen whales sustain their enormous bulk on a relatively scanty diet of krill, ploughing the seas at a speed of 48 kilometers per hour (higher, more often than not, than that of a nuclear-powered icebreaker). A swordfish or tunny can move through the water at 100 kilometers per hour; the frigate bird can fly at 200 kilometers per hour—but the peregrine falcon swoops at 320; a gazelle or a leopard can run at 100 kilometers per hour. Many smaller-scale feats sound less striking because their dimensions are tiny in human terms, but we cannot build miniature machines capable of such performances: the scarab beetle can carry on its back a load equal to 850 times its own weight; the stag beetle can hold 200 times its own mass in its mandibles; the hummingbird can beat its wings 60 times a second; the spider can spin a thread 1,000 times longer than itself. Maximum use of energy is the natural propensity of Life, no matter what its size. If a single protozoan, which weighs a millionth of a milligram and reproduces by fission, encountered no obstacles, it could exhaust the planet as successfully as any other species; unchecked, its descendants would equal the volume of the Earth in one month, and that of the Sun in five weeks.

Similarly, the sense of smell, which is the most primitive of animal senses, pushes reality to the bounds of belief. A dog's nose may be a million or even two million times better developed than ours. All that a Labrador needs to find its master 1,200 kilometers away is the few molecules that must inevitably filter through his boots or the body of his car. When a female butterfly emits a few thousandths of a milligram of its pheromone, it will infallibly attract all the males from 11 kilometers around; it is as if a chemical detector could pick up the presence of two cubic meters of a mixture at the opposite end of the earth. Imagine a volume of water 58 times the size of Lake

Constance; an eel placed at one end could smell a single cubic millimeter of diluted attar of roses at the other end. Moreover, smells do not function only as signals, they also act. For example, when a nest of termites fight, the insects' characteristic odour decreases, triggering the rapid metamorphosis of inoffensive young termites into fierce new warriors.

The power of living organisms is coupled with complex controls that mimic conscious activity. A striking example is the megapode hen; it maintains its nest, in fermenting compost, at a meticulously constant 35° C. When an experimenter varied the surrounding temperature by 2° C every two minutes, the megapode hollowed out air vents and enlarged or closed exhaust holes so that the internal heat of the compost heap did not vary. The megapode's control device is its tongue, which can detect infinitesimal variations in temperature. Many species of fish taste the environment in a similar way; salmon are thus able to sample an almost infinite number of fluvial waters and recognize the one that comes from the river of their birth. The rattlesnake, thanks to two small, thermo-receptive cavities beneath its eyes, can distinguish temperature variations of a thousandth of a degree and precisely determine the position of a heat source. Human beings might be able to duplicate the performance—with the help of a complete laboratory; the rattlesnake deprived of all other senses would strike its prey just as accurately.

To complete this brief panorama, one must mention some even more baffling enigmas. How does a termite that has been buried in a combination isolation box and Faraday cage (which eliminates all magnetic influence) manage neverthless to feel the commands of its queen as though she were right in front of it? Why does it fall into a coma if the queen is killed, or dig obstinately in her direction even when it has a clear path to food in the opposite direction? How do most migratory birds navigate by the stars, even in a planetarium? How does a puffin find its way back to Wales after being transported with its eyes sealed to Boston, 7,500 kilometers from its starting point? When migrant turtles head for the Mexican coast, they make a series of random choices from a hundred days of the year, 300 kilometers of coastline, and any of the twenty-four hours that make up a day; how are they unfailingly anticipated by thousands of turtle-egg-eating coyotes that never frequent the seashore at other times but congregate there shortly before the arrival of the turtles? (The turtles swim without surfacing, which rules out the possibility of their giving off an odour the coyotes can sense.) How do countless animal species manage to know that earthquakes are coming long before they register on seismographs?

It would be rdiculous to talk of miracles. The material world is an ensemble of laws that operate without violation. They do not make themselves disappear, any more than one can "vanish" the musical instrument on which one is playing, which exists only because it resists. "Know thyself" is the motto of the Universe; the whole of Nature is its most important accomplishment.

II

One might call the ensemble of Nature's successes the Diving Technology, but it must not be confused with the Mind, which tangibly manifests itself therein. Life's methods are of unparalleled ingenuity, but, like our own techniques, they must be based on what is possible. The real mystery is not only that finality beyond which no science can go, even when it believes it is doing so. The mystery to end all mysteries is the immeasurable, absolute knowledge that this finality almost forces us to postulate. It shines from one end to the other of the immense universe of the instincts, not as if Matter were animated or manipulated from the outside, but because it is, as we saw in another chapter and shall see again shortly, *the exteriorization of Mind.*

The botfly lays its eggs on the shoulders of a horse; when the horse licks itself, it transfers the larva into its digestive system, the only place in which this insect can develop. The fly does not deliberately choose a horse rather than a cow, nor does it foresee that the horse will lick itself or that this is the only way in which its eggs can reach the only place in which they can develop. Similarly, the oft-cited Sitaris lays its eggs at the mouth of the underground tunnels dug by one particular kind of bee, the anthophore; when the male comes out of the tunnel, the larva attaches itself to the bee until the nuptial flight, when it passes from the impregnating male to the impregnated female; when the female lays her eggs, it jumps into one, which serves it as a raft on the liquid honey; next the larva devours the egg, then metamorphoses so that it can float by itself; it eats honey, becomes a nymph and then an adult Sitaris—which will later begin the whole cycle over again. Although we are tempted to say the larva "waits" for the right moment at many of the stages, we know it does not do so in any volitional or conscious sense of the word; it acts entirely on instinct, without choice and without foresight. Instincts neither choose nor foresee anything; we know this quite surely because an animal is as infallible as it is blind, and so it can be fooled by simulation.

But what does not think must be thought. This is as true of instinct as it is of mimesis. To crystallize our ideas, let us take another look at a case of the latter, a simple one that gives a perfect résumé of all the others, the simulated owl's eyes on butterflies' wings. Now, we know from De Vries that Evolution proceeds by sudden mutations, which are generally attributable to cosmic, ultraviolet, or other rays. By definition, they can modify an animal's genetic code only by chance. We saw earlier that the idea of Chance is that of randomness—in other words, the opposite of the idea of Finality. But even as we try to use this traditional meaning, we are obliged to exclude it: the number of designs a butterfly's wing could reproduce is infinite, whereas the design of an eye is unique, so the probability of its appearing is practically one in infinity—in other words, nil. But whenever we speak of Chance, we risk confusing the dice players with the game they play, taking the appearance of good numbers for their stock in hand, believing that what is chosen *from* Chance is chosen *by* Chance. In fact, Chance never had a single chance of making a pair of eyes appear on the wings of a single species of butterfly. Moreover, the number of insect species that use mimesis is astronomical (on close examination, nearly the whole of living Nature turns out to be an exercise in camouflage).

Now, suppose that the wings of the butterflies in question became ornamented with imitation eyes *progressively* through orthogenesis —i.e., by a series of oriented mutations. The idea of Chance immediately becomes superfluous because an orientation is a finality. At some stage of Evolution, the eyelike simulacra must have been merely rough sketches that would not have served to put a predatory bird to flight. What then was the genius of the species that grasped the necessity of continuing to evolve in the same direction, until veritable imitation eyes finally appeared? What could such a genius be if not an exterior awareness?

The reality itself contradicts the hypothesis of Chance. Mimesis regularly goes well beyond the level of the strictly necessary. Dissuasion does not require anything like the absolute resemblance of stick-insects to the twigs on which they perch, the striking similarity of the folded wings of one kind of butterfly to the chewed leaves of a certain real species of plant, the perfect copy of the owl's eyes. The birds that have to be kept away would find a much sketchier representation sufficient to make them believe in the presence of an owl—unless they are not taken in at all by any mimesis (a theory that postulates their detecting their prey by superior, nonvisual mechanisms, most frequently olfactory).

Only a single possibility remains, more unlikely than all the others. A sudden mutation could have transmitted to the insect's chromosomes, at one fell swoop, the complete plan of a pair of wings disguised with owl's eyes. This is the very type of divine intervention, inexplicable because it must be intentional. It is something that Science does not have to examine and that the scientific world does not generally admit.

It doesn't matter. Whether one attributes an example of mimesis to a series of imperceptible mutations or to a single, qualitatively richer change, the principle remains the same: one is describing not the operations of Chance but the intervention of a finality, of intentions, of a knowledge—none of which are human.

Now this finality, this knowledge—if not these intentions—would be evident even if Life did not exist. I have already shown that Time, being unable to be causal, is final in itself. And Matter, although it is the support of sensations, is not a sensation itself and cannot be other than a concept; all its forms are thus conceptual forms—in other words, a knowledge. Pythagoras' statement, "Everything is sentient," does not mean that Matter thinks, but that it *is* thought, even that it is a part of absolute Thought.

Whether Mind percolates through a molecular grouping or is swallowed up by a brain, it then discovers itself. The whole history of the cosmos is merely this anamnesis. Absolute Thought creates a ground for itself: *it remembers itself*. One must picture the ensemble of the living world as a prodigious series of machines whose user and overall objective are unique. The same Being simultaneously uses the butterfly and its predator, argument and counterargument, bees and nectared flowers, idea upon idea, owls and trees, discovery after discovery. To use something is to live within it. The love that animates and uplifts Matter is penetration. The deeper this penetration, the more we see awareness emerging—an awareness that is not Mind but simultaneously comes from it and returns to it, contains both its origin and its objective, and finally thus *doubles* itself in its reflective, human form.

Instinct is merely the superficial—and hence solidified—layer of a knowledge that has already spread throughout the Universe. It is perfectly logical that animals should be connected to this knowledge *to the degree that they lack awareness.* Inert matter is not connected to it but blended with it. Similarly, primitive tools required a human presence and direct action, whereas more perfect machines have increasing autonomy and thus become separated from us; we must spend time behind a spade, but a computer can do it without our presence entirely. Such is the process of Evolution. Its most rudimentary creations are under the direct influence of what I called earlier on, for want of a better term, absolute Knowledge. With humans, Mind has taken on its greatest risk: it has cut all its moorings, then shut itself up almost completely. Our freedom and awareness are the beginnings of the creative Mind's most grandiose awakening in the midst of its creation. Certainty implies a conclusion, freedom supposes doubt. Perhaps we could receive the same finishing touches as the butterflies, but only on condition of renouncing our freedom, annihilating our Ego. In this case, the Supreme Ego, *one* of whose ideas we are, would recast its story the other way round: it would debase itself instead of being launched, by us, on its proper pursuit.

If the roots of words had the same nutritive function as those of things, the Word that was in the beginning would not require any long analyses to reveal a part of what should be our purpose. In Latin *Natura* means "what will be born" and *Universum* means "turned in one way" or "combined into one whole." How could the Romans, who did not suspect the existence of Evolution, have invented expressions of such force? By doing what all the butterflies with eyes and all the flowers with butterflies had done before them: turning towards the unique source that is also the source of our awareness. It lies, with the final causes, in the only direction that has ever interested Life: the future. . . .

III

The know-how of the living animal certainly transcends ours, but its know-how is not its own, while ours comes from a still higher knowledge. An animal's intelligence can be astonishing—and its stupidity even more so. A hen will mistake a stone for its egg and push its own young out of the nest because they have been dyed a different colour; any female bird will feed a fledgling of another breed but peck one of its own to death because it has been slightly disguised; a prairie dog will confuse a stag beetle and an eagle. When we think about this behaviour, we realize we must rate the *autonomous* awareness of the individual animal very low indeed—if it comes onto the scale at all. The anthill is more intelligent than the ant.

What is true of the living individual is even more true of the story of Life—Evolution. Basically, we know it in two versions— Lamarck's and Darwin's. In their present forms both versions owe a great deal to the mutationism of Hugo De Vries and T. H. Morgan. In order to understand why no theory radically different from mutationism can be envisaged within the limits of scientific speculation, the best course is to examine all three hypotheses succinctly. They do not suffer much from being simplified down to their bare bones, for their principles are simple, and we are dealing only with these principles.

Lamarck, chronologically the first of the avowed, systematic evolutionists, held that all past and present variations in Life demonstrate as many efforts on the part of animate matter to adapt to its environment. Thus, he presupposed finality. It goes almost without saying that Lamarck's vitalism was naïve. Everyone is familiar with the classic examples of his rule, which can be abbreviated to "the function creates the organ." According to the usual illustrations, the giraffe's neck grew gradually longer so it could more easily reach the high branches where the leaves are most plentiful; camels and warthogs, by dint of constant kneeling, ended up being born with protective calluses on their knees, just as the soles of human feet are merely thick epidermal layers that have become hereditary. It is not difficult to understand how Lamarckism became the first evolutionary theory. Its appeal is immediate; we ourselves instinctively connect the Black's dark skin with a pigmentation against the sun that individuals have passed to the species by the effect (incomprehensible and thus concealed) of repetition. Moreover, the least of our organisms suggest that Life is an adaptative system: Our bodies produce antitoxins; our external temperatures can be regulated; our skin renews itself, scars over, modifies itself in a lasting fashion, as necessary.

But even if Lamarck's truth were an explanation rather than an extremely hazy interpretation, it would still be far from a general theory of evolution. Millions of variations—in colour, height, coat, muscular morphology, and even the nervous system—do not visibly adapt an animal to anything. The lazy, who can only survive where they have no predators, are thus an aberration. Terns, cormorants, and frigate birds have a well-developed palmation that is useless to them since they spend their lives in the air. The near blindness of sharks, stags' monstrous antlers, the useless wings of penguins and ostriches are apparently defects. Moreover, it is contradictory to assume that an organ such as the eye could have come into being by an adaptation to light—which is not light without an eye. Finally, what could the first animal that flew have been adapting to, when its peers remained on solid ground and prospered none the less for that? Why does Life tend to emerge from water, where its possibilities are practically boundless? The lungfish is endowed with both branchial and pulmonary breathing; what effort to adapt (except the wrong way) is involved in its annual attempt to attain dry land, which often costs it its life and invariably fails.

Lamarckism received its coup de grace when biologists following Jordan and others had to acknowledge a truth that attacked its very principle: none of the characteristics, however infinitesimal, that an individual acquires during its lifetime is ever transmitted to its descendants. Science then had to divide living matter into two watertight compartments: the *soma* or ensemble of features proper to an individual and the *germen*, the genetic program of the species. The *soma* is highly modifiable so an organism can register and adapt to extraordinarily varied situations, but nothing of all its experience filters through to the *germen*. Therefore, to take the simplest of examples, it is necessary for the child of a pianist to learn how to play the piano. And therefore, it is not apparent how the adaptation to the environment that Lamarck postulated, however strong it may be in individual animals, could profit those that followed. (Of course, even if the distinction between *soma* and *germen* is justified, there is no obligation to admit that it is strict—or that it is not.)

In Darwin's view, Lamarckism's great defect was its teleological (and hence theological) appearance. Life that is continually making an effort to adapt itself to its environment seems too much like a person; unicellulars can have only the shadow of an awareness and, in consequence, of an intention. And, of course, it is impossible to base a science on the notion of finality, which the Lamarckists were compelled to use.

Darwin hoped to get rid of this finality by suggesting that Life does not make an effort to produce anything, that it varies in a *haphazard* fashion, and that amid the innumerable variations that have marked Natural History, only the most favourable survived to pass themselves on. Thus mimesis, for example, has nothing voluntary about it; it starts as a fortuitous resemblance to a species' environment and is passed on because of the automatic elimination of individuals that do not have it.

We have already seen that the existence of so many fortuitous imitations is so unlikely as to be impossible. Various other reasons also make Darwin's thesis unacceptable. First, mimesis is not always useful. Neither is it always present; though the thornback and the turbot blend in with the ocean depths, there are other fish that are clearly distinguishable but have survived nevertheless. Second, mimetic tendencies are not always geared to an environment. Perhaps even more frequently they are aimed at reactions peculiar to *one* particular predator, and the animal mimic can often strengthen them itself. For example, the viperine colubrid can, at will, accentuate its already close resemblance to a viper—but colubrids and vipers *do not form part of the same environment*. Myriad species use other animals as tools without their survival depending on this action. The *melia* crab, for example, holds a live sea anemone in each pincer and uses its poison to paralyze its victims; the *trenoctopus* clothes itself in the body of a jellyfish; certain flatworms eat jellyfish and integrate their poison-bearing nematocysts into their bodies as weapons. All three cases are more one-upmanship than necessity.

The water beetle, which travels underwater in horseponds on a bubble of air, and the water spider, which lives inside this bubble as in a diving bell, also contradict Darwinian logic; both have means of survival other than performing such miracles. In the vegetable kingdom the stinging of the nettle is a method of defense for individual plants, but the poison of the colchicum only becomes active after the death of the plant—a very subtle form of dissuasion. Moreover, if one sort of plant needs poison to survive, the survival of any non-poisonous species seems inexplicable.

In any case the finality that Darwin thought he had kicked out the door immediately came back in through the window, landing in the big melting pot of natural selection in which the principal ingredient is the struggle for life. The phrase, which is not Darwin's but is Darwinian, means "struggle with life as the *objective*." But Evolution reduced to the idea of survival immediately becomes contradictory; one cannot explain self-development by preservation of the status quo. If Life had aimed only at preserving itself, nothing could justify its having gone beyond single-celled entities. Moreover, the objection to Lamarckism on grounds that acquired characteristics cannot be transmitted applies just as forcefully to Darwinism. How is the increased fitness of the survivors to be introduced into their genes?

Finally, if there is no finality, how does natural selection work? What are the criteria for increased fitness? The hedgehog's bristles were started as unusually thick hairs, and the palmation of the otter was originally rudimentary. Though bristles are now an incontestable advantage for defense, a palmation is for swimming, merely thick hairs are, on the contrary, a defect, as are a few centimeters of skin between the fingers. So Darwinian natural selection should never have let the hedgehog's and the otter's ancestors survive, much less allowed them to increase their defect. Now consider the slowness of adaptation. For example, the polar bear's colour is an advantage against the ice floes, but what happened while it was developing? Unless a camouflage comes into being at one fell swoop, the animal remains visible. Again, amphibians very likely came from a fish. But for an amphibian-aspiring fish to have had any superiority over its congeners, it would have had to have been instantly endowed with lungs and differentiated locomotive organs. If they only appeared gradually (and Darwin's theory does not allow any other hypothesis), the first batrachians were heroic cripples; rather than favouring them, natural selection should have doomed them all to death.

All that is left to Darwinism is the loophole of mutationism. First De Vries discovered that, over a sufficiently large number of generations, changes that are *minimal* in themselves affect individuals and simultaneously write themselves into the genetic code. Then Morgan induced hundreds of mutations of this sort in the common drosophila or fruit fly, proving that X rays, gamma rays, ultraviolet rays, even magnetism and temperature could bring them on. Of course, these mutations took place "by chance" and were nearly all regressive; the animal gained no fitness from them. But, the biologists reasoned, if one hypothesizes a similar series of positive changes all in the same direction (an orientation that, as we have seen, excludes the idea of chance), one could imagine the slow metamorphosis of one species into another. Thus, they developed an improved version of Darwinism whose basic equation is: hereditary mutations plus survival of the fittest equals Evolution.

Most of the objections that ruled out pure Darwinism hold true here, too. Another widespread one is worth mentioning. Suppose that Chance, against its very definition, did progressively transform the ocular spot of the first vertebrates into the human eye. How could the same Chance have caused the same evolution among the cephalopods, which have no genetic relationship with the vertebrates, but whose eyes are constructed of the same materials, according to the same principles, and nearly as meticulously?

The idea of fitness, which Darwinism uses too freely, is an essentially finalist idea, like the idea of machine, or organism, and of Chance. All these ideas imply an objective, an attempt, a function, and thus an end. When we say that a structure is fitted for certain conditions, we understand not that the conditions are causes but that the structure is an objective. If this were not the case, an extinct species would be just as fitted as any other to the conditions that brought about its death—its death would have been a mere adaptation. Moreover, Darwinism supposes that at a given instant of Evolution, certain species showed themselves "fitter" for a life that did not yet exist, since it was they who inaugurated it. That is putting the cause of a transformation after the transformation itself —and what could be a better definition of finalism?

Be that as it may, scientists' references to Chance are inevitably attempts at obscuration, exactly like the "explanation" of divine intervention. If one cannot solve an enigma, one gives it a name. Science's first error is its belief that the law of causality is valid in Time, and it commits a second error by setting finality against Chance as an ensemble of causes too intricate for any approach other than probabilism. Thus when Science says, after Democritus, that everything comes from Chance and Necessity (the latter being the ensemble of the laws that we know), it is saying that everything comes from causes that we cannot know and from causes that we can know—which is hardly an unexpected conclusion. Moreover it is false, for nothing *comes* from causes, known or unknown. In the first place the law of causality explains only identity, while Time means change. Second, Time has not happened in its entirety and is made up only of presents. Third, the present produces the past, not the other way round; everything was present *before* it became past.

Even if one were to admit provisionally (at the cost of a thousand contortions) that there is no finality save in human awareness, what would one gain except a temporal respite and a quantitative reduction? Since human awareness does exist and consequently forms part of the universe, if there had never been more than one human in the cosmos, the cosmos would nevertheless have brought finality into being. Whether awareness appears sooner or later in the story of the world is of no importance from the moment one has to admit its necessity. Can one say that a physical law is *not* a law of the universe if it *practically* never manifests itself?

Science cannot account for either Evolution or, as we have seen elsewhere, the principles of Life. Lamarck overlooked the role of obstacles, Darwin saw nothing else. Neither of them could admit that Life invents and improvises. The former saw the fact of adaptation but did not know what to attribute it to. The latter realized that

Life is a series of obstacles surmounted, but understood nothing else. He did not notice that some surviving species have never surmounted anything over millions of years while others that showed much more perfect adaptation are extinct. Awareness is never recognized in the world except as a sort of blemish, a fault of taste that one can only explain through faith (which explains nothing) or deny through bad faith (which denies itself).

Thus, the religious and the atheistic attitudes converge, like pessimism and optimism. The idea that Humans are brought about by Chance is as absurd as the idea that they are brought about by God. Both serve as the same sort of padding. Omnipotent causality and omniscient Providence are the same determinism. Explanation by what is behind and justification by what is ahead both reduce the present to the same absence. Some deny Mind because it is not visibly manifested, the others worship it because they believe that it is; to both, Mind is Matter. Some refuse a God exterior to the world, the others have recourse only to this exteriorness; for both, the world is dead. Some declare that Humans are alone in the Universe because they see no helping hand descending from the heavens to write its decalogue in starry letters; the others believe that Humans have been succoured and delude themselves in seeing the hand and the law of God. The atheists say that the world is a clock; the mystics think of the clockmaker. When one speaks to them of Mind, the former sees Jehovah and his priests and reacts with disgust; the latter sees the same things and reacts with enthusiasm. They argue over the existence of Nothing, as though one of them were claiming that numbers are even and the other that they are not. These two blindnesses now face to face must be turned about so that they are back to back. The God of the religions does not exist; neither does the Chance of the agnostic. If the mask falls, its reverse falls with it.

Evolution, the majestic and pathetic aurora of awareness, calls upon us once again not to confuse awareness with Mind. Awareness is what *results* from the passage of Mind through a body; Mind was at the entrance, awareness is at the exit. Matter is merely an object for awareness, but for Mind, it is Mind itself. The absolute Ego thinks *itself* as subject, as object, and as a synthesis of the two—and my contact with Matter is a part of its contact with itself, just as I am a part of itself. Thus, the phrase "appearance of awareness" as a description of Life is misleading. By nature, awareness, which is pure subject, can neither appear nor disappear; to disappear, it would have to have appeared, and to appear, it could not be that through which everything appears and disappears.

It is correct to say that since finality exists in Humans, it exists in the Universe, but to say that it has existed there forever makes no sense because a principle does not live in Time. Like a billion suns, the supreme end of the Universe shines for all eternity above and below Matter in torment, and Life is merely an uninterrupted effort to see it from a closer vantage and to melt into it. In other words, Life is *introspection* by which the supreme Ego discovers itself. Before the formation of atoms, then when they existed in isolation, then when they grouped themselves progressively into molecules, into amino acids, into cellular structures, Matter was always pulled in one direction (the meaning, let us remember, of the word *universe*). Under the influence of this magnet, it became more and more translucent, allowing awareness to filter through with increasing ease. Even the principle of entropy merely highlights this double progress in opposite directions; at the beginning, Matter was at its maximum and Mind manifest at its minimum; the former decreases while the latter increases, and Mind will attain its zenith when Matter has reached its nadir.

Thus Life does not need to be explained; it alone explains. The same is true of the Ego, which we are—our bodies being a means for us to be it. I shall never know "why" Mind uses my brain to produce my mind. All the possible whys are but its creation; the only explanation of its existence is that it exists, and its presence explains the others while all the others imply its presence. Since without awareness there are no colours, no shapes, no positions, no Space, no Time, no Matter, and since a universe that was not thought nor felt nor imagined nor supposed would be literally *nothing*, the absolute Ego, of which we represent an infinitesimal part quantitatively but the whole qualitatively, is postulated here once again. There is no object without subject; when I admit that the world existed before the appearance of awareness and that it would have existed even if nobody knew about it my certainty supposes another: that of the absolute Subject, of which my own awareness forms part. When I imagine this world without awareness, it is still my awareness that is imagining it; I *cannot* abolish this awareness substitute without abolishing the world itself.

To create the world is first of all to be that without which the world does not exist. I am that. Humanity is the Creator of the Universe, not in person, but in persons. *Persona* means "mask," and every living individual is a mask of Mind. But a mask is never more than a resemblance; the only acceptable end of Evolution is an endless ecstasy, just as its only limitation is having no ecstasy at all.

What has always attracted Life *takes part in it* in the perpetual *present*. It could be called the absolute Magnet, provided that we remember that Object and Subject are two things in one, just as magnetism, which is one, comprises two poles—and that the French word for magnet is *aimant,* the *present participle* of *aimer,* to love.

IV

The time has come to review several essential theses.

1. Cause and effect are simultaneous and therefore identical, for if any time elapsed between them, the effect would "come from" this temporal interval and not from the cause. Now, Time is chance and succession—the reverse of identity and simultaneity. Consequently it cannot be casual. Every real chance is finalist—that is, spontaneous.

2. Thus, determinism is a fiction. At any given moment laws and facts constitute the world. The laws are identities, the *described* facts are immobilities. From this whole of laws and facts one can only infer the world itself—*immobile and identical.* No determinist foresight—not even divine foresight—is possible. To "foresee" is to know in advance not what will change, but *what cannot change.* For example, Newton's Laws will still hold good tomorrow, and two plus two will still equal four.

3. Science is forced to play a double game. From probabilism, it supposes that a single cause can produce *several* effects (e.g., before the coin is tossed, heads and tails are equally possible). From determinism, it postulates that a given cause can have only *one* effect (once tails has appeared, it necessarily *had* to appear). In its prob-

abilist role, Science is right *before* the event; in its determinist guise, it is right *after* the event. The reality is the event itself—during which Science abstains.

4. The present is the fixed point in relation to which everything is oriented. Without the present, no date—past or future—has any meaning. The question *when* is never applicable to a verb in the present tense, but it always relates to it. The real arrow of time may be shown thus:

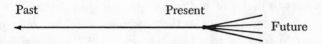

In other words, Time goes from the present to the past, for everything is present before it is past. The past does not produce the present; that which is no longer does not produce that which is. On the contrary, it is the present that ceaselessly produces the past. The world of yesterday is not the cause of the world of today; it is merely that which, in the world of today, has *not* changed and thus is *not* of today. A change refers to what went before it; to say that it results from it is absurd. The ball is not displaced by the shock it receives; it receives this shock because it is displaced. Indeed, the displacement *is* the shock, for it alone measures the shock and thus gives it existence. The determinist law of causality presides over topsy-turvydom; to see in the present the effect of the past is to imagine that a body in motion is propelled by its trajectory or a boat by its wake.

5. Because we are obliged to modify the present *in order to* attain the objective to come, we believe that what comes before generates what comes after (whereas it merely announces it, and generates only itself). In doing so, we have given the Universe an anthropomorphic law of causality—a travesty of finality that explains the living by the dead.

6. In reality, the present eternally precedes the past. Creation is not only continuing, as Malebranche and Descartes held, but strictly continuous. It is the perpetual Now that cannot have begun, for everything begins *in* in. The future flows ceaselessly into the present, and thus the first cause of the world (the fountainhead of this flow) is also its final destination. Alpha and Omega are but one.

7. We call Chance that which is without an objective (in reality, it is without an objective known to us). Yet it is our idea of Chance that provides access to that of Finality. If I play roulette and wait for *any* number to come up, no matter what, its appearance is a *certainty*; Chance is excluded. Chance is involved only when I wait for a *specific* number to come up; that number is then the objective of my wait—which is Finality. Chance is the relationship between two finalities, one known and the other unknowable.

8. Time is not that which passes; it is the relationship of that which passes to that which does not pass. It thus demands, *in order to exist* not only in me but in the objective world, a fixed, nontemporal point in relation to which the course of things unfolds. This point is the present. Since all movement is merely relative to an immobility, every passage from one instant to the next can refer only to what is found *in* one instant and the next, without *being* one or the other. The hour does not change if the clock face goes around with the hands. Time carries the intemporal within it. We live—and the world changes—in eternity, which is one of the two poles of the present, one of the terms of the relationship called Time. Eternity is not that which lasts without end but that which does not last at all. Temporally, zero and infinity are the same reality.

9. As Time could not exist without a nontemporal point of reference, neither could space exist without a nonspatial referent. The world that surrounds my body cannot lie within my brain, even as an image. A colour, which is vibration outside my brain and an electric current inside it, is not colour *anywhere*. All we have "in our heads" are differences in potential. The body is a machine; Mind is its user and awareness its use. The eyes do not see, the ears do not hear, the brain does not think. The world as I see it and the Ego that perceives it are neither spatial nor temporal. We are divers submerged in Matter, and hence in Space and Time. The intoxication of the depths has made us forget the open air, from which we come, to which we return, which we *are* fundamentally and which alone permits us to breathe here and now.

10. The intemporal, which makes Time possible, is the very basis of memory, which postulates the eternal presence of past *reality*. If I recognize one memory as more accurate than another, it cannot be with the help of a third memory. If it were, then *by what* would I

recognize that third memory as more accurate than the first two? It is the same when I remember a word that my memory did not know—because it was searching for it. In both cases, the final criterion can only be the past itself; thus, this past is completely *here*, completely present. More generally, if the memory—the image of a past event—must have a model, this model *cannot* be another image, which would itself have to have a model, and so on. In fact, everything that has an awareness, animal or human, has lived, is preserved—though *preservation* is really an inappropriate word since preservation implies that which lasts. The past *is* once and for all in the zero and the infinity of Time, and this circumstance—that multiplicity endures in uniqueness—is illustrated by the fact that multiplying any number by zero or infinity never yields anything but zero or infinity. Contingent memory recalls, forgets, or deforms what was, but this no more affects the past than the fact of being looked at or ignored affects an actual landscape.

11. The very principle that makes memory practicable is independent of my present awareness. Because my awareness dives deep in Time, it neither can nor wishes to possess absolute memory, which exists outside of Time and would in any case make awareness impossible. If each instant were merely the remembrance of the one before, then Time could not elapse. So although any awareness depends upon this absolute memory, it does not depend on my awareness, which is to say that it does not depend on my brain, my body—*or my life*.

12. In conformity with the principle of entropy, any quantity of information must decrease as it passes from one machine to another. Life is the absolute negation of this law. For three billion years information has passed from cell to cell (and so, strictly speaking, the cells from which our bodies are made have lived since the beginning of Creation). This vital information never stopped increasing in organisms, and it is infinitely richer in the youngest. Thus, life grows younger as it grows older. As leaves on this genealogical tree, we are doomed to destruction, but as parts of the tree we contain its principle. I find myself more *aware* than I was last year, though my brain and my body are less well organized; my awareness progresses, while my cerebral computer grows less efficient; I know more at the end of a sentence than I did at the beginning. But entropy does

its work evenly from beginning to end. Through an unbroken series of improverishments, I obtain an unbroken series of enrichments. Like Life itself, I do more with less. Let us turn once again to etymology. *Ich mag* in German, *ya magou* in Russian mean "I can" (from the Greek root for our word *machine*). *Magic* signifies power, and the power of Life is this absolute memorization by which Mind doubles itself or—as we saw above, remembers itself. Memory is the essential *member* (cf. re-*member*), and its principle is divine. The Greek root for "memory" is related to the word for "divination." Divination is the memory that raises itself to the infiniteness of the past to observe the indefiniteness of the future, that intel-*ligent* and re-*ligious* transparency that lying makes opaque by playing its role of separator (*dia-bolos*). Our personal aging results from false cellular information; our collective agony is the work of our personal falseness. But Awareness challenges both and fights what it challenges, accepting every risk—including the worst.

13. Were old age to blunt all my faculties, the absolute memory, intemporal and eternal, that is my complete past and that underlies my durability and conditions it would be expanded none the less. To do more with less—such is the function of Life and the objective of Mind. The path of my existence must, therefore, be either a flight or a fall. Ballast falls by itself. To change the metaphor: the virtuoso who masters a run using all five fingers can only progress by mastering it with four. Paganini used to impress audiences by removing strings from his violin and playing just as well on the remaining ones. The aging process never stops removing our strings: you have less—now, do more with it. On each step of the stairway the stakes become bigger, a fall more likely, and upward progress more difficult. One is not "fixed" in one's habits—one falls into the void those habits make. Habitude in itself is a liberating condition: to learn is merely to habituate oneself. But habits grow and impose themselves. If awareness does not profit thereby and open its eyes to vaster curiosities, it falls back into pointless repetition and its time is cut short, for every habit is an abbreviation.

14. Concept and sensation are the two poles of reality (affections and sentiments are only products of their synthesis). What is not concept is sensation, and vice versa. All pure concepts are objective, all pure sensations are subjective. A concept is necessarily the same

for every mind; the number three, space, a pebble are independent of the ways in which people think of them or in which they are perceived. Here we have the only possible definition of objectivity: that the representation of the thing *is not* the thing itself. It is impossible for "twelve" to mean different things to two people without their noticing the difference. It is likewise impossible for one person to take as "time" what another subject would take as "space." And though I may perceive a pebble as a pane of glass and you the same object as a point, we nevertheless understand that we are talking about the *same* pebble, or rather the same object. On the other hand, it is impossible to know whether the word *blue* signifies the same colour to you as it does to me. Through concept we are One; through sensations we are unique.

15. Matter, which can only be described as the *support* of sensations (and the independent support, it goes without saying, of the sensations themselves) is thus a *concept*. It is even Concept in itself, or rather outside itself. The Universe is the body of God, or its double: *Duo in deo.* To object that this concept is "concrete" is pointless, for one rightly calls "concrete" that which is material. To say that other concepts, such as numbers, are "abstract" is no less futile. Take the planets of the solar system—are they or are they not *concretely* nine in number? Matter is a palpable concept in that the act of touching is a material concept; it is the material that touches, and naturally it touches only itself.

16. Concepts go from the less general to the more general, and each is contained by another, wider in scope, that defines it because it encloses it. The ultimate container is the concept of Concept, which is the ultimate reality. Of itself, as a unity of subject and object, this concept can only be an Ego—and here, the absolute Ego. As matter, I am an Object facet of the absolute Ego; as mind, I am a Subject facet of the same entity. Any awareness whatever is the whole of Mind, as each drop of water in the ocean is the ocean.

17. All mind is one; all awareness is one single awareness. A split personality, even an infinitely divided one, suffers only from being many *in one*. The absolute Ego—of which we are a quantitative part but the qualitative whole—is thus many in one, yet aims towards being no more than one in many. All possible awarenesses

are varied kinds of content, but their container is identical. My Ego is infinite. As soon as I name myself or think myself, it is not I *whom* I am naming or thinking, but I *who* am naming or thinking. "I say that I know that I see myself seeing myself see myself, etc." However long a sentence of this nature may be, the real Ego is never found in it—though it looks for itself in it.

18. Every state of my awareness, however hesitant or dim, *is* my awareness. Thus, the most contemptible of humans or the most primitive of arthropods *is* the absolute Ego—that is, God. Although I shrink from using that name, sullied as it is with all the baseness and materialism of religions, no better one exists. One does not adopt a pseudonym merely because one has been vilified. "Mind" and "absolute Ego" remain vague entities, "Supreme Being" is an abstraction, but God lives. And the living God aims at the Good because he *is not* Good. From one side, God always appears as though he were aiming, from the far side as though he were being aimed at. He wants everything because he cannot achieve everything; he wishes neither to dispose of what he imposes on himself nor to make himself a present of what he intends to win—for Best is the absolute enemy of Good, just as 'still more" is the absolute enemy of "enough already." He is wrong, makes mistakes, does harm, detests this harm once done, gives *himself* nothing, forgives *himself* nothing, does not reward *himself*, and does not admire *himself*. Everything that is dead, everything that has lived, is a memory of the same Ego, of which my individual ego is but a moment. That Ego judges itself, and that judge will be I. I do not forgive my own bad memories; I do not cherish something of which I am ashamed. The best I can do is to forget: I forget the contemptible being I was because I hate him, *without end*. To see perfection in the living God is an insult, for a perfection is immobile. To see Good in him is another insult, for evil is a price paid, and the law of morality does not play tricks with itself—rather, it takes risks. The flames of Hell and of Pentecost are the same fire. All natural prodigies are born from billions and billions of sufferings, faux pas, errors, failures, and distresses. Nobody will help us because we are the living God, and nobody has ever helped God.

19. Thus, death must be a birth or a miscarriage. We have nothing to expect from it except our whole lives, compared, confronted,

and associated with all the lives ever lived in the infinity of Time and Space. To think of that is possible (even the only thing that is possible) but to represent it is not. For however prodigious, any attempt to represent an ideal is merely the reverse of that ideal— and the exact representation of Life is Death. Life, the living God, cannot tend towards the past. It can aim itself only at that which does not yet exist and only in the real, divine environment of Space, Time, and Matter. Everything that is born is the reincarnation of the living God. The only epitaph worthy of a living being is this: "I was mind and matter. Do not weep for matter, for it does not live, nor for mind, for it does not die."

The only ideal figure on our horizon is Prometheus. Ascending among the gods to steal Fire, he found only extinct ghosts and stole Mind instead. Real Creator of Life and of the human race, pinned to Mount Caucasus as an impious slanderer and blasphemer, victim of all the World's cults, Prometheus cries out to the end of time that every religious pose is a desertion, that every creature has in reality created itself and has nothing to look forward to except itself, that each awareness is God and that God is to be born (*Natura*), that nothing is guaranteed, that the entire Universe can founder, and that Life is an insurrection. Prometheus bound suffers death each night. Aeschuylus has him say to Hermes, representative of all the esoterisms, all the hermetic secrets, all the initiations, and all the sects, "I hate the gods." But his defiance continues: "I would not exchange my misfortune for your servitude."

Prometheus has already died billions and billions of times in each plant, each animal, each man. While he gazes at the world with his sleepless eyes, clinging to everything with his bleeding hands and crying out his love and fear as he awaits the dawn, thousands of priests watch yawning from the other side, asking Nothing for benefits, favours, and pardons. The Titan peers into the night. He watches it for signs of the cataclysm that fills him with horror and longing. His own death does not frighten him; he already knows it from one end to the other. His only hope is that, by dint of massacres and holocausts, the ghost gods will finally flee Olympus and dawn will break. Then Prometheus unbound will breathe, for the first time, free and triumphant. His head will sparkle like a thousand cities, his veins will be rivers, his hair will be mountains and forests, his mind will be that of Earth, and every human life will march in step with his. Set Prometheus free!

V

Let us return now to the idea of Evolution, which we left by the wayside. Since its beginnings, Life has been a quest for increasing complexity and thus for increasing organization. Now, nothing is more complex or more organized than the nervous system; each step forward there justifies a step forward in awareness. The zoologists have known this for a long time. When they classify living beings according to their cephalic indexes (their cerebral capacity and the probable number of cortical cells that it implies), they find that a list of increasing complexity is almost the exact reverse of a list by age. In other words, the most elementary nervous systems are chronologically the most primitive.

Very early on, Evolution favoured awareness over instinct. Now, we have already seen that instinct is infallible but can vary only with the genetic code—that is, over millions of years. Awareness, on the other hand, is fallible, but it can be trained and can thereby, in principle at least, change direction instantaneously. By making what amounts to the genetic code undergo training, Life gains a vast amount of time and a more or less unlimited flexibility. But the price is exteriorizing an increasing amount of what had been interior, making the individual more and more dependent on the social group that surrounds and shapes him.

What separates instinct from intelligence in living beings is comparable to what differentiates two machines in cybernetics. One can carry out a given program perfectly but does nothing else, while the other can choose its program according to the situation, but its criteria for choice are very imprecise. Thus programming is unnecessary for insects and of very short duration for simple mammals, but infancy lasts about one year in the dog, four in the chimpanzee, and fourteen or so in Humans. (This long period of dependence is the origin of the mother's specialization—and, correlatively, her extreme feminization—as well as of the extreme physical and instinctual destitution of Humans.)

A termite born and raised far from any termitary could function like a normal termite, after a few olfactory searches, but a dog deprived of canine training would not be completely a dog, and a chimpanzee left to itself would not survive. Human Beings, as we know from the instances of wolf-children, need complete human society to become human, and they need it throughout the whole of their life to remain human. Adaptability, fragility, and dependence are inseparable. An external skeleton imprisons the living creature while protecting it; an exchange for an internal skeleton frees it and by that very fact exposes it. Being cold-blooded automatically reconciles a creature to its environment but to that alone; when it becomes hot-blooded, it interiorizes this environment and carries it around within itself, thus placing itself at the mercy of delicate and complex controls.

All animals save Humans—the least primitive—carry out their function with the aid of a body that serves as a specialized tool and consequently plays only one single role. Human destitution is still an amplifying liberation. Where the animal was a pile driver, a pair of shears, a dagger, a toothed trap, or a poisoned spear, Humans have rid themselves of specializations and acquired the general principle, thereby giving themselves an unlimited choice of alternative roles. In this way they activate the vital process that generalizes the objective while particularizing the instrument: the more complex the machine becomes, the larger the target it aims at; the more ramifications there are in a sentence, the wider its scope. The conceptual series that rings reality in concentric circles thus passes from the general to the particular only to bring the latter *nearer* to the former. Human language thus attacks the absolute singularity of sensations and impressions; it forms concepts from them, thereby fulfilling one of Evolution's most fantastic challenges: to communicate the incommunicable, and thus to create an identity of individual Egos. At the peak of this challenge are ethics and aesthetics, which give an inkling of what is at stake. Art is trying to say: I am thou. I am thou, thus we shall be All.

All is, therefore, merely generalization. Algebra generalizes arithmetic and discovers a whole universe; the machine generalizes the tools, and automation generalizes the machine; awareness gradually rids itself of everything that is mechanical by nature and is thus not awareness itself. Libraries, record libraries, film libraries are collective memories, school and education our common genetic code. The more widespread all this becomes, the greater the release, the more enormous both the hope and the threat. Each step can be a fall, each machine is an obligation. Watch out, freedom!

It is to language, the social product par excellence, that we owe all exteriorization of thought. It is impossible to think without language, but the more refined it becomes, the greater the risk of its thinking in our place. We have adapted to a number of situations in a way inconceivable for all preceding forms of life, even though they were all better equipped than ourselves. We move in the air, under the seas, on land—and yet each of these paths is, in itself, a blind alley. Technology is a spur to progress under threat of asphyxiation; it *had* to come, yet is not responsible for *anything*. Anyone who levels accusations against it, as Heidegger has done, is reasoning like someone who lends a monkey a machine gun and then blames the result on the machine gun. Science is an honour to the human race when it is not mistaken for a philosophy; it offers us amplification of all our powers, but with each power comes a danger: reflection or death. The chief danger is scientific ideology itself. And would we really prefer an indefinite prolongation of the history of torturers and diviners, of willing victims and legalized predators, of theft as an institution, of State imposture and judicial carnival? History prefers death to this living lie and gets ready for its preference by the only possible means: aggravating every ignominy.

The person who attacks things *ipso facto* defends people; the one who objects to this method is seeking to excuse (as the ideology of humility has always done) the startling vulgarity of our objectives. Moral law itself has logical and evolutionary implications. Lying divides the memory in two and accordingly diminishes it, obliging it to retain the false rather than the true. The true and the false together spread confusion, lead gradually to contradiction and nonsense, cut information short, turn Society cloudy and cancerous. Egotism and jealousy sleep on their secrets and lose them. Theft slows down exchanges, falsifies products, makes lying obligatory. Murder calls for murder, immobilizes energy in defensive stagnation, dulls the mind to losses, complicates to emptiness, and unbalances the world. The day comes when all Humanity is swimming in night and fog, when it oscillates between senility and madness, when it loses its dignity and its knowledge, when it preaches universal rubbish in billions of deserts simultaneously, when it succumbs to all automatisms and all absurdities, when it is slashed down in its tracks and thus finds itself, once again, face to face with itself.... *Ecce Homo*.

VI

The symbol is a second sight. Etymologically it is conjunction and conjecture, but it does not offer the one in the other. Rather, the mists of time throw out glimmers whose meaning appears only with the dawns and dusks that follow them. Perhaps we shall get enough out of this section to risk using the analogy....

The history of the last two thousand years is merely the tracing of a single cycle developed around a single center: the idea of the Individual. The cycle itself is comparable to the stages of vegetable life. The ground has been fertilized by Greek philosophy, by Stoic morality, and in a still more profound way, by Roman law. The irreducible concept of the Individual was first spread like seed by Christ (whose total reality is obviously unaffected by whether his material reality was this, that, or the other, just as the influence of *The Odyssey* does not depend on the identity of Homer). What a law thinks through approximation, a mystique lives through death. For the first time a religion fashioned God as a man, a seditious attitude as a superior attitude, and the Kingdom as a future. It is difficult for us to realize what a momentous leap forward this was; we want to go on from the principle to the facts and from souls to beings, but that step would not be attempted until 1789, towards the end of the cycle. The sowing of the concept of the Individual was an absolute prerequisite.

If the seed die not, said Jesus, nothing can grow—and Jesus died. The Individual sacrificed remained open-armed. He would be the call, the welcome, and the triumph of the God-Man and of the Man-God—everything that added to the immediate image of suffering, in the sign of the cross. The slave gallows had already been planted in the heart of the world, multiplying by the thousands the death rattles along the trade routes. Now God held out his hand to sons of Spartacus; martyrdom signifies bearing witness, but bearing witness signifies certainty. The new religion was rebellious from its birth, and that alone made it political, if not revolutionary and utopian. It was not for nothing that Rome, which tolerated every other cult, from that of Osiris to that of Baal, persecuted the Priscillas, the Judes, the Callixtuses. Tertullian testifies to the fact that Power was obsessed by Christianity without knowing why—and more often than not, without the Christians themselves knowing why.

The seed was planted, and its first task was to get its roots into the soil. The story of Christianity began underground, repeating Christ's descent into Hell; he had thereby led the way for thousands of his followers among the slaves, and his victorious emergence foreshadowed the victory of the new spiritual order. The catacombs were simultaneously refuges, tombs, and underground cells. While the world above, the world of the Roman institutions, was crumbling away amid its triumphs, and the whole expanse of an empire was changing into an excuse for a civilization, the world below, the world of the oppressed, was in ferment. A millennium of silence and apparent immobility followed. Rome became an empty city, with goats browsing on the Capitol and wolves sheltering on the Palatine Hill. The ravages of successive onslaughts of barbarians were like a mighty tilling; the mixing of peoples was like turning the soil with a plough; each crack in Rome's marble pavement opened the way for a rootstock that would become a language, then a culture, then a vital spirit. The old world, which seemed lost, was merely dozing, and while it dozed, it dreamed. Gregory of Tours was half waking, half walking in his sleep. Antiquity, thrown to the four winds, nourished itself silently in every soil. Its widely scattered lore germinated in those surface catacombs—and cloisters—ridiculous utopias in the midst of the jungle now without a name, scraps of the City of God in the heart of the Kingdom of Satan where night multiplied ghosts by chimeras and errors by terrors.

The Middle Ages were the time of sprouting and budding. Sprung from the mixed and the hybrid, and figures were still strange, crawling, embryonic. The Gothic world was a profound Orient with Germany as its Far East. Nothing makes a face so gargoylelike as a fetus, and the bud, encased in its own folds, is distorted beneath its sticky lacquer as though by an iron collar. The Middle Ages were no more a fall than a quick sketch in a finished caricature. They were uncouth like a child, while the world of antiquity had been depraved like an old roué. The most murderous of jousting tournaments was not the carnage of the Circus; serfs were no longer absolute slaves. Evil had lost its former frankness; it had acquired a guilty conscience and no longer had any recourse except hypocrisy. Superstition was not paganism: the demons had ceased to be gods, and the gods had ceased to be God.

One by one, the buds opened. The vernaculars burgeoned, quite distinct from church Latin. The sacred stopped permeating the universe and began to come together into a divine unity, thus forming a pole within the profane that called to the other or opposite pole. Medieval reasoning, at first entirely theological, discovered a virgin space all around itself that cried out to be filled; ignorance is flexible, because it cannot prejudge, and no appeal is more pressing than an appeal by the void. Finally the leaves unfolded. To general amazement, much more was discovered in the pattern of their veinings than the old hidden universe of Phidias and Virgil. They were the projection of that universe multiplied, amplified, rejuvenated, softened.

Two segments of the spiral of history overlapped here. Theology had brought about a rebirth of philosophy through Thomas Aquinas, which is to say Aristotle. Then the need for literalness that had made Aristotle stick to the letter caused the first blossoms of Science to open at the very moment when the letter was retreating before the spirit. The theologians possessed the knowledge of Antiquity; Copernicus and Galileo had its freshness. These overlapping segments themselves suggested the name of the Renaissance, although the word was misleading. It was not only a matter of recreating Rome or Athens (in fact, it was necessary to go back to the Etruscans or the Aegeans). History repeats itself only in the manner of a never-ending sentence in which the same words and the same rhymes keep recurring. The Roman Empire and the perfection of Greece were what everyone wanted to see revived—but what is born at its maturity is fashioned to go further than its early old age. The Renaissance made everything turn green again, but History does not content itself with mere leaves: it demands the full flowering.

The Individual took another step upwards. Reformed—in other

words, made secular—it became its own, sole judge and its own anchorage. The Roman Catholic world would later find itself caught in a tempest because it had ignored the first raindrops; from them came the Enlightenment, the Encylopaedia, militant atheism, and the Revolution. Knowledge and social life were already intercommunicating through the work of such men as Gutenberg, Da Vinci, and Huyghens, and Bacon elevated this intercommunication into ideology. For better or for worse, Humans were about to join forces with this ideology, and nothing would prove worse than what they dreamed was best. But this union was slow, and individual free thought reached its zenith in the nineteenth century, after having travelled, in the fields of art, philosophy, and science, over the widest horizons ever displayed before the mind of humankind. The early part of the century was a period of unbelievable expansion of genius in all spheres; we owe nearly everything to its hundreds of peaks, some of which were of almost uncanny height: Beethoven, Hegel, Hugo.

Towards the end of this splendid century, everything began to look like the approach of nightfall. Baudelaire, Mallarmé, Verlaine in poetry, the post-Wagnerians in music, Nietzsche as a moralist—all understood perfectly what was happening when they classed themselves as decadent or as the last of the poets, the last of the musicians, the last of the philosophers. The petals had begun to fade, the fragrances became languorous, heavy, and intoxicating, all the splendours of the age were on the wane. A little while later, the scientism of Taine, Berthelot, Claude Bernard, and Haeckel would capitulate before radioactivity, the speed of light, quantum, and non-Euclidean geometries. Riemann, Russell, Planck, and Einstein would shake the very basis of logic. Nerval, from deep in the cells of Doctor Blanche, had not cried out in vain, "The universe is in the dark of night."

One could extend this allegory backwards by another, much more hazy, that links up with myth: the allegory of astrological eras. Nothing could be more natural than that, here and there, myth should support History, for History has secreted myth. The Christian era was known from its beginnings—and especially at its beginnings—as that of the Fish. The letters of "ichthys," the Greek word for fish, form an acrostic of the words "Jesus Christ, Son of God, Saviour," and the first adepts adopted the fish as their symbol, drawing it as a secret sign of fraternity on their doors and even scribbling it as graffiti in the catacombs. But the sign of Jonah doubled also represents Pisces, the Fishes of the Zodiac. The end of the era of Aries, the Ram, recurs no less constantly in the form of the Paschal Lamb, the Lamb of God, the Lamb of the Apocalypse. Nearly two thousand years earlier, the era of the Ram was vaguely represented by the myth of the Golden Fleece, which had ushered it in approximately in the days of Moses, who put an end to the era of Taurus, the Bull, by banning the cult of the Golden Calf, parallelled by Egypt's worship of Apis. A final correspondence ties in the preceding era of the Twins, the Gemini, with the dual religion of Ormuzd and Ahriman, gods respectively of the day and the night, good and evil, equal and alternate. These myths are of no importance save by virtue of their past significance, and that hardly manifests itself except in the appearance of the first Christian sects. The Fish as a symbol was associated with various features including fertility, multiplicity, diversity, a passionate and passive character, a sacrificial end. Hundreds of stained glass windows in the cathedrals of Europe continue this theme.

The Christian era has been immensely fertile, immeasurably multiple, prodigiously diverse. But it has also been, and increasingly so, the era of the division that the Gospels seem to foretell. "I came not to bring peace, but a sword." If that was prophecy, all the Christian mind needed to know was itself. It held the seeds of defiance, revolt, carnage, the auto-da-fé, excommunication; all were expressive of mutual intransigence, itself an implication of certainty.

The Christian era had to rekindle the ancient, scattered spark of Greco-Roman science, to make it either the promise of a new dawn or the beginning of a conflagration. It is this choice we face today. The epoch of the Fishes, the ultimate water sign, may devolve into that of Aquarius, the Water Bearer, the ultimate air sign, and air overlays water as mind overhangs passion or as intelligence dominates instinct. To pass from one era to another, with or without astrological symbols, would amount to unifying by the mind what passion was holding apart—namely, human beings themselves, whose solitary story is thus ended or rather completed. This continuous Creation that is the Universe, in which night always comes before the dawn, did not stop at the number seven. We are in the twilight of its eighth day, a day both historical and geographical: its dawn in the Orient led to the midday of Greece, where justice and accuracy were nicely balanced; then came Rome to upset this balance; finally Christian Europe shattered the first Unity into infinite details, the interiorized spiritual Sun multiplied by the total number of human beings. Now we are entering upon the eighth night, and it depends on us whether this night shall be eternal, or whether tomorrow, if tomorrow dawns, the ninth day shall shine, world without end.

All the themes that I have pursued in this book are irrational, pertaining to the passions, interested in origin. To convince interest by reason would be like squaring the circle, were it not that they must converge in the end. Bad faith turns to uneasiness by becoming guilty conscience, and the hour of universal guilty conscience is on the point of striking. Nor can this tolling be silenced. The fact that the era of the Individual is finished does not mean that we must return to the tribal collective—its solitary individual history was precisely what led us to abandon it forever. What it does mean is that henceforth the human individual and the human community must be one. I need not become more and more We, except to make us become more and more I; it is not the mirror we must look for, but transparency. It was, of course, easier for the One to become multiple than it is for the multiple to return to being One. But that return will be to the second power—in other words, without any loss of multiplicity. And the very difficult means that what awaits us, what is already tearing at us, is perhaps more important than the beginnings of Christianity or any other turning point in History. In fact, it is no longer History speaking, but Evolution.

Henceforth, it is no longer possible for one empire to give birth to another. Our only empire is Earth, rendered jointly liable towards, against, and by us in its dirtiness and in its death throes. The barbarians besetting it today bear chemical names; they want nothing, they will not negotiate, they do not wait, they do not argue. Like the things they are, all they do is reflect one single barbarism: our own. We are victims of a decadence that will be perpetual from now on and that can no longer be anything but global, for we inhabit a world shut in upon itself, all hatches battened down. The Orient can no longer replace the Occident or vice versa. The East and West—as, elsewhere, the Collective and the Individual, which they symbolize—no longer have any choice but to unite for everlasting light or to dissociate themselves in nameless darkness. It has been said that the Humanity of tomorrow will be metaphysical; in reality, it must go much further than that if it is to survive at all. And first its basic metaphysical character must be an obvious fact, something neither the religious faiths nor the traditional philosophies ever were.

I have described many extinguished lights in this book. It was by design that I first cited the light of Art, which has been put out forever. Lying at the junction of the individual and the sphere of the passions, Art has produced an accumulation of marvels that no human being could exhaust in a single lifetime. The end of the era of the Fishes saw a miraculous draught of fishes, or, if you prefer, the seed of Individuality has produced all its flowers. Our mistake is to want to add ours to them at all costs, even though the only choice left to us is that between postiche and pastiche, given our belief that a ship should sing of its shipwreck instead of avoiding it. Our immense past is within our reach—all we have to do is grasp it. Art calls loudly; what is lacking is a proper response to its call. No one has any idea of what could make a terrestrial society really intimate, united, warm; no one can guess how many masterpieces such a society could fashion from what it had lived through by means of transparency, which we have seen to be either magic or divine, and enthusiasm, whose very name means "having God within oneself."

Schiller did not write his "Ode to Joy" with its "*Seid umschlungen, Millionen*" ("Be embracéd, O ye millions") with the idea that this embrace would never take place. Hugo did not keep returning to the theme of Future Earth merely to cherish a dream, any more than he meant nothing when he described a liberated Humanity in these words:

> It has the divine and chaste function
> Of forming on high the only nation
>   At once the first and the last,
> Of initiating flight amid the radiance,
> And making liberty soar into the light,
>   Intoxicated by the fault of heaven.

Or again, elsewhere:

Already, in the ocean of shade that God dominates,
The gloomy archipelago of prison hulks lights up;
  God is the great magnet.
And the globes open their sinister eye
To the immensities of the eternal dawn
  And slowly turn.

The rising sun of *The Magic Flute* is not a stylistic fancy. The "ardent sob that rolls from age to age" in Baudelaire's "Phares" is not weeping just for show. Honegger's *Liturgical Symphony* is not a sonorous blueprint. Claude Lorraine's landscapes do not make one think of spatial structures. The "Gloria" of Bach's Mass in B Minor is not an exercise in counterpoint. *What Art has dreamed, we must do.*

Here, of course, we have entered the age of metaphysics. Henceforth, our field is that of ideas and of the whole human race. In Art, some lookouts keep crying "Land-ho!" but we must make sure the landfall is success. The objective is the same, but the methods are contrasting. Society, scarcely emerged from its night, offers all the incoherencies of all the passions. Its interests curb its reason, which gradually grows weaker and is lost. Its contradictions cry out to be dissolved in a light they finally find impossible to turn aside. Until now Art and Philosophy have been but ornaments. The idea was extraterrestrial, morality did but jest, the dream aimed at distracting. Then, on their last legs, Art and Philosophy themselves teetered between gratuitousness and charlatanism. While we were waiting, we could occupy ourselves with our affairs. But now the ideal, the jest, the dream have become as serious as a question of life or death. It is precisely at the end of our affairs that we catch a glimpse of a morality so disembodied that it leaves us no choice save that between itself and nothing. The seers of the past could do nothing. Mozart was a lackey, Bach a plodder, Rembrandt a hireling of merchants and provosts. The world of the Masters did not budge; profit, beastliness, injustice, lying, and egotism were at their peak, while Art filled in the gaps.

It was *necessary* that towards the end of the last century the doors of Matter should be opened wide with the development of technology, that all the old world of oppressors, warriors, and usurers should rush towards this promised land, and that it should close upon them—and upon us. It was *necessary* that chemistry should turn flight toxic and that the atom should bestow on it the face of murder. It was *necessary* that everything on all sides at once should grow worse, physically, intellectually, and morally. Life does not spare itself—even if it should wish to do so, it could not. People considered themselves good because they were anonymous; they considered dreams great when they were merely interested. Everything had to appear in its realized reality—ignoble, vulgar, murderous, and lying. The conqueror was merely a bookkeeper, the adventurer an ambitious swindler, the sorcerer's apprentice a fly-by-night manager. The apparently great were merely gross, the apparently celestial earthbound after all. All that futility, taken at its word, could do was to accuse the word—and the trap that caught it. The early Christians had awaited what is happening to us as the arrival of Christ the King, and they knew the role of evil: *Felix culpa* ("fortunate sin"), the liturgy proclaimed on the subject of Adam, and St. Augustine chained Lucifer to the divine millstone: *Omnia cooperant in bonum, etiam peccata* ("Everything, even sin, worked together for Good").

The radio made us believe what it left to our imagination; it spoke in the dark and created a common auditory hallucination with its Bacchic frenzies. Hitler's rantings were the voice of the world multiplied by itself in this nightmare at high noon. The flattery, the enthusiasm for everyone, the cheap Paradise only needed a tool made to their measure to unleash every type of Fascism. The cult of power, the Ego infinitely swollen by repercussion and reverberation, unreasoning resignation in dull hatred, empty triumphs in the race to nothing—all these principles have always created, in every arena and in every stadium, the same sinister entertainment, and they wrung a gloomy festivity from the death camps. All that was needed was the foolproof instrument of technology and the transference of that bloody baseness known as religiosity. Paleolithic society wanted its tanks; it got them—and it was the fault of the tanks. Peter the Great, haloed with technique, became Stalin—and it was the fault of the technique. People clung stubbornly to war, to national borders, to the immovable social order of work and the family; they got the nuclear Erebus—and it was the fault of Science. The famous men of past centuries had been princes, true enough, but they had also been creators; those of this century were still princes, but also millionaires, swindlers, comedians, boxing champions—and the fault lay not with the public but with the media. Television brought individuals and people closer, but we looked better from a distance—and it was the fault of television. And so on and so forth. . . .

So let optimism and pessimism come together, here and now, in the inaction that prepares for death. Henceforth, we know, the axiom "Everything is possible" is inseparable from and complementary to "Nothing is certain." We have the means for a unified world; it is the end that is lacking, and it is the end that is lying. We have the means for a society whose first objectives would include the progressive transfer of all servile work from humans to machines. We have the means for a terrestrial community that would have as its goals the abolition of all differences of profit and power and the final removal of all national boundaries. We have the means for a unified human nation in which children could grow up together, in which each person could benefit from his or her singularity. We have the means for social institutions that would one day overcome all jealousies and enable men and women to live in communion in the same calm and serene fervour. We have the means for relationships that would at last rebaptize love, which alone enables two, three, a thousand *minds* to be alike, to be attached to each other, and to be liberated by their attachment. We have the means for knowledge that would allow us to face death with certainty and no longer with faith alone. All these means we already have. Arms could be made to look ridiculous throughout the world. All violence could become useless. The countryside could be beautiful again. Our life could become the meeting place of action and contemplation. Nature could become what it has never been—our identity. We could marvel at our own works as we do at Nature's. Tomorrow every man could become free for dreaming, meditation, studying. Competition could disappear in friendly sport. We could cooperate for the same ends instead of just cooperating. We could arrange things so that there would no longer be any money to be made in either the means of expression or the sciences, and so that nobody had any more interest in falsifying any information whatsoever. We could accomplish the first conscious step of God on Earth. . . .

But who will give up his car? Who will accept a decrease in

possessions, even as a wager on an increase in being? Who will envisage love without sexual monopoly, much less without any sexuality at all? Which of the parasite professions will scuttle themselves? Where are the men and women who will recognize that their ideal is an interest and that this interest is bad faith? Where are the mistaken ideologists who will admit that their future lies behind them? Where is the passion that will not resort to a lie in answer to an argument? Who will stop us from fawning on heads of state, from respecting law and order, from trembling before our superiors, from simulating and dissimulating, from reresponding to warnings by hoarding, to crises by withdrawal, to prosperity by wild stampedes, to fashions by fashion, to general expectation by a supplementary expectation, to a cry for help by quibbling?

The choice is clear. Before our very eyes lie the means by which Life will either attain its ideal or succumb to its defeat. I am writing these lines on a Sunday in spring in Paris. Automobile after automobile is passing beneath my windows. Tons of tetraethyl lead have been added today to the tons of benzopyrene that rain gently down onto the fields, forests, and seas. A few kilometers from here, a nuclear breeder reactor, banned for the time being in America, is being built in France. Two couples are walking along the street, their arms about their partner's waists as though immobilizing their prey. My window frames a belfry; just a few moments ago its bells were ringing out a call to a cult ceremony in which the faithful would pray to Nothing for the success of their own interests. Across the way, TV sets light up, one above the other, in the family cells that are the living rooms of a twelve-storey apartment building. In the North Sea, a drilling rig is spilling out 4,000 tons of oil per day. The newspapers that tell us about it are eating up hectare after hectare of Scandinavian forest. Tomorrow the people in the street below will go back into the industrial jungle to hunt for spoils, just like Neanderthals. Arms will continue to accumulate in the warehouses of their Swiss manufacturers, not far from the offices of the Red Cross. Factory chimneys will start spewing out their toxic products again. Cabinet ministers will get together to combat rising prices. Early tomorrow morning we shall all fight our way through traffic so as to continue serving our sentences in factories that live, as we do, on theft and pollution, in the offices that administer the factories, in the banks charged with raking in the spoils to enrich others, or in the universities that are the antechambers of this collective success. Here someone will chew over a sentence of Kierkegaard's, there over a vector equation, somewhere else over Mendel's laws, somewhere else again over the fine points of property law, and elsewhere over theology—a science that consists in studying God. The walls are plastered with Marxist slogans against the rich, feminist denunciations of men, bourgeois appeals on their own behalf— all out for themselves. Posters denounce torture (*in Brazil*), Israeli oppression (*in the Near East*), and anti-Christian censorship (*in the U.S.S.R.*). In millions of cells prisoners await the hour of their daily torture—or that of their death. At this very moment the audience at a variety show is chanting "La-la-la," under the direction of a male singer costumed in white satin. A manager's family is relaxing on the patio of a villa, while a few kilometers away some Italian tenants are watching TV in a stifling attic. In a nearby arena, a crew of TV stagehands is putting up a huge set for televised international games that will feature sack races and cultural jousts for the entertainment of all Europe; the whole thing will cost only as much as three hectares of reforestation. Stickers proclaim "Stop Nuclear Power: Fight for Your Life" and "Save the Seas" from car bumpers, a few centimeters from the exhaust pipes. Soldiers are reporting back to their barracks; tomorrow's exercise will simulate an atomic attack. The World Council of Churches calls on the world to pray for peace, but several million Catholic integralists insist upon their right to pray in Latin. A folk music festival has just begun, and the words *freedom, love, brothers,* and *sisters* ring out; tonight the participants will drive back to their homes couple by couple—just as they did ten years ago. An art gallery is exhibiting the work of an abstract painter who expresses the agonies of the times—and most of his canvases already carry "sold" stickers. A celebrated octogenarian pianist is going to play all Mozart's sonatas for the hundredth time. Evening falls. After having communed by the hundreds of millions in the same vacuum of chauvinism, men and women come out of the stadiums and pass each other in the streets, care-laden, absorbed in their own problems. They dare not look each other in the eye; depending on their sex, it could only mean an invitation to copulate or to gossip. Women who hear someone following increase their pace: they are afraid. Lone men look away as they pass each other: they are afraid.

Our life no longer has any direction—but then it never had any. The screw turns, and we descend step by step towards the sticky night, the noxious proliferation of evasions and lies, the growing ignominy, the infernal cacophony of a thousand voices in which individuals cannot even hear their own. We have never stopped saying that we cannot do otherwise, but History cannot do otherwise either—because History is ourselves. At the bottom of the nameless gulf into which everything is hurling itself is inscribed a motto that is easier and easier to read: Death or Transfiguration. We have begun with Death, and we are forced to pursue this route.

What is to be done? Unanimity as to the ends, and the means will follow. Unanimity: one single *anima*, one single soul. The price is crazy, the risk is even more so, but this craziness is the soul itself—and a soul has no price. The false transfigurations that we have invented have been answered by Death—and it is Death that will always answer them, untiringly. As long as we wait, our lives are no more than parades that pass from the derisory to the sinister at the echo of the terrible trumpets of the Last Judgement, which comes like a thief when no one is expecting it, where no one sees it. Perhaps we will choose transfiguration when death leaves us no other way out.

Prometheus bound contemplates the reddish glow of the hyperborean night, watches the colossal black statue of Pluto raising itself gradually before the gates of Hell. He smiles at the god of damnation. Anticipation had finally completed its work of weariness. The crucial moment was worth more than a crucifying eternity, and it was necessary that once in the history of the world—for the first and last time—it should be so. So be it. . . .